COLLABORATION IN FRANCE

COLLABORATION IN FRANCE

Politics and Culture during
the Nazi Occupation, 1940–1944

Edited by
Gerhard Hirschfeld *and* **Patrick Marsh**

BERG
Oxford/New York/Munich
Distributed exclusively in the US and Canada by
St. Martin's Press, New York

First published in 1989 by
Berg Publishers Limited
Editorial Offices:
77 Morrell Avenue Oxford OX4 1NQ UK
165 Taber Avenue, Providence R.I. 02906, USA
Westermühlstraße 26, 8000 München 5, FRG

© Berg Publishers 1989

British Library Cataloguing in Publication Data
Collaboration in France: politics and culture
during the Nazi occupation, 1940–1944.
1. World War 2. French collaboration
I. Hirschfeld, Gerhard, *1946–* II. Marsh,
Patrick
940.53′163′0944
ISBN 0–85496–237–9

Library of Congress Cataloguing-in-Publication Data
Collaboration in France : politics and culture during the Nazi
occupation. 1940–1944 / edited by Gerhard Hirschfeld and Patrick
Marsh.
p. cm.
"Developed from an international workshop entitled 'France and the
German occupation, 1940–1944: collaboration—politics and culture,'
which was held in London in September 1987"—Pref.
Includes index.
ISBN 0–85496–237–9
1. World War, 1939–1945—France. 2. World War, 1939–1945–
–Collaborationists—France. 3. France—Politics and
government—1940–1945. I. Hirschfeld, Gerhard, 1946–
II. Marsh, Patrick.
D802.F8C578 1989
940.53′44—dc19   88–39474
                                                                         CIP

Printed in Great Britain

CONTENTS

PREFACE

The French response to the Nazi Occupation during the Second World War remains one of the most fascinating and controversial chapters of recent political and cultural history. It is perhaps understandable that, for many years, public and scholarly attention (both inside and outside France) has focused almost exclusively on the activities of the French Resistance. There was a need to restore confidence in a country that had known the trauma of occupation, and the ensuing internal strife and division.

Nearly half a century has passed since Hitler's armies invaded France and the French capitulated – time enough to allow a different picture to emerge: that of the activities and ideas of some, often distinguished, French men and women, who chose to collaborate actively with the German occupiers.

This book examines in some detail the political, cultural and literary aspects of French collaboration during the years of German occupation and hopes to present a reasonably balanced account of various scholarly views and interpretations of this period. It developed from an international workshop entitled 'France and the German Occupation, 1940–44: collaboration – politics and culture', which was held in London in September 1987. The unusual choice of venue (the Architectural Association at Bedford Square) and the 'regrettable discretion' of French participants perhaps indicate the persistent reticence that is still felt when dealing with an issue that has become both emotive and topical. The workshop was, however, highly successful and the number of those attending exceeded all our expectations.

We should like to thank the French Embassy in London and in particular Mme Lewis-Soubignac, head of its cultural section, for initial support and help towards financing the conference. The Architectural Association offered us their splendid facilities at very short notice and we enjoyed their hospitality. Thanks are also due to Niamh Kinsella for her help with the translation of some papers and to Geraldine Cremin and Susanne Bluhm for their secretarial assistance.

Preface

We are particularly grateful to our publisher Marion Berghahn, who not only generously supported our workshop but also proved to be a constant source of encouragement throughout some of the more difficult stages of the publication process.

Finally we take this opportunity to thank again all contributors for their willingness to participate in what turned out to be a truly interdisciplinary intellectual venture and the patience with which they have awaited the outcome.

Gerhard Hirschfeld   **Patrick Marsh**

ILLUSTRATIONS

Photos 8 and 9 appear by kind permission of Comédie-Française

ix

Abbreviations

ACJF	Action Catholique de la Jeunesse Française
CGOJ	Commissariat Générale aux Questions Juives
CIMADE	Comité Inter-Mouvement Auprès des Evacués
COES	Comité d'Organisation des Enterprises de Spectacle
CNE	Comité National des Ecrivains
ERR	Einsatzstab Reichsleiter Rosenberg
FNA	Front National des Arts
GMR	Groupes Mobiles de Réserve
IDHEC	Institut des Hautes Etudes Cinématographiques
JAC	Jeunesse Agricole Catholique
JOC	Jeunesse Ouvrière Catholique
LVF	Légion des Volontaires Français
MBF	Militärbefehlshaber Frankreich
MRP	Mouvement républicain populaire
PPF	Parti Populaire Française
RKK	Reichskulturkammer
RNP	Rassemblement National Populaire
SD	Sicherheitsdienst
SOL	Service d'Ordre Légionnaire
SS	Schutzstaffel
STO	Service du Travail Obligatoire

1. Pétainist propaganda poster thanking the Légionnaires for joining the German-led 'crusade' against the 'Bolshevik peril'

2. The entrance of the anti-Semitic exhibition 'Le Juif et la France' at the Palais Berlitz in September 1941

3. Joan of Arc as a symbol of anti-British propaganda

4. 'Joan of Arc window' – Vichy propaganda

5. *Kamaraden* by Arno Breker

6. A scene from Marcel Carné's *Les Enfants du Paradis*

7. A scene from Jean Grémillon's *Remorques*

8.   A scene from Claudet's *Le Soulier de Satin*

9. A scene from Montherlant's *La Reine Morte*

1

COLLABORATION IN
NAZI-OCCUPIED FRANCE:
SOME INTRODUCTORY REMARKS

Gerhard Hirschfeld

Collaboration with the enemy is as old as war and the occupation of foreign territory. Whenever an army enters another country there is co-operation and a certain degree of fraternisation between the occupied population and the occupier. A statute of Edward III, enacted in the year 1351 'at the request of the lords and commons', defined treason as a form of collaboration with the enemy: 'if a man do levy war against our Lord the King in his realm or be adherent to the King's enemies in his realm giving them aid and comfort in the realm or elsewhere', he was considered guilty of treason. (It was, incidentally, this same law against treason on which almost five hundred years later the prosecuting counsel for the Crown, Sir Hartley Shawcross, based his case against William Joyce, the British broadcaster and Nazi collaborator during the Second World War.)[1]

The French Revolution and the proclamation of the principle of People's Sovereignty replaced the traditional concept of loyalty and faith, based on the monarchy and the church, with a new notion and new terms of reference. 'La trahison', as Talleyrand, master of political pragmatism, remarked, 'c'est une question du temps'. The nineteenth century and the rise of nationalism witnessed further changes in the meaning of loyalty, disloyalty, confidence, faith, and treason.[2] Betraying one's country, so it seemed, was by no means worse than attempting to overthrow any particular régime.

The current political and historiographical perception of collaboration (or collaborationism, as some historians and political scien-

1. See Rebecca West, *The Meaning of Treason*, new edn, London, 1982, p. 17.
2. See Margret Boveri, *Der Verrat im XX. Jahrhundert*, vol. I: *Für und gegen die Nation – Das sichtbare Geschehen*, Hamburg, 1956, pp. 15–18.

tists prefer to call it) is not even fifty years old. One can even give a precise date for its origin: the modern concept of collaboration was born on 24 October 1940 at a memorable meeting between the German Führer Adolf Hitler and Maréchal Philippe Pétain in Montoire. Six days later Pétain went on French Radio and declared: 'une collaboration a été envisagée entre nos deux pays. J'en ai accepté le principe'.[3] It was the formal acceptance of this political principle which gave rise to the modern definition of collaboration and which, unfortunately, led to numerous historical misconceptions and misinterpretations. Collaboration was seen as a political arrangement between two nations: the victorious one which had occupied foreign territory and the defeated nation which tried to preserve as much independence as possible. This narrow definition automatically excluded all other forms of co-operation between victor and vanquished, which were then left open to moral judgement and, in most cases, moral condemnation.

The introduction of the word 'collaboration' with this specific connotation into the everyday language of politics led to a further semantic erosion. Frequently, the term is used simply to expose and discredit a political opponent, to accuse him of committing the second most terrible crime after being a Fascist, that is, being a collaborator and/or a traitor to the national cause. In recent years, public attention in some countries which were occupied by Nazi Germany during the Second World War has returned to the issue of collaboration. The impassioned debates preceding and accompanying the trial of the former Gestapo chief of Lyon, Klaus Barbie, in May 1987 illustrated this trend, as did the unmasking of certain famous 'collaborators' in the Netherlands in the late 1970s. However, the explosive effect of public debates on political affairs in these countries tended to prevent any sober historical and scholarly analysis of the issue.

In post-war Europe early attempts to come to terms with the phenomenon of collaboration were largely overshadowed by political considerations. The first 'après-guerre' debate in France and elsewhere focused almost exclusively on what should be done with collaborators, rather than on what they were and what collabor-

---

3. Text of address in Jean-Pierre Azéma, *La Collaboration 1940–1944*, Paris, 1975, pp. 86–8. Probably the first official use of the term collaboration in the sense of 'continuing co-operation' between Germany and France occurs in a memorandum by the French Foreign Minister Paul Baudouin at the beginning of July 1940; see *The Private Diaries of Paul Baudouin*, London, 1951, p. 182.

ation consisted of.[4] Despite an ever increasing amount of literature
on the history of the Second World War in general and of Nazi rule
in occupied Europe in particular, there is still no real agreement on
the exact meaning of the term 'collaboration'. Indeed, contradictory
assessments of it have been made. In the majority of cases 'collaboration' has been understood to describe political and ideological
co-operation between Nazi occupiers and Fascist or semi-Fascist
factions among the native population. Economic, social and cultural
issues are dealt with only peripherally or are largely left to specialised studies. There are few overall surveys dealing with all forms of
collaboration, and moreover, there has been no convincing comparative investigation extending beyond the level of individual
nations and their particular responses to the German Occupation.[5]

As far as the historiographical interest in French collaboration
during the Second World War is concerned, the various Vichy
governments and their policies certainly dominated most historians'
attention, as if collaboration with the German authorities had
existed only within the geographical and temporal bounds of that
regime. In any case, painstaking historical accounting started relatively late, despite earlier attempts such as Robert Aron's mod-
erately 'pétiniste' *Histoire de Vichy* (1954) and Stanley Hoffmann's
brilliant analytical essay 'La Droite à Vichy' (1956).[6] Among the
works which cast new light on the political power structure of the
Vichy régime and on the background of Franco-German co-operation during those years were important studies by three non-
French historians (Eberhard Jäckel, Alan Milward and Robert O.
Paxton).[7] All these authors, whose respective books dealt with
different aspects of the occupation, concluded that it was first and
foremost the French and not the Germans who wanted to collaborate. According to Henri Michel, one of the most ardent pro-
moters of scholarly research into the French wartime record, the
Vichy leadership's political calculations were based, right from the

4. See Michael Kelly's contribution to this volume: 'The View of Collaboration
during the "Après-Guerre"', pp. 239–51.
5. See the introduction to my book *Nazi Rule and Dutch Collaboration. The
Netherlands under German Occupation 1940–1945*, Oxford/New York/Hamburg,
1988, pp. 1–3.
6. Repr. in *Essais sur la France. Déclin ou renouveau?*, Paris, 1974 (Engl. trans:
Decline or Renewal? France since the 1930s, London, 1974).
7. E. Jäckel, *Frankreich in Hitlers Europa*, Stuttgart, 1966; A. Milward, *The New
Order and the French Economy*, Oxford, 1970; R.O. Paxton, *Vichy France: Old
Guard and New Order, 1940–1944*, New York, 1972.

Gerhard Hirschfeld

start, on a fatefully wrong diagnosis: they assumed that there would be a decisive and final German victory.[8] Michel and other French historians paid considerable attention to the question of continuity between pre-war and wartime France as well as to the specific ideological character of Vichy's régime and the 'Revolution nationale' it propagated.[9]

The economic and social implications of the collaboration years have been the subject of a number of local studies, but few historians so far have attempted to present a reliable national picture of French society during the German Occupation and of the overall role and responsibilities of industry in Vichy France and elsewhere.[10] With regard to the policy of collaboration vis-á-vis Nazi persecution of the Jews, a field in which the comprehensive studies by Michael Marrus and Robert Paxton, Maurice Raijsfus and Serge Klarsfeld are gradually being supplemented by regional studies, there seems to be little left to investigate, while Vichy's compliant and often accommodating attitude towards the German requisition of French labour still requires further research.[11]

Collaboration and French Fascism have been well served by political historians, and a number of analytical and descriptive interpretations are available, for example, those by Jean-Pierre Azéma, Pascal Ory, Claude Lévy, Bertram M. Gordon, Zeev Sternhell, John F. Sweets and others.[12] By contrast very little has been

---

8. H. Michel, *Pétain et le régime de Vichy*, Paris, 1978.

9. See, among others, Yves Durand, *Vichy (1940–1944)*, Paris, 1972; Roger Bourderon, 'Le régime de Vichy était-il fasciste?', in *Revue d'histoire de la deuxième guerre mondiale* 91, 1973, pp. 23–45; H. Michel, 'La Révolution nationale. Latitude d'action de gouvernement de Vichy', in *Revue d'histoire de la deuxième guerre mondiale* 81, 1971, pp. 3–22; Fondation nationale des Sciences politiques, Travaux et recherches de science politique, 18: *Le gouvernement de Vichy (1940–1942)*, Paris, 1972.

10. See numerous articles on regional and local economic developments during the occupation period in *Revue d'histoire de la deuxième guerre mondiale*, in particular vols. 79 (1970), 95 (1974), 102 (1976, special issue), 107 (1977), 120 (1980), 141 (1986).

11. M. Marrus and R.O. Paxton, *Vichy France and the Jews*, New York, 1981; M. Raijsfus, *Des Juifs dans la Collaboration, L'UGIF, 1941–1944*, Paris, 1980; S. Klarsfeld, *Vichy – Auschwitz*, 2 vols., Paris, 1983/1985. For the mobilisation of French labour see Jaques Evrard, *La déportation des travailleurs français dans le IIIe Reich*, Paris, 1972; Ulrich Herbert, *Fremdarbeiter. Politik und Praxis des 'Ausländer-Einsatzes' in der Kriegswirtschaft des Dritten Reiches*, Berlin/Bonn, 1985.

12. Azéma, *La Collaboration (1940–1944)*; P. Ory, *Les Collaborateurs, 1940–1945*, Paris, 1976; idem, *La France allemande. Paroles du collaborationisme français (1933–1945)*, Paris, 1977; Cl. Levy, *'Les Nouveaux Temps' et l'idéologie de la collaboration*, Paris, 1974; B.M. Gordon, *Collaborationism in France during the Second World War*, Ithaca, 1980; Z. Sternhell, *Ni droite ni gauche. L'ideologie fasciste en France*, Paris, 1983; J.F. Sweets, *Choices in Vichy France*, Oxford/New York, 1986.

done on various cultural and social aspects of the so-called collaborationist milieu. David Pryce-Jones's popular account of everyday life in occupied Paris (1981) and a number of fascinating case studies, not least by British scholars, some of whom are represented in this volume, offer a wealth of research material for a synthesising approach.[13]

The following preliminary remarks are in no way intended to provide a stringent definition, which would restrict the use of the term collaboration. They should rather be seen as general observations and assessments, which might allow us to gain some insight into the nature and range of collaboration in Nazi-occupied France.

France ostensibly assumed a very special status within the German sphere of domination in Europe. The country was divided into four areas with little or no communication between them and, as far as its administration is concerned, each area requires a case study of its own. Alsace-Lorraine, comprising the former three French départements Moselle, Bas-Rhin and Haut-Rhin, was annexed and governed by a Gauleiter from across the Rhine, while the cut-off Départements Nord and Pas de Calais with Lille, Cambrais and Arras were placed under German military command in Belgium (General Alexander von Falkenhausen). The largest part of the country, the north and west including the capital Paris, was also subjected to military rule (Generals Otto von Stülpnagel and Carl-Heinrich von Stülpnagel), but alongside the Militärbefehlshaber Frankreich there existed a number of other military and political agencies whose positions and jurisdictions were by no means obvious. Certainly the most obscure and fascinating of these institutions was the German Embassy in Paris under Otto Abetz. The remaining and by far the most important area was the so-called 'free' zone of Vichy France, which comprised approximately two-fifths of the country south and east of a line running from Geneva – Dole – Chalon-sur-Saône – Moulins – Bourges – Langon to Mont-de-Marsan.

This complicated and often confusing political and administrative situation suggests that it is necessary to assess collaboration in the context of German political and ideological conceptions and to confront the reality of Nazi rule in the occupied territories. Hitler,

---

13. See for example Roderick Kedward and Roger Austin (eds), *Vichy France and the Resistance: Culture and Ideology*, London and Sydney, 1985; for the relationship between literature and politics also Jürgen Sieß (ed.), *Widerstand, Flucht, Kollaboration. Literarische Intelligenz und Politik in Frankreich*, Frankfurt a.M./New York, 1984.

preoccupied with his attack on England, clearly favoured a political solution and initially saw France as a mere pawn in the negotiations he expected to have with a defeated Britain; his lack of interest in the administrative affairs of the occupied territories very soon became obvious. The Wehrmacht leadership and the German Army High Command demanded the total occupation of France until a final peace treaty was concluded. This attitude reflected a strong desire for security, but was also born out of revenge for Germany's defeat in the First World War. The humiliation of France was also high on the agenda of Propaganda Minister Josef Goebbels, who wanted to reduce the occupied country to the status of an 'enlarged Switzerland' (Goebbels), a holiday resort for Germans travelling abroad. The German Foreign Minister Ribbentrop on the other hand favoured a diplomatic solution which would have left France more or less intact and formally independent. This solution was to be achieved by using the earlier contacts of a small group of German Francophiles surrounding the later Ambassador, Otto Abetz. Abetz, certainly one of the more imaginative Nazi figures, proposed close co-operation with French Fascist and nationalist organisations and support for regional minorities. The Economics Ministry, a number of other economic agencies and the office of the Four-Year-Plan under the second most powerful man in the Third Reich, Hermann Göring advocated the total economic exploitation of France in one way or another. One proposal was to cut off the industrial centres of the North and East and turn France into a purely agrarian state. And then there was Reichsführer-SS Heinrich Himmler, with his SD and Gestapo bloodhounds, whose first concern was the extradition of all German emigrants who had found shelter in France. All these Reich organisations and a few more besides now became involved in administering and governing occupied France, constantly fighting each other for better positions and political advantage.[14]

All these German institutions had their own contacts and personal connections within the inner circle of the collaborationist milieu, thereby supporting different factions at different times and naturally fostering different solutions for the future political shape of France. These rivalries and inconsistencies within the German camp favoured the emergence of various collaborationist groups

14. See Jäckel, *Frankreich in Hitlers Europa*; also Lucien Steinberg, *Les autorités allemandes en France occupée*, Paris, 1966; Hans Umbreit, *Der Militärbefehlshaber in Frankreich 1940–1944*, Boppard am Rhein, 1968.

and organisations and, needless to say, complicate the history of French collaboration during the Second World War.

Thus it follows that a history of the collaboration of the people of an occupied country is always a history of the occupying power as well; any preoccupation solely with collaboration as such would be futile. Just as resistance in all its forms cannot be seen in isolation from the conditions of repression in which it arises, so collaboration cannot be separated from the social and political conditions which enable it to develop. However, a 'challenge-response' model of this kind is in danger of producing an analysis which divides resistance from collaboration according to the following dichotomy: those who do not collaborate are members of the Resistance, those who do collaborate can of course have nothing to do with the Resistance. In fact, the boundaries between individual forms of collaboration and opposition or resistance are actually quite fluid and rigid classification seems appropriate only in the areas of 'Fascist collaboration' and 'illegal (underground) resistance'.[15]

In addition, such an interpretation overlooks the fact that the postulated antithesis of collaboration – resistance presents an inadequate set of alternatives, at least for the first period of the German Occupation. Under the impact of German military successes, the prevailing attitude in most western European countries was one for which the French have coined the term 'attentisme': a cautious waiting approach, a form of playing for time. This reaction, however, was rapidly supplemented by a growing willingness to reach agreement on a modus vivendi with the victors in the interests of maintaining peace and order, thus accepting that the entire political and military situation had been totally transformed. As André Gide remarked (5 September 1940) 'to come to terms with yesterday's enemy is not cowardice but wisdom, as well as accepting what is inevitable'.[16] But such apparent accommodation often also revealed signs of a specific political orientation.

French contemporaries described the willingness to accept German domination as a form of collaboration, and consequently regarded 'attentisme' or 'accommodation' and 'collaboration' as a single mode of conduct. Alfred Fabre-Luce, the propagandist of a 'New Europe', wrote in his *Journal de la France 1939–1944*: 'L'at-

---

15. See Hirschfeld, *Nazi Rule and Dutch Collaboration*, Introduction, p. 5.

16. André Gide, from his *Journal 1939–42* as cited in D. Pryce-Jones, *Paris in the Third Reich*, London, 1981, p. 8.

tentisme déclaré, c'était, virtuellement, l'acceptation de l'occupation intégrale. La collaboration, c'était le véritable attentisme.'[17] By contrast, I regard political accommodation as neither a variation of nor an alternative to collaboration. Instead, it should be seen as a response characteristic of the first period of the Occupation, a stage at which important elements of the subsequent collaboration were being formulated, but also when early indications of a later (mostly conservative) opposition and resistance can be traced. We find evidence for this thesis in various areas of economic and administrative collaboration as well as in the co-operative attitude of a number of social groups and organisations. However, motives for accommodation were soon eclipsed by motives for collaboration, specific to the individual institutions and organisations concerned. An example of this is the so-called 'New Order' debate amongst Dutch, Belgian and French industrialists and civil servants. This debate relates to the anticipated collective 'Re-orientation' to the new political and economic realities created by the Reich, in particular, the dismantling of a national economic system, the development of new spheres and methods of production, the reorganisation of the national social system, and the possible restructuring of the administrative spheres after the removal of parliamentary control.[18] The discussion was ultimately dominated by fear of economic and social chaos, and concern for the maintenance of industrial production and jobs, even though rudiments of the 'political accommodation' of the first phase of the Occupation continued to be apparent.

Economic collaboration provides a very good test case for demonstrating the ambiguity of arguments and attitudes during the Occupation period. There were both entrepreneurial as well as more general economic reasons for ensuring the continuation of production and intensive economic co-operation with Germany. These included an interest in maintaining companies as viable entities; a desire to safeguard invested capital – including its potential future proceeds – from possible seizure by the occupying power; and the aim of preventing the penetration of the French economy by German big business (capital interpenetration). The

17. A. Fabre-Luce, *Journal de la France 1939–1944*, repr. Paris, 1969, pp. 511–12. On Fabre-Luce see Ory, *Les Collaborateurs*, pp. 27, 160.

18. See Jean Freymond, *Le Troisième Reich et la réorganisation économique de l'Europe, 1940–1942. Origines et projets*, Geneva, 1974; Milward, *The New Order*; John Gillingham, *Belgian Business in the Nazi New Order*, Ghent, 1977; Hirschfeld, *Nazi Rule and Dutch Collaboration*, ch. 5.

closure of factories might have led to the distmantling and transportation of machinery, goods and whatever raw materials were still available. Moreover, the workers who lost their jobs in this process would have had to face the prospect of being sent to Germany as part of the slave labour programme. A high level of industrial production, on the other hand, provided a tolerable livelihood and relative security for many employees. Besides, those goods and finished products which were not intended for export to Germany benefited the native population.[19]

But there was more to this than just the aim of maintaining production and keeping enterprises alive. All major studies (Milward, Kuisel, Frank) and new research on French industries at local or regional level have pointed to an overall increase in output and profits during the first two years of the Occupation; some entrepreneurs were even able to expand after 1943 when general economic decline had become obvious.[20] The process of modernisation intensified and the monopolisation of industries, already well under way before the war, increased as a result of measures taken by the Vichy government and the German authorities in co-operation with larger companies and industrial groups. Particularly the French aircraft industry, which by June 1940 already commanded one of the highest international growth rates, achieved large-scale expansion in production and major technical innovation as a result of Franco-German 'joint programmes' that were agreed upon in July 1941.[21] There was certainly something seductive for many businessmen and politicians about linking France with a vibrant, renovated European economy as an equal or near-equal partner. The reality, however, was quite different. As Adrian Jones has recently shown, once French industry had entered the path of close economic collaboration and had become dependent upon German orders, there was an 'inevitable erosion of national sovereignty which no prospect of an

---

19. Hirschfeld, *Nazi Rule and Dutch Collaboration*, pp. 318–19.

20. Milward, *The New Order*; Richard Kuisel, *Capitalism and the State in Modern France: Renovation and Economic Management in the Twentieth Century*, New York, 1981; Robert Frankenstein (i.e. Robert Frank), 'Die deutschen Arbeitskräfteaushebungen in Frankreich und die Zusammenarbeit der französischen Unternehmen mit der Besatzungsmacht, 1940–1944', in Waclaw Dlugoborski (ed.), *Zweiter Weltkrieg und sozialer Wandel. Achsenmächte und besetzte Länder*, Göttingen, 1981.

21. See Peter F. Klemm, 'La Production Aéronautique française de 1940 à 1942', in *Revue d'histoire de la deuxième guerre mondiale* 107 (1977), pp. 53–74; Patrick Facon and Françoise de Ruffray, 'Aperçus sur la Collaboration Aéronautique Franco-Allemande (1940–1943)', in ibid. 108 (1977), pp. 85–102.

Gerhard Hirschfeld

eventual full partnership in a European order could replace'.[22]

Purely ideological motives for economic collaboration were rare. The establishment of a new industrial structure adopted by Vichy France with Organisation Committees and Distribution Sections modelled along German lines was no exception and only demonstrated the extent to which Vichy had already copied Nazi German institutions. Instead economic considerations dominated and attempts to gain increased profits were by no means limited to a few 'economic profiteers' who knew how to exploit the occupation system to their advantage.

The verdict of the Czech historian Tomás Pasàk that every Fascist – some probably later than others – has inevitably been a collaborator, but that not every collaborator has been a Fascist is of course also valid with regard to the Nazi occupation of France and the policies of Vichy. But it is exactly here that the problem begins.

As far as various Fascist movements are concerned – among them Déat's Rassemblement National Populaire (RNP), Doriot's Parti Populaire Français (PPF) and Darnand's Milice Française – the case seems to be quite clear. There is no doubt that the line separating Nazi occupation policy and Fascist collaboration remained very fine, in so far as they did not actually overlap as the result of ideological identification. Some Fascists went so far as to propagate a Nazi racist view of France and French society as 'enjuiviée', 'négrifié', miserably latinised. While French Fascists, too, saw 1940 as humiliating and dishonourable, defeat at the hands of the Germans nevertheless seemed to offer a chance to restore France's 'gloire' and greatness in a new and European Fascist order. Collaboration with the occupying power was thus regarded, though perhaps with differing intensity and conviction, as an ultimate objective: either as a long-term and unlimited co-operation with Nazi Germany or (for a small faction of the Fascist movement) as a total absorption into a future Germanic empire, created under the auspices of Himmler's SS.[23] Like the pre-war Fascists, the wartime Fascist collaborators held rather diverse and heterogenous convic-

22. A. Jones, 'Illusions of sovereignty: business and the organization of Committees of Vichy France', in Social History 11, 1 (January 1986), pp. 1–31, here p. 29.
23. For a summary of French Fascism see J. Plumyène and R. Lasierra, Les Fascismes Françaises, Paris, 1963; Eugene Weber, 'Nationalism, Socialism, and National-Socialism in France', in French Historical Studies 2 (1962), pp. 271–307; Zeev Sternhell, 'Strands of French Fascism', in St. U. Larsen et. al. (eds), Who were the Fascists? Social Roots of European Fascism, Bergen 1980; Robert Soucy, French Fascism: The First Wave, 1924–1933, New Haven/London, 1986.

tions, which even allowed some of them, at times, appear to be social revolutionaries and modernisers.[24] But despite their progressive rhetoric and youthful sounding slogans of 'revolution' and 'socialism' these 'revolutionary Fascists', like the mainstream of the French Fascist movement, remained strongly reactionary and largely anti-modernist.

The French political scene during the occupation was the logical and to a large extent inevitable consequence of the political events and constellation of the 1930s. This is certainly true of the French Fascist movements that embraced collaboration after 1940 in order to settle some of their longstanding controversies with political enemies once and for all, a situation which then led to the violence of a 'Franco-French' civil war in 1944.[25] But the element of continuity also applies to Vichy's 'Revolution nationale', which Pétain constantly evoked as the only way of achieving the intellectual and moral renovation that the country needed and which proved to be a source of permanent illusion. Although the National Revolution – as Bertram Gordon has remarked, 'meant different things to different people', and, one might add, at different times, there was one underlying assumption which all representatives of this system shared. Vichy's 'pluralistic dictatorship' (Stanley Hoffman) began with Pétain's reactionary-patriarchal regime (1940–2), was followed by Laval's authoritarian-technocratic rule (1942–4) and ended with Darnand's open-Fascist system (1944). But despite different motives and diverse approaches all the protagonists of a National Revolution and their followers favoured close collaboration with Germany as providing the only operational basis for their policies.

In all cases, however, the potential as well as the limits of political collaboration subordinated to the interests of the occupying power. Nazi Germany in turn was interested neither in creating a genuine Fascist state in France nor in honest co-operation with organised French Fascism going beyond existing personal contacts. The occupation authorities regarded political collaboration (and, incidentally, any other form of collaboration) first and foremost as a useful means of achieving their own selfish and destructive goals. Concessions were only temporary and never constituted any real change

24. See Gordon, *Collaborationism in France*, Introduction, p. 21.
25. See Stanley Hoffmann, 'Collaborationism in France during World War II', in *Journal of Modern History*, 40 (1968), pp. 376–7.

of policy.

One of the arguments for political collaboration (put forward quite forcefully by its practitioners) has always been that things would have been worse if collaboration had not taken place, in other words that collaboration had a moderating effect on the repercussions of Nazi occupation. This argument later became known as the 'shield' theory, meaning that measures taken by French authorities and the Vichy government had shielded the country from even greater repression by the Germans.

But such deliberate decisions to support certain German initiatives in order to prevent worse ones would have required intimate knowledge of German intentions which no French politician or official could have had. Furthermore, historical facts point in a different direction. By far the gravest events of the occupation period, the deportation of Jews from France and the implementation of the slave labour programme on French soil after 1943 (in the so co-called 'Sauckel' actions) give no indication that French authorities exerted any moderating influence. On the contrary: Vichy's anti-Jewish legislation and 'Aryanisation' measures, directed particularly against all foreign Jews, were already well under way before the Nazis ordered the segregation of Jews as the first step towards the Final Solution. Initially the Germans even disapproved of French initiatives adopting their own anti-Jewish policies since they regarded France merely as a dumping ground for Germans Jewish refugees. In this respect, Vichy's treatment of foreign Jews was not at all in line with German concepts but clearly amounted to a rival action. As Marrus and Paxton have shown, there was a constant struggle with the occupation authorities in the Vichy government's attempt to assert its own sovereignty in anti-Jewish matters, and to keep the advantages of property confiscations and refugee control for itself.[26]

Once the Germans has secured the overall initiative and finally embarked on their policies of persecution, the French authorities and the Vichy government did everything in their power to support them in their effort to rid the country of unwanted outsiders. By doing so, they clearly hoped to retain some sort of authority in this matter and they even welcomed the involvement of French police. Since there were relatively few German staff available to handle the deportation of all Jews, the SD had to rely on extensive co-oper-

26. See Marrus and Paxton, *Vichy France*, ch. 4.

ation by the native police and civil administration to administer its barbarous task. French police soon rounded up Jews, both foreign and other, held them in camps and finally saw the convoys off to the East. If a vague hope of saving French Jews by sacrificing all refugees ever existed it was soon frustrated. The fact that the French persecution rate (of murdered Jews) was relatively low in comparison with other countries (France: 75,000 murdered Jews or 20 per cent of its former Jewish population; Belgium: 24,000 or 40 per cent; Netherlands: 102,000 or 75 per cent) had nothing to do with the collaborative attitude of French authorities, but was clearly the result of geographical circumstances, administrative difficulties created by conflicting German interests and the different pace of deportations from Western Europe.[27] Only the military defeat of Nazi Germany brought the deportation trains to a halt. Collaboration had not prevented the worst from happening but rather had made it possible and in any case had paved the road to Auschwitz.

The same negative conclusion must be drawn for Vichy's involvement in the Nazi requisition of French labour, where the government and the authorities had adopted a similar attitude. Neither the 'Relève' of June 1942 (exchanging one French prisoner of war in Germany for three Frenchmen volunteering for work there) nor the 'Service du Travail Obligatoire' (STO), which Laval had ordered in February 1943, worked as anticipated. Instead of offering protection to the majority of French workers it led to an ever increasing circle of demands and concessions. Again, the fall in the numbers of workers destined for Germany was not due to Vichy's 'successful' labour policies, as Laval claimed, but the consequence of more and more workers going underground or joining industries and organisations that were exempt from the compulsory conscription of labour, such as the mining industries, the so-called 'S-factories' (Sperrbetriebe) and the police. Some STO-workers did not even shrink from applying for work with the German construction units of the Organisation Todt in France, while only a minority – contrary to some tenacious legends – joined Resistance groups in the maquis. In general most French workers did not mind working *for* Germany as long as they did not have to go *to* Germany.[28]

27. Idem, 'The Nazis and the Jews in Occupied Western Europe, 1940–1944', in *Journal of Modern History* 54 (1982), pp. 687–714; Hans Blom, 'De vervolging van de Joden in Nederland in internationaal vergelijkend perspectief', in *De Gids* 6/7 (1987), pp. 494–507.
28. See Frankenstein, 'Die deutschen Arbeitskräfteaushebungen', p. 216, basing

But the balance-sheet of the 'Vichy government' not only reveals the immense French contribution to the German slave labour programme and the active support of its authorities involved in the deportation of more than 75,000 French and foreign Jews. It also lists the internment of 70,000 suspected 'enemies of the state' (among them many refugees from Nazi oppression), the dismissal of 35,000 'untrustworthy' civil servants and the trials of approximately 135,000 French people between 1940 and 1944.

The history of collaboration and its protagonists within and outside the realm of Vichy furnishes ample proof that there was no other occupied country during the Second World War which contributed more to the initial efficiency of Nazi rule in Europe than France. This is not to belittle French resistance against Nazism and the German occupation and to depreciate the heroic acts and daily suffering of many thousands of French men and women who fought and died for their country. But while resistance remained strong as a constant reminder of the 'other' France so did collaboration with the enemy in all its variations and appearances.

It is therefore no wonder that the Vichy-syndrome, the collective repression and occasional recollection of the years between 1940 and 1944, remained a traumatic experience for many French people throughout the post-war period, for some even to the present day.[29]

The following essays examine in great detail important political and cultural aspects of French collaboration with the Germans during the Second World War. They stress the inevitability of collaboration for a country that had never fully recovered from the trauma of the defeat of 1940. But these essays also confirm the ambiguity of collaboration though, as Roderick Kedward has pointed out, ambiguities in intention do not necessarily produce ambiguous actions.[30] None of the authors make any attempt to justify the events nor to attribute moral blame. Unfortunately – as the tenor of debate in recent years has revealed – this is a comment which still needs to be made.

---

his comments on some unpublished regional findings of research directed by the Comité d'Histoire de la Deuxième Guerre Mondiale.

29. Henry Rousso, *Le syndrome de Vichy. 1944–198 . . .*, Paris, 1987.

30. Roderick Kedward, Introduction to Kedward and Austin (eds), *Vichy France and the Resistance.*

2

PARIS DURING THE
GERMAN OCCUPATION

David Pryce-Jones

In the summer of 1940, one among tens of thousands fleeing from Poland, Gustav Herling found himself in the Soviet Union, not in a refuge as he had hoped, but in prison. One June day, as he tells in his memoirs *A World Apart*, a man was brought into the crowded cells, where red-eyed he burst out with the news that the Germans had captured Paris, and not a shot had been fired. The prisoners wept.

It was indeed as though hope were dying in the world. 'Liberté', 'Egalité', 'Fraternité, the great French inspirations to the universal heart and the universal mind, had come to this – Hitler's army, impassive and disciplined, was marching unchallenged past the Arc de Triomphe and down the Champs Elysées. So might was right, and there would be no more justice. This was not a conquest like any other between comparable states. Expressed in political and historical terms, an advanced industrial democracy had been matched for the first time against a totalitarian state. A verdict of an absolutely humiliating kind had been given against democracy.

The question was then, and is now: was a democracy such as France a social organisation suited only to the nineteenth century in which it had been evolved? If so, this was a momentous turning-point, and a brand new concept of progress would be required. The Mass-Age had begun. Stalin, for one, certainly thought so. The messages of congratulation that he conveyed to Hitler on the capture of Paris were genuine. In the logic of the Hitler–Stalin pact, Nazism and Communism were two halves of an arch, theoretically in tension, actually mutually supportive in crushing societies built upon respect for the individual.

The disintegration of France has been analysed in a variety of

15

David Pryce-Jones

perspectives, political, military, institutional; all contain their elements of truth, and from them one generalisation emerges: at the outbreak of war Frenchmen in all walks of life were ignorant of the real nature of totalitarianism, and specifically, what the Thousand Year Reich implied for them. Hitler's threat to the French way of life had been represented as a repeat of Bismarck's threat, of Kaiser Wilhelm's threat: the Boches were always the same; the past remained the guide to the future. By the time that this fundamental misconception was apparent, it was too late for remedy.

The leadership's inadequacy in the crisis of June 1940 was at once translated into general panic, into a military and civilian rout. The government, and with it official Paris, packed up at the approach of the German army, and fled southwards during the night of 10 June. Following after them, three million of the five million inhabitants of the city and the surrounding Seine département took to the roads in an uncontrollable exodus. According to some estimates, 40,000 civilians may have died, or in other words the casualties were equivalent to perhaps as many as half the number of soldiers killed in the actual fighting. Physical abandonment of home brought with it unprecedented abandonment of spiritual values, sometimes of civilised behaviour altogether. Here, some nurses about to evacuate their hospital, administered lethal injections to patients who could not be moved; there, a brave tank commander, preparing to defend a bridge across the Loire, was killed by the local inhabitants in the hope of propitiating the incoming Germans. For weeks afterwards newspapers carried advertisements for babies who had been lost, or found without means of identification.

The distinguished historian Henri Michel remarks upon the population's profound wish to avoid the horror of war. Goebbels' Ministry of Propaganda sensed as much, putting up throughout the occupied zone a poster showing a child cradled safely in the arms of a smiling and obviously 'Aryan' German soldier. This projection of childlike dependency as the basis of the new relation of the conquered to their conquerors proved a clever psychological stroke. The caption, demanding that these 'abandoned' people take confidence in the German soldier, rubbed in the point.

In a matter of weeks dependency was complete. France was where Hitler wanted it: two-fifths of the country under direct military rule, Alsace and Lorraine governed by Gauleiters for the Reich, eighty-year-old Marshal Pétain, head of the government in the southern remainder of the country, the so-called Vichy Zone,

16

declaring that he was entering upon the course of collaboration. On 24 October Hitler and Pétain met, and photographs of the two men shaking hands appeared everywhere.

The pre-war Third Republic had simply been turned inside out like an old coat, and the New Order fitted straight into it. Of course the overwhelming sensation was relief. By the autumn Paris was superficially itself once more; the theatres had reopened, also the schools, the Bourse, the museums and offices and factories. Unemployment was temporary. Policemen were back on duty. Over the Assemblée Nationale, however, converted to German administrative offices, floated a banner 'Deutschland siegt an allen Fronten'. And still not a shot had been fired. The military governor, the Militärbefehlshaber in Frankreich, reported to Berlin such incidents as random cutting of telephone wires, brawls in bars and heated exchanges about women, but nothing that he considered to be outright sabotage. Maintenance of discipline among the German garrison in so pleasure-loving and lax a city exercised him more than potential disobedience among the French. On 11 November 1940 some students paraded in commemoration of the previous, and quite different, Armistice Day of 1918. Over a hundred of them were arrested. During the four years in which Paris was occupied this was the one and only public demonstration of its kind. Rarely in its history has Paris been so little turbulent as when it lay at Hitler's mercy. During the first eighteen months of the Occupation no Germans were purposely killed by anyone French, and one single Frenchman was wrongly accused of jostling Germans on the street, and summarily shot.

What the French role in Europe had been, and what it ought to be over the coming thousand years, was frequently and closely discussed in Hitler's circle. It was agreed in principle that the standing and influence of this hereditary enemy had to be eradicated once and for all. What distinguished Hitler from his predecessors Bismarck and Kaiser Wilhelm, was that satisfaction of national claims could never be sufficient. Nazi ends were the permanent and irreversible aggrandisement of power for its own totalitarian sake, and the practice of racialism. French Jews were suspected of having played a particularly powerful part in building up their society, and to have been successful at assimilation, which in the context meant sinister concealment. Significantly, early estimates by the SS put the Jewish population in France at 800,000 or more, at least twice the actual numbers. The resources of France and its labour force pri-

17

marily attracted Hitler and his associates. Profitable exploitation notwithstanding, Göring hoped that the French would remain perpetual providers of food and wines, the good things of life. Goebbels preferred to represent them as a nation of 'couturiers'. Rosenberg believed that the French had invented class warfare with the 1789 Revolution, and they would have to be made to put the clock back. When indulging his favourite sentimentality that he was an artist by nature, Hitler found occasion to patronise French architects and town planning, but that was all. The eyes of the French would pop out of their heads, Goebbels one day reported, if they knew what plans Hitler really had for them.

Rather than just let their eyes pop out of their heads, of course, they might have resisted. Until June 1940 the concept of Frenchmen collaborating most willingly in turning over their country's resources of labour and raw material to Germany would have been unimaginable. Yet the Blitzkrieg and then the immediate swift return to a new order as part of Hitler's Europe opened the way to ideas and practices which until then had been abhorrent and marginal.

What happened in France during the early part of the Occupation illustrates that sleight-of-mind that so fascinated George Orwell, whereby people under totalitarian control rationalise and justify what they are being forced to do, when they would rebel if asked to do the same thing in a society with the usual democratic constraints. To adapt Orwell's imagery, there had been a Two Minute Hate, after which, and by means of which, the dreaded enemy had been transposed into the benevolent saviour and partner. The process was well understood by the German authorities. Their soldierly performance was allowed to speak for itself, and now the population at large, through the mouthpiece of the Vichy government, was invited to consider what sort of favour could be done, what gratitude earned, in order for France to plead for generous treatment in the peace conference to which Hitler was looking forward with confidence.

So procedures and policies which the Germans knew to be exploitation pure and simple were presented by Vichy for general acceptance on the grounds that French self-interest was being served. The deception is fully illustrated in the single detail that France was ordered to pay for the costs of the German Occupation a daily sum of 400 million francs – in other words, financing its own spoliation. In this deception lay the human desire to avoid some undefined great sacrifice by making a series of smaller concrete sacrifices. Such had been the logic of pre-war appeasement as well, whereby from a position of comparative strength in 1938 Czechoslovakia had been delivered to Hitler for fear of something even worse happening.

The Vichy régime's extension of appeasement, from a truncated zone in which it was best tolerated with cynicism by its overlords, proved a mechanism for inflicting injuries upon itself. That this could ever be defended as a political process was a measure of illusion about the nature of Nazism even in the face of experience. Between sixty and a hundred per cent of French agricultural and industrial production was diverted to Germany; two million labourers were also compulsorily sent there. Confiscations, chicaneries and frauds, controls, official purchasing agencies that were concealed cartels, black markets connived at by the German authorities, bled the country. The Germans used every illegality and violence to enrich themselves – the very thing which they were accusing the Jews of doing.

A number of French Nazis declared themselves to be unequivocally on the winning side, as they saw it. Such men came from all levels of society; some were sincere, some were dupes, some were gangsters and some were fools. Three or four hundred thousand Frenchmen enrolled in German military organisations, including the Waffen SS, or as French 'gestapistes', agents in German pay, and as members of such Fascist movements as the Parti Populaire Français (PPF), run by the ex-communist Jacques Doriot, or the rival Rassemblement National Populaire (RNP), run by the ex-socialist Marcel Déat. The danger of these people derived from their mass-identification with Hitlerism. The rest of society, the majority whose motivations were too complex for generalisation, found in practice that choices had been made for them – choices that proved indispensable to Nazism as often as not. Conscientious bureaucrats in the administration, for instance, had been converted into traitors, whether they liked it or not, by Vichy's collaboration. Between eight and nine million Frenchmen in one way or another worked directly for the Germans, building the Atlantic defences with military roads and blockhouses and pens for U-boats, or in factories producing aircraft and armaments and vital components for the Nazi war-machine, or growing food for Germany.

Collaboration, then, facilitated rather mitigated Nazism. A number of studies have shown this to be the case, and strikingly so

19

where persecution of Jews was concerned. *Vichy France and the Jews*, by Robert O. Paxton and Michael R. Marrus, concludes beyond all doubt that collaboration did not ward off the French contribution to the Holocaust, but on the contrary made certain of it.

Before 1940 there were several thousand anti-Semites who would have practised racialism if offered the opportunity. They belonged to fringe associations of their own. Some of them were in touch with anti-Jewish pressure groups operated out of Erfurt by Julius Streicher whom they liked to imitate, and they had attended occasions such as the annual Nuremberg rallies. But even the extremists among them could hardly have visualised the public remaining indifferent to officially-sanctioned persecution of Jews.

Collaboration brought these anti-Semites to the fore. Moral checks had been removed at a stroke. Since the German intention to persecute had been evident for some years before the war, Jews were to that extent already hostages to fortune. Now, according to the Vichy attitude, the concrete sacrifice of Jews was acceptable, in the expectation of receiving compensatory concessions in some other sphere. One or two Vichy ministers, notably Raphael Alibert, the Minister of Justice, and Peyrouton, the Minister of the Interior, were anti-Semites by conviction, and urged it upon their colleagues. Pétain had not previously had occasion to give the Jewish question much thought and his feelings were probably expressed in his remark: 'Un juif n'est jamais responsable de ses origines; un Franc-Maçon l'est toujours de son choix'.[1] Laval, his deputy, made no bones about the fact that he could see the elements of an advantageous bargain or deal in the German anxiety to lay hands on the Jews. The effect of the Two-Minute-Hate, to continue Orwell's image, was to make the Jewish question an essential test of collaboration. Put another way, democracy had been an essential factor in the previous security of Jews.

By 1940 there were perhaps 350,000 Jews in France, of whom half were French citizens by birth. Numbers are disputed but, during the 1920s and '30s when comparatively liberal immigration laws applied, as many as 150,000 Jewish immigrants may have reached France, though a proportion would then have moved on futher. One authority gives the figure of 55,000 Jews entering France in the decade after 1933.

---

1. Pétain quoted in Pierre Chevallier, *Histoire de la Franc-Maçonnerie française*, Vol. III (1877–1944), Paris, 1975, p. 349.

Be the statistics as they may, this was the very first group of people against whom Vichy moved. The compulsion to do so came entirely from within, as an integral step in accommodating to the Germans. The Germans themselves had not yet begun anti-Jewish measures in the occupied zone, where paradoxically they even had to restrain PPF youths from attacking Jewish shops. The Germans had put no pressure at all upon Vichy to begin organised anti-Semitism. Persecution of Jews was therefore a matter of voluntary propitiation of Hitlerism, an early offering of goodwill, one of those favours which it was hoped would be one day recompensed.

Between August 1940 and March 1941 previous legislation was repealed and the French equivalent of the Nuremberg laws were passed. Jews were excluded from the public service, and allotted a secondary position under the law. Numerous further restrictions were deliberately imposed in order to harass them. What in Germany had taken five years was achieved in France within eight months by means of seventeen laws and twenty three decrees. This was the main administrative thrust from Vichy during the opening stage of the German occupation, regardless of what other and more realistic problems and political considerations had to be faced. By March 1941 a Commissariat Général aux Questions Juives (CGQJ), had been set up, at its head an anti-Semite of long standing, Xavier Vallat. A war veteran, Vallat did not care for the Germans, and was to a considerable extent motivated by the sentiment that national honour required him to show the Germans how these things were done. Special anti-Jewish police forces were recruited and placed at his disposal, with powers of entry and arrest.

One step behind Vichy, quite separately, the apparatus of the planned persecution was installed in the occupied zone in conformity with Hitler's intentions. At the end of September 1940 Hauptsturmführer Dannecker of the SS arrived in Paris. He was only twenty-seven, and even to Vallat his anti-Semitism seemed 'frenzied'. His superior in Berlin was Eichmann, who was directly responsible to Himmler for running the anti-Jewish department within the Nazi police complex, the Reichssicherheitshauptamt (RSHA). In the Paris offices Dannecker was in charge of a section of not more than thirty men. The co-operation and goodwill of the French authorities were therefore indispensable to him.

Addressing himself to the Préfecture de Police in Paris, Dannecker arranged to liaise with the special new anti-Jewish police squads. By 22 February 1942 he was reporting back to Berlin: 'Les inspecteurs français formés et instruits en collaboration avec notre service des Affaires juives constituent aujourd'hui une troupe d'élite et les cadres d'instruction pour les Français détachés, à l'avenir, à la police antijuive. Pour la zone occupée, notre service a entièrement assuré son influence sur la police antijuive.'[2]

No obstacles had been put in their way. In October 1940 on Dannecker's behalf the French police ordered a census of the Jews. Everyone Jewish was obliged to register in alphabetical order at police stations, providing details of their profession, nationality and domicile. Henri Bergson's reply had a resonance all its own: 'universitaire, philosophe; prix Nobel; juif.'[3] The results of the census were kept by a civil servant named André Tulard, and were therefore known as the 'Tulard dossiers'; more properly they were death-files. (After the war, incidentally, Tulard, like so many others, was considered to have done merely his bureaucratic duty; he rose to the top of his profession and eventually died loaded with honours.)

The looting of pictures and works of art from Jewish owners had begun the moment the German army arrived. Otto Abetz, for example, arriving at the German Embassy to take up his appointment as ambassador, spent the opening weeks of the occupation sorting out and crating up for despatch the choicest collectors' items, destined for German museums, for Göring, and even for Hitler himself. In October, with the census-taking, this plundering was placed on a more systematic footing. Owners of Jewish businesses, from the largest industrial enterprises down to small workshops, were obliged to register. Instructions to the Militärbefehlshaber were to suppress Jewish influence in the French economy. Whatever served or supplied the war-machine was expropriated. Numerous companies were deviously transferred into German ownership. 11,000 buildings owned by Jews, and 27,000 businesses were sequestrated on behalf of French 'commissaires-gérants', managers approved by the occupation authorities. In many cases they acquired title and full rights. Indeed these particular war-profiteers formed an association to lobby for security of ownership in the event of the dispossessed Jews one day returning to reclaim what was theirs. Vichy was anxious lest this transfer of wealth created lost opportunities, and Germans enriched themselves where Frenchmen might have done. Similar measures, often justified as being in defence of

2. Dannecker quoted in Claude Levy and Paul Tillard, *La grande rafle du Vel D'Hiv*, Paris, 1967, p. 245.
3. Bergson quoted in Henri Michel, *Paris Résistant*, Paris, 1982, p. 30.

French interests, were therefore undertaken through the CGQJ in the unoccupied zone. One of the reasons for Vallat's downfall in 1942 was the corruption of his inspectors, too frequently caught lining their pockets with money stolen directly from Jews.

Frenchmen were subsidised by Dannecker to launch a variety of anti-Semitic institutions, which served not only to obscure SS purposes but also to heighten the impression that the French could give a lead when it came to attacking Jews. Quite separate from the Vichy CGQJ, an Institut des Questions Juives was founded in Paris on SS money, under the chairmanship of Paul Sézille, a former colonial officer. Its function was to uncover all and any Jewish elements, wherever they might be, and publicise them, as though spontaneously. Nothing was too small to escape the notice of this glorified and paranoid police informer. In a letter dated 16 July 1942, a year or so after his Institut had come into existence, Sézille was writing to an official at the German Embassy to explain that a subsidiary 'Friends of the Institut' had been formed, containing 31,287 vigilantes. Among other organisations promoted by Dannecker and Sézille was the Association of Anti-Jewish Journalists, which numbered 3,000 members.

By August 1941 various concentration camps had been prepared, of which the most central was Drancy, in an uncompleted housing-estate close to Le Bourget with its airport and railway station. The camps, Drancy included, were staffed and administered by French police under instruction from Dannecker.

The translation into actuality of these carefully conceived facilities for persecution came with the invasion of the Soviet Union in June 1941. The expediency of the 1939 pact was laid aside. Taken unawares, Stalin appealed for help from every quarter, thus dispensing Communists everywhere from the earlier obligation to collaborate. The first shots were now fired at Germans in Paris, by Communists, some of whom were also Jews. The Militärbefehlshaber thereupon imposed a collective fine of a billion francs upon the Jewish community, and arrested and sent to Drancy several hundred of the more prominent Jewish personalities. Far from being held as hostages, on 27 March 1942 these were the first French Jews to be deported to Auschwitz.

To simulate a favourable climate for operations, the SD, stage-managed a Paris version of the Kristallnacht. On the night of 2 October 1941, squads of hired French Nazis were provided with explosives, with which they blew up seven synagogues. This was intended to signal widespread resentment by the Parisians of the Jews living among them, and to be followed by massive demonstrations on the part of the public. Anti-Semitism, it was hoped, would look popular. In fact, the subterfuge was so transparent that it set the Militärbefehlshaber and the Nazi Party at loggerheads. This power struggle, for such it essentially was, remained unresolved until May 1942, when General Carl Oberg was appointed to Paris, with the title of Höherer SS und Polizei-führer. Oberg was a personal friend of Himmler. He had come from murdering Jews in Poland, notably at Radom.

Xavier Vallat had been curtly informed that Jews were now to be deported from France, and that his CGQJ was to be available to carry through the necessary measures in conjunction with the SS and the SD. Vallat's response was considered insufficiently enthusiastic. He preferred anti-Semitism with a French accent, and on these quasi-nationalistic competitive grounds he hesitated. Impatiently the Germans took the occasion to insist that he was replaced by one of their paid agents, Darquier de Pellepoix, a man with a record of anti-Semitic agitation. At the moment of their choosing, the Germans had simply incorporated Vichy's parallel mechanism of persecution. So much for the defence of French interests through collaboration.

On 5 May 1942 a large gathering took place in the Ritz Hotel in Paris, at which Heydrich, then head of the Sicherheitsdienst, introduced Oberg to the ranking SD and SS officers in France, as well as to selected senior personnel from the staff of the Militärbefehlshaber. Heydrich explained to them what had been decided a few months previously at the Wannsee Conference. He then described in detail how the policy of mass-murder was developing in Eastern Europe, and what part in it would be expected of the German administration and the Vichy régime. Urgency was impressed upon his listeners; the war did not allow them to be leisurely; the Jews were to be deported and killed by the end of the year.

To clarify how this was to be done, Heydrich had a further meeting with the Prefect of Police in Paris, René Bousquet. In order to suppress resistance and deport Jews for the 'Final Solution', Heydrich demanded that the regular French police forces should be subordinated directly to Oberg. A precedent for such a step existed in Belgium. A witness of this encounter was Fernand de Brinon, the delegate-general of the Vichy government in Paris, and the most outright of collaborators. He wrote: 'Heydrich dut avoir une sorte de penchant pour Bousquet qui se présentait à lui plein de bonne volonté, affirmant son désir de collaboration avec les autorités allemandes afin de lutter contre le communisme. Bousquet professa, en paroles tout au moins, une grande admiration pour le courage de la S.S.'[4]

The French police, as Bousquet and Heydrich arranged in the event, would do what was required, but there would not be a joint police bureaucracy to formalise their mutual understanding. Such conduct painfully reveals the expedients to which the Vichy régime was driven in order to screen ugly reality. After the war, Bousquet was condemned for collaboration and simultaneously reprieved and decorated for resistance – a double-faced judgement characteristic of the times.

On 29 May only three weeks or so after the Heydrich–Bousquet accord, German preliminaries were finalised with the decree that Jews would have to wear a yellow star on their clothing, as in Poland and Germany itself. This symbol, the German authorities believed, would segregate and alienate Jews from the French. Eichmann himself now arrived in Paris to activate deportation.

The French government was provided with summary demands for the delivery of Jews according to German requirements. Some prevarication took place on the part of Laval, who tried to draw distinctions between Jews who were French-born, and therefore full citizens of the state, and those who were foreign-born, now deprived of legal rights of any kind. His hesitations were insincere. In the perspective of Vichy, the Jews had value only in that the Germans seemed to want to have them so badly. Not even time was gained.

The first mass arrests, known as 'la grande rafle', started on the night of 16 July, and lasted for twenty-four hours. Five Paris arrondissements were sealed off, disrupting the life of much of the city. Some 27,388 names had been selected from Tulard's files though about half of these managed to avoid arrest, because absent or in hiding. Nearly 900 teams of French gendarmes, the familiar blue-uniformed men, were assisted by bands of PPF youths. Fifty buses, the familiar green-and-white buses, were requisitioned from the Compagnie des Transports. So it came about that what the SD had instigated was performed entirely by the French themselves. No German was observed to be playing a part.

---

4. Fernand de Brinon, *Mémoires*, Paris, 1949, p. 148.

From that moment until the Liberation of Paris at the end of August 1944, transports left Drancy at regular intervals. At every step gendarmes continued to do exactly what was demanded of them. There are reports of bystanders applauding, and there are reports of bystanders weeping, but no recorded instance of interference, or even active protest. There are also reports of gendarmes overcome by emotion, but no authenticated instance of a single one who preferred to resign rather than be so degraded.

Late in 1943, by which time Dannecker was away in Bulgaria and had been replaced by Hauptsturmführer Roethke, and by which time also the worst had already happened, the SD formally took over the running of Drancy, though still employing French gendarmes there.

Le Mémorial de la déportation des juifs de France, compiled name by name by Serge Klarsfeld from German records of the transports, has established the fact that eighty-five convoys left Drancy containing 75,721 Jews, of whom about one-third were French-born. This is a minimum number. As Klarsfeld emphasises, there were deportations incompletely recorded from the Vichy zone, as well as the shooting of hostages and other atrocities for which he has been unable to provide named victims.

What did the French people make of it? That Jews were being plundered and arrested with every brutality, and then deported to the East, was common knowledge. Crowds would gather to watch daily scenes, not only the dramas of Drancy, but for instance the convoying of Jews under armed guard to the huge Lévitan department store in the centre of Paris. Once Jewish-owned, this place had been sequestrated and was used as a depot where clothes and furnishings from Jewish homes were sorted out and packed up to be despatched to Germany. Three days after the 'grande rafle', Claude Mauriac, son of the famous novelist, was seeing his mother off at the Gare d'Austerlitz. 'Un long train de marchandises, cerné par des forces policières imposantes, avec de pâles visages d'enfants pressés aux étroites ouvertures des wagons à bestiaux. Voilà ce que j'ai vu hier matin.' And he added in his diary: 'Maman est bouleversée par ce spectacle.'[5] So no doubt were the thousands of other travellers at the station that day.

What would happen in the East was not known. The Jews themselves were uncertain about their fate upon leaving French soil.

---

5. Claude Mauriac, *Les Espaces Imaginaires*, Paris, 1975, p. 238.

One widely accepted deception, spread by the Germans, was that a magnified ghetto was being created in the vicinity of Lublin, where Jews would work the land. This was implausible, to say the least, if only because of the implied wastage of skills. There was also an undercurrent of persistent rumour that Jews were being systematically killed. The likelihood, though it is beyond proving, is that this information filtered down from the upper echelons of the German administration, from those men who had listened to Heydrich's briefing and discussed it afterwards in ever-widening circles. And the truth also sounded implausible, though validated by the inhumanity of contact with the Germans.

At the individual level, decent impulses often prevailed when French men and women saw others worse off than themselves. It may be reasonably asserted that some thousands more Jews might have gone to their deaths had it not been for papers counterfeited for them, false identities and alibis provided, and accommodation offered in farms, schools, monasteries, cellars and attics – France, like all countries under Nazi occupation, had its share of brave and desperate people.

The Catholic church was divided in its response. As a rule, the higher prelates advocated passivity or outright collaboration, some of them going so far as to draw attention to anti-Semitic utterances dating back to the earliest historic times of the papacy. On the other hand, on 23 August 1942, Mgr Saliège, archbishop of Toulouse, gave instructions that a text of his be read aloud in the churches of his diocese, calling for an act of conscience in regard to Jews. 'Ils font partie du genre humain'[6] was one of the tragic sentences which he found himself reduced to uttering. Laval sent for the papal nuncio in order to protest against this text.

At about the same moment, Pastor Boegner, head of the Protestant community, sought an interview with Laval, to plead for Jewish children in particular, because they were being separated from their parents. He returned to report, 'Je lui parlais de massacres; il me répondait jardinage.'[7] Laval had by then had a number of meetings with Oberg and other leading SS and SD officers, and certainly was fobbing off his importunate visitor.

Outright resistance naturally included Jews; there were some exclusively Jewish groups. The number of Jews summarily executed

6. Archbishop Salièges quoted in Henri Amouroux, *La grande histoire des Français sous l'occupation*, Vol. 5 *Les passions et les haines*, Paris, 1981, p. 336.
7. Pasteur Boegner quoted ibid., p. 333.

in France, either as hostages or as armed militants captured by the Germans, is 1,100 according to Serge Klarsfeld. Once again, he stresses that this is the minimum figure which can be established.

The more widespread response, however, was either to shelter under Vichy policy and turn a blind eye to what was happening, or to encourage it in ways which were sometimes furtive and anonymous, sometimes active and open. The idea that Jews might indeed be going to their deaths in the East was circulated with approval in print, as in this article on 19 November 1942 – it is hard to believe that its author, Maurice de Séré, had not been informed of Heydrich's briefing.

Mais maintenant, juif, que les hommes qui te combattent a mort ont pénétré dans ton fief, cette demi-France que tu avais cru pouvoir barder en espérant réoccuper bientôt l'autre moitié, que vas-tu faire? Envahi par la terreur, tu sais quel est le sort qui t'attend. Tu t'enfuis dans les montagnes et tu te caches dans des coins secrets. Mais prends patience, juif, tu ne perds rien pour attendre et, tu le sais, ton sort est réglé, tu disparaîtras jusqu'au dernier de ta race.

Au pilori, the weekly magazine in which this appeared, specialised in gutter racialism. No insinuation or prejudice was too vile for it. One of its earliest slogans immediately after the German entry into Paris, had been 'Les juifs doivent payer pour la guerre ou mourir'.[8] Its columns were always pointing the finger at Jews or crypto-Jews, insisting that penal measures be taken against them. Here, in short, was an organ for denunciation, what is more one subsidised by the government in that official advertisements were inserted in it. Sales were also high, probably at least 100,000, comparable to its German parallel, *Der Stürmer*.

On 13 August 1942 *Au pilori* was giving advice: 'De nombreux lecteurs nous demandent à quel organisme ils doivent s'adresser pour signaler les activités occultes ou les frandes des juifs. Il suffit pour cela d'adresser une lettre ou une simple note signée au Haut-Commissariat aux Questions Juives ou à défaut aux bureaux de notre journal qui transmettra.' Signed letters obviously committed the writers. Not only *Au pilori* but every paper carried its column aimed at tipping off the police. *Je suis partout*, which correctly proclaimed that it had gathered a team comprised of the leading Nazified intellectuals, expressed the sentiments of *Au pilori*, but in

8. *Au pilori*, August 1940.

better French. At the height of its wartime popularity, its circulation was an astonishing 300,000.

'J'irai le dire à la Kommandantur' was the title of an article by the poet Robert Desnos in the paper *Aujourd'hui* as early as September 1940 – Desnos himself was eventually deported and died in a German camp. It was in this sudden and growing practice of denunciation that the totalitarian state was proving the kind of power it exercised over the individual, corrupting private standards of civic behaviour and destroying solidarity. Desnos did not use such explicit language but his meaning was clear, and to stop denunciations he appealed to 'the sense of dignity'. In the well-known satirical novel *Au bon beurre*, by Jean Dutourd, published after the war, the married couple who are its central characters think nothing of posting off an unsigned letter to the Kommandantur to give the address where an escaped prisoner of war can be picked up, a man who happens to be the son of a neighbour and a customer at their grocer's shop against whom they have a temporary grudge.

Even today, after the ceaseless weeding of evidence and the construction of alibis, thousands of these anonymous denunciations survive to bear witness to fear and jealousy. This was what moral collapse really looked like.

This letter to the CGQJ was on Ministry of Interior writing-paper: 'J'ai l'honneur de porter à votre connaissance, à toutes fins utiles, qu'un appartement, situé 57 bis, boulevard Rochechouart, appartenant au juif Gresalmer, contient un très beau mobilier.'[9]

Zeitschel was the counsellor in the German Embassy responsible for dealing with all matters Jewish, and this is an example of his correspondence from Frenchmen: 'Ainsi que j'apprends de source confidentielle un magasin juif (fabrication et vente de bas) ferait des affaires sous un propriétaire Douilheb, Magandu, 42, rue du Fg St-Honoré. Il paraît également que la fille de ce juif travaille continuellement dans le magasin, en outre, ce juif aurait des dettes importantes.'[10]

Dr Laurent Viguier was a full-time activist at Sézille's Institut des Questions Juives, and unlike many, he delighted in signing his name to letters of denunciation to the Germans. 'Etant donné l'ordonnance qui interdit aux employés juifs d'être en contact avec le public, il faut que Madame S. . . soit destituée de sa place de concierge.'[11]

---

9. Quoted in Lévy and Tillard, *La grande rafle*, p. 242.
10. Quoted in André Halimi, *La Délation sous l'occupation*, Paris, 1983, p. 53.

In his book *La grande histoire des Français sous l'occupation*, the historian Henri Amouroux has collected numerous examples of spiteful or self-seeking collaboration, in one chapter especially to which he has given the title 'Le Cancer des Âmes.' The following letter is signed 'Quelqu'un du quartier.' 'Il y a... rue Pierre-Demons, au quatrième étage gauche des meubles en garde, les propriétaires N... sont très amis avec les juifs Blum. Ils racontent que les meubles sont à eux. Les conciergent [*sic*] reçoivent des produits contingentés par colis a partager avec les N... La concierge déteste le maréchal Pétain. Il n'y a qu'à la faire parler.'[12]

A seventeen-year-old schoolboy offered his services to Sézille as an informer because another boy in school had said to him, 'Il y a des juifs qui sont plus français que toi.'[13] An eighteen-year-old boy wrote to the German Embassy to promote himself as a specialist in detecting Jews not wearing their compulsory yellow star. Roethke, who in 1942 replaced Dannecker and took over Drancy, wrote a note on 14 November 1943 requesting a police permit for side-arms 'pour le citoyen Bertrand L... qui a été menacé par des juifs et des personnes à opinion pro-juive. Il a livré d'excellents matériaux contre les juifs et s'est montré également antijuif sans limite, à l'étranger.'[14]

The motivation for what was effectively murder through the agency of others lay, in Amouroux's opinion, in simple envy and a sense of failure for which the individual did not hold himself responsible. Personal conflict could be wished upon others to resolve. A professor from Toulon wrote to ask for the arrest of his wife's lover on the grounds that the man was Hungarian, a Jew and a Communist. In contrast, a woman denounced her husband's mistress:

Puisque vous vous occupez des Juifs, et si votre campagne n'est pas un vain mot, voyez donc le genre d'existence de la fille M...A..., ancienne danseuse, actuellement en hôtel, 31, boulevard de Strasbourg, ne portant pas l'étoile. Cette personne, *non contente d'être Juive*, débauche les maris des vraies Françaises et sachez donc de quoi elle vit [?]. Défendez les femmes contre les Juives, ce sera votre meilleure

11. Quoted in Amouroux, *Les passions et les haines*, p. 270.
12. Ibid., p. 270.
13. Ibid., p. 262.
14. Ibid., p. 264.

propagande, et vous rendrez un mari français à sa femme.[15]

There were of course monetary rewards as well. Depending on local factors, denunciations of Jews and other wanted people might be recompensed with sums ranging between a hundred and three thousand francs.

Human nature no doubt remains constant down the ages, but which aspects of it will be expressed depends upon social organisation. When instituting its own brand of anti-Semitic repression, Vichy may well have had confused motives to propitiate, to take the easy advantage, perhaps to keep the Jewish question in its own hands. What it achieved was the condition legitimising persecution. It was characteristic of totalitarianism, of Nazism in particular, that the quite ordinary men and women who wrote those denunciations or worked for the CGQJ or the police, had been brought to conceive their contribution to genocide to be a matter of useful duty and service to the state.

Bousquet, for one, knew it as he is on record telling Oberg, just before the 'grande rafle' that the fact that this man-hunt was to be undertaken by his men was embarrassing for Paris. Connivance in murder, in other words, was clearly perceived. At that time, the German authorities maintained three battalions of SD police in France, mustering fewer than 3,000 men. Of these, few were fluent French speakers or had specialist knowledge of the country. Their parade of power masked considerable helplessness. Oberg reported to Berlin that politically speaking he could do as he liked where deportations were concerned, but to be effective in practice he asked for a reinforcement of 250 men. He had to make do with just four. Manpower demands for the surveillance of frontiers, as well as for counter-resistance and security measures, and finally for the processes of deportation and mass-murder, far exceeded capacity to meet them. As the war turned against Germany these resources were stretched thinner still. After the occupation of the Vichy zone in November 1942, the same police forces had to spread over about twice as much territory. Increasingly the task of persecution fell upon the obliging French themselves.

The deportation from France of Jews depended in the final analysis upon enough Frenchmen consenting to take part in it. The few had assured the complicity of the many.

15. Quoted in David Rousset, *Le Pitre ne rit pas*, Paris, 1979, p. 39.

3

THE VICHY OF THE OTHER PHILIPPE

H.R. Kedward

We are coming to accept the idea that Vichy should be presented in the plural, though it is not all that easy to put the concept into a book title. Eventually 'the governments of Vichy' might be preferred to 'the Vichy régime', but I suspect that the plurality will normally be laid out in the chapter headings, like the different entrées which make a 'Menu à 80 Francs' into several alternative meals. The strands within Vichy do not, however, have to be presented as alternatives. Although examiners still like to ask 'Vichy France: Old Guard or New Order?', Robert Paxton was, in fact, ahead of the field in stating that Vichy was not one or the other, but both,[1] and most recently Denis Peschanski has explicitly written about 'Vichy in the plural' and talks of 'le premier Vichy' from 1940 to some point in 1942 as if there must be a second, a third or even a fourth Vichy to come. Or were they all there concurrently? And either way, how do you label such a plural régime? Was 'le premier Vichy' Fascist, Peschanski asks. There is no quick answer, for experts are constantly pluralising the concept of Fascism, so that we are faced not with one issue but with many. Which Vichy? What kind of Fascism? Readers could despair at this point, but Peschanski has a positive conclusion, welcoming the plural concepts in the interests of history, which thrives on making detailed distinctions.[2] In an age when the values of history are challenged by a new and aggressive utilitarianism the historical profession must continue to insist that nothing is ever as simple as it seems.

Least simple of all was the apparent simplicity of Philippe Pétain's Vichy, which claimed to be above, or outside, politics, even above, or outside history, in the sense that Pétainism was seen to

1. Robert Paxton, *Vichy France: Old Guard and New Order*, London, 1972.
2. *Vichy 1940–1944. Archives de guerre d'Angelo Tasca*, Paris, 1986. Introductory study by Denis Peschanski, 'Le régime de Vichy a existé', p. 12 and pp. 47–9.

32

correspond to something supra-historical in the French nation, to relate to an essentialist code of national and familial values, which the highly political régime of the Third Republic was accused of subverting in the interests of faction, class and party. It was the court chronicler, René Benjamin, who excelled even the kingmakers of Action Française in establishing the olympian nature of Philippe Pétain. After Maurras, Léon Daudet and Robert Havard de la Montagne had made the superhuman, divine claims for the Marshal, Benjamin gave flesh and blood to the myth of Pétain in his vastly popular *Le maréchal et son peuple*.[3] He had already demonstrated his talents as a hagiographer in 1937 with his *Mussolini et son peuple*, the first lines of which introduced the Duce as a kind of sun god,[4] but what is important about his adulation of Pétain is that it registered a norm in public opinion, not an extravagant exception. Pétain was insulated not only from the usual trappings of history, but also from the usual expectations of political action. The letters to Pétain which Benjamin finds most endearingly ingenuous are those from simple people asking for help or material aid, an extra ration of chocolate, more potatoes or an increase in family supplement. Only slowly did the phrase 'l'oeuvre du Maréchal' come to mean what Pétain was doing for France: in the first year of Vichy it more often meant what France – French men, women and particularly children – should do for the Marshal.

Shortly after Benjamin's exaltations came *La seule France* from Charles Maurras, which took Pétain not only out of politics but out of rational enquiry altogether, but Maurras did give the Marshal an historical place in his utopian version of French history which he called his 'uchronie', a version which left out all the revolutionary and republican events of the previous 160 years as 'un-French', and jumped from the grandeur of the ancien régime to the marvels of classical authority reborn in the rule of Pétain.[5] No historians outside the tradition of Action Française have taken this chronology seriously. On the contrary most historians since the war have insisted on giving Pétain and Pétainism a detailed political dimension within the right-wing history of the Third Republic, if not

3. René Benjamin, *Le maréchal et son peuple*, Paris 1941.
4. Idem, *Mussolini et son peuple*, Paris 1937, p. 2.
5. Charles Maurras, *La seule France*, Lyon, 1941, pp. 234–5. For an analysis of his 'uchronie' and his concepts of 'French' and 'un-French', see H.R. Kedward, 'Charles Maurras and the True France' in R.J. Bullen et al. (eds), *Ideas into Politics*, London 1984, pp. 119–29.

always with the polemical intention of Albert Bayet whose *Pétain et la 5e Colonne* of 1944 gave Pétain a scurrilous role in the underworld history of the Cagoule and other quasi-Fascist organisations of the 1930s.[6]

Historians still have much to do in exploring Pétain's Vichy, particularly in revealing the effects, rather than the intentions, of Pétain's Rénovation, or Révolution, Nationale, in such areas as family life, women's employment and town/country relationships; and there will always be historical disagreement on the extent of Pétain's involvement in the different stages of collaboration. But despite the growing availability of archives Pétain's Vichy will probably appeal relatively less to historical research in the next ten years or so. By contrast the Vichy of the other Philippe will soon be under siege, and it is the intention of this chapter to introduce a topic which will undoubtedly attract the revisionists, if it has not already done so.

Philippe Henriot was not the choice of Philippe Pétain for the Ministry of Information and Propaganda in December 1943. It was German pressure for the entry of Henriot and Joseph Darnand into the Vichy government, and Laval's acquiescence, that secured his appointment. Pétain did not put his name to the authorisation: he was said to detest Henriot. On the other hand he did not attempt to dismiss him. It was one more forced humiliation for the Marshal, but also one more concession. Henriot had been broadcasting regularly on Radio-Vichy for over a year: he was a frequent contributor to the collaborationist pages of *Gringoire* and *Je suis partout*, and in the provinces he was a roving lecturer at the invitation of local branches of the Milice, whose black shirt he wore on most public occasions. He was also to be seen attending meetings of lepidopterists, his private passion.

Born in 1889 into a Catholic military family, to a father who was a colleague of Pétain's at Saint-Cyr, Henriot did not follow the family line into the army, but embraced its staunch Catholicism, first as a teacher in a Catholic school in the Gironde and then as a politician and deputy for Bordeaux, sitting with the right-wing Fédération Républicaine in the 1930s and opposing the Spanish Republic, Communism and particularly André Marty, against whom he used his very considerable oratory in the Chamber as if engaged in a personal vendetta. Just as fervently he supported

6. Albert Bayet, *Pétain et la 5e Colonne*, Paris, 1944.

Munich in 1938 and the Armistice in 1940, and immediately rallied to Pétain and the Révolution Nationale. Everyone is agreed that the Nazi invasion of Russia in June 1941 liberated and further radicalised his anti-Communism, and by 1942 Henriot's collaborationism was overtly proclaimed in Parisian and Vichy circles, leading directly to his career as a radio propagandist. From January 1943 his broadcasts revealed him as Pétainist, devout Catholic, Milicien (after March 1943), anti-Semite and anti-Communist, and his voice, style of delivery and dialectical power earned him a page of grudging or glowing admiration in most memoirs of the period, bringing Vichy a last and vigorous flicker of popularity in the midst of its decline and disintegration.

Lucien Rebatet, nihilistic, barbed and cynical about many of his co-collaborators, was unambiguous about Henriot. 'Il s'imposait par le talent', he wrote in his *Mémoires d'un Fasciste*, and he speculated that if D-Day had been delayed by a few more months and the allied raids had continued, Henriot would have won over two-thirds of Gaullist supporters in France.[7] More often quoted is Maurice Martin du Gard's gossipy but informed *Chronique de Vichy* which estimated Henriot's broadcasts to be compulsory listening: 'Henriot est écouté par tout le monde, adversaires ou convaincus. Des familles décalent leurs heures de repas pour ne pas le manquer. Il n'y a plus personne dans la rue à l'heure où il parle.'[8] Guéhenno listened, so did Galtier-Boissière, so did Pétain and still more Madame Pétain, la Maréchale. The French in Algiers and London listened (except for Jean Oberlé), so too did 94 per cent of the 426 people clandestinely questioned by Max Barrioux in April 1944, all of whom were sympathetic to the Resistance.[9]

His voice, said Rebatet, was 'présente, bien timbrée, jamais théâtrale'[10]; to Guéhenno it was 'solide, méprisante et un peu nasillarde'.[11] Martin du Gard found it 'étonnante, grave, pleine,

---

7. Lucien Rebatet, *Les mémoires d'un fasciste*, vol. 2, 1941–47, Paris, 1976, p. 170.

8. Maurice Martin du Gard, *Chronique de Vichy, 1940–44*, Paris, 1948, p. 433. It is this quote that Henri Amouroux uses in his seventh volume of his *La grande histoire des Français sous l'occupation. Un printemps de mort et d'espoir, Novembre 1943–6 juin 1944*, Paris 1985, p. 67. Martin du Gard is also the main source for an earlier, and also much-quoted, study of Vichy by A. Brissaud, *La dernière année de Vichy, 1943–44*, 1965, pp. 240–2.

9. Amouroux, *grande histoire des Français sous l'occupation*, vol. 7, 1985, p. 70.

10. Rebatet, *Les mémoires d'un fasciste*, vol. 2, 1941–1947, 1976, p. 170.

11. Jean Guéhenno, *Journal des années noires, 1940–44*, Paris 1947. Folio edition, 1973, p. 421.

soignée',[12] while Sisley Huddleston, the Ex-*Times* correspondent, who was doing his own pro-Vichy tours of the French provinces, described it as a voice of 'metallic resonance, seizing one in the grip of steel'.[13] Amouroux concludes from Barrioux's unique opinion poll that Henriot's impact was probably greatest among employers, but Rebatet judged that his skill lay in presenting complex subjects with a clarity and directness which engaged the peasant, the mechanic and those who had retired.[14] Jean Oberlé, in his memoirs of 'Les Français parlent aux Français' on the BBC, claimed he never personally listened to Henriot but read the transcripts of his talks every day in order to reply in detail to his propaganda, since Henriot's major tactic was to present himself as the voice of reason within France correcting disinformation from abroad. Henriot's arguments, said Oberlé, were designed 'pour gens timorés, pour gens apathiques, et dans beaucoup de cas, ceux que l'on appelle des petits bourgeois'. But it was not a class he appealed to, continued Oberlé, rather a social attitude, the attitude which responded to the rallying cry of Charles Maurras, 'la France, la France seule'.[15] As for the survey by Crémieux-Brilhac and Bensimon, thirty years after the war, they found the clergy and the upper classes admitted most readily to having been impressed by Henriot.[16]

Nasal or metallic, appealing to the bourgeois or the petit bourgeois, Henriot's broadcasts were a daily, or twice daily, event of dynamic importance for the history of Vichy. It is not just the interest they aroused or the media personality he made for himself. Far more important is the way in which Henriot defined or exposed the basic rationale of Vichy's collaboration, which reduced the high-minded Vichy of Pétain, and the Vichy of barter and compromise led by Laval, to a simple populist formula. Sisley Huddleston, whose judgements have been largely discredited due to his credulous admiration for Pétain and his subsequent wish to sit on as many fences as possible, was accurate when he wrote,

12. Martin du Gard, *Chronique de Vichy, 1940–44*, p. 432.
13. Sisley Huddleston, *France. The Tragic Years*, London, 1958, p. 260.
14. Amouroux, *grande histoire des Français sous l'occupation*, Vol. 7, p. 71, and Rebatet, *Les mémoires d'un fasciste*, Vol. 2, 1941–1947, 1976, p. 10.
15. Jean Oberlé, *Jean Oberlé vous parle. Souvenirs de Cinq Années à Londres*, 1945, p. 212.
16. J.L. Crémieux-Brilhac and G. Bensimon, 'Les propagandes radiophoniques et l'opinion publique en France de 1940 à 1944', *Revue d'histoire de la deuxième guerre mondiale*, January 1976, pp. 3–18. See also the chapter by Pierre Sorlin 'The struggle for control of French minds', in K.R.M. Short (ed.), *Film and Radio Propaganda in World War II*, London, 1983, pp. 245–70.

Few men have been listened to with such passionate interest for a few months as was Philippe Henriot. He drove his admirers into ecstasy and his antagonists into frenzy. Whenever I was asked, and I was often asked, by admirers or antagonists, what I thought of him, I could only reply that it was highly regrettable . . . that the gulf between Vichy and Algiers should be widened by verbal violence. That was the fatal mistake. Henriot rendered all rapprochement of Vichy and Algiers . . . impossible.[17]

He is right, not because there was the potential for co-operation between Vichy and Algiers that he envisaged (there he is a prey to his own wishful thinking) but rather in his observation that Henriot's broadcasts gave stark definition to the war between Vichy and the Resistance. They did so because Henriot went further than any official Vichy authority before in giving Vichy's collaboration a clear justification and a pre-history with which huge numbers of French people could identify, not least because they themselves had contributed to it.

The pre-history of Pétainism, from Verdun onwards, did not lead clearly and directly to Pétain's handshake with Hitler at Montoire, nor to his continued existence as Chef de l'Etat once the Germans had broken the Armistice and occupied the whole of France in November 1942. For the French to understand that Pétain might be collaborating with his old enemy Germany necessitated an almost religious suspension of rational faculties, close to the belief that 'God moves in a mysterious way'. Equally, the nationalists of Action Française appeared badly qualified for an adventure in collaboration by their pre-history of vehement and dogmatic anti-Germanism. Even in 1944 the Germans were still suspicious of the French nationalist Right, and Pétain's apologists, such as Isorni, and Maurras himself at his trial, attempted to use their pre-history before the Vichy period as a kind of self-evident proof that they could not have collaborated. It is true that Laval's collaboration appeared to make more sense to the French public, but not because of the irresistible logic of his history before 1940 – he had after all 'collaborated' or negotiated with Britain and Russia as well as Italy and Germany – but more by the nature of his political personality as the foremost horsetrader of his generation.

By contrast, Henriot's broadcasts set the collaboration of Vichy firmly within the history of political struggle against Communism which half of France's electorate had in some way endorsed over the

17. Huddleston, *France. The Tragic Years*, pp. 260–1.

previous thirty years. Unlike the élitist tradition of the Old Guard with its aristocratic pretensions and its evocation of a distant eighteenth-century glory, the history which Henriot established for Vichy started well within memory of 1917, and was still acutely relevant to those who experienced everyday fears of Communist power.

On 17 January 1943 in one of his first broadcasts, Henriot set out what he called the Soviet plan to dominate Europe in which the International Brigades sent to Spain were the open vanguard of Bolshevism, but in which there was a sinister role for the Trojan Horse of Popular Frontism, designed to penetrate the weak régime of the Third Republic. 'Vous avez vu le Front Populaire mené par Moscou', he stated, 'la Chambre de 1936 manoeuvrée par Moscou, la guerre décidée par Moscou, la défaite organisée par Moscou', and now the Communist deputy, Fernand Grenier is speaking on the British radio and Stalin holds de Gaulle, Giraud, Roosevelt and Churchill on the end of a rope. Nothing has changed since 1917, he concluded. 'Marty et la mer Noire. Et Bela Kun et la Hongrie. Et la Pasionaria et les crucifixions espagnoles, et les cachots de la Tchéka, Moscou, Budapest, Barcelone, vingt-cinq ans de larmes, de détresses et de sang.'[18]

Such a monistic view of recent history was common fare in *Gringoire* and *Je suis partout*; it was the very essence of most propaganda emanating from collaborationist circles in Paris, notably round Jacques Doriot and his Parti Populaire Français (PPF); it was there in the notorious sentence of Laval's broadcast of 22 June 1942,[19] and it was there in pamphlets disseminated from Vichy throughout 1943. It was an ideological offensive far from invented by Henriot, and its importance throughout the whole of the Vichy period has been conclusively demonstrated.[20] But such was the power and attraction of Henriot's broadcasts that he convinced unnumbered thousands of listeners that this obsessive fear of Communism was their own rational good sense. Throughout 1943 everything that happened, not least the dispute for leadership of the French in Algiers, was fitted by Henriot into this historical vision of Bolshevik conspiracy, and at the end of the year he realised what

18. Philippe Henriot, *Et s'ils débarquaient?*, Paris, 1944, pp. 16–18.
19. 'Je souhaite la victoire de l'Allemagne, parce que sans elle le bolchévisme s'installerait partout.'
20. E.g. by Pierre Laborie in his local study of the département of the Lot, *Résistants, Vichyssois et autres*, Paris, 1980.

a trump card he had in his hand: popular ambivalence at the effects of Maquisard activity and the steadily mounting figures of civilian casualties due to allied bombing.

These were sensitive areas of collective concern, in village and urban quartier, in which long-standing prejudices were easily mobilised. From January 1944 Henriot supplied the families and neighbours of the victims with a mixture of official sympathy and visceral accusations against those whom he labelled the assassins of the skies and the woods and the alien leadership of the Maquis. He flaunted his Catholicism, putting a photograph of Cardinal Liénart of Lille, and one of his moralising equivocations, on the most circulated pamphlet from his Ministry,[21] and he played on every element of ingrained suspicion that behind all destruction and chaos lay the unseen hand of Communism. This demonology had been well-cultivated in the inter-war years and had become almost universal with the Nazi–Soviet pact of August 1939. Now in 1944 Henriot's commanding radio presence allowed it to be displayed as a respectable part of the home, alongside the crucifix on the bedroom wall and the portrait of Pétain in the living room. His defence of collaboration was thus emotionally and intellectually built on the respectable pre-war attitudes and fears of substantial classes and sections of French society, who had voted against the Popular Front, who had learnt to see Communism in a rather shadowy way as the nightmare of the twentieth century, and who now needed little encouragement to believe that the Bolsheviks were about to break down the doors of their homes.

Philippe Henriot's Vichy was starkly political. There were no Olympian myths, and no hidden agenda of negotiation and 'double-jeu'. Unlike Vichy polemicists before him Henriot did not try to hide the existence of the Gaullists abroad nor the dissidence at home, he did not try to minimise the Russian victories in the East, on the contrary he exaggerated the strategic threat they posed to France. Gaullist and Allied propaganda gave him the substance of his broadcasts; it was simply, but consistently, turned on its head: if they landed, he insisted, it would not be a liberation but an invasion, not a victory but a defeat; Moscow would have arrived on the beaches of France. Indeed, he claimed, its fifth column was already deeply entrenched in the camps of the Maquis.[22]

21. 'Pourquoi ces Attentats?'
22. There are substantial quotes from Henriot's 1944 broadcasts in Delperrie de

But would the 'débarquement' in the West ever come? Vital for the history both of Henriot's Vichy and of the Maquis is the growing impatience and disillusionment of the French people in the autumn and winter of 1943–4, waiting and waiting for the allied landing thought to be so close. By the spring of 1944 it had almost become a bad joke. Not surprisingly, therefore, the high point of Henriot's polemic and the peak of his, and Darnand's, Vichy were reached in March and April 1944.

The avowed context of what were now twice-daily ministerial broadcasts was the surge of occasionally desperate but growingly adventurous Maquis activity; but historians should pay just as much attention to the unadmitted context of intensified German reprisals and atrocities. These were not just in direct response to Maquis and other Resistance attacks, which is what is normally claimed by Vichy and Nazi apologists, but equally in pursuit of Germany's barbarous racial objectives, and in search of forced labour. German occupation tactics, ruthlessly established in 1941, were to execute an arbitrary selection of French people for any assault on their personnel, their installations or their transport, and to this was increasingly added the deportation of Jewish men, women and children and the round-up of men for labour in the Reich. In the winter of 1943-4 German punitive raids on villages and towns were commonly accompanied by indiscriminate shootings and the firing of buildings, a pattern of reprisals which the French Milice came to imitate and even to exceed. The wholesale deportation of men from the town of Nantua at the end of 1943, after the Maquis had staged a one-day parade in the nearby town of Oyonnax, was reported by the Prefect as terrifying proof that the Germans had decided on an extension of terror in the belief that activities by the Maquis would cease only when the local population came to fear the Germans more than the Maquis.[23]

The opposite, in fact, proved to be the case, but Henriot neither referred to German tactics of terror and brutality nor to their failure. What he used was the evidence supplied by Prefects and the Renseignements Généraux that where the Maquis were able to

Bayac, *Histoire de la Milice, 1918–45*, Paris 1969, especially in chapters 11 and 13. The essence of his accusations against the Maquis can be found in the Vichy pamphlets, 'Pourquoi ces Attentats?' and 'L'Armée de la Libération', author's photocopies from Archives Départementales, Hérault, 172 W35. See also the important article by J.L. Crémieux-Brilhac 'La Bataille des Glières et la guerre psychologique' in *Revue d'histoire de la deuxième guerre mondiale*, July 1975, pp. 45–72.
23. Archives Nationales (AN) FIC III 1135, Ain. Report of January 1944.

operate with impunity, or in periods when the German troops and Vichy police were less in evidence, varying levels of public hostility to the Maquisards could easily be discerned. This hostility prompted the local authorities to call for increased police presence and protection. Such calls were motivated by a fairly universal wish among Vichy officials to rediscover the independent status of Vichy which they had seen steadily eroded since November 1942, but this motivation had two quite separate aims within it. On the one hand there were those who called for a swift increase in the numbers of French police as a preventative measure to stop the Germans from taking action, and on the other there were Prefects who urged Vichy to send an ever larger contingent of armed police to carry out repressive raids into the countryside of equal force to those mounted by the Germans.[24]

It was one thing to try and cover yourself administratively from German accusations that you were inadequately policing the département, quite another to try and take responsibility for eliminating the Maquis altogether. Here, as so often, historians are forced to confront the unknown, and probably unknowable, levels of sheer administrative bluff in the reports of Prefects to Vichy. It makes the local archives particularly difficult to handle in the nine months prior to the Liberation. It was part of administrative survival, at all levels, to make the maximum protest when faced with a 'coup de main' by the Maquis. The Maquis themselves frequently encouraged such protests both to protect the officials whose tacit co-operation they increasingly secured, and to advertise their strength, but there was also the infiltration of the Milice into police intelligence which Darnand promoted after his ministerial appointment. Both factors made Prefects zealous in reporting incidents involving the Maquis. A scrupulous level of complaint at such incidents does not, therefore, by itself indicate an active commitment to Vichy repression, nor should the thousands of extracts from the postal censorship disapproving of Maquis 'attentats' be quoted by historians in isolation from extracts which qualify their meaning. In May 1944 in the Hérault, for example, 4,833 expressions of disapproval or disquiet at Maquis actions were noted, but there were only 457 extracts approving the government measures of

24. Compare, for example the report from the Dordogne for 27 March 1944 in AN. FIC III 1151, with reports from the Lozère for 8 July 1943 and 5 May 1944 in AN. FIC III 1165 and from the Gard for 2 February and 24 April 1944, in AN. FIC III 1153.

repression.[25]

But for Darnand and Henriot the indications of increased Resistance strength and the scope of Maquis operations, which progressively filled the pages of prefectoral reports and the Contrôle Postal, provided them with what they saw as an unanswerable case for a major Vichy initiative.

On 22 March 1944 Darnand wrote to General Oberg, the head of the SS:

> J'ai l'intention de procéder au cours des semaines qui viennent à un certain nombre de coups de main contre des nids de terroristes et des groupements de résistance. Pour que ces coups de main réussissent il y a intérêt à mettre sur pieds des unités très maniables, bien armées, pourvues de moyens de transports, capables d'agir avec la plus grande rapidité et un secret absolu.

What he proposed, in specific terms, was the creation of a 'groupe franc de la Garde' under his direct control.[26] The Garde was already at that very moment participating in the police campaign against the Maquis of the Glières in the Haute-Savoie, which Darnand had initiated in January and which was showing few results by the middle of March. Some 7,000–8,000 Miliciens under the leadership of de Vaugelas were sent by Darnand to reinforce the Garde and the local police, but by the date of his letter to Oberg it was clear both to Darnand and the Germans that his combined French forces would be unable to break up the Maquis by themselves. German troops were therefore sent in on 26 March, and the last tragic act of the Glières Resistance quickly unfolded, with the Milice largely reduced to picking off isolated Maquisards and torturing and killing prisoners and local inhabitants deemed to have supported the Maquis.

On 31 March Oberg rejected Darnand's proposal,[27] showing the continued caution of the Germans towards any increase in French military strength, so that Darnand was left with mainly the Milice, the Groupes Mobiles de Réserve (GMR) and the courts martial which he had introduced in January with which to continue the repression. To these was added an intensification of Henriot's radio propaganda. In a series of broadcasts, which provided the only information many French people received on the Glières, Henriot

25. AN. F7 14932.
26. AN. F7 14894.
27. Ibid.

glorified the role of the Milice in securing what he richly embroidered as an historic victory for French discipline and order over a rag-bag mixture of bandits, assassins and cowards, and he gave his reportage a certain on-the-spot credibility by going to the Haute-Savoie and interviewing some of the captured Maquisards, whose features he graphically described as twisted, stupid and evil.

Whatever the exact role of the Milice in the Glières, the only obvious benefit from the operation for Vichy was the relative triumph of Henriot's propaganda. Given all the problems of interpreting the archives, there is no missing the fact that report after report for April 1944 comments on the impact of his broadcasts. Not untypical is the evaluation of the Prefect of the Vaucluse that whereas two months before the people were ready to join the Resistance en masse, now opinion had swung back.[28] From the Var came details of 'réfractaires' from the compulsory labour service (STO) who had given themselves up due to Henriot's persuasiveness.[29] In the Dordogne his oratory and reasoning were said to have gained him a wide following, and in the Bouches-du-Rhône his appeal was seen to be restoring credibility to Vichy after a disastrous collapse of public confidence in 1943.[30] Only the Haute-Savoie provided a negative reaction when the Prefect wrote that the broadcasts of Henriot were much listened to, but the people were not convinced, reproaching him for having distorted the truth when he spoke about the plâteau of Glières.[31]

This corrective from the only local authority which was in a position to check the veracity of his broadcasts appears to have caused Henriot little anxiety, for he continued throughout the month to build on the media success with which he had been credited by most other regional administrators. 'Grâce à l'action de M. Philippe Henriot,' wrote the Prefect of the Loiret, 'il est indéniable que le sentiment gaulliste et giraudiste est, sinon en régression, du moins stoppé.'[32] In Vichy itself, Henriot is said by Martin du Gard to have cultivated the good opinion of Madame Pétain 'qu'il éblouit par sa voix'.[33] This is probably accurate, for it

---

28. AN. FIC III 1195, Vaucluse. Report of 3 April 1944.
29. AN. FIC III 1194, Var. Report of 1 April 1944.
30. AN. FIC III 1151, Dordogne. Report of 27 March, and FIC III 1143, Bouches-du-Rhône. Report of 5 April 1944.
31. AN. FIC III 1187, Haute-Savoie. Report of 4 May 1944.
32. Quoted in Amouroux, *grande histoire des Français sous l'occupation*, vol. 7, 1985, p. 68.
33. Martin du Gard, *Chronique de Vichy, 1940–44* 1948, p. 476.

was at this period that Henriot had set out a speech for Pétain to read to the nation condemning the actions of the Maquis. The German diplomat, von Renthe-Fink, who cut an absurd as well as bullying figure at Vichy, had been unsuccessfully demanding such a broadcast from Pétain since the events at Glières began, but Pétain had refused to use any phrase which might echo Laval's proclaimed wish for a German victory uttered two years before. By 26 April, the day of Pétain's first visit to Paris since 1940, the Marshal seems to have accepted the necessity of some kind of broadcast, for tactical reasons urged on him by Laval, but few people close to Pétain were prepared for the words he did finally use on 28 April.

All the 'mots clefs' of Henriot's propaganda were there. Pétain's speech reproduced charges of odious crimes committed against peaceful rural communities which spare neither women nor children; the menace of civil war; the mirage of the so-called Liberation; dissidence which opens the floodgates to Communism, and finally words which did indeed echo Laval's, an expression of gratitude to Germany whose 'défense du continent' was credited with protecting French civilisation from 'le danger que fait peser sur elle le bolchévisme'.[34]

According to Brissaud, Pétain knew in advance that these final words would be unacceptable to the French people, but his opinion on the earlier phrases condemning the Maquis is unknown.[35] Tasca leaves no doubt that the speech was written by Henriot and was imposed on Pétain[36], but why, after two months of refusal to make similar statements, did Pétain capitulate so completely? Was it tiredness, ill-health, fading mental powers? Perhaps it was all of these, but it was also a measure of Henriot's widespread reputation as reported from the provinces, and testifies to the inroads Henriot had made into the consciousness of Pétain himself. It was less than a month later that General Serrigny claims to have heard Pétain privately eulogise Henriot in no uncertain terms.[37]

In effect, the speech of 28 April 1944 brought the two Philippes together. Arguably it was the lowest point of Pétain's Vichy: unquestionably it was the pinnacle of Henriot's. Advisers to the

34. The speech is not reproduced by authors sympathetic to Pétain, e.g. Isorni's presentation of Pétain's speeches in *Quatre années au pouvoir*, Paris, 1949, but most of it can be found in Amouroux, *grande histoire des Français sous l'occupation*, vol. 7, 1985, pp. 456–8.
35. Brissaud, *La dernière année de Vichy, 1943–44* 1965, p. 346.
36. *Vichy 1940–1944. Archives de guerre d'Angelo Tasca*, p. 580.
37. Amouroux, *grande histoire des Français sous l'occupation*, vol. 7, p. 76.

Marshal had expected him to make some form of distinction between the Resistance he found acceptable and the acts of civil violence which he abhorred. By not doing so Pétain gave his public sanction to the circular from Darnand's ministry a few days later directing the Regional Prefects to make no further distinctions between different types of Maquis units, but to furnish information on all dissident organisations directly to the German authorities.[38]

This document (dated 2 May 1944 and signed for the Ministry by Clemoz) can be found in a poor copy in the Archives Départementales at Nîmes, and doubtless elsewhere, but its existence and importance appear to have been overlooked. Apparently giving full official cover to the collaborationism of certain Prefects and certain chiefs of police, it can be said to confirm the final polarisation of Vichy and the Resistance, to which, as Huddleston argued, Philippe Henriot made such a decisive contribution. This polarisation led to the urgent demand, not just from the internal Resistance but also from Algiers, that Henriot should be killed. On 28 June he was assassinated at his house in Paris in front of his wife. It was said, as if it proved some deep-down innocence, that he had spent the previous day chasing butterflies in the woods near Vichy.

'Une foule énorme', reported Brasillach, 'se pressait rue de Solférino, au ministère de l'Information, pour saluer le corps, émue aux larmes.'[39] The same level of emotion perhaps explains why Henriot was given a funeral mass in Notre Dame, which led Cardinal Suhard into a good deal of trouble at the Liberation; and it certainly explains the ferocity of the revenge killings unleashed by the Milice at Macon and in several other towns which climaxed in the murder of Georges Mandel.

In Vichy itself the cast of the black comedy which had been playing in the town for four years took to the streets and disputed the name of rue Président Wilson, which the Milice decided to rename rue Philippe Henriot. The Milice put up the new plaque by night and the municipal council took it down by day.[40] There was a similar fracas in Paris between supporters of Henriot and, in this case, rue George V. Other epitaphs can be found in the carefully doctored Henriot file in the police archives, where there is a tapped telephone call from someone in the Hôtel du Parc at Vichy using the name 'Triffaux', speaking to an 'Altier' at the Hôtel Matignon in

38. Archives Départementales, Gard, CA 367.
39. R. Brasillach, *Journal d'un homme occupé*, 1955, p. 268.
40. *Vichy 1940–1944. Archives de guerre d'Angelo Tasca*, p. 600.

Paris, which reveals the two speakers delighted at the assassination of Henriot, and there is a note to the Minister of the Interior which reported that the police chief at Nogent-sur-Marne had publicly declared that if he knew who had murdered Philippe Henriot he would shake him warmly by the hand.[41] From Tasca came a wry entry into his cahier by way of a final word: 'On a décidé de faire imprimer aux frais de l'Etat les "oeuvres complètes" de Philippe Henriot en quatre volumes. Mais puisque le papier manquait, on s'est adressé aux autorités allemandes de Belgique, qui disposaient des 30 tonnes de papier nécessaires. Celles-ci seront livrées, à la condition d'un troc avec 30.000 bouteilles de Bénédictine.'[42]

There are two other brief points by way of a postscript. Firstly the unbridgeable gulf between Vichy and the Resistance created by Darnand and Henriot undoubtedly led to a more violent purge of Vichy supporters at all levels between July and September 1944. Vichy by then meant unequivocally the Vichy of the Milice, torture and enthusiastic collaboration, not that of the distant days of 'Maréchal nous voilà' and the hopes for youth and sport epitomised by Lamirand and Borotra. Secondly, Henriot's impact did not disappear with the Liberation. Clearly the Maquis created ambivalent feelings in many areas of France, and to some people the violence of the 'Epuration' seemed to vindicate Henriot's propaganda; but after the war many French people who had no personal experience of the Maquis, many writers, film- and television-programme-makers, several historians even, who have never studied the Maquis, have nevertheless continued to give the Maquis a dubious rôle and a 'mauvaise réputation'. Nor has Henriot's seamless history of Communism lost its power to convince. But the history of the Maquis is as plural as the history of Vichy, and the history of Communism is even more so. The cry of the Prefect of the Corrèze after the SS had barbarously devastated his region was both poignant and incisive when he asked how he and his administration could possibly balance a hypothetical bolshevik threat against the reality of the German hangings at Tulle.[43] In the summer of 1944 the Vichy of Philippe Henriot had no defensible answer to this. Neither, after his speech of 28 April, did the 'other' Philippe.

41. AN. F7 14895.
42. *Vichy, 1940–1944. Archives de guerre d'Angelo Tasca*, p. 606.
43. AN. FIC III 1147. Report of July 1944.

4

THE IDEOLOGISTS: VICHY FRANCE, 1940–1944

Paul J. Kingston

One definition of ideology has been formulated in an admirably succinct way by the British historian Roderick Kedward: 'Ideology is in this sense a body of ideas forming the basis of a distinct set of policies and one which could be the projection of class interests, but is not necessarily so.'[1] If one adopts this notion as a useful guideline in identifying the ideologists of Franco-German collaborationism, then one needs to move from consideration of political thinkers to consideration of politicians, for to propound a set of policies is normally to aspire to their implementation. Implementation requires political power. The terms of reference of this chapter are, therefore, limited to those who sought actively to gain political power in France from 1940–4 and who accepted and promoted the cause of Franco-German collaboration in that quest for power.

It is significant that the so-called 'ideological precursors' of Vichy whose writings were quoted to qualify an acceptance of Franco-German collaboration were only sparsely cited by collaborationists in the Northern Zone during 1940 and 1941, whereas in the Southern Zone the ideological antecedents of the Révolution Nationale were extensively quoted throughout the period 1940–4.[2] Vichy propaganda in all its guises and throughout the evolution of that régime maintained a certain consistent reliance on the writings of past French thinkers; in the Northern Zone such 'nostalgia' and 'backward-looking' exercises were considered to be more of an impediment to collaboration with Hitler's Germany than in any way a

---

1. R. Kedward and R. Austin (eds), *Vichy France and the Resistance: Culture and Ideology*, London/Sydney, 1985, p. 3.
2. Foreign Office, *The Review of the Foreign Press 1939–45*, Series D. and F. (France), London, 1980.

justification for such collaboration in that they manifested a France-centred mentality. The centenary of the death of Louis de Bonald (on 23 November 1940) illustrates the different approaches of collaborationists in the two zones; numerous Vichy figures and journalists stressed the importance of L. de Bonald whose efforts to discover the laws which governed the moral and social order of society were in contrast with the a priori doctrines of the French Revolution. De Bonald's emphasis on the need for stability in the family, adherence of society to the moral and social principles of Catholicism, but especially on the need for continuity in the structure of the state was noted. The Paris press and ultra-collaborationist figures grudgingly acknowledged de Bonald's relevance to the new régime but regarded his statements as minor points of reference in the framing of a history of French political thought rather than as a means of awakening some form of consciousness of the moral objectives of the Révolution Nationale. Renan, Taine, René de la Tour du Pin, Joseph de Maistre, Mistral, Balzac and numerous other French figures were quoted in the Southern Zone as proof of the particularly 'French' lineage of Vichy principles. Not merely did the past offer a buttress against accusations of anti-patriotism launched against Pétain's régime, it also served as a means of transposing the 'alleged' realities of economic and political subservience to a foreign occupying force into a mysterious context of the 'flow of history' with the ebb in the tide of France's fortunes being presented as only of passing importance.

The Defeat and the Armistice

The defeat of France in June 1940 and the occupation of the country by Nazi Germany signalled not only the demise of parliamentary democracy in France and the establishing of the Vichy state, but also, in the opinion of a small, active and articulate minority, the inevitable and even necessary humiliation of a country which had chosen what were perceived to be illusory ideals of the French Revolution. Democracy was equated by these individuals with disorder in the social, political and moral domains. The anti-parliamentary riots of February 1934 had provided an opportunity for the principles of 1789 to be rejected; the opportunity had not been seized by those from both poles of the political spectrum. The greater trauma of national defeat with its concomitant social and political dislocation offered an even greater possibility of realising new or well-rehearsed 'strategies for power'. Counter-revolutionary tenets masqueraded in June 1940 as they had in 1815, 1848–52 and 1871, under the apparent conjunction between Reaction and Revolution, but the human reality of political and economic opportunism needs to be weighed carefully against claims to ideological continuity made by many of the actors on the political stage in occupied France between 1940 and 1944.

To understand the motivation and dynamism within the major collaborationist movements one needs to examine each movement separately and then draw contrastive conclusions in order to discover whether or not claims such as 'there were as many forms of collaborationism as collaborators' or that collaborationism in France was essentially 'the ideological acceptance of fascism' are valid.[3]

It is important to remember that the Armistice which came into effect on 25 June 1940 did not demand anything other than administrative collaboration from the French authorities towards the German occupying forces. One cannot interpret article 3 of the Armistice Convention as being anything other than an invitation to the French public and governmental services to act in such a way as to facilitate the administration of France by the Germans. It is further necessary to point out that article 3 of the Convention applied only to the occupied zone. The legitimacy of the armistice has not been called seriously into question by historians except in as much as an armistice indicates that a country has temporarily ceased hostilities with another but that the two countries are nevertheless legally still at war.[4]

Questions have arisen as to the validity of the vote accorded Marshal Pétain on 10 July 1940 in Vichy by a joint meeting of Senators and Deputies by which they granted full executive powers

3. S. Hoffmann, 'Collaborationism in France during World War II', *Journal of Modern History* 40 (September 1968), p. 375, and B.M. Gordon, *Collaboration in France during the Second World War*, Ithaca, NY/London, 1980, p. 17. See also R. Girardet, 'Pour une introduction à l'histoire du nationalisme français', *Revue française de science politique* vol. 8, no. 3, (1958), p. 527; and A. Siegfried, 'Le Vichy de Pétain, le Vichy de Laval', *Revue française de science politique* vol. 6, no. 4, 1956, pp. 737–49.

4. P. Dhers, 'L'Armistice: L'Assemblée Nationale', in H. Michel (ed.), *La France sous l'Occupation*, Paris, 1959, pp. 1–12 and A. Scherer, 'La Collaboration' in H. Michel (ed.), *La France sous l'Occupation* Paris, 1959, pp. 13–38. See also R. Kedward, *Occupied France: Collaboration and Resistance 1940–1944*, Oxford, 1985, pp. 2–3; and P. Ory, *Les Collaborateurs, 1940–1945*, Paris, 1976, pp. 36–54.

to Marshal Pétain (by 569 votes to 80). Such a vote was clearly the destruction of a republican régime and the installation of a non-democratic, non-parliamentary authoritarian structure. Pétain was, therefore, the régime – at least in the eyes of most ordinary French people. The cult of Pétainism was a cult of 'realism'. The Marshal provided 'de sa personne' a 'bouclier' against German excesses. It was his human and specifically French qualities which were projected as being the credentials of his respectability as the representative, and at times the incarnation, of France. Pierre Laval, on the other hand, was far more of a political animal. As an independent socialist he had held various senior ministerial posts including Président du Conseil between 1935 and 1936 for a period of six months. Laval's opposition to France's entry into the war against Germany identified him after the defeat as one of the most important politicians capable of negotiating a peace settlement and building a new political structure in France to replace the allegedly 'evident' failure of the parliamentary system. Laval possessed a European vision which required that France would come to an arrangement with Germany to the mutual benefit of both nations. Pétain, on the other hand, appears to have been more concerned with the moral regeneration of France and the protection of national identity against eventual settlements of frontiers and economic markets after the war.

The meeting between Hitler and Pétain at Montoire on 24 October 1940 signalled the acceptance by Pétain, at least publicly, of the need for more extensive collaboration than that envisaged under the Armistice Convention.[5] However, Pétain himself and his advisers distrusted the Europeanist ethic of Laval (which in 1940 meant a particularly pro-German stance) and Laval was dismissed from office on 13 December 1940. Laval was not reinstated in office until April 1942 and during the intervening period much of the social legislation for which Vichy has become well known was implemented, with the emphasis being placed on the national rather than international strength of France. This situation pleased the Nazi occupiers in as much as it accorded them a relatively orderly society to govern.

5. D. Veillon, *La Collaboration*, Paris, 1984, pp. 67–98.

Collaborationist Movements

Three major collaborationist movements have been identified by historians amid the plethora of minor groupings all claiming to possess the strategy necessary for regeneration of a defeated France. These three movements all claimed the need for a single party in order that national unity could be achieved without dispersion of political affiliations. The Rassemblement National Populaire (RNP) was finally created in the early months of 1941 by Marcel Déat who had failed in his efforts to establish a single-party structure in France during the late summer months of 1940.

A further spur to the creation of the RNP was the dismissal of Laval in December 1940. The second major political party/movement was that of the Parti Populaire Français (PPF). Unlike the RNP the PPF had existed in pre-war France and had enjoyed a measure of popularity with some 200,000 supporters estimated in 1937. The Munich crisis and the decision of the PPF to support the Munich accords brought about a significant reduction of its members in 1938. The leader of the PPF, Jacques Doriot, was himself a former Communist who had evolved into the most ferocious of anti-Communist demagogues. The PPF faced an ideological dilemma from June 1940 to June 1941, i.e. until the breaking of the Germano-Soviet Pact, and was unable to mobilise its full forces until the latter part of 1941 using the crusade against Communism as a prime argument for its support of the collaborationist cause.

The creation of the Milice in 1942 under the nominal leadership of Laval but under the control of Joseph Darnand came about as a consequence of the failure of political movements such as the RNP and the PPF to gain control of the levers of power in occupied France. The Milice had as its prime function the maintenance of civil order and was essentially a paramilitary organisation. Its claim to notoriety focuses around its battles with members of the Resistance in France in the final days of the German Occupation.

The difficulty that French collaborationists experienced in unifying pro-German elements within France was no doubt due to Nazi aims of 'dividing the better to rule'. It also stemmed in part from the fluctuating definitions of political allegiance in inter-war France and had much to do with the loss of face of authoritarian movements in the 1934 anti-parliamentary riots. Most importantly, it was related to the divisions brought about in the ranks of these groups by the Munich agreement in 1938 whereby nationalism was subju-

51

gated in certain instances to the desire for ideological solidarity with National Socialist Germany and with Fascist Italy. It has further been maintained that these authoritarian movements were manned by individuals isolated from the main political parties in France and who had experienced only 'oppositional politics', being unable to develop political strategy except in counterpoint to an already defined programme of policies created by their ideological opponents.[6] Both Doriot and Déat had, indeed, rejected Marxism prior to the Second World War but had viewed appreciatively the emphasis on nationalism and social cohesion in the Fascist and National Socialist states on the borders of France.

Right-wing figures such as Darnand and Eugène Deloncle had evolved away from the impotence, as they perceived it, of the Action Française in pre-war French society. One of the means to achieve social cohesion in the view of both Déat and Doriot was by strengthening the executive to the detriment of the parliamentary system. Doriot's acceptance of appeasement at Munich and Déat's article 'Faut-il mourir pour Dantzig?' place them in the ranks of the so-called 'pacifists'.[7] These 'pacifists' argued against confrontation with Germany and pointed to the social disruption and lack of unity in democratic France as indications of France's retarded political evolution. The models of Germany and Italy were cited as necessary adaptations of industrial countries to the modern world. In France the Action Française provided a source but not a cohesive agent for the development of extra-parliamentary leagues. A degree of apparent unity had been achieved in 1936 on the declaration of the Spanish Civil War, but again the Munich accords substantially undermined the tenuous links which had been developed by these fragmented rightist groupings.[8]

It is important to realise not merely to what extent Déat and Doriot resembled each other in their support of a powerful, autonomous executive, but also to make clear the differences in perspective of both political leaders. Déat was an enthusiastic supporter of an authoritarian Republican régime whereas Doriot, whose earlier Communist affiliations and PPF activities had always kept him

6. Z. Sternhell, *Ni droite, ni gauche*, Paris, 1983, pp. 234–45 and 296–9.

7. M. Déat 'Mourir pour Dantzig?' in *L'Oeuvre*, 4 May 1939. See also Eugen Weber, 'Nationalism, Socialism and National-Socialism in France', *French Historical Studies*, vol. 2, no. 3, 1962, pp. 272–307; M. Seliger, *Ideology and Politics*, London, 1976.

8. J.-P. Azéma, *De Munich à la Libération*, Paris, 1979.

outside of the political power centres of the French Republic, was anxious to see the destruction of Republican principles and organisation. Doriot viewed Déat as an opportunist attempting to prolong the life of a moribund political system while claiming to bring revolutionary proposals for a new France to the French people. The British attack on the French fleet at Mers-el-Kébir in Algeria on 5 July 1940 caused Doriot to seek a national force greater in its appeal than his own PPF. Accordingly, he launched the Rassemblement pour la Révolution Nationale. However, political activity in the occupied zone was not favoured by the Germans, and indeed, in the unoccupied zone Pierre Pucheu, the Vichy Interior Minister, had restricted the PPF to a minimal level of activity. The appointment of Otto Abetz (later to be named German Ambassador to France) put a stop to Doriot's single party ambitions as Abetz, a former socialist, distrusted the 'excessive' statements of Doriot, preferring the more traditional political 'types', such as Laval and Déat.[9]

The anti-German sentiment of the Action Française during the 1930s caused many of its more youthful members a degree of ideological difficulty for many of them saw similarities between the régimes in Italy and that in Germany and felt that the evidently impotent and ageing Maurras was not the man to lead them into the overthrow of the republican régime. One of these followers of Maurras was Eugène Deloncle who created in 1936 a secret organisation known as the Comité Secret d'Action Révolutionnaire (CSAR).[10] CSAR maintained that France was in danger of being taken over by Communists who had infiltrated the major bastions of French social structures, such as the army and the political parties. The organisation became widely known for a series of allegedly political murders during 1936 and 1937. Its nickname, the 'Cagoule', was given to it by Maurice Pujo from the Action Française who regarded it as a form of terrorist organisation. The Cagoule was broken up at the end of 1937 but it formed an interesting model for the active militancy of offshoot groupings from the Action Française.

Deloncle had much in common with Doriot, and although they attempted to link forces, by September 1940 they had come to the decision that they were unable to work together. This was hardly

---

9. O. Abetz, *Pétain el les Allemands*, Paris, 1948, pp. 44 and 53.

10. P. Bourdrel, *La Cagoule: 30 ans de complots*, Paris, 1970; and G. Loustaunau-Lacau, *Mémoires d'un Français rebelle, 1914–48*, Paris, 1948.

surprising, given Doriot's Communist background and the fact that Deloncle had been the organiser of political murders which had concentrated on anti-Fascist political agitators, many of whom were, or had been, Communists. Deloncle did not succeed any better than Doriot in securing governmental responsibilities in the new Vichy régime, and returned to Paris, along with many of the more pro-German political leaders, leaving Maurrasian Germanophobia well installed in the Southern Zone. It is worthy of note that the fragmentation of political parties which had occurred in France during the 1930s was given a new dimension with the polarisation along the Paris–Vichy axis. The physical division of France mirrored the ideological divisions existing in the French political domain.

In all discussion of ideological differences between collaborationist groupings in occupied France one needs to remember the fact that different German services of occupation promoted the interests of different collaborationist groups in France. To an extent, and as has often been noted, this promotion was orchestrated by Berlin inasmuch as Germany could rule a divided country more easily than one united in demanding greater but unwelcome participation in the German war effort. There is, however, a further dimension to this German support of various collaborationist movements which has not received a great deal of scrutiny. German individuals or agencies supporting French collaborationist interests were often working for the promotion of their own careers or political importance. The case of Abetz is relevant in this instance. Abetz represented Ribbentrop and the German Foreign Ministry in France. He supported Laval and Déat believing that his own position would be improved vis-à-vis other German services in France if Laval were to be 'at the helm'. Laval's dismissal in December 1940 meant in effect that Abetz's own position was weakened and he strove to reinstate Laval, eventually being successful in June 1941. By the end of 1942, however, a power struggle within France by the various German services had been won by the SS and the Sicherheitsdienst. Although Laval remained in power after 1942 Abetz was unable to exert the form of influence he had hoped with senior Nazi leaders in Berlin.[11]

11. O. Abetz, *Das offene Problem*, Cologne, 1951, pp. 275–7.

The Rassemblement National Populaire

Pierre Etienne Flandin replaced Laval after 13 December 1940 but enjoyed minimum German confidence and was himself replaced by Admiral Darlan in February 1941. At this stage of the war the German military leaders were considering their attack on the Soviet Union and did not wish to improve the political status of France to some form of collaborationist affiliation, preferring instead to use the resources of France to strengthen their own war effort in the east. Under Admiral Darlan, therefore, economic collaboration became the order of the day. At this most unpropitious of moments the establishing of the Rassemblement National Populaire was announced on 1 February 1941 with Marcel Déat as the leader of what purported to be the union of Leftist groupings such as former socialists and trades unionists with members of the Union Nationale des Combattants, which was on the right of the political spectrum, as well as members of Deloncle's MSR party (Mouvement Social Révolutionnaire).[12] This new movement was encouraged by Abetz and was assisted by Laval who saw in it the means of threatening Vichy authority with a potentially more viable and sympathetic political movement with which the Nazi occupiers could deal.

The RNP wasted a lot of its energies in the early months of 1941 campaigning for Laval's return to power and did not itself attempt to build up an independent power base preferring to link its own ascent to power with that of Laval. Deloncle did, in fact, plan a march on Vichy similar to that undertaken by Mussolini in his march on Rome in 1922 but this move was opposed by the Germans who felt that it might give rise to the resignation of Pétain which would have been antithetical to their political strategy in France. Without total German support, however, the RNP was doomed from the outset. Given that Doriot enjoyed SS support as opposed to the Embassy support accorded Déat, that the RNP could not operate in the South, and that within the movement itself there were extreme tensions between individuals and sub-groupings which only a few years previously had been in vehement opposition to each others' political programmes, it was difficult to see how the RNP could achieve its goal of a single party, though the RNP did

12. R. Paxton, *Vichy France: Old Guard and New Order 1940–44*, London, 1972, pp. 238–44.

create a network of affiliated sub-sections responsible for the politicisation of as many sectors of French society as possible. Déat
himself attempted to win working class support by arguing strongly
in favour of trades unions being accorded equal status with that
already granted to employers' associations by Vichy's corporate
policy. Darlan, however, was not prepared to admit this equality.

Déat faced a monumental task in gathering working-class support
because physical and material conditions deteriorated in France
during the course of 1941. Tensions arose in the RNP and became
critical during the month of May 1941 when Deloncle refused to
disband his MSR party and made clear his desire to be the sole
leader of the RNP. This threat to Déat's leadership could not be
taken lightly. The German invasion of the Soviet Union in June
offered Deloncle a means of releasing his energies while retaining
political status. Accordingly, in early July 1941, the Légion des
Volontaires Français contre Bolchévisme was created in Paris, Deloncle becoming the Chairman of its Executive Committee. In spite
of the feverish activity involved in the establishing of the Legion,
Deloncle still had time to plot the removal of Déat from the Head of
the RNP by means of a 'car accident'. Paul Colette very nearly
achieved the same aim by his attempted assassination of Laval and
Déat on 27 August 1941. Déat had information relating to Deloncle's plots to take control of the RNP movement and from his
hospital bed started to organise the exclusion of Deloncle and his
supporters from the RNP. Déat ordered the vacating of all party
offices by Deloncle's supporters and made clear his desire that any
member of the RNP who wished to leave the party with Deloncle
should immediately do so. The removal of Deloncle from the RNP
caused that party's withdrawal from the prominent position it held
on the French political stage inasmuch as the RNP had been
weakened significantly by the reduction in rightist support which
had previously been brought to it by Deloncle and other rightist
sub-groups. By the end of the year the RNP was constituted
primarily of middle-class members, retained an anti-Communist
trades unionist base, but lacked the militancy of the MSR and the
PPF. It had, in effect, had its teeth drawn and the ideological balance
of the movement had been destroyed.

Although Déat espoused a form of anti-Semitism, it cannot be
maintained that he identified his programme with that of other
more racist collaborationist groupings. Déat followed a more traditional Maurrassian line, believing that a prioritisation was possible

among Jews which permitted those who had fought on behalf of France during the First World War and with distinction during the Second, to be considered 'bon Juifs'.[13]

The RNP can be distinguished from the other collaborationist parties in that it attracted and deliberately campaigned for the support of teachers and others engaged in the field of education. One of the organisations established by the RNP in its attempt to permeate all sectors of French society with its political programme, was the Union de l'Enseignement which campaigned for increases in salaries for teachers, the removal of Catholic influence in French education and the promotion of National Socialist training of French youth. It is because of the strength of the network of organisations and subsidiary units previously created by the RNP that the movement maintained its strength during 1943 and 1944. Déat's personal influence was enormous through his editorials for the newspaper *L'Oeuvre*. He did not, however, deal with the day to day administration of his movement, unlike Doriot, and to that extent was more of an ideological leader than the 'Chef' image cultivated by Doriot. Membership of the RNP is difficult to estimate (as it is for most collaborationist organisations given conflicting assessments of numbers and the mode of calculation of membership at different points during the Occupation period). However, it is generally believed that between some 20 and 25,000 members registered with the RNP during 1942–3.[14] The RNP remained principally in the Northern Zone and was not allowed until November 1942 to become active in the Southern Zone. This may account for its lack of popularity among the 'paysans' section of French society. An interesting factor is the number of women members of the RNP which is significantly higher in relation to women's support for other collaborationist groupings. Déat himself was opposed to women's suffrage, but also campaigned against Vichy's attempts to reduce educational opportunities for women, confining the role of the woman to mother and wife.

Laval returned to power in April 1942 and rewarded Déat for his unflagging support during the former's period in 'the wilderness' by subsidising the RNP with government funds (as he did for numerous other collaborationist movements in the occupied zone). Such

13. S. Grossman, 'L'Evolution de Marcel Déat', *Revue d'histoire de la deuxième guere mondiale*, no. 97, 1975, pp. 22–3.

14. Ory, *Les Collaborateurs*, p. 113; and Gordon, *Collaborationism in France*, pp. 119–22.

'patronage' had the same divisive aims as those of the Germans. He did not, however, reward Déat with a governmental position. This, together with the fact that it became clear that Laval did not intend to transform France into a mirror-image state of Nazi Germany or Fascist Italy and that the programme of the RNP was in many ways unacceptable to Laval's system of balancing principles with realism, inspired Déat to try once more to form a single party. In September 1942 he announced the creation of the Front Révolutionnaire National (FRN) which would act as a unifying federalist structure, putting pressure on the Vichy régime to adopt National Socialist principles and only after this pressure had been applied would discussions, so Déat proposed, take place between its various constituent movements on the subject of the creation of a unitary party.

The crucial element governing the success of this FRN structure was the integration of Doriot's PPF. Doriot was himself very ambitious and had no intention of allowing his party to be subsumed into a greater, more amorphous movement which would be of no benefit to himself, nor in fact to his political aspirations for France. Accordingly, he rejected the offer made by Déat and made clear that the PPF was in the best possible position to assume power among all the collaborationist movements of that period. It has to be recognised that this claim was not mere verbiage but was supported by a systematic attempt by Doriot to create grass-roots collaborationist unity, allegedly in preparation for the possible invasion of France by allied troops, but also as a means of structuring an integrist network of supporters, to be used in the eventuality of the PPF seizing power in France.

It is interesting to note the difference in strategy between Déat and Doriot – Déat attempting to impose unity on collaborationist movements by an umbrella organisation/single-party structure, whereas Doriot attempted to use the areas of common fear and aspiration of ordinary collaborationists in France to build a form of movement which was not avowedly that of a single party. The leftist persuasion of most of the executive members of the RNP contrasts with the National Socialist programme it promoted in occupied France. The apparent opposition which exists between the pre-war ideological positions of these individuals and the stance they assumed under the Occupation may be explained by definition of the term 'socialism'. For them, socialism was essentially anti-Marxist.[15]

---

15. A. Bergounioux, 'Le néo-socialisme – Marcel Déat: réformisme traditionnel ou

Many of them had demostrated their anti-Communist beliefs after the Munich accords and others among them had broken from the French socialist movement describing themselves as independent or neo-socialists. The prime preoccupation, however, of the RNP was the need for France to adapt to a modern, industrial society and to play its full role in an industrialised Europe. The strong elements of pacifism which had been espoused by many of the individuals who later joined the RNP resemble closely Vichy 'attentisme'.

The conservative policies of Vichy contrasted radically with what was the perceived need for a modern view of the world to be taken by the French government, according to RNP members. With the refusal of Laval to grant Déat a ministerial post after April 1942, the RNP saw itself increasingly isolated and unlikely to gain sufficient popular or German support to pose a major threat to the stability of the Vichy régime. Through its support for Laval the RNP dissipated much of its energy which would normally have been directed against the more reactionary policies of the Pétain government. This support for Laval lasted until 1943 and by then it had become clear that the RNP did not enjoy sufficient German support, nor have the necessary militant arm to seize power in France or to pose more than an apparent threat to the Vichy régime. In other words, the danger from the movement lay more particularly in its potential exploitation by German services as an alternative to Pétainism and not as a viable, 'independent' movement with its own well-defined ideological programme.

The Parti Populaire Français

The hold which Jacques Doriot maintained over the PPF movement was more charismatic than ideological. Doriot himself an ex-Communist had all the fervour of the convert to anti-Communism and had oratorical skills far superior to those of Déat, the intellectual. A point of some importance is that Doriot spent significantly more time on the Russian Front between June 1941 and August 1944 than he did in France. The declaration of war against Russia by Germany caused Doriot to throw himself wholeheartedly into recruiting for the Légion Anti-Bolchévique. The Légion itself was permitted to exist by Vichy as it provided a useful escape valve for

esprit des années trente', *Revue historique*, October-December 1978, pp. 389–412.

the more militant extreme collaborationist elements within French society who could expel their frustrations and energies in battle against the Soviet régime on the Russian Front rather than constantly harassing the Pétain government. Anti-Communist, Doriot certainly was; he was also a nationalist. In fact, his nationalism had borne him away from the anti-Fascist broad-based alliance of the Left which he had tried to establish against Russian directives in 1934 and towards German and Italian authoritarian expressions of nationalist fervour.[16]

The PPF was only allowed to operate in the Northern Zone with 'authorised status' from October 1941, whereas the RNP had been granted such status some eight months earlier. This delay in German approval being accorded the movement is an indication of the reticence felt, particularly by Abetz, towards the strength of nationalist sentiment to be found in the PPF ranks. Although the PPF groups in Tunisia succeeded in assuming a pivotal role in opposing the Allied landings of November 1942, it became clear that directives from Berlin were to maintain Laval in power in France in order that the social order be maintained but also to allow the continued existence of the PPF as yet another threat to the long-term viability of the Vichy régime, were it to prove unsatisfactory in meeting the demands made by the Nazi authorities. The PPF possessed an internal structure far more sophisticated and equipped for taking power in France than that to be found in the RNP. Most of the executive members of the PPF were former Communist agitators whose ideological training in propaganda techniques and subversive activity stood them in good stead in their new anti-Communist, but nevertheless isolated, political role in occupied France.

The physical militancy of the PPF also lent itself to the possible overthrow of the established order in France, although it must be admitted that membership of the PPF was no greater according to recent estimates than that of the RNP, in other words, not exceeding some 25,000 members.[17] The links between the PPF and the SS in Paris had strengthened Doriot's belief that German support would be forthcoming in due course to allow him and his organisation to assume power in France. Laval was aware of SS support for

16. D. Wolf, *Die Doriot-Bewegung. Ein Beitrag zur Geschichte der französischen Faschismus*, Stuttgart, 1967, p. 56.
17. Foreign Office, *French Basic Handbook: Part III*, 1944, p. 144, cited in H. Amouroux, *La vie des Français sous l'occupation*, vol II, Paris, 1961, p. 386; also cited in Gordon, *Collaborationism in France*, p. 145.

Doriot and attempted to reduce the possibility of direct confrontation between Vichy and the PPF by not dismissing out of hand demands for ministerial positions made in discussions between himself and the members of the PPF executive. Doriot's statement that the Relève was too weak a measure to ensure sufficient manpower supplies to Germany to enable that country to meet its massive war effort and his argument that compulsory work service should be required of French citizens did much to reduce his popularity in France. Nevertheless, the PPF did operate clandestinely in the unoccupied zone under the title of Mouvement Populaire Français. Fears that the movement would be outlawed by the Germans or by the Vichy régime itself as well as anticipation of operational difficulties in the event of an Allied invasion, resulted in the structuring of local units of the PPF along similar lines to the Communist 'cell-structure', whereby members were grouped in sections of four with a fifth member being the commander of the section, and the section itself known as a 'main'. Such an organisational structure permitted the continued existence of the PPF in liberated France and the perpetration of terrorist acts after August 1944. The socialism of the PPF harped back to that defined and espoused by Proudhon and Barrès. The movement, however, cannot be described as revolutionary in its social ambitions. Active before the war, it had adopted corporatist policies first announced in France by La Tour du Pin as well as a level of anti-Semitism which was a conscious attempt to use the racist sentiment as a cementing agent to achieve class cohesion within France. The death knell for Doriot's short-term aspirations came on 21 September 1942 in a telegram from Ribbentrop to Abetz informing the latter that Hitler preferred Laval to Doriot in terms of the maintenance of social order in France.

Although Doriot had made overtures to Costantini's Ligue Française at one point during the Occupation, it was, in fact, the unwavering single-mindedness of the leader of the PPF that made certain his lack of success in the political arena of occupied France. For without compromise no single collaborationist movement could muster sufficient popular and/or German support to pose more than a minor threat to the Vichy régime. In addition, Hitler's pronouncement in favour of Laval in September 1942 meant effectively that Doriot was excluded from the levers of power in France as well as being physically removed from his own country for most of the crucial period 1941–4. Doriot, in his naiveté, was more 'absolute' in his ambitions and direct in his actions than Déat.

The Milice Française

In the heat of the polemical exchanges and threats from ultra-collaborationist movements in occupied France, Laval felt himself to be exposed both personally and politically by not having a unitary force which could be used in a defensive or, indeed, offensive way against his own political enemies. It appears that at a meeting with Hitler in December 1942 Laval requested permission to create a movement which would be under his personal control in Vichy and which would militate in favour of Vichy government aims as well as those of the occupying forces. Hitler agreed to the establishing of such a movement, partially on the grounds that it would be used against the increasing power of the Resistance groups in France.[18]

The man chosen to head this organisation, to be known as the Milice Française, was Joseph Darnand. Darnand's military credentials were excellent, having distinguished himself in both World Wars. An ex-member of the Action Française he had evolved through the Cagoule organisation to take up position by the outbreak of the Second World War on the extreme right of the French political spectrum. Darnand pledged loyalty to Marshal Pétain when he became a member of the Légion Française des Combattants in the autumn of 1940, eventually becoming the leader of the Nice contingent of the Légion. The Légion, however, rapidly became little more than a nominal grouping of pro-Pétain individuals. Pétain's meeting with Hitler at Montoire and the subsequent declaration of collaborative intent by the Marshal was sufficient grounds for Darnand to overcome his previous Germanophobia and to accept the 'realism' of the Pétainist stance.

The invasion of Russia by German forces in June 1941 compounded this commitment to collaboration with the occupying power as it satisfied Darnand's own anti-Communist principles. (In fact, one of the major factors in dissuading Darnand from becoming active in the Resistance in France during the Second World War was the Communist presence, made active after June 1941.) By the late summer of 1941, Darnand had become disillusioned by the

18. J. Delperrie de Bayac, *Histoire de la Milice*, Paris, 1969, p. 182.

Légion and sought a more dynamic framework for collaborationist activity. Together with senior French army officers he created in the Alpes-Maritimes Department a secret military organisation which was to be used in the event of Italian aggression attempting to seize further regions of France. The name given to this organisation was, the Service d'Ordre Légionnaire.[19] Although local at first, the movement spread rapidly throughout the unoccupied zone and became an important force by the end of 1941. It was given official blessing in January 1942 by the Vichy government, not as a military unit but as a means of protecting France from external and internal aggression. The political programme of the SOL was, to say the least, sketchy: 'Contre l'Apathie, pour l'Enthousiasme . . . Contre l'Oubli des Crimes et pour le Châtiment des Responsables.'[20] The degree of vagueness inherent in this political programme resembles closely the generalist statements of many collaborationist movements during the period 1940–4. It should be remembered that the SOL was a strongly Pétainist movement and not, therefore, under the direct control of Laval. In the view of some attentistes, the SOL provided a further body of men who could be called upon at moments of crisis to defend French interests. Former members of the SOL have, indeed, maintained that they joined the organisation as an alternative form of Armistice army.

At the same time as granting official recognition to the SOL, Pétain gave Darnand overall charge of the organisation in the unoccupied zone. In the late summer of 1942 Darnand visited members of the Légion Anti-Bolchévique in Poland and came back convinced of the greater Russian threat to Europe than that posed by the German war-machine to French national integrity. Darnand set about encouraging members of the SOL to sign up for military duty on the Russian Front. By so doing, he moved even closer to identifying himself with the Nazi cause in Europe. By January 1943 it was clear that the militant PPF and more extreme members of the RNP were in danger of taking the initiative in forming anti-Resistance groups in France. This further encouraged Laval to arrange for the transformation of the SOL into the Milice Française on 31 January 1943.

Darnand's nomination as the head of the Milice was, for him, the justification and apogee of his struggle to gain credibility in the

19. Ory, *Les Collaborateurs*, pp. 245–50.
20. Ibid., p. 249.

French political arena. He was, however, an inexperienced and naive political 'player', unable to break from the allegiance he had sworn to Pétainist ideals which were, in essence, chivalric. Inevitably he came into conflict with Laval, who viewed the new organisation as a form of personal defence force to be used in the maintaining of social order, not merely in opposition to Communists and other Resistance 'terrorists' but also to be used at will against the more militant members of other collaborationist movements that threatened Laval's own political position. The high wages and youthfulness of a significant proportion of the Miliciens cause one to doubt the ideological convictions which brought individuals to join such a movement in 1943. Nevertheless, it cannot be argued that political opportunism was of prime significance in their decision, inasmuch as the Allied invasion of North Africa in November 1942 had sounded warning bells all over Europe for collaborationist circles as to the possibility of German defeat. The involvement of the United States of America in the Allied war effort was a further body-blow to the myth of a Nazi Millenium. Less than a year after the creation of the Milice, Darnand was brought into the Vichy government as Minister 'au Maintien de l'Ordre'. The appointment was the result of German pressure, for the Nazi authorities were becoming concerned that Vichy might shift its direction towards a policy of neutrality rather than one actively supporting the German cause.

During the summer of 1943, as increased Resistance activity led to assassinations, bombings and attacks on Miliciens and their property, Darnand's pleas for the arming of his movement met with no success. Laval blocked each request to the French government and, as titular head of the organisation, Laval was the correct person to request arms for the Milice. Events on a broader canvas, however, caused the Germans to seek the creation of a Waffen-SS battalion in France and the Milice was seen as an ideal source of recruits and one which gave respectability to the previously unthinkable sight of a Frenchman in an SS uniform. An arrangement was arrived at whereby arms would be granted to a limited number of Miliciens in response for co-operation from the executive members of the Milice in recruiting soldiers for the new unit of the Waffen-SS. Indeed, the Milice was merged under the control of the SS when in August 1943 Darnand took the oath of personal loyalty to Hitler and became a Sturmbannführer. It was not until January 1944 that the Milice was allowed to operate in the Northern Zone where its recruitment was far less successful than in the South.

It is difficult to identify the ideological roots of an organisation which acted as an umbrella movement, welcoming individuals as well as groups from the authoritarian Right. The task is only apparently simplified by consulting the published 'Twenty-One Points' which the Milice inherited from the SOL and which formed the credo of that organisation. The 'Points' demanded of members a spirit of faith, a sense of community, an appreciation of hierarchy and the need for authority and discipline as well as identifying the usual rightist statements common in inter-war France of the importance of placing the need to resolve class divisions over capitalism; the need for active racism in France and moral acceptance of Christian society. It is in its emphasis on Christian belief that the Milice to a degree separates itself from other collaborationist movements which all paid some attention to respecting the Catholic tradition of France while attacking the allegedly pernicious influence of the church in politics. The Milice, on the other hand, used Christian imagery and adopted a crusade-like attitude in its public campaigns.

The Milice was even less able to determine its fate than other collaborationist movements, for although the latter were also in receipt of subsidies from the Vichy government, they did not have Laval as titular head of their movement. Secondly, the German army were extremely distrustful of Darnand and the Milice and a jockeying for position between the Wehrmacht and the SS (who supported the Milice) further limited the effectiveness of the organisation until Resistance activity reached such a level that the Miliciens served as a useful 'adjunct force' in the policing of the now totally occupied country.

Both the RNP and the PPF recognised the potential attraction of the Milice and attempted to undermine Darnand's movement by infiltrating their own members as Miliciens – even though Déat and Darnand were seen together at public meetings and spoke at the same meetings. Darnand, however, could not forgive Doriot his Communist origins and never accepted the possibility of links between PPF and the Milice. Both Déat and Darnand had limited political ambitions, seeking ministerial posts in Laval's government, whereas Doriot had greater pretentions to power and could not envisage being subordinate to Laval.

It was personal allegiance to Marshal Pétain and a belief that a threat greater than German hegemony lay over Europe, namely that of Communism, which brought the nationalist Darnand into German uniform and eventually into exile at Sigmaringen. The Milice itself has been estimated as having a maximum of 30,000 members; however, this figure cannot be said to be truly representative in that it groups Miliciens and Miliciennes.[21] It also enjoyed the paradoxical quality of being provincial in its locations yet urban in its recruitment of members. It may be suggested that the Milice was far more a paramilitary organisation than a political movement. The contention would be correct if it were not for the fact that from January 1943 to August 1944 ideology and armed struggle within France became synonymous at the extreme ends of the political spectrum. Darnand and his Miliciens may be regarded as 'Les Actifs de l'Idéologie de la Collaboration'.

Other Collaborationist Movements

We have now considered in general terms the three major collaborationist movements in France between 1940 and 1944 which sought much closer union with Germany than that envisaged by the Vichy régime. These movements also saw as a necessary first step to the achievement of integration of France into a German dominated Europe, the establishment of a single-party system in France. In addition to the RNP, PPF and the Milice, there was a plethora of minor collaborationist movements which rose and fell according to the political climate of the time during the occupation period. Some of these had been active in pre-war France and had, at that time, nationalist and pro-Fascist sympathies expressed through propaganda and street demonstrations, thus principally voicing their views outside of the parliamentary forum. Less politically aware, but equally collaborationist in their ideological stance, were another set of groups which acted as cultural/intellectual platforms for the expression of support for an alliance between France and Germany.

Marcel Bucard's Francistes, Eugène Deloncle's Mouvement Social Révolutionnaire, Pierre Costantini's Ligue Française, Pierre Clémenti's Parti Français National-Collectiviste, Jean Boissel's Front Franc, financed in pre-war years by big business and to some extent by 'foreign subsidy' – all these movements received some degree of

21. Ibid., p. 250. A detailed breakdown of Milice membership in the Southern Zone appears in Gordon, *Collaborationism in France*, pp. 186–7, 355–6.

financial support from the Vichy régime. They were manipulated through this support to undermine (by their adhesion or withdrawal from greater collaborationist movements) the realisation of a single-party alternative to the Vichy régime. As both catalysts and retardants these organisations served both German and Vichy purposes in rendering the union of collaborationist parties an impossibility.[22]

The best known of the organisations which had principally (or, at least, avowedly) cultural/intellectual aims rather than narrowly political ones in the realm of Franco-German collaboration was the Groupe Collaboration headed by Alphonse de Châteaubriant and by Jean Weiland (the organisation's Director General).[23] Europeanist in focus, with a strongly spiritual and indeed anti-materialist ethos, this movement supported the moral regeneration which the National Revolution was to bring to a Europeanised France. Strongly middle class in its membership, the Groupe Collaboration was primarily an organisation which promoted artistic, cultural and intellectual activities such as the arranging of lectures, screening of German films, promotion of German literature, as well as organising public discussions and other social events. The membership of this organisation may have achieved the very significant total of 100,000 by mid-1943. (The military and civilian records relating to the Groupe Collaboration conflict in their estimates of membership.) Some historians ascribe the popularity of this particular movement to the fact that its anti-Communist stance was not followed through in any overtly political way, except via its youth movement, Jeunesse de l'Europe Nouvelle, which was at variance with the parent organisation in seeking to become more of a militant organism than the executive of the Groupe Collaboration perceived the role of their organisation to be.[24]

Far less important than the Groupe Collaboration were other propagandist agencies such as the Comité d'Action Anti-Bolchévique and the Centre d'Action et de Documentation which strove to acquaint the French population with German efforts in the anti-Communist and anti-Jewish/anti-Freemasonry domains. By providing information on these subjects, these agencies attempted to

22. J.-P. Cointet, 'Marcel Déat et le parti unique', *Revue d'histoire de la deuxième guerre mondiale*, no. 91, 1973, pp. 1–22.

23. C. Maubourget, *Alphonse de Châteaubriant*, Paris, 1977, pp. 239–333, and Foreign Office, *French Basic Handbook*, pp. 151–2.

24. Foreign Office, *French Basic Handbook*, pp. 151–2.

promote the adoption of virulent anti-Communist and racist views by the French population.[25]

It is usual when considering collaborationism in France to see November 1942 as a turning-point in the evolution of collaborationist parties. The Allied invasion of North Africa on 8 November 1942 was the first of several setbacks suffered by the Germans who only a few months later were being repelled by Soviet army offensives and suffering defeat at Stalingrad. The American presence among the Allied forces had made itself felt and the capability of the American war machine was beginning to become apparent. What remained, however, was a pervasive fear of Soviet 'liberation' of Europe. Among anti-Communist circles in pre-war France the 'Mieux vaut Hitler que Blum' slogan had been modified to 'Mieux vaut Hitler que Staline'. Concomitant with this attitude was the suppression of nationalist sentiment, for to prefer Hitler and a Nazi occupation to liberation by Soviet forces one had first to suggest that French national interest was in some way closer to that expressed in a German-dominated Europe than that to be found under Soviet 'liberation'. Ideological espousal of the principles of a foreign political doctrine was apparently preferable to the limited and unsatisfactory maintenance of a 'France Seule' policy. There was, of course, a third option, namely that of affiliation/adherence to the Allied cause. Democracy, however, even under Anglo-Saxon guise, had proved itself inefficient in the eyes of French collaborationists, who considered that political system to be detrimental and injurious to the moral health of France and to the health of their own political careers.

In September 1943, exasperated collaborationists including Déat, Darnand, Luchaire and others drew up a 'Plan de Redressement National Français'.[26] The plan warned the German authorities that France was liable to join the Allied cause unless Laval and his government were dismissed from office and a single-party system, led by Darnand and executive officers from the Milice, were installed in power in France. Vichy's response to the Plan was expressed by Marshal Pétain who attempted to recall the Assemblée Nationale which had not met for over three years in order that he, Pétain, could validate the legitimacy of his government and place himself above reproach were the Allies eventually to invade France.

25. See M.R. Marrus and R. Paxton, *Vichy France and the Jews*, New York, 1981.
26. A. Brissaud, *La derniere année de Vichy*, Paris, 1965 pp. 82–6 and pp. 541–61.

Clearly, this was unacceptable to the German authorities, who prevented Pétain from making public his desire to re-establish the Assemblée Nationale. Berlin responded rapidly to the threat of France joining, albeit indirectly, the Allied camp by insisting on the promotion to ministerial status of Déat, Darnand, and Philippe Henriot.

The appointment of Darnand and Henriot took effect in January 1944, that of Déat in March of the same year. Laval undermined to an extent the power wielded by Darnand and Henriot by arranging for sympathetic subordinates to undertake to delay or only partially implement the directives from the newly-appointed ministers. Déat was a different matter. Laval perceived Déat to be a significant threat to his own status and continued power in France. Accordingly, he created the post of Ministre du Travail et de Solidarité Nationale for him. This was, to say the least, a highly unpopular area of Vichy's activity. German demands for French workers had become difficult to resist, given the previously agreed Relève contract whereby for every three French workers who volunteered to go to Germany one French prisoner would be released. This arrangement, however, did not achieve its targets (not unsurprisingly given the popular understanding of the atrocious working conditions and status of French workers in Germany). It is to Déat's credit that a minimal number of French workers were, in fact, sent to Germany during his tenure of office. Déat did also attempt to implement his worker-based organisations to counter the previous advantages accorded employers through the creation by Vichy of corporative associations. The Allied invasion of France, however, cut short his attempt to redress the unequal representation of workers on these allegedly representative professional bodies.

The Dénouement

The D-Day invasion by Allied forces in Normandy on 6 June 1944 was the most traumatic factor in deciding the polarisation of French political groupings. Vichy declared that France was to be considered neutral, thereby directly aiding the German military effort. Most collaborationists, on the other hand, called for the immediate engagement of the 'enemy' by their forces and mobilised their members in support of the German military machine. Darnand rose to even greater heights when he was appointed Secrétaire d'Etat de

69

l'Intérieur by dint of pressure on Laval by both the German authorities and collaborationist organisations. In July, with the Allied invasion forces moving nearer, an apparently united collaborationist front, including Doriot and Déat attended a large rally in Paris where the tenets of the previously agreed Plan de Redressement were once again reiterated. Laval successfully outmanoeuvred this attempt to overthrow him and it was not until the end of July that Berlin was beginning to take seriously the claim by ultra-collaborationists that they were better guarantors of French collaboration than Laval.

The approach of the Allied forces caused an exodus of ultra-collaborationist members and leaders from Paris. Both Pétain and Laval were forcibly removed from Vichy against their will and taken to Sigmaringen castle in south-west Germany.[27] They were joined there by most of the ultra-collaborationist leaders. On 1 September 1944 Hitler announced his intention to nominate Doriot as the leader of this 'French government in exile' much to the dismay of Déat and Darnand who had considered their own ascent to power to be an indication of German preference for their particular political abilities. Although both Darnand and Déat intrigued continuously at Sigmaringen to undermine Doriot's position, it was clear by the start of 1945 that Doriot was considered by Hitler to be the unchallenged leader of the French Delegation. The mysterious death of Doriot – his car was strafed by a plane in February 1945 – served to accelerate the disintegration of the loose political grouping which existed in the highly unusual context of Sigmaringen Castle. Darnand carried on the battle against the Allies in Italy with some members of his Milice, while Déat and the remaining leaders of the PPF engaged in political struggles for power until the Allied approach again caused them to flee. This time, however, their flight was final. Franco-German collaborationism disintegrated and as the major French figures in the drama dispersed, seeking refuge from the advancing Allied armies, their belief in the justness of their cause burned as strongly as ever and would be given expression at their trials in the following months and years.

What had started out for many as either a pre-war belief in Fascist or National Socialist values or as an allegedly 'realistic' appreciation

27. L. Noguères, *La dernière étape: Sigmaringen*, Paris, 1956 and E. Jäckel, *Frankreich in Hitlers Europa. Die Deutsche Frankreichpolitik in Zweiten Weltkrieg*, Stuttgart, 1966, pp. 354–9.

of the political situation of France in June 1940, had degenerated by the spring of 1945 into a stubborn refusal to accept that the National Socialist régime imposed by Hitler on so many European countries had not been the solution or fulfilment of internationalist aspirations nor a pathway for the realisation of ideological beliefs. The supposedly proven inefficiency of a democratic parliamentary system in France, the belief in the moral revolution published by Pétain under the banner of a national revolution; an impatience with the evident reluctance of the Vichy régime to apply the tenets of its programme to the international domain, in other words, to look outwards rather than inwards; the rejection of the Allied camp because of the presence therein of the Soviet Union with its threat to Western European civilisation, the post-rationalising of collaborationism through economic collaboration, these were the means whereby individuals and groups were drawn into the collaborationist camp. There appears to have been an inexorable progress by the politically ambitious and the ideologically convinced down the road to Sigmaringen castle.

Of the three 'ideologists' under scrutiny, only the intellectual Déat retained coherence and a significant degree of consistency in his set of policies in spite of the constraints on political life in occupied France. The essentially reactive and crass political consciousness of Darnand found militarisation a sufficient surrogate for social policy. Doriot's organisational and political skills were undermined by the uncompromising approach he took to gaining political power. All three individuals lived the illusion shared by most collaborationists, namely that French patriotism and German National Socialism were not essentially antithetical. Sigmaringen finally broke the illusion and rendered the ideologists victims and prisoners of their policies and their acts.

5

FRENCH CHRISTIANS AND THE GERMAN OCCUPATION

W.D. Halls

The deep-seated incompatibility of National Socialism and Christianity caused Rosenberg, that theorist of barbarism, to speak of the 'Judeo-Roman Church'. The Nazis perceived the danger of allowing to co-exist a creed more ancient, more transcendental, and more international than their own, backed by an organisation more powerful and more influential than the NSDAP. In a nation such as Germany, divided between Protestantism and Catholicism, one priority after the Machtübernahme had been to neutralise the churches. The promotion of the Deutsche Christen movement on the one hand, and the signing of a Concordat on the other, had been the chosen means for temporarily suppressing religious dissent to Nazi policies. Hitler's aim, after a successful war, was nothing less than the eradication of Christianity. But resistance remained, and could not be stifled. Although the dissident Confessional Church was made illegal and its head, Pastor Niemöller, imprisoned, others continued to speak out, as did Catholic leaders such as Cardinal von Galen. When German forces occupied France in 1940 the authorities therefore anticipated difficulties with the predominantly Catholic leaders and were on their guard, but did not believe they would run into real trouble, provided that the church was made to keep out of political matters.

French Protestants had kept up contacts with their German counterparts. One link was through Karl Barth who, driven out of his professorship at Freiburg, had accepted the chair of theology at Basel. Barth's doctrines, with their emphasis upon the primacy of Christian exigencies over any demands of the state, became known in France through Pastor Maury, who translated his work. His ideas were also spread through reviews such as *Ici et Maintenant, Foi et*

Vie, and *Le Semeur*. Relief workers such as Madeleine Barot, working for the Protestant relief organisation CIMADE, were in touch with Pastor Niemöller and Gustav Heinemann, a future president of the Federal Republic, both prisoners of Hitler.[1]

The Holy See had expressed its concern over Nazism. In a Christmas message to the College of Cardinals in 1936 Pius XI had spoken out against the persecution of German Catholics. In 1937 he not only condemned Communism in the encyclical *Divini redemptoris*, but in another encyclical, addressed to the German bishops, *Mit brennender Sorge*, he likewise condemned Nazism. In France Catholic newspapers devoted two-thirds of their space to the anti-Communist document, as compared with one-third to the anti-Nazi one[2], which surely reflects priorities at the time. On the other hand, the position in the secular press was exactly the opposite. And younger Catholics attached equal importance to both documents, affirming that they were 'nourished on both texts'.[3]

What was the strength of Christianity in France in 1940? Disregarding what might be termed Catholic rites of passage, the number of active Catholics was perhaps ten million. They included a disproportionate number of the elderly, and women and children. The bourgeoisie – 'Black France' – was also disproportionately represented. Peasants predominated over industrial workers. Geographically Catholicism prospered in the west and north-west, in Alsace and in French Flanders. Protestants numbered about 600,000 and were widely scattered. The biggest concentration was in Alsace-Lorraine, but they were also strong in Doubs, Gard, Drôme and Ardèche, S. W. Garonne and Saintonge, as well as big cities such as Paris and Lyon. Again the industrial proletariat were under-represented, as compared with the peasantry. Some influential members of the upper bourgeoisie, bankers and financiers in

1. *Eglises et Chrétiens dans la deuxième guerre mondiale. La région Rhône-Alpes*, Actes du colloque de Grenoble, 1976, ed. X. de Montclos, Lyon, 1978 (henceforward Actes: Grenoble), p. 211. This and the other two records of colloquia proceedings following are essential reading. The present writer has drawn freely upon them. See also Louis Allen, 'Jews and Catholics' and W.D. Halls, 'Catholicism under Vichy: A Study in Diversity and Ambiguity', in R. Kedward and R. Austin (eds), *Vichy France and the Resistance: Culture and Ideology*, London/Sydney, 1985.

2. *Eglises et Chrétiens dans la deuxième guerre mondiale. La France*, Actes du colloque de Lyon, 1982, ed. by X. De Montclos, Lyon, 1982 (henceforward Actes: Lyon), p. 31.

3. *Eglises et Chrétiens dans la deuxième guerre mondiale*, Actes du colloque de Lille, ed. Y-M. Hilaire et al., *Revue du Nord*, Nos. 237 and 238, April-June and July-September 1978 (henceforward Actes: Lille), p. 563.

particular, were Protestants.

Since Protestants were to play a disproportionately large part during the Occupation, some analysis of their composition is appropriate. Organisationally, the Eglise Réformée was the strongest group, with Pastor Marc Boegner, later a notable advocate of ecumenicism, at their head. His was a voice to which Pétain – and Catholic leaders such as Cardinal Gerlier – listened attentively. A small independent group, the Eglises Réformées Evangéliques Indépendantes, was less liberal in tone. Outside Alsace, where it was strongest, the Eglise Lutherienne, of the Augsburg Confession, had centres in Montbéliard and Paris. Smaller Protestant groups – Methodists, Baptists and Plymouth Brethren – had united with the Eglise Réformée. Their English origins meant, with reason, that they were automatically suspect to the Occupation authorities. This held good also for the Salvationists – The Armée de Salut – one of whose members, 'Major' Georges Flandre – fled to the Midi, where under the 'nom de guerre' of Montcalm, he became a notable Resistance leader.[4] The American-based Jehovah's Witnesses, a few of whom lived in Northern France, had already been banned in 1939 by the Daladier government because of their pacifism, and later suffered almost as cruel a fate as the half million French Jews. The mainstream Protestants, who had always had a feeling of being a minority 'outside the nation' – France was, after all, 'the eldest daughter of the Church' – rallied strongly to Pétain in 1940, but saw no contradiction in being anti-German; these dormant sentiments were aroused, which dated back at least to 1871, because of their strong links with the annexed Eastern départements. Although they took their theology from Germany, their liberalism inclined them towards Britain.

What emerges from this 'battle order' of French Christianity is that the religious situation with which the Occupation authorities had to deal was considerably more complicated than that within the Reich itself.

Hitler, however, did not appear to attach much importance to the posture the Germans in Paris should adopt towards French Christians, although his attitude was always conditioned by 'his distrust of the French, which had never disappeared'.[5] This

4. H. Clavier, *The Duty and Right of Resistance* (Dale Lectures, Oxford, 1946), Oxford, 1956, p. 97. 'Montcalm' was captured by the Gestapo, branded with the Croix de Lorraine and finally shot in August 1944.
5. E. Jäckel, *Frankreich in Hitlers Europa. Die Deutsche Frankreichpolitik im*

mistrust seeped down to the three German administrations in France that had most to do with Church matters from 1940 onwards. The Militärverwaltung, the administrative arm of the Militärbefehlshaber in Frankreich (MBF), consisted of largely Wehrmacht personnel, some of whom were civilian experts hastily put into uniform to administer occupied France. In 1941 the MBF, nominally in overall charge, delegated to the Sicherheitspolizei and Sicherheitsdienst (SD) the task of surveillance of the church and any anti-German activities involving ecclesiastics. These police bodies were also responsible ultimately to Himmler. The third group concerned were the diplomats, led by Abetz, the German 'ambassador' in Paris, who also reported to Ribbentrop. Most of the staff, including Abetz, Gerlach (information section), Epting (cultural affairs), Grimm (propaganda) and Sieburg, a former Paris correspondent of the *Frankfurter Zeitung*, had had pre-war experience of France. But between this triple division of authority, there were 'unklare Befugnisse', and rivalry particularly between the SS 'police' and the Embassy. Within the MBF itself there was also an office concerned with the sequestration of French Jewish property and another group, Kultur und Schule, which was a thorn in the side of both French public and private education. In such circumstances it was difficult to formulate a unified policy towards Christians.

Initial words and actions showed that the Occupation authorities sought first to establish its authority in church matters. Already in June 1940 Grimm declared: 'Our enemies are the clergy of both denominations, the Jews and the upper bourgeoisie.'[6] A fortnight before Montoire, where Pétain and Hitler met to discuss collaboration, Abetz reported that 'the French government finds its widest support among the army and clergy, the majority of whom, however, oppose the policy of Franco-German collaboration towards which that government is heading'.[7] Two of the three pastoral cardinals had their episcopal palaces searched by the SD. Cardinal Suhard, of Paris, was told that it was to unearth the papers of his predecessor, Cardinal Verdier, who had been been a well-known anti-Nazi. In Lille Cardinal Liénart protested in vain to the military

---

Zweiten Weltkrieg, Stuttgart, 1966, p. 148. All quotes from German sources in this chapter are my own translations.

6. H. Umbreit, 'Les services d'occupation allemande et les églises chrétiennes en France,' Actes: Lille, p. 301; H. Michael, *Paris allemand*, Paris, 1981, p. 40.

7. O. Abetz, *Pétain et les allemands*, Paris, 1948, p. 17.

governor against the search of his palace. Bishops' palaces elsewhere suffered the same indignity during the autumn. By the end of 1940 arms caches had been uncovered in a few presbyteries, and Abetz reported this time that the lower clergy and the teachers in Catholic schools were 'our most dangerous enemies'.[8] Not without justification: the Resistance later acknowledged its debt particularly to priests in rural areas. The bell of the isolated presbytery tugged in the depth of night by a desperate fugitive from the Gestapo was hardly ever rung in vain.[9]

The dismissal of Laval by Pétain in December 1940 aroused German indignation. One historian comments, 'in internal politics Laval was unwelcome to circles in the Army, the Church and high finance'.[10] It is most likely that influential Catholics at Vichy such as Alibert and Chevalier, Pétain's godson, influenced the Marshal to dismiss his over-zealous collaborationist first minister.

The climate of hostility between church and Germans was sustained throughout the war. German 'sitreps' ('Lageberichte') reported suspicions of such Catholic youth leaders as Lamirand, Pétain's secretary-general for youth, and Borotra, his commissioner for sport. In early 1941 another source stated that only about one-quarter of lower- and middle-ranking clergy favoured collaboration.[11] Catholic schools were again castigated as 'centres of Germanophobia'. Laval, after his reinstatement, discussed with Abetz in May 1942 his intention of dismissing from the Légion des Combattants those leaders who had chauvinist and clerical leanings, replacing them by others who were more anti-English. In March 1943 Kuntze, the SS chief, stigmatised all priests as anti-German resisters who should be 'broken'. The following September the Bordeaux Abwehrstelle continued to refer to 'the very dangerous activities of the clergy'. The Germans regarded the so-called Révolution Nationale as clerically inspired, and were gratified when Catholics occasionally fell out with Vichy over matters such as aid to Catholic schools.

A number of well-known Catholic priests made no secret of the abhorrence they felt for Nazi doctrine, particularly in the unoccupied zone, where they were somewhat freer to express their views.

8. Umbreit, 'Les services d'occupation', p. 306.
9. *Cahiers du Témoignage Chrétien*, Nos. 26–7, 'Exigences de la Libération,' May 1944.
10. Jäckel, *Frankreich in Hitlers Europa*, p. 148.
11. Archives Nationales (AN.) AJ.40.563. Gestapo report, Paris, 13 May 1941.

Père Doncoeur preached a sermon on Palm Sunday, 1941, in which he condemned 'atrocious doctrines' attempting to destroy Christianity.[12] Père Riquet spoke out strongly against the second Statute on the Jews, and went on to demolish Nazi racial theories. He was eventually deported to Mauthausen.[13] Père Dillard, who before the war had inveighed against the semi-pagan character of the Hitler Jugend, noted that after the total occupation of France in November 1942, at the sight of German uniforms the good citizens of Vichy perceived that 'the house was still in ruins'.[14] He eventually died in Dachau. Such men demonstrate that between collaboration, slavish submission to the régime and the Resistance proper, there was another alternative: to remain within the system and speak out fearlessly.

Relations with Protestants were little better. Karl Barth, in an essay directed to the French after the defeat, declared that nothing had changed. Nazism remained what it had always been: 'lies and cruelty', 'persecution of the Jews, and concentration camps', 'attacking and poisoning the Christian church'.[15] Marc Boegner, the French Protestant leader, although supporting Pétain, even to the extent of serving on the Conseil National set up for constitutional reform, was the first Christian cleric to speak out against Vichy's anti-Jewish measures and continued to make his voice heard when the persecutions were taken over by the SS. His own son joined de Gaulle in England in June 1941. A note of defiance was expressed in the utterances of Protestant pastors. Henri Hatzfeld declared, in the face of defeat, that it should 'suscite dans nos coeurs une neuve vaillance';[16] the sermons preached at the heart of French Protestantism, the Oratoire du Louvre in Paris, by such pastors as A–N Bertrand, P Vergera and G Vidal convey the same undercurrent of resistance. When the Occupation authorities closed down the Salvation Army 'citadels'[17] Protestant pastors ensured their mission continued. Boegner was considered to be the key figure

12. Actes: Lyon, p. 239.

13. M. Riquet, *Chrétiens de France dans l'Europe enchaînée*, Paris, 1972, p. 89; R.R. Lambert, *Carnet d'un témoin, 1940–43*, Paris, 1985, p. 129, n. 47.

14. *Cité Nouvelle*, quoted in AN. 2 AG 75, 'Note' (Secret), 26.3.43. Correspondence et documents de Ménétrel.

15. K. Barth, 'Eine Frage und eine Bitte an die Protestanten in Frankreich', reprinted in *Eine Schweize Stimme 1938–1945*, Zurich, 1945.

16. Quoted in E. Léonard, *Le Protestant français*, Paris, 1953, p. 236.

17. See *Voix chrétiennes dans la tourmente*; also M. Boegner, 'A–N Bertrand', in M. Boegner (ed.), *Le Pasteur 'A–N. Bertrand': Témoin de l'unité évangélique, 1876–1946*, Nîmes, n.d., pp. 182–3.

behind such words and actions, and there was even a suggestion in June 1943 that he should be arrested. But this was deemed imprudent: it would merely reinforce the position of Cardinal Gerlier, since the two men worked closely together, and it would have been disastrous to arrest also the senior Catholic of France, the Primate of the Gauls.

Among lay Catholics who, like the priests mentioned above, were not afraid to speak out, was Jacques Chevalier, who nevertheless cuts a sorry figure in the history of the Occupation. For a short while Vichy's minister of education, he was a close friend of Pétain, and of Bergson, the famous Jewish philosopher, who at the close of his life, was very near to Catholicism. Upon Bergson's death in Paris in January 1941, he sent a telegram of sympathy 'in the name of the Head of State' and, unable to obtain an 'Ausweis' for the occupied zone himself, had himself represented at the funeral. As minister he promulgated a decree exempting from the anti-Semitic laws a number of distinguished Jewish academics such as Robert Debré and Marc Bloch. The Germans riposted by declaring the decree null and void in their zone. Moreover, they knew of Chevalier's connexions with Lord Halifax – a pre-war relationship that facilitated Vichy's negotiations with the British, but eventually proved abortive, in the autumn of 1940.[18] The Occupation authorities in Bordeaux in February 1941 characterised the rather ingenuous minister as anti-German ('deutschfeindlich')[19] and drew attention to one of his books in which Chevalier, an academic philosopher by profession, had declared that German aims were world conquest.

It is estimated that perhaps two per cent of the French 'collaborated' in the sense of coming out openly on the German side. Catholics and Protestants were no exception. Among the laity were a few well-known as Catholics. The leader of the Franciste movement, modelled upon Italian Fascism, was one. Before the war Bucard had spoken on Catholic platforms such as meetings of the Fédération National Catholique (FNC). He had originally been destined for the priesthood. Executed after the Liberation, he had gone to his death singing: 'Je suis chrétien, voilà ma gloire.' His henchman was Guiraud, whose father was on the editorial staff of La Croix. This Catholic background undoubtedly attracted others

18. Public Record Office (PRO) FO 371. File Z255.
19. AN. AJ 40.560 Report, Bordeaux, 2 July 1941.

to their movement. Another politician, Philippe Henriot, an ex-deputy, and also a former stalwart of the FNC and one–time Catholic school teacher, found his niche in the media, becoming the most well-known commentator of Radio-Vichy until he was assassinated by the Resistance just before the Liberation. He had joined the Groupe Collaboration started by Alphonse de Chateaubriant and patronised by such notorious collaborationists as Bonnard and Brinon. Less 'political' were men such as Robert Vallery-Radot, an 'integrist' Catholic who, with Bernard Faÿ, undertook to root out freemasons from public life, and was assisted by a few renegade freemasons such as Jean Marques-Rivière, a pre-war Catholic convert.

Whereas the Catholic element at Vichy before April 1942 was strong, with men such as Baudouin, Alibert, Chevalier and Lamir- and taking a large part in public affairs, after the return of Laval to government, this Catholic presence dwindled away.

The Catholic-inspired press numbered a few collaborationist journals, although its most influential journal, *La Croix*, almost ignored the German presence north of Moulins, and was in no way pro-German. In unoccupied France a Lyon daily, *Le Nouvelliste*, adopted a deferential tone towards Nazism, deemed Montoire 'une journée historique'[20] and presented the war against the Soviet Union as a crusade against barbarism. It even established contact with Doriot. 'Le grand Jacques', ex-Communist turned collaborationist, was then fighting in Wehrmacht uniform on the Eastern Front. Its views on the 'crusade' against Russia were shared by *La Croix de Savoie*,[21] but were rarely openly expressed by other Catholic periodicals appearing in the 'free' zone.

In occupied France the most notorious pro-German periodical was the Bordeaux-based *Soutanes de France*, run by Abbé Bergey, who had founded before the war a league of ex-servicemen priests, the Prêtres Anciens Combattants (PAC). His journal specialised in attacks upon Churchill. Also appearing in the Bordeaux area were *La Liberté du Sud-Ouest*, edited by Canon Peuch, who also co-operated with Paul Lesourd in publishing *Voix Françaises*. This weekly distinguished itself in its very first number (17 January 41) by announcing under the heading 'Notre Programme' that France's future was as 'une collaboratrice de premier ordre pour l'établissement

20. Actes: Grenoble, p. 99.
21. See *La Croix de Savoie*, 24 March 1943.

d'un ordre nouveau en Europe'. For allowing priests in his Bordeaux diocese to produce such tendentious publications, and for allowing the local *Semaines Religieuses* occasionally to present Germans in a favourable light, Archbishop Feltin was very much condemned after the war.

Elsewhere minor Catholic publications exhibited the same pro-German tendency. Père Gorce, a Dominican, published *L'Emancipation Nationale*. Gorce distinguished himself after the deportation of General de la Porte du Theil, the head of the Chantiers de la Jeunesse, by writing to Bonnard, then Education minister, proposing himself for the vacant post, because 'un curé collaborationiste vaut bien un militaire revanchard'.[22] Père Bruno, a Carmelite, the director of *Etudes Carmelitaines*, also wrote for the collaborationist scandal sheet, *La Gerbe*.

Anti-Bolshevism was a slogan that misled a few other prominent Catholics. A friend of Henriot, Canon Polimann, a courageous soldier of the First World War and deputy for the Meuse since 1933, came out strongly in support of the Légion des Volontaires Français (LVF), fighting for the German cause in Russia.

A few key laymen, and even fewer prominent clergy, thus favoured collaboration. These were mainly men in public life before the war, politicians who acted out of conviction or self-interest, or both, and those connected with literature, the press or radio. Their influence was disproportionate to their numbers, and this counted against the church after the Liberation.

The hierarchy, bishops, archbishops and cardinals, had to be more circumspect, not only because they were watched closely by the Occupation authorities but also because they had to tread a delicate line between their absolute loyalty to Pétain, a more wary attitude towards the Vichy régime as a whole – not all shared Maurras' view in 1941 that the new order in France was a 'divine surprise' – and public opinion which, on the whole, continued to mistrust the occupiers. 'Attentisme' was, at least from December 1941 onwards, after the entrance of the United States into the war, the prevailing state of mind.

Who were the Church leaders at the time? Since the First World War a new generation of bishops had emerged, reckoned to be more 'social'. Between 1936 – the year in which the Vatican had condemned the Action Française – and 1939, 39 new episcopal appoint-

22. AN. F17.13347. Correspondance de Bonnard.

ments had been made; of these 28 were ex-servicemen. In 1918 the Assembly of Cardinals and Archbishops (ACA) had been constituted. Although at first meeting separately in the two zones, its voice was an extremely important one. Four of its members were cardinals. Verdier, who died in 1940, had been succeeded in Paris by the then archbishop of Reims, Suhard, a cardinal since 1935. Liénart, bishop of Lille, esteemed because c his championship of the industrial working class, had been promoted to the purple in 1930. Gerlier, of Lyon, titular Primate of the Gauls, who had close relations with Pétain, had been made a cardinal in 1937. These were the 'pastoral' cardinals. In addition, there was the aged Cardinal Baudrillart, Rector of the Institut Catholique in Paris. Among the most prominent archbishops were Feltin (Bordeaux) and Saliège (Toulouse). In 1936 the ACA had spoken against the Popular Front, and made no secret of its rightist sympathies. Nevertheless, there was not one of its members, with the possible exception of Baudrillart, that the SS did not view with suspicion.

Baudrillart came out strongly in favour of Nazism, especially after the attack on the Soviet Union, which, like others, he viewed as a religious crusade. Doriot, on leave from the Eastern Front, came in 1942 to consult him regarding a recruiting campaign for the LVF. His Eminence also shared with two other members of the Académie Française the doubtful honour of membership of the Groupe Collaboration.

Here it is appropriate to mention the colourful figure of (Count) Mgr Jean de Mayol de Lupé. This cleric, approaching seventy, had served with distinction in the First World War and had been a chaplain of Marshal Lyautey. He had met Abetz before the war. He became the Chaplain General of the LVF. Having some misgivings about donning German uniform, he had consulted Cardinal Suhard, who had replied: 'Allons donc, ce n'est qu'une contingence.'[23] A proud figure on horseback, the pectoral cross and the swastika around his neck proclaimed his dual allegiance. He won the Iron Cross. His presence among the French mercenaries reassured many young Catholics, who through the Milice eventually found themselves fighting in enemy uniform for what they were assured was the future of Europe and civilisation itself. Mayol's assistant was Abbé Verney, who ministered to the LVF officers, who regarded themselves as 'catholiques et français toujours'.

23. J. Mabire, *La Division Charlemagne*, Paris, 1974, p. 80.

One bishop removed from his see after the war – and then not specifically because of his collaboration but because the Holy See held him to be 'in odium populi' – was Mgr Dutoit, Bishop of Arras. It was his excessive allegiance to Pétain that led him astray. After Montoire he sent out a pastoral letter that set out a reasoned argument for collaboration, which, he declared, the French had misunderstood.[24] It was a line from which he never wavered: even in January 1944 he was proclaiming that only by collaboration could the spread of Communism be halted. Six professors of the Lille Catholic faculties criticised the bishop's initial statement as 'appearing difficult to reconcile with the requirements of patriotism' but were rebuffed by Cardinal Liénart.

As the war progressed, the hierarchy began increasingly to distinguish between the Marshal and Laval, now committed beyond recall to total collaboration. This was not lost upon the Germans. Cardinal Suhard's case is not untypical. He was reckoned to be among the most pliable of the higher clergy. After the Allied invasion Abetz noted in July 1944 that Suhard now thought that Germany should try to come to an accommodation with Britain and had shown himself more reserved ever since de Gaulle had received the bishop of liberated Bayeux. Moreover, he had been cautious in his condemnation of the assassination of the collaborationist Philippe Henriot. But a few days later the ambassador reported that Suhard had veered in his opinions once more, since he now believed that a German understanding with Britain was impossible, because of the detestation the Allied bombings had aroused in the Reich.[25]

The Germans found themselves in direct or indirect conflict with the church in at least four matters, which can only be touched upon briefly here.

The first concerned the small separatist movements that thought the collapse of France might serve their aims. In Brittany in 1940 the activities of Olivier and Mordrel, who returned to their native heath from Germany under military protection, received no ecclesiastical support. The bishop of Quimper even took part in a counter-demonstration against the so-called Congress of Pontivy, called to set up a Breton state.[26] In a profoundly Catholic region

24. H. Claude, 'La hiérarchie catholique, le gouvernement de Vichy et l'occupant' in: Actes: Lille, p. 271.
25. Foreign Office (FO) Archives No. 6455 GM2. Telegrams No. 3410, signed Abetz 14 July 1944; No. 1543, signed Hilger, 17 July 1944.
26. Jäckel, Frankreich in Hitlers Europa, p. 50.

such episcopal opposition must have weighed heavily. Likewise Abbé Gantois, who, from Lille, and with some German connivence, had headed a pre-war pro-German movement to carve out a new 'dietsch' satellite state to include French Flanders, was shunned by the church and forbidden by Liénart to exercise any public ministry. It is noticeable that after mid-1941 German support for these two separatist movements dropped dramatically, and it is reasonable to assume that this was in part due to the church's attitude.

The question of the *de facto* annexation of Alsace-Lorraine also aroused strong feelings in ecclesiastical circles. In 1940 the bishop of Metz, Mgr Heinz, had been pushed over the new 'frontier' and forbidden to return. The same interdict had been placed upon Mgr Ruch, the bishop of Strasbourg, who, exiled to unoccupied France, represented, together with Terracher, the rector of the Université de Strasbourg, the lost provinces. The arbitrary transferral of Strasbourg cathedral from Catholic to Protestant hands, who refused to accept this 'gift', was bitterly resented. News of Nazi measures seeped through: the closure of confessional schools, the expulsion of their staffs, the obligation laid upon parents to request religious instruction for their children, and the closure of the two confessional faculties at Strasbourg. In effect, the former Concordat, which had continued to apply in Alsace after 1918, was brushed aside. The French church took note of all this, and silently condemned.

The second matter concerned the young. Petty irritations such as the requisitioning of their schools (state schools likewise suffered), and cases of local German NCOs censoring Catholic school history books by tearing out pages considered derogatory to Germany, stimulated priests to protest to their ordinaries and to react also in petty ways, such as refusing to celebrate mass, or at least refusing communion, when German soldiers were present.

However, the major confrontation concerned the Catholic youth movements, by far the largest organised body of young people with whom the Germans had to deal, and capable of being regulated by the church, if needs be, with as much discipline as applied in the Hitlerjugend. The Occupation authorities' fear was that they might become the nucleus of an army of revenge. The Action Catholique de la Jeunesse Française (ACJF) comprised perhaps as many as 116,000 young Catholics in organisations such as the Jeunesse Ouvrière Catholique (JOC: 40,000 members) or the Jeunesse Agricole Catholique (JAC: 35,000 members).[27] In addition, there were by 1941 some 40,000 Catholic Scouts (Scouts de France); there were also some 25,000 young Protestants in youth movements. Thus the total number of organised Christian youth fell not far short of 200,000, if smaller organisations are included.

The Occupation authorities realised the potential danger from the beginning. An ordinance of 28 August 1940 forbade all such associations, the wearing of distinctive badges and the display of flags. The ordinance of course applied only to the occupied zone.

Two or three Catholic youth groups came in for special attention. The scouts, with their para-military tradition, merited special surveillance, but nevertheless covertly carried on their activities. Occasionally the authorities pounced. Thus one luckless chaplain in the state lycée of Bourges was gaoled for attempting to restart a scout troop.[28] The Abwehrstelle at Bordeaux signalled the 'very dangerous' activities of the clergy, who operated scout or rover troops under the guise of names such as the Amis de Saint-Michel or Amis de Notre-Dame, particularly on the coast; in Normandy it proposed to 'provide assistance and a reception organisation for any intended British landing'.[29] Camping was also carried on surreptitiously. The 5th Lille troop, the Troupe Lyautey, and the 1st Tourcoing troop camped twice a year throughout the war. In 1942 the latter pitched tents in Calvados and sang the jingle:

> Aux Allemands elle [la troupe] n'a pas dit
> Qu'elle campe en Normandie.[30]

Parish youth clubs (*patronages*) were tolerated provided activities were confined to religious matters. The prefect at Tours was rapped over the knuckles when it was found that those in his area were engaging in sport. Likewise the Germans questioned even the legality of the 'colonies de vacances'.[31]

But it was the organisations of the ACJF proper that were the most closely watched. The hierarchy had agreed that they should

27. AN. AG II 654. File A308: 'Jeunesse' gives the figures for each movement in detail.
28. AN. AJ 40.557. File: VKult 405 [former German file]
29. Centre de Documentation Juive Contemporaine (CDJC.) Carton CDXCIV–7–8. Report of 27 September 1943 to Abwehrleitstelle Frankreich, Paris.
30. CDJC. Carton LXXVIII - MBH in Frankreich, 24 March 1942.
31. AN. F17. 13379 Letter from Feldkommandantur 588, Indre-et-Loire to Prefect, Tours, 21 May 1947.

function in private, but stated meetings should take place in church and take the form of prayers, religious songs and a homily. Despite a warning from the Secrétariat à la Jeunesse in May 1941 that absolute compliance with Germans wishes was required, nothing was done. Finally the Germans, losing patience, raided the JAC offices in Rennes, arresting some officials, who were only released through the intervention of Mgr Roques. Later that month the church thought it had at last secured permission for the movements to function, provided that they carried on no political activity and restricted meetings to fewer than 300 people. But the position remained unclear.

On 31 March 1943 the SS officer Kuntze had arrested two chaplains of the 'Coeurs Vaillants', a Catholic junior movement for boys aged between nine and fourteen. This raised once more the whole issue.[32] Kuntze maintained that he knew nothing of the 1941 agreement. Since 1 June 1942, he claimed, the German Embassy, which had signed the agreement, had had no standing in the matter – a significant example of rivalry between the two occupation authorities. Although he was prepared to re-consider the position, he added darkly that in his view all priests were anti-German resisters who should be shot. Cardinal Suhard intervened with Bonnard, the minister of education. Since the position of other organisations, and particularly the JOC, had become very precarious, on 25 October 1943 the cardinal wrote to the Germans asking for a decision. He received no immediate reply.

The JOC had been under suspicion since 1942, when the Germans asked the prefects for reports on the movement. But the bishops refused even to supply the names of local leaders. Well-known ones, such as Abbé Masse of Dijon, were then arrested. In May 1943 JOC chaplains in the Quimper diocese were threatened, and finally Abbé Guerin, the JOC national chaplain, was arrested. Suhard urged other JOC leaders to hide. Oberg, although releasing Guérin in December 1943,[33] pointed once more to the 1940 ordinance, and also to a local one of the Kommandant of Gross-Paris specifically banning the JOC. Not until 27 March 1944 did the Germans give formal permission under very strict conditions, for the youth movements to operate.

32. AN. F17. 13346. Correspondance du ministre [de l'Instruction publique], 1943-1944.

33. Cardinal Suhard (ed. O. de la Brosse), *Vers une Eglise en état de mission*, Paris 1965, p. 103.

By then the JOC was very active, particularly in helping young workers deported to Germany. One commentator has said that it felt 'un besoin irrésistible et combien séduisant de "rouler" l'occupant'. The Commissaire aux Renseignements Généraux at Lille had already reported in April 1943 that its 'influence politique est d'autant plus marquante que cette organisation calquée sur l'organisation communiste s'oppose à elle et tend même à la noyauter . . . il faut bien ajouter qu'elle s'oppose également à la pénétration allemande'.[34] Structuring into Communist-like cells and the adoption of the 'need to know' principle were particularly effective for the movement's clandestine activities. Eventually some Jocistes joined their fellow-Frenchmen in Germany, others enrolled in the Francs Tireurs et Partisans.

On the two other matters in which the church was forced into confrontation with the Germans, the persecution of the Jews[35] and the Service du Travail Obligatoire, much has already been written. Here only a few aspects can be highlighted. In these matters Pétain had become the 'shield' behind which the hierarchy could shelter to justify their actions – or their inertia. For their part, the bishops still exhorted the faithful to rally around Pétain. Incidentally, their loyalty hardly extended beyond the war. At the Marshal's trial only three out of the sixty-three witnesses were clerics. One, Abbé Rodhain, merely gave an account of the treatment of French workers in Germany. Pastor Boegner appeared on behalf of French Protestants, but appeared reserved towards Pétain, particularly at the latter's failure to stop the deportation of Jews. Only Cardinal Liénart testified – by letter – to the rectitude of the actions of the former head of state, but nevertheless concluded with an appeal for the nation to rally round 'son libérateur, le Général de Gaulle.'[36]

The ambiguous and vacillating attitudes of Catholics towards the treatment of the Jews have already been thoroughly explored. Here observations will be confined to matters that link the church and the Germans directly, although Vichy was the prime initiator of the persecution, and when it was taken up by the SS continued to give it its backing.

Anti-Semite groups were not lacking among Catholics. Among

34. Archives Departementales (AD.) du Nord, R. 2410, Letter to Prefect 28 April 1943.

35. See the outstanding study by M. Marrus and R. Paxton, *Vichy France and the Jews*, New York, 1981.

36. Pétain, *Compte rendu du procès Pétain*, 22 vols., Paris 1945.

the nominally Christian intellectuals were writers such as Brasillach, Châteaubriant, Robert de Beauplan, Béraud and La Varende; among 'political' Catholics were men such as Henriot, Clémenti and Vallat. With the exception of the last-named, all were tainted with collaboration. Many bishops, moreover, still perhaps unconsciously influenced by the 'death of Christ' slur, considered there was a Jewish 'problem', particularly through the influx of refugees.

The three main German authorities in France each had a section dealing with Jewish affairs. In the offices of the MBF Dr Blanke dealt with the sequestration of 'non-Aryan' businesses. In the Embassy part of Consul General Schleier's office was devoted to 'Jewish questions' and was run by Zeitschel, who had promoted the notorious 'Jews and France' exhibition in Paris in September 1941. However, the main Occupation authority concerned was the SS, headed from 1942 onwards by Oberg. Under him was a 'Judenreferat' run until July 1942 by the notorious Dannecker, and then by Rothke.

The first religious protest came from the Protestants. Pastor Boegner's letter to the chief Rabbi (23 March 1941) deploring the measures against his co-religionists became widely known. By November 1941 Protestants were urging Catholics to join in their protest. Boegner approached Pétain on a number of occasions, but there are indications that the Marshal was indifferent to the anti-Jewish measures. Another Protestant, René Gillouin, who had been Pétain's speechwriter in 1940, wrote no fewer than a dozen letters of protest before fleeing to Switzerland.

Since the Vichy police were acting as agents for the Nazis, protests had to be either public or addressed to the head of state. The church in the occupied zone remained strangely silent, despite the fact that Liénart had spoken out before the war against racism. Indeed the *Semaine religieuse* of Evreux even published, at the behest of the Propagandastaffel, a note in which it 'justified' historically the anti-Jewish measures. In July 1942, somewhat tardily, Catholic protests began to be heard. On 16 July Suhard, and on 22 July Gerlier, protested against the massive Vel'd'Hiver round-up in Paris. Other deportations, particularly that of children from Vénissieux, stimulated further protests. Saliège, archbishop of Toulouse, caused a letter to be read from the pulpit, but German sources reported that only half his clergy complied.[37] He was

37. FO. Archives. Ref: no: 220323. Telegram 3732, signed Abetz, 28 April 1942.

closely followed by the remarkable Mgr Théas, bishop of Montauban, who spoke in ringing phrases: 'Tous les hommes, aryens ou non-aryens, sont frères parce que créés par le même Dieu.' Gerlier spoke out afresh on 6 September, as did Mgr Delay and Mgr Moussaron, bishops respectively of Marseille and Albi, in the same month. Yet overall, in the unoccupied zone, only somewhat less than half the prelates protested. By October German sources could report that on the Jewish question, 'a section of the clergy, particularly Suhard, Archbishop of Paris, have shown greater understanding in this matter than other bishops'.[38] Flying squads, led by SS but comprising also the Milice, continued to seek out Jews right up to the Liberation.

The feats of two priests, Père Glasberg and Père Chaillet, a Jesuit Superior, in saving Jewish children and others in the Lyon area are well documented and need not be repeated here. Chaillet was eventually arrested on the orders of Laval, who reported the fact to Abetz on 1 September 1942. Abetz's comment is interesting: 'This is the first time for a long while that such a high-ranking cleric has been arrested in France, and the measure should have an even more lasting effect, because Chaillet is the right-hand man of the very anti-German Primate of the Gauls, Archbishop Gerlier of Lyon.'[39] This throws an interesting light on Gerlier, but probably exaggerates his relationship to Chaillet.

As the furore arose about forced labour in Germany, which affected almost every French family, the persecution of Jews faded somewhat into the background. By 1943 many bishops would have liked to do as Gerlier adjured the faithful to do, to work, to pray, to keep silent. It was not to be. The young catholic sought guidance as to whether he should comply with his call-up for the STO. The advice given was, to say the least, ambiguous, although some bishops, such as Mgr Dutoit, came out in favour of out-and-out acceptance. Perhaps noteworthy is the attitude expressed by Christian student leaders at a conference in Lyon in April 1943, who urged revolt. They declared that it was to the honour of France that it had declared war on Germany in 1939 and 'il ne peut être question d'un relèvement de la France avant l'écrasement de l'Allemagne nazie, et tous nos efforts doivent tendre vers sa défaite,

38. FO. Archives. Ref: no: 220498. Telegram 4340, signed Abetz, 30 September 1942.
39. FO. Archives. Ref: no: 220345. Telegram 3818, signed Abetz, 2 September 1942.

même au prix de toutes les compromissions'.[40] The rank and file clergy undoubtedly shared this hostility. In 1944 Déat asserted in exasperation: 'Une fois de plus, le clergé fournit des arguments aux réfractaires et des justifications au maquis'.[41] The activities of Jocistes who went to Germany on what they regarded as an apostolic mission, and of the priests sent clandestinely to Germany to minister to the spiritual needs of French youth are also well-known. Both gave rise to unease on the part of Himmler, who feared the effect upon German Catholics.

By 1944 the most that the Occupation authorities could hope for regarding Christians was to neutralise their now open hostility. However, the French Milice, who had become the helots of the SS, reflected a certain Catholic element. The young bourgeois Catholic who had volunteered in all innocence in it early days, even with paternal approval, found himself associating with later recruits drawn from the dregs of society, and sucked into a whirlpool of criminality and brutality – this despite the fact that the Milice newspaper, *Combats*, continued to project the image of the crusading Christian.

As the Occupation wound to a close high- and low-ranking ecclesiastics alike began to be arrested almost indiscriminately. Ironically – for he was firmly anti-Allied – the first episcopal victim was Mgr Puguet, bishop of Clermont-Ferrand, who was arrested for allegedly having sheltered a fugitive priest[42] and deported eventually to Dachau. On 9 June, Mgr Théas, bishop of Montauban, was arrested because, as regards terrorism, he had told the local Kommandant, referring to Gestapo atrocities: 'Si le vainqueur pratique le terrorisme, il est disqualifié pour l'interdire'. At Front-Lager 122, near Compiègne where he landed up, he found Mgr Bruno Solages, rector of the Institut Catholique of Toulouse, with three of his staff. Other internees in the camp rejoiced at having – at last, as they put it – a bishop among their number. They were joined by Mgr Rodié, bishop of Agen, who had been arrested on June 15, as had the bishop of Albi. Later all

40. For an account of the STO as it affected young men see W.D. Halls, *The Youth of Vichy France*, Oxford, 1981, ch. XIV.; AN. F17. 13349. Report by Brunereau, Chef de la Propagande universitaire, to Creyssel, Commandant Chapuis and de Laugauzie, 17 April 1943. His report, when received at Vichy, was pencilled across in red: 'Gaullisme'.

41. FO. Archives 898/212, 1943-1944.

42. J.F. Sweets, *Choices in Vichy France*, Oxford, 1986, p. 57.

save Théas were shipped off to Germany. Some 80 Oblate friars then joined Théas, until they were freed by the Allies. With the exception of the bishop of Limoges, arrested on 7 July and detained for only two weeks, the Occupation authorities arrested in all only four bishops.

The Liberation marked the close of an eventful period in French Christianity. The high hopes with which Catholics had welcomed the Vichy régime, whilst regretting the defeat that had occasioned it, but trusting to regain the eminence the church had lost under the Third Republic, were not fulfilled. As regards the Nazi element among the occupying forces, to whom Christians were always suspect (not always justifiably so), it was forced to react eventually to exorbitant actions and demands. But the strength and quality of that reaction was fiercely criticised at the Liberation. Whilst on the whole the rank-and-file clergy were not impugned, it is nevertheless difficult to accept Mgr Théas' verdict given at the time, 'Le clergé est le corps social le plus atteint par la Gestapo.' Given the potential of Christianity, and in particular of an internationally-linked church, it is remarkable how successful the Occupation authorities were, with a few notable exceptions, in stifling religious opposition – with the magnificent exception of those Christians engaged in the armed or passive Resistance, the scope of which lies outside this study.

Excessive timidity and hopelessness, the sub-conscious idea that the Occupation was almost a divine visitation upon the French, the feeling that it was best to 'wait and see': these explanations are inadequate. Did the fault lie in church leadership? Were the leaders misled by Pétain? The coolness between de Gaulle and Liénart, both Lillois, may be traced back to this. But the cardinal could not be accused of pro-German sentiments. Not only his whole past career but also his condemnation of the SS atrocities at Ascq, near Lille, in 1944 confirm this. Cardinal Suhard, from the few reports of his activities that have emerged, is a more dubious case, although, being in Paris, he had necessarily to temporise more with the occupiers. The cardinal archbishop was nevertheless excluded from his own cathedral on 26 August 1944, when a solemn thanksgiving service was held in Notre Dame, in de Gaulle's presence. The immediate pretext for this snub was that only a few weeks earlier he had welcomed Pétain there; he had also presided over the funeral service for the assassinated collaborationist, Philippe Henriot; and had said masses for the LVF that had fallen on the Eastern Front. It would seem that later Théas intervened on Suhard's behalf with de

Gaulle, who afterwards received the cardinal cordially. Gerlier was said to be constantly anti-German, despite the innuendoes cast against him at the recent Barbie trial.

Mgr Théas, who seems to have been taken up by de Gaulle at the Liberation, advised against any 'Epuration' of the church. Despite this, the General approached the Vatican in 1946 to ask for the deposition of one-third of all bishops. This was of course totally unacceptable, because their main crime was 'collaboration' with the Vichy régime, and not the enemy, and hence with a régime that Pius XII, through the presence of his nuncio to the very end, had recognised. A list was also drawn up of lesser lights who might be chargeable with treason. It contained the names of Mayol de Lupé, the Abbé Bergey, Canon Peuch, Père Forestier, who as chaplain to both the scouts and the Chantiers de la Jeunesse had insisted upon strict compliance with the STO, and Père Bruno, the Carmelite. The roll-call is notable for its brevity.

Among the bishops Mgr Dutoit was forced to resign. Latreille,[43] the distinguished historian who was appointed Sous-directeur des Cultes for a while after the Liberation, gives the names of bishops whose removal was considered desirable; a first list (Liste A) included Suhard; a second (Liste B) added Liénart and Gerlier. His own conclusion, moderate and well-informed, must be respected: '. . . on ne peut pas dire qu'aucun des évêques maréchalistes (mis à part le cardinal Baudrillart) soit jamais tombé dans la Collaboration'.[44] The Germans, hostile throughout to the church, would certainly have endorsed this judgement. With the exceptions mentioned, none of the standard works on collaboration, such as those by Ory, Cotta and Gordon, indict a single bishop. Gordon, however, adds a somewhat intriguing aside: 'It is not surprising that in Catholic France, there were many Catholics in the collaborationist movements but there seems to have been a proportionately large number of collaborationists strongly grounded in Catholic education.'[45] How many is 'many'? How large is 'large'. His statement must be taken with a pinch of salt: collaborationists, it will be recalled, numbered perhaps no more than two per cent of the population as a whole.

43. A. Latreille, *De Gaulle, la Libération et l'Eglise catholique*, 1978, pp. 26ff.; Actes: Lille, p. 289.

44. Actes: Grenoble, p. 360

45. B. Gordon, *Collaborationism in France during the Second World War*, Ithaca, NY / London, 1980, p. 336.

6

THE CULT OF JOAN OF ARC UNDER THE VICHY RÉGIME

Gerd Krumeich

The historiography of this important and fascinating theme is extremely limited. Marina Warner's *Joan of Arc: the Image of Female Heroism* does not deal with this problem; neither does Regine Pernoud mention it in her numerous essays on the cult of Joan of Arc. The almost exhaustive catalogue *Images de Jeanne d'Arc* does not go into detail on the subject; the recent history of Fête d'Orléans by Bauchy pays no attention to the years 1940–4; and the all important study by Marot ends before this period.[1] The great Czechoslovakian historian Frantiček Graus, who has written a fascinating book about the cult of national heroes in general and that of Joan of Arc in particular, confines himself to the statement, albeit clear-sighted, that the cult of Joan did not spread very rapidly during the Second World War, as 'Joan could not become the decisive symbol of the fight for liberation' because of the propagandist image of her projected by the Vichy régime. But from this remark Graus draws an interesting conclusion:

> The role of Joan of Arc as a symbolic figure was limited at the time and has always been put into question by the fact that the remembrance of Joan has been identified with certain tendencies of French domestic policy. However, she has always remained a great if enigmatic personality. Her fate is too individual to be truly integrated into a collective legend, whether Roman Catholic or nationalist.[2]

1. See Marina Warner, *Joan of Arc: The Image of Female Heroism*, New York, 1982. R. Pernoud and M.V. Clin, *Jeanne d'Arc*, Paris, 1986. R. Pernoud, 'Jeanne et son image', in *Images de Jeanne d'Arc. Hommage pour le 550e anniversaire de la libération d'Orléans et du Sacre*, Paris, 1979. Jacques-Henri Bauchy, *Une fête pas comme les autres. 550 ans de fêtes de Jeanne d'Arc*, Orléans, 1979. Pierre Marot, 'De la réhabilitation à la glorification de Jeanne d'Arc: Essai sur le culte de l'héroïne en

These remarks will be referred to again, but first the general state of research must be defined.

Claude Ribéra-Pervillé's article 'Jeanne d'Arc au Pays des Images', illustrates the attempts of the Vichy régime to appropriate Joan and examines the reasons for their relative failure. Many aspects, which are to be found in this article, can be found in that analysis.[3] In a further remarkable essay entitled 'Jeanne d'Arc et les Juifs',[4] Michel Winock sets out to show how the patriotic cult of moderate republicans, who wished to use the image of Joan of Arc as a means for obtaining consensus in a divided country, was finally used: 'Au moins en partie par cette lignée de journalistes et d'écrivains qui se sont employés à diffuser le mythe du Juif en France ou plus tard à y naturaliser les délires nazis.' Winock also tries to show how the myths attaching to Joan of Arc in many ways complemented the myths surrounding the Jews during this period. Finally, the detailed and subtly pioneering study by Patrick Marsh of the performance of plays concerning Joan of Arc during the Vichy years must be mentioned.[5] A more comprehensive documentation provided by Gabriel Jacobs comments on the double meaning of the famous play by Vermorel, *Jeanne avec nous*, which can be interpreted either as a play of Resistance or of Collaboration (according to how it is acted and to the perception of the play by the audience). Nick Atkin, on the other hand, draws the following conclusion in a more succinct study of the presentation of Joan of Arc in French *lycées* during the Occupation:

> But, because Joan embodied so many causes, Church and State would soon stumble across yet another problem with her cult: that of ambiguity, especially as a symbol of patriotism. Subsequently, as the war dragged on, ambiguity of this kind became more and more difficult to contain, and would slowly eat away at the fragile unity Church and State

France pendant cinq siècles' in *Mémorial du Ve centennaire de la réhabilitation de Jeanne d'Arc, 1456–1956*, Paris, 1958.

2. See Frantiček Graus, *Lebendige Vergangenheit. Überlieferung im Mittelalter und in den Vorstellungen vom Mittelalter*, Cologne/Vienna, 1975, p. 304.

3. Claude Ribéra-Pervillé, 'Jeanne d'Arc au pays des images', *L'Histoire*, 15 September 1979, pp. 7–11.

4. Michel Winock, 'Jeanne d'Arc et les Juifs' in *L'Histoire* 3, 1979, pp. 227–37.

5. Patrick Marsh, 'Jeanne d'Arc during the German Occupation', *Theatre Research International* 2 (1976–7), pp. 139–46. Gabriel Jacobs, 'The Role of Joan of Arc on the Stage of Occupied Paris' in R. Kedward and R. Austin (eds), *Vichy France and the Resistance: Culture and Ideology*, London and Sydney, 1985, pp. 106–22.

had been so desperate to preserve through the figure of Joan.[6]

Atkin's opinion about the relationship between church and state should be regarded with caution, but the theme of ambiguity is fundamental to the whole question.

Furthermore, there are important iconographic sources preserved at the Musée d'Histoire Contemporaine de la Bibliothèque de Documentation Internationale Contemporaine as well as the dossiers about Vichy which are kept at the Centre Jeanne d'Arc at Orléans; these last are not all that numerous, but they are particularly interesting as far as the celebration of Joan of Arc during the years of the Vichy régime is concerned. Moreover it is important to try to place these attempts by the Vichy government to appropriate the figure of Joan of Arc back into the tradition of her particular cult as it had developed during the Third Republic. This will allow us to judge whether the Pétain régime finally succeeded in creating something new, or to what extent its attempts at obtaining a historical legitimacy by 'adopting' Joan of Arc were doomed to failure because they met with opposition from old-fashioned and traditionalist elements. In the light of these documents, and in the context of the history of the cult of Joan of Arc, the attempts by Vichy to create an authentic and significant view of the national heroine appear somewhat impoverished and ineffectual, particularly when compared to established ideological stereotypes.

This chapter is therefore a good opportunity for showing the inherent limits to a Pétainist construction of a new order, 'Joan under Vichy' serving as a concrete example for the general definition of Pétainism offered by J.P. Azéma:

> Le pétainisme, c'est avant tout la convergence d'idées lointainement reçues des droites, badigeonnées de quelques ingrédients empruntées aux années trente. Ce pessimisme fondamental, ce moralisme sentencieux, cet élitisme antidémocratique, cette construction organisatrice de la société, ce nationalisme défensif et replié sur lui-même ont un fondement bien réactionnaire. C'était un pot-pourri . . . d'idéologies fleurissant à la fin du XIXe siècle . . . sans que ce syncrétisme qui se prétendait régénérateur fasse une part démesurée au système de Maurras . . .[7]

6. Nick Atkin, 'The Cult of Joan of Arc in French Schools, 1940–44', in Kedward and Austin (eds), *Vichy France and the Resistance*, pp. 265–8.
7. Jean-Pierre Azéma, *De Munich à la Libération*, Paris, 1974, p. 80.

This is the reason why it is also important, in order to situate Pétainism in relation to Joan of Arc, to outline the overall course of the 'battle of Joan of Arc' during the Third Republic.

After the discovery of the 'national' significance of the story of Joan of Arc at the beginning of the romantic period in the early nineteenth century, Joan was, in the first instance, something of a heroine of the Left. Above all, it was the progressive authors who rallied to her banner who discovered, by dint of reinterpreting well-established source material and the addition of new material, a Joan whose image fitted in well with the anti-monarchist, anti-clerical character of the liberal and republican movement. Sismondi, Michelet, Henri Martin and many others discovered a Joan who was a 'fille du peuple', betrayed by her king (and the great lords) and burnt by the church. Was it not the case that Joan had been hindered from pursuing her mission of liberating the whole of France? And had she not been found guilty by an ecclesiastical court? For a time Joan was a rallying point for republicans and the idea of establishing a national holiday to honour her came from radical republican circles. In contrast, the old view of Joan persisted in Catholic circles (particularly at Orléans): Joan of Arc was above all a faithful servant of the King (and, on occasion, she was accordingly promoted to the ranks of a 'royalist') whose mission it was to have the King crowned at Reims. In consequence her tragic end was often considered to be a punishment that God had meted out to her for having 'transgressed' her divine 'mission'.

From the 1870s this royalist, Catholic, traditionalist and secular view was partially revived: Joan remained the faithful servant of the King, but the divine character of her mission was stressed up to the time when her canonisation was proposed in 1869. The problems of this procedure need not delay us here and Joan was finally canonised in 1920; this was a move approved of by moderate republicans because, since the 1890s, Joan had no longer been regarded so much as a protagonist of the 'popular' republic but more as an element of 'centrist' consensus with the Right. In a certain way the image of Joan of Arc had always shifted between those who supported the Establishment and those who were for progress, and for this reason it corresponded to the general trend of political life in the Third Republic.[8]

8. François Goguel, *La politique des partis sous la 3ème République*, Paris, 1947. For the historical and general background see Gerd Krumeich, *Jeanne d'Arc in der Geschichte: Historiographie – Kultur – Politik*, Stuttgart, 1989.

It is interesting to note (as Martha Hannah has done in a recent study of Joan and the Action Française)[9] the way in which the image of Joan evolved at this end of the political spectrum. Before the First World War the Action Française used Joan in the struggle against the internal enemy, the Jews, and all other possible enemies. But during the twenties Joan became for the Right a means for maintaining the status quo: 'Parades, formerly excuses for anarchy, became an expression of order.' And when, after 1924, the government revised its policy towards the English, Joan suddenly became the standard bearer for all those who were united in the struggle against perfidious Albion. The Action Française, which was then in opposition as a result of the 'cartel des gauches', exalted the young woman who had rebelled against the established order, and after the banning of the Action Française, Joan became for them an innocent young girl, betrayed by those in power. Georges Bernanos, at that time a supporter of the Action Française, has expressed this attitude very well:

> Et pour avoir cru surprendre en péril, un moment, un seul moment, l'honneur français, ton doux honneur, plus frais qu'un lis, ils nous laissent de toi la fade image d'une rosière inoffensive, à faire rêver les séminaires . . . Vous faisiez autour de la martyre un rempart de ventres, de cuisses grasses, de crânes polis comme l'ivoire . . . [10]

But inspite of the activities of the Action Française, it is obvious that the conservative and clerical discourse of the established order with regard to Joan of Arc has persisted since the 1920s; any attempt to construct it anew was doomed to failure. The myth of Joan of Arc has been of service to many political and ideological ambitions, and has been taken over both by the Right and the Left, although it must be remembered that the Right has been dominant since the 1920s. But it must not be forgotten that Joan was made a saint in that decade, and that her Catholic legitimacy has since become more clearly established than it had been before: a Thalamas affair would not have been conceivable in the 1920s or '30s.

This fact is very important for understanding the phenomenon of the Fête Jeanne d'Arc at Orléans. Indeed, from the very beginning in the fifteenth century – it has always been the town of Orléans

9. Martha Hannah, 'Iconology and Ideology: Images of Joan of Arc in the Idiom of the Action Française, 1908–1931', *French Historical Studies* 14 (1985), pp. 215–39.
10. Georges Bernanos, *Jeanne relapse et sainte*, Paris, 1934 (new edn. 1969), p. 44.

that has preserved and enhanced Joan's memory by instituting in particular the annual celebration and the panegyric preached in the cathedral. This panegyric is an institution in itself, and clearly indicates both the stable and the ephemeral aspects of the cult of Joan of Arc. It is characteristic of the 'discourse' of this panegyric during the German occupation that it did not make any concessions to the ideology of the Vichy régime. This is all the more remarkable because the temptation of power was fundamental to that particular event.

The first Fête during the Second World War took place just at the end of 'la drôle de guerre', a few days before the arrival of German troops outside Paris. For this reason the traditional procession was replaced by a procession inside the cathedral of Ste Clothilde. All that is known is that Mgr Fellion, the archbishop of Bourges, addressed himself in particular to the young people in the congregation, presenting Joan of Arc to them as an example to be followed.[11] But the celebration of 1941 – the first to take place during the Occupation – is far better documented as it was reported in the *Républicain du Centre*: 'Les fêtes de 1941 ont été marquées par des cérémonies discrètes' when the public maintained 'une réserve parfaitement naturelle' dictated by the circumstances. But that particular year a public ceremony took place among the ruins – even Joan of Arc's house had been partially destroyed. In his opening address the mayor made reference to 'la grande pitié du Royaume de France' from which Joan herself had suffered so much, and – after reviewing the great events in Joan's life (which had been the practice since the sixteenth century) – the mayor ended with the following remark: 'Puissions, Français, méditer la leçon qui nous est donnée par la Pucelle, apprendre par la vie de celle qui détestait la guerre [!] et la mena sans haine de l'adversaire que ce n'est que par les efforts incessants et le sacrifice le plus absolu . . . que se font les choses grandes et durables.[12]

After these few well chosen words – which avoided all mention of a new or Pétainist order – there followed the panegyric in the cathedral given that year by the Rev Father Bouley of the Oratory. He began his sermon with an appeal, 'Du fond de l'abîme j'ai crié vers toi, Seigneur', and continued, insisting on the fact that Joan was truly 'la Sainte de la Misère Nationale'. After this unusual remark, he carried on in the following way:

11. In *Journal du Loiret*, 7 May 1940.
12. *Républican du Centre*, 11 May 1941.

On ne saurait voir en elle un chef de guerre à la manière d'un Condé ou d'un Bonaparte. C'est avant tout une sainte que Dieu envoie à la France et c'est par des moyens de sainteté qu'elle agit . . . . Une idée merveilleusement simple la dirige en toutes ses entreprises: Ceux qui n'ont pas le droit d'être là doivent s'en aller, de gré, sinon de force. Telle est la justice de Dieu; telle est la loi de Jeanne.

The Reverend Father Bouley also explained that 'Dieu voulait d' abord redonner à la France une âme. Il fallait donc non un grand capitaine, mais une sainte.'

One should keep in mind that at the time, Orléans was occupied by the Germans and that Pétain had come to the town for the ceremonies the day before.

It is no surprise to find in the same panegyric some remarks about Pétain himself:

Rien ne sert de multiplier les machines de combat ou les puissances économiques d'un pays si l'on ne réussit pas à lui redonner une âme . . . Le meilleur culte que nous puissions aujourd'hui rendre à Jeanne, c'est de travailler par un effort quotidien à nous transformer nous-mêmes selon sa ressemblance. La France peut continuer de décliner demain si nous répugnons à la tâche de restauration spirituelle dont l'urgence est manifeste.

It is in that particular sense that Pétain is described as the 'glorieux vieillard', who had come to Orléans the day before:

Nous avons connu hier une faveur inattendue, une joie inespérée. Le drapeau tricolore a flotté sur Orléans. Les rues et les places ont retenti des cris de 'Vive la France! Vive le Maréchal! Vive Jeanne d'Arc!' L'hymne national a salué vingt fois le glorieux vieillard dont personne ne niera qu'il ne porte dans son coeur la souffrance de la patrie comme il incarne en sa personne le vouloir vivant du Pays.

Are these sentiments equivocal or overtly Pétainist? Or are they nothing more than the usual conservative and Christian discourse which seeks to summon up the memory of a military leader and the saviour of 1917? But by putting the emphasis mainly on the liberation of the country by Joan of Arc, the speech avoids mentioning any possible plan of constructing a new order.

Nothing is known about the panegyric of 1942, but at the festival for Joan of Arc in 1943 we again find the same emphasis being put on the 'simplicité discrète qu'imposent les circonstances' as mentioned in the 'Annales' of the diocese of Orléans. Another panegyric must be mentioned here, in part at least, to avoid the accusation of having put too much emphasis on one isolated incident and of having taken a part for the whole . . . In this instance they are the words of the bishop of Saint-Dié, Mgr Blanchet, who began his sermon with words that could have alluded to the Marshal: 'L'histoire de Jeanne d'Arc nous présente le spectacle d'un pays qui reprend vie parce qu'il a entendu l'appel d'une âme . . .' But he continued in the following totally unexpected fashion: 'On ne régente pas davantage les hommes; il faut les gagner . . .' And he went on to explain how it was the simplicity and the modesty of Joan that won the hearts of the people of France: but Joan is not simply 'à l'aise', she is a 'vraie chrétienne dont les vertus se définissent de la façon suivante':

> Jeanne refuse de s'en tenir aux antithèses faciles où on veut l'enfermer. Elle n'oppose pas, elle ordonne: elle n'exclut pas, elle prend à la fois les vérités complémentaires, et sauve ainsi, comme il se doit, les droits nécessaires de la conscience personnelle comme ceux de la véritable Eglise. Cette humble fille, sans savoir technique, mais de juste sens chrétien, excelle à faire de l'ordre, et ses réponses comme son exemple font, en ces temps agités, un sûr équilibre, comme sa mission a fait un durable établissement. . . . O Jeanne, notre soeur plus claire et plus vaillante, faites-nous entendre votre voix, écho de celles auxquelles vous avez été fidèle. Voyez la misère non seulement de ce pays, mais de ce monde qui pour avoir oublié son âme, est en train de perdre jusqu'à son corps. En ce temps où il semble qu'on ne veuille choisir qu'entre des excès humains, ô vous la plus simple, la plus proche, et pour prendre l'un de vos mots, la plus 'gentille' des Saintes, aidez notre pays à trouver sa route: apprenez-lui par votre exemple qu'on ne choisit pas entre l'ordre et la conscience humaine, mais qu'il les faut aimer et servir l'un et l'autre, en servant Dieu; et obtenez-lui de donner à ces tragiques problèmes, pour son honneur, pour le bien du monde entier, la solution qui, étant à l'image de votre âme, sera la plus humaine, parce qu'étant la plus chrétienne, elle sera aussi la plus française. Ainsi soit-il.

The message is categorial, and it is clear: Catholicism and individualism are united in a synthesis 'à la Jeanne'. Though this panegyric is based on a considerable number of well established arguments which have often been heard before and which have often been contradicted, it is a secular speech which does not make the slightest concession to the spirit of Vichy. On the contrary, it is interesting to note that there is quite clearly no increase in political conformity here on the part of a church dignitary despite the fact that so many churchmen kowtowed to the secular authorities during the eighteenth and nineteenth centuries.

The foregoing can be summed up as follows: it is obviously not enough to rely on the official events organised by those in power during the Vichy régime to understand the significance of the cult of Joan of Arc.

Of course, such events were organised, and there was a definite attempt to appropriate Joan of Arc and derive from her historic stature a certain legitimacy as well as a much needed and suitable means of propaganda for the war effort and national unity. There was, for instance, a propaganda leaflet printed on a double sheet of paper produced 'pour le Bureau de documentation du Chef de l'Etat'. On the cover, beneath some rather archaic designs, there is the following sentence: 'Suivez-moi! Gardez votre confiance dans la France éternelle.' The back page shows a duel between two knights with the insignia 'Jeanne / Du Guesclin / Bayard', and inside the leaflet there is a gallicised picture of Pétain, who makes the following speech:

A tous je demande les efforts qui feront de la Jeunesse Française une jeunesse forte, saine de corps et d'esprit, préparée aux tâches qui élèveront leur âme de Français et de Françaises. C'est sur la jeunesse et par la jeunesse que je veux rebâtir notre Pays dans l'Europe Nouvelle. Pour cette grande oeuvre, je fais appel à tous les jeunes.

The message is crystal clear: Joan, Bayard and Du Guesclin representing the heroic history of France, are watching over the Marshal's great plan.

If such reminiscences and exhortations appear relatively inoffensive, doing nothing more than encouraging the reconstruction of France and a type of sacred union – à la Poincaré – we are immediately aware of a characteristic to be found in any Fascist or extreme right-wing discourse in Pétain's language: the naming of the enemy against whom the effort of reconstruction must be made. Patrick Marsh has mentioned one of Pétain's phrases concerning Joan of Arc which is highly significant:

Pourtant elle ne connut pas le succès tout de suite. Trop d'égoïsmes l'entouraient. Trop de lâchetés, trop de scepticisme, trop d'intrigues. Il lui fallaint lutter durement avant de voir se rallumer les énergies . . . C'est seulement après de rudes efforts qu'elle eut la joie de se sentir suivie. On comprenait enfin la nécessité de se grouper derrière le Chef et d'abandonner les chimères de l'étranger . . .[13]

And the enemy within is quickly named: Pierre Pascal, an uncompromising ideologue, published an article on 7 May 1942 – the day of Joan of Arc's Fête – which was an appeal to the 'Sainte de la Patrie' in which he denounced all traitors from the Jews to the politicians of the Third Republic, and calls for them to be punished by 'la Justice':

> Or, la justice n'est pas incarnée. Certes elle inspire l'âme, la vie et le feu quotidien du Maréchal de la Patrie: un contre tant! Mais il manque à la France un véritable officier de justice, une sorte de héraut du Maréchal, capable de faire juger, fustiger et mener au supplice ceux qui, volontairement, avaient voulu défaire, détruire et réduire en charbons l'oeuvre même de Sainte Jeanne: c'est-à-dire la France et son étonnante unité, la France jadis chrétienne et européenne, bien pensante et bien conseillante.

Here the Marshal is put on a par with Joan of Arc; *L'Appel* of 7 May 1942 makes the following point: 'Si Jeanne n'avait en vérité qu'une volonté: chasser la trahison par le sacre de son roi; le Maréchal n'a qu'une volonté: chasser la trahison par le sacre de la justice.'[14] (N.B. It is worth remembering the words of the panegyric given the same day in which it was pointed out that Joan had only one aim: to chase the occupier out of 'sa doulce France.')

It is not at all difficult to find – in any police state – people who settle old scores on an internal political level under the guise of supporting the so-called spirit of renewal. And, when all is said and done, it is not easy for historians to distinguish between misplaced sincerity and bad faith resulting from fear or ambition. But to monopolise Joan of Arc for internal political ends was in no way an invention of Vichy, and it is quite probable that people were able to see the difference. Such attempts at taking over Joan of Arc were certainly of less interest to them, given the tradition of using the national heroine for biased political aims, than the historians of Vichy would like to make out. We should not take these historians

---

13. Marsh, 'Jeanne d'Arc during the German Occupation', p. 141.
14. *L'Appel*, 7 May 1942.

too seriously when, for example, they exclaim that Joan was used most unjustly by the régime which favoured capitulation whereas she was, they argue, a symbol of the Resistance;[15] Joan had been used for more than three centuries for various political and ideological ends, and moreover this is the reason why, hand in hand with all the veneration, goes a certain irony and sarcasm, which brings to mind the 'images d'Epinal' and certain advertisements (e.g. Camembert Jeanne)[16] when her name is mentioned.

The only original contribution that Vichy made to the image of Joan of Arc consisted in conferring on her a ferociously anti-English character. In no sense had this been a predominant theme during the nineteenth century and during the first forty years of the twentieth century. Of course, Joan had fought against the English and it was the English who had burnt her – and this was a fact that could be usefully used in the political circumstances. But had not Joan said that she did not hate the English? It was only during the Vichy régime that Joan was presented as being hostile to England which became her 'seul ennemi'. On 13 May 1944 the government published a series of stickers and posters with the text: 'Pour que la France vive il faut comme Jeanne d'Arc bouter les Anglais hors d'Europe.'

All this borders on the ridiculous, but it seems that great play was made of this idea, particularly when the bombing of Rouen was mentioned. But it is precisely here that the history of the period is at its most ironic as it was this very idea that had been used again and again during the First World War to describe the barbarity of the Germans who had shelled the cathedral at Reims at the beginning of the war. Hundreds of posters, postcards, etc., bear witness to an event which deeply traumatised the collective French soul. But the fact that Vichy used ideas and themes that had been exploited in other circumstances and in a quite different sense points to a lack of originality on their part, and the ultimate failure of this campaign.

Joan cannot be the standard bearer for politically innovative movements; for the collective memory of the French she has always been and will always remain 'la Sainte de la Défense Nationale'.

15. Winock, 'Jeanne d'Arc et les Juifs', p. 229.

16. Collection of documents in the Centre Jeanne d'Arc at Orleans; the *Bibliothèque de documentation internationale contemporaine* (BDIC) in Paris-Nanterre has an important collection of postcards and posters on this theme too. I am grateful to Mlle Coutin and Mme Laure Namer-Barbizet for granting me access to these documents.

7

COLLABORATION IN THE FINE ARTS, 1940–1944

Sarah Wilson

> Je vous salue Breker. Je vous salue de la haute partie des
> poètes. Patrie ou les patries n'existent pas, sauf dans la
> mesure ou chacun y apporte le trésor du travail national . . .
> dans la haute patrie ou nous sommes compatriotes vous me
> parlez de la France.
> Jean Cocteau, 'Salut à Breker', *Comoedia*, 16 May 1942

The official face of artistic life in occupied Paris extending to the
salons and the beaux-arts policy makers embraced a formal academicism that had been forecast by trends increasingly apparent in
the 1930s. The picture of overt collaboration, 'laissez-faire' and
'artistic revolution' in Pétain's terms take their place against the
backdrop of salon and Sunday painting, a time-honoured French
activity, the emergence of the 'jeunes peintres de tradition
française', the clandestine flourishing of movements such as surrealism and here and there the genuine stirrings of a new art: Jean
Dubuffet's graffiti-inspired painting and Jean Fautrier's moving
'Hostage' series for example. Picasso, the only artist of international
stature to remain in Paris moved into the bleakest and most intense
period of his work. The major dada and surrealist artists, Duchamp,
André Breton, André Masson, Salvador Dali, Jean Tanguy along
with Fernand Léger and Jean Hélion had escaped to New York;
older artists such as Braque, Rouault, Matisse, Bonnard, Jacques
Villon continued to paint outside Paris. While the quietism of
Villon or the religious themes of Rouault may be interpreted in the
light of response to national defeat, they cannot be read as 'collaborative'. The pioneer of the dada period, Francis Picabia, who
stayed on the Côte d'Azur for most of the war, painted very
saleable, kitsch works that at their most 'proto-Fascist' are delib-

erately problematic. This much richer context provides the background to the discussion of co-operation and collaboration as such in the fine arts from 1940–4.[1]

The museums' administration had been mobilised to safeguard artistic treasures as early as 1936, with the first plans for the evacuation of the Louvre, and during 1938, literally thousands of cases were constructed and numbered, while paintings on exhibition were designated with red and green spots – those to be taken down first of all and those of secondary urgency. After a false alarm in 1938, when certain works were packed up after Munich, the museums were definitively closed in August 1939, and their contents sent to the Château de Chambord. The Louvre was responsible for around fifteen other museums and buildings in Paris. Subsequently, the law of 10 August 1941, bringing provincial museums under the jurisdiction of the Direction des Musées de France, facilitated the coordination of the evacuation projects. In all approximately seventy-seven per cent of the 'trésors mobilier' were successfully protected.[2]

Just as the threat of war had provoked action in 1936, reports from Germany concerning the 'entartete Kunst' policy were widely available. The Nazi campaign against so-called 'degenerate' art was deliberately spelled out by Christian Zervos, editor of the luxury review *Cahiers d'Art* in 'Réflexions sur la tentative d'Esthétique dirigée du Troisième Reich', nos 6–7 (special *Guernica* issue) and nos 8–10 of 1937. Zervos quoted extensively from E. Wernert's detailed account *L'art dans la Troisième Reich*, Centre d'Etudes de Politique Etrangère no 7, which laid bare the dictatorial policies of the Reichskulturkammer or RKK.

At this time, the German painter Otto Freundlich, an abstract artist based in Paris for many years, set up an association to help refugees and alerted his fellow artists to the existence and the consequences of concentration camps in Germany. Immediately he

1. See my articles 'La vie artistique à Paris pendant l'Occupation' and 'Les Jeunes peintres de tradition francaise', in *Paris-Paris, Créations-en-France, 1937–1957*, Paris/Munich, 1981–2, with collected texts. The former provides a basis for much of this article, but also lists the avant-garde exhibitions in Paris, 1940–4. For surrealism see Michel Faure, *L'histoire du Surréalisme sous l'Occupation*, Paris, 1982. For Picabia see Yves Alain Bois, 'De Dada à Petain', *Macula*, 1976, no. 1, pp. 122–3 and Bernard Blistène, 'Francis Picabia: In praise of the contemptible', *Flash Art*, no. 113, Summer 1983, pp. 24–31.
2. Adeline Hulftegger, 'Les Musées en Guerre', *Le Jardin des Arts*, no. 32, vol. 2, June 1957.

suffered the consequences: one of his sculptures was used as the catalogue cover for the 'Entartete Kunst' exhibition of 1937 in Munich, and in 1943 he was deported to Poland dying in or on the way to the extermination camp at Lublin-Maidanek.[3]

While official Soviet Socialist Realism was embodied by Boris Iofan's pavilion and its contents at the Paris World Fair of 1937, so official Nazi art was on display in Albert Speer's German pavilion which confronted its rival across the Champ de Mars. Based on neo-classical mausoleum imagery, its portals were flanked by grim and muscular nudes by Josef Thorak. Close by, Picasso's *Guernica* in the Spanish pavilion spelled out the real intentions of Fascism. However, the prevailing academicism in much of the art on display in 1937 was both a foretaste of art under Occupation and Vichy and the natural result of the increasing nationalism and 'return to order' in the arts.[4]

From the 1920s onwards the so-called 'rappel à l'ordre' countered the revolutionary movements of cubism, dada and surrealism with a return to figuration, neo-classical ideals and a taste which mingled the conservative with the decorative. Accelerated by the Wall Street Crash of 1929, which had profound repercussions on the Parisian art market, this change of taste was exemplified by the 1937 exhibition. 'C'etait le goût du temps, la tradition classique héritée de Rude qui triomphait, avec le style classique de 1925, de l'impressionisme de Rodin. Ne trouvez-vous pas que le Palais de Chaillot et l'ancien musée d'Art Moderne, quai de Tokyo, ressemblent étrangement aux mastodontes de pierre élevés par Albert Speer à Nuremberg?'[5]

Long before Paris itself was occupied, on 11 May 1940, Count Franz Wolf Metternich was appointed to head the 'Service de Protection Artistique' or 'Kunstschutz'. On 22 June 1940, Arno Breker, Hitler's official sculptor was flown to Paris to give the Führer an artistic tour of the city, from the steps of the Opera to the Madeleine, the Champs Elysées and the Invalides, where before Napoléon's tomb Hitler apparently mused 'I would like my

3. For Freundlich see *Exposition Résistance-Deportation*, Chancellerie de l'Ordre de la Libération, Paris, 1980, entries nos. 135 and 150.
4. See *Exposition Internationale des Arts et des Techniques dans la vie moderne – Paris 1937 Cinquantenaire*, Musée d'Art Moderne de la Ville de Paris, 1987.
5. The quotation is by Arno Breker from 'Un sculpteur maudit', *Figaro Magazine*, 24 January 1981. For the 'rappel à l'ordre', see *L'art dans les années 30 en France*, Musée d'Art et d'Industrie, Saint-Etienne, 1979, and *Les Réalismes entre Révolution et Réaction*, Paris, 1980.

ashes to be laid to rest on the banks of the Seine, in the midst of these French people I have loved so dearly.' It was a year precisely to the day when the Germans invaded Russia and Breker, according to his memoirs, foresaw Hitler's defeat.[6]

Breker had first attracted Hitler's attention with his decathlon athlete and a female 'Victory' bearing an olive branch created for the Berlin Olympics in 1936. Two warrior heroes, by Breker, representing the party and the army flanked the portals of Speer's new Chancellery by 1937. From 1937 Breker was based in Berlin and received numerous commissions for sculptures and bas reliefs for monuments and museum projects in Berlin and several other German towns. As an habitué of Montparnasse of the 1920s his role in fostering collaboration in the Parisian art world was absolutely central.

After the Armistice, Breker's first visitor in Berlin was Jacques Benoist-Méchin, a former friend, now a minister in the Vichy government, who immediately extended an invitation for a Paris exhibition. At once Breker attempted to liberate Eugène Rudier, the famous caster in bronze of sculptures by Rodin, Maillol and Bourdelle, who had been sent to the prison at Fresnes for refusing to turn his foundry into an arms factory. A telephone call to the Propagandastaffel led to the reunion of Breker and Rudier in Berlin. Albert Speer reassured Breker that the necessary sums for the exhibition could be transferred to Paris via the Banque Worms.

'Certificats de laideur' had been issued for statues commemorating First World War triumphs, which were promptly melted down to be recast as armaments. Breker's power as intercessor was revealed almost at once. Thus he claims that thanks to a personal protest to Hitler, the statue of Maréchal Ney and Carpeaux's *Quatre parties du monde* were spared the fate of Edith Cavell and General Mangin who had been destroyed as early as June 1940.[7]

On 30 June Hitler ordered the 'mise en sécurité' of all art objects belonging to the state, private individuals and above all the works of art belonging to Jewish collectors. In July Otto Abetz, the German Ambassador, ordered the 'seizure of the totality of the museums in Paris and the provinces along with the entirety of their collections', and the 'Einsatzstab Rosenberg' was created to control operations. On 5 October 1940 a law issued from Vichy gave the French

6. See Arno Breker's memoirs: *Im Strahlungsfeld der Ereignisse*, translated into French by Dominique Deroux as *Paris, Hitler et moi*, Paris, 1970, pp. 96–105.
7. Ibid., pp. 133–6.

government 'la gestion, et le cas échéant, le droit de réaliser les biens sans séquestration de tous les émigrés'. The systematic appropriation of artworks as war booty had a long tradition – one has only to recall the provenance of paintings in the Louvre or to remember the sequestration by the French of the German dealer Kahnweiler's collection during the First World War . . . Now it was the collections of the Baron Edouard de Rothschild and others that fell into Nazi hands. On 2 November 1940, Jacques Jaujard, Directeur des Musées Nationaux, was forced to offer Count Metternich the Jeu de Paume Museum in which to store the mounting number of pillaged art works, with the proviso that a double Franco-German inventory of the works be kept. On 3 November the first 'private view' was held for Göring's delectation. By 5 November Göring had drawn up a complete code for the 'Einsatzstab Rosenberg's' exploitation of pillaged collections. On the basis of 'la loi juive du talion', Gerhard Utikal, Chef de l'Etat major spécial du Reichsleiter Rosenberg proclaimed: 'Le Juif avec ses biens . . . se trouve hors de tous droits, parce que depuis les milléniums il a de son côté considéré tous les non-juifs comme dépourvus de droits.' Göring, in fact was to appropriate all real power from the Reichsleiter Alfred Rosenberg until summer 1942. During the course of ten visits to the Jeu de Paume in 1941 and four in 1942, Göring reserved for himself ten Renoirs, ten Degas, two Monets, three Sisleys, four Cézannes and five Van Goghs. Obviously what was considered 'degenerate' for the masses could be enjoyed by their masters. The squabbles for the direction of operations between Abetz, Göring and Alfred Rosenberg, finally Hitler himself, with Martin Bormann at his side resemble the dividing of spoils by medieval robber barons. Metternich, a distinguished art historian, had initially attempted to bring some sense of justice and decorum into the proceedings – in vain.[8]

An 'Epuration' of Jewish artists was the counterpart of the appropriation of Jewish collections. The 'Ecole de Paris' of the 1920s had owed much of its prestige to artists such as Chagall, Soutine, Lipchitz whose works were no longer to be seen. The

8. See Rose Valland, *Le Front de L'Art, Défense des Collections françaises, 1939–1945*, Paris, 1961, pp. 43–53 for a detailed treatment of the very complex situation. The relevant legal documents are quoted in extenso. See also Jean Cassou, *Le Pillage par les allemands des oeuvres d'art et des bibliothèques appartenant à des juifs en France*, Paris, 1947; James J. Rorimer, *Survival, the Salvage and Protection of Art in War*, New York, 1950. Recent work includes Norman Stone, *The Great Art Dictator*, written and presented for BBC 2, 14 December 1981, and Bernard Denvir, 'Monster and Maecenas' (Hermann Göring), *Art and Artists*, February 1983.

official *Revue des Beaux Arts de France*, organ of the Ministère de l'Education Nationale and the Secrétaire Générale des Beaux Arts, appeared first in October/November 1942 – a fascinating and often depressing account of the collaboration of the French museums bureaucracy with the orders to sequestrate Jewish collections, 'reorientate' the Manufactures Nationales at Sèvres and Aubusson, etc.

By 10 November 1942, *Beaux-Arts* directed by Georges Wildenstein, the chief arts magazine which flourished throughout the Occupation, contained advertisements for one 'Vanderpyl's *L'Art sans patrie, un mensonge, le pinceau d'Israël*. Camille Mauclair, a right-wing critic who had been writing since the 1920s excelled himself with *La Crise de l'Art Moderne,* 1942, a complete espousal of anti-Jewish/'degenerate' Nazi aesthetics transposed as an analysis of the Parisian art scene. Its opening paragraph announces the general tenor of the publication:

> Il y a eu de grands poètes, de grandes savants, de grands philosophes juifs, mais peu ou point d'artistes juifs: à peine deux ou trois composi-teurs notables (Mendelssohn, Meyerbeer, Dukas), et des virtuouses du piano et du violon: en peinture et en sculpture, rien que les imitateurs plus ou moins habiles, dont Israels et Pissarro sont les plus notoires. L'art plastique n'a jamais été le fait des juifs. Cependant, comme l'oeuvre d'art est, en même temps qu'une creation de l'esprit, un objet materiel dont la vente nourrit son auteur, les 'juifs, pour qui tout est possibilité de commerce, ont songé à ce domaine de leur activité.
> . . Ce qu'on peut reprocher aux juifs, c'est d'avoir introduit dans le commerce de la peinture des procédés de malhonnêteté et de cor-ruption . . .

The invasion of French art is dated from the 1891 number of the *Revue Blanche* 'où tout le monde était juif . . . '. The conspiracy is detailed to the 1930s:

> Mais il faut maintenant en venir à un aspect plus grave du debat: l'aspect politique et social. La peinture obeissait sous l'impulsion des juifs, eternels chambardeurs internationalistes et apatrides, au slogan 'toujours plus à gauche'. Elle ne se contentait plus d'être anti-academique: elle se voulait enemie du pretendu 'art bourgeois'. Et sous ces mots se dessinat une attaque contre la tradition et le goût de la France, que l'on affectait de confondre avec la mediocrité d'un Institut qui ne representait plus rien. Cette haine du bourgeoisisme mal defini créait une liaison entre certains artistes d'avant garde et les agitateurs révolutionnaires qui cedaient de

plus en plus au bolchevisme sous le Front Populaire. Il devenait bon ton de sympathiser avec les 'rouges', parce qu'on faisait de la peinture extrémiste. On en arrivait à proner un 'art international'.

The Maison de la Culture, the Association des Artistes et des Ecrivains Révolutionnaires, 'organismes protégés par le ministre juif Jean Zay' are similarly the focus for specific attack.

The arrangement of Mauclair's illustrations, a 'fou' from the Villejuif hospital with a Braque, a Picasso and a Chagall labelled 'UN TALENT FOU!!' deliberately imitate the rubrics of the 'Entartete Kunst' exhibition and the 'Franc-maçonnerie' and 'Le Juif et la France' exhibitions that had been held in Paris, despite the fact that most of the (late post-cubist) objects of anathema were created by non-Jews.

The debate between the Ecole Française and the Montparnasse-based, largely expatriate Ecole de Paris, which had become increasingly acute with the rise of nationalism in the 1930s, surfaced at the Salon d'Automne of 1940, rudely ousted from the Grand Palais, and organised in seventeen days.[9] Jewish artists were absent: while exemplifying a will to continuity, the Salon demonstrated a covert form of censorship. The 'Appel aux anciens' in the Salle d'Honneur was dominated by Rodin and his disciple Bourdelle; the 'générations nouvelles' were represented by Wlerick, Yencesse, and Charles Despiau, the 'maître' of Arno Breker in his Montparnasse days.

Contrary to the image of artistic standstill 'Vanderpyl' wrote in *Beaux Arts* no. 39, 10 October 1941: 'Notre vie est envahie par la peinture, notre vie est envahie par les Salons annuels, voire par les expositions particulières... Presque sans interruption – juste le temps qu'il faut pour un accrochage plus ou moins soigné – se succèdent, depuis le mois de mars, les Salons au Palais de Tokyo... Quelle est le signification de ce déluge d'expositions?' It was true, the 2,447 works exhibited in the 1941 Salon d'Automne was a record not to be repeated in the forties. With no transport facilities and very little money, painting and looking at painting became a significant leisure activity of the 'parisien moyen', while with currency unstable, no imported luxury goods, fortunes made and lost on suspicious black-market transactions, paintings became for

9. See Romy Golan, 'Ecole Française, Ecole de Paris', *The Circle of Montparnasse*, Jewish Museum, New York, 1985.

others an easily transportable form of converted cash – and the art market had never flourished so well. It was hardly the time to have ethical concerns about the fact that both Picasso and Léger had been denied 'les cimaises officielles'. Claude D'Arcy's series 'L'Art Indépendant' provides an idea of the painting that was sold on this kind of market. He shows the various salon contributions from 1941–5 (fifteen volumes), including the Salon de l'Art Religieux or the new Salon des moins de trente ans: quite a contrast with the impressionist or 'degenerate' masters which were creating colossal profits in Swiss auction rooms.

While the organisation of the 'return' of German national treasures was being negotiated, there was the cold comfort of the possibility of loans from Germany: Monets from Berlin and Bremen were added to the Monet–Rodin retrospective organised by the Musées Nationaux in November 1940. By this time, however, the Petit Palais was housing the German propaganda exhibition 'Secrets de la Franc-Maçonnerie'. The Grand Palais prepared for the huge 'Exposition de la France Européenne' which opened in June 1941. On 4 September 1941 the curator Yvon Bizardel was afforded an extraordinary vision of the basement of the Petit Palais, where fire had broken out: 'La ferraille nickelée (boulons, écrous, pièces de rechange) scintillait dans les vitrines, les murs revêtus de papier doré portant des oriflammes écarlates à croix gammées. De loin en loin se dressait des autels à Hitler, dont le buste en simili-bronze se détachait sur un éventail de drapeaux, parmi les offrandes de fleurs et de verdure.'[10]

Some museums retained their independence. As early as August 1940, the Musée de l'Homme which mounted exhibitions throughout the Occupation became one of the first centres of Resistance activity in Paris. Tracts were produced in its basement, and *Résistance* was edited by Claude Aveline, Jean Cassou, Marcel Abraham and Agnès Humbert. By the start of 1941, many of the group were imprisoned; the women were finally sent to concentration camps and many of the bravest men, such as Boris Vilde and René Senchal were shot.[11]

Seemingly compliant curators could none the less subvert the plans of the occupying forces. In July 1942, after overhearing that the Germans intended to take over the prospective Musée d'Art

10. Yvon Bizardel, Preface to the Salon d'Automne of 1947 reprinted in *Paris-Paris*, p. 102.
11. See Jean Cassou, *Une vie pour la Liberté*, Paris, 1981.

Moderne for a radio base (proximity to the Eiffel Tower being a prime consideration), the curator Bernard Dorival with his superior Pierre Ladoué, arranged for the premature opening of the museum, which was inaugurated by Abel Bonnard on 6 August 1942. The Vichy authorities were led to imagine of course that this was all part of the policy which required the preservation of a 'normal' cultural life in the occupied capital. Approximately half the number of works evacuated to the Château de Valençay were hastily summoned back leaving the older Matisses, Braques, Rouaults and Dufys in safety. In the 1942 catalogue, we see Neo-Impressionists, Nabis and Fauves all well represented, with some later Cubists, but the general impression of contemporary painting was provided by the Walch, Goerg, Desnoyer spectrum, augmented by the painters who gathered under the aegis of the 'Maîtres de Demain' monographs, published by Editions Sequana. These former doyens of the Ecole Nationale des Arts Décoratifs of 1914, then of the Salons d'Automne and the Salon des Tuileries from the 1920s onwards, Planson, Chastel, Brianchon, Leguelt were the darlings of *Beaux-Arts'* 'Calendrier des Galeries' and second-rate at their most decorative.[12]

Reverting to 1940, during the summer months *Signal*, the Paris edition of the *Berliner Illustrierte Zeitung*, appeared – as was also the case in other occupied countries. Together with frightening photographs of bomb damage and of German military strength, articles on show business and general 'faits divers', it promoted the Nazi aesthetic throughout the Occupation. It regularly covered exhibitions at the so-called 'Maison des artistes' in Berlin, the 'Maison de l'Art Allemand' in Munich. German artists were interviewed in their studios: 'Grace et pesanteur, une visite chez Georges Kolbe', 'La vie et force d'un peintre allemand' (Paul Mathias Padua), 'Une femme sculpteur' (Milly Steiger). Critical articles appeared about non-German art, for example 'L'Art Soviétique. La niaiserie dans la simplicité' and in particular 'Aux Etats-Unis, propagande et protestation, "L'Art décadent"' illustrated by Mondrian, Léger, etc. In August 1940 one of the first numbers put the sculptures of Arno Breker into the context of their German contemporaries: His *Prêt au combat* at the Haus der Kunst in Berlin took its place alongside Prof. Fritz Klimsus' *Olympe*, Prof. Georges

---

12. Interview with Bernard Dorival, 12 January 1981 and 'Ouverture partielle du Musée National d'Art Moderne', *Revue des Beaux-Arts de France*, p. 77ff.

Kolbe's *Amazone* and Prof. Joseph Wackerle's sculpture for Hitler's summerhouse at Obersalzberg.[13]

Besides a flourishing art press, an even wider audience was reached in the cinema newsreels: 14 August 1940 covered an exhibition of German art in Munich and the Wagner festival at Bayreuth – the exhibitions which now appropriated the most hallowed exhibition spaces in Paris were given ample coverage: 'Secrets de la Franc-Maçonnerie' at the Petit Palais was filmed in October, the Exposition de la France Européenne at the Grand Palais was transmitted in June 1941, the pernicious exhibition 'Le Juif et la France' at the Palais Berlitz appeared in the cinemas in October 1941. Cinematic preparations for Breker's exhibition were carefully planned. On 16 January 1941 'Sculptures allemandes présentées par le professeur Thorak' recalled the works of the type shown around Speer's pavilion and gave a foretaste of things to come. Most importantly, the notorious tour of Germany by French artists was given footage that was carefully spaced as a prelude to Breker's triumphal return to Paris. 'Berlin – Peintres et sculpteurs français visitent l'Allemagne' was shown on 26 November 1941.[14] The artists visited art schools and exhibition halls in Munich, Vienna, Dresden, Berlin and Dusseldorf and the stadium at Nuremberg.

Bernard Poissonier gave his account of the voyage in *Beaux Arts* for 28 November 1941. He listed Despiau, Derain, Dunoyer de Segonzac, Othon Friesz, Landowski, Bouchard, Lejeune, Vlaminck, Van Dongen, Belmondo, Leguelt, Oudot. It must be said that the former 'fauvists' of 1905 – Derain, Vlaminck, Friesz had all been interested in artistic developments in Munich before the First World War, and besides visits of the 'fauve' painters to Germany, there had been French connections with the Blaue Reiter movement. Although the official claim was that the tour was purely artistic, desperate letters to the 'Epuration' committee of the Front National des Arts mention promises to release French prisoners of war. Moreover it has been revealed that André Derain's canvas *Le Retour d'Ulysse* bears no fewer than six persuasive bullet holes. Derain agreed to participate. The sculptor Paul Landowski was

13. *Signal* for 10 August and 25 September 1940, no. 1, March 1941 (Kolbe); no. 2, April 1941, no. 2, July 1941 (Padua); no. 1, November 1941 (Milly Steiger); no. 1, January 1942 ('Art sovietique'); no. 1, June 1942 ('Aux Etats Unis'). See also explanatory publications such as F.A. Kauffmann, *La nouvelle peinture allemande*, Brussels, n.d.

14. See *La cinemathèque de l'ORTF Archives provenant des Actualités Françaises*, no. 1. *La Guerre, 39–45, août 1940– août 1944* Institut National d'Audiovisuel.

explicit: 'En réalité ce voyage n'était que le prélude à l'opération de propagande pour l'exposition du sculpteur A. Brecker [sic], du printemps 1942, avec toutes les suites que cette exposition comportait.'[15]

It was in late 1941 that the first programme for Pétain's artistic revolution was published in *Atalante, revue de l'art et de la culture*. René Borelly's opening article on 'L'Art au service de la révolution nationale' declared optimistically:

> La révolution, telle que l'a conçue le Maréchal, implique qu'architecture, sculpture, peinture ... au service de l'Etat ... doivent transformer la vie sociale et la vie privée ... Il faut que les artistes expriment désormais notre sens de la vie, non point celui que la révolution nationale condamne, mais qu'elle approuve, celui qui triomphe de toutes les résistances parce qu'il sera le seul possible, le seul admis. ... Des autostrades, des ouvrages d'art, des stades gigantesques, des monuments grandioses vont être prévus et réalisés.

This financial dependence on state patronage and complete censorship would thus be harnessed to a policy directly paralleling the totalitarian architectural excesses of Nazi Germany. Borelly continues: 'L'Art doit traduire pas ce que nous sommes, mais ce que nous voulons être, exprimer le courage, l'énergie, la santé morale et physique, et nous rendre le culte de la Beauté.'

Berthold Hinz's study, *Art in the Third Reich*, has demonstrated how this 'courage and energy' was manifestly linked to the ideology of war of aggression, how this 'beauty' was again a device for alienation, perpetuating not only the worst salon pieces but a return to allegory in which the female nude, bereft of all erotic or sensual suggestion became a mere vessel of abstract content such as Breker's *La Victoire*.[16] To revert to *Atalante*, 'L'Art avec un A majuscule' of

15. Letter from Paul Landowski to the Front National des Arts, 6 October 1944, André Fougeron archives.

16. René Borelly, 'L'Art au service de la Revolution Nationale', *Atalante, Revue d'Art et de la Culture*, no. 1, December 1941. This seems to be the only number in existence. *Les Cahiers Français*, no. 1 (n.d.: late 1941 or 1942), contains Henri d'Amfreville's rather unspecific 'Les Arts et la Revolution'. See in general the first two chapters of Laurence Bertrand-Dorléac, *Histoire de l'Art, Paris 1940–1944*, Paris, 1986 with bibliography, including Luce Namer, *La Politique artistique du Gouvernement de Vichy, hommes et structures*, memoire de D.E.A., supervisor Pascal Ory, Fondation Nationale des Sciences Politiques, Paris, 1983. Mary Macleod's *Le Corbusier, From Regional Syndicalism to Vichy*, PhD, Princeton University, UMI Research Press 1985 contains a sensitive chapter on Le Corbusier's frustrated attempts to work with the Vichy administration. See also Berthold Hinz,

the Révolution Nationale implied a policy of selection, directions from 'les grands maîtres des Beaux Arts, au-dessus des groupements', decentralisation, and, of course, 'chantiers innombrables'. In fact *Chantiers*, the organ of the Commissariat à la lutte contre le chômage had been published since June 1941 and held its first exhibitions of paintings that October. Its policy was to emphasise 'l'artisanat': '"La France restaura les antiques traditions artisanales qui ont jadis fait sa gloire" dit le Maréchal.' Endless articles on 'le maréchal-ferrant', 'le tailleur de pierre', 'bourrelliers et selliers' went hand in hand with illustrations from medieval manuscripts and woodcuts – expensive to reproduce at a time when *Les Lettres Françaises* or *Humanité Clandestine* were mere leaflets. The emphasis on the 'métier bien fait', regional identity, the history of guilds and apprentices, etc., provided the ideological basis behind a deliberate attempt to refeudalise relationships in a country governed by a war economy with a daily debt of 500 million francs paid to the occupying forces from November 1942 onwards. *Chantier's* artistic policy, while designed to appeal to 'les petits gens' who constituted the work force for France and the Service de Travail Obligatoire displayed the basest anti-intellectualism and, en passant, deliberately eradicated the history of avant-garde art: 'C'est méconnaitre le bon sens, et parfois même le goût du peuple que de lui infliger de tels enfantillages [Miro's *Le Faucheur* in the Spanish Pavilion at the 1937 World Fair]. . .C'est chercher á le dégoûter définitivement de l'art, et c'est finalement de l'insulter.'[17] Just as Robert Leforestier goes on to attack the Louvre in this article, so Jean de Beer in 'Notes sur l'Art Vivant', 1943, continues: 'Le monde croule sur les musées. . . il vaudrait mieux faire des chef d'oeuvres que les admirer. . Il y a des jours où l'esprit se surprend à souhaiter des desructons [sic] des musées, des hétacombes de trésors, des charniers des merveilles. . .'

The old battle-cry of the avant-garde to burn the Louvre, has become curiously the expression of a dilemma (faced later by the French Communist Party) – the use of art as a term, in arguments of

---

Art in the Third Reich 1979 (revision of the 1974 German version). While this has no separate section on sculpture it provides the context for the degenerate art debate in Germany, and comparative material on National Socialist aesthetics in mythological, genre and battle painting, photography and the mass media and architecture.
17. Robert Leforestier, editorial, *Chantiers* no. 14, 15 December 1941. Material from *Chantiers* and *Le Rouge et le Bleu, Revue de Pensée Socialiste*, directed by Charles Spinasse is discussed at length in Bertrand-Dorléac, 1986, chapters 1 and 2.

revolutionary appeal to a culturally deprived worker-base. The outrageous remarks at the end of his article show De Beer trapped into acknowledging an elitist dictatorship – precisely what happened in politics and the arts in Nazi Germany, and what Pétain and his artistic advisers envisaged for France: 'Il ne s'agit pas de supplier, il s'agit de vaincre. L'art est une dictature qui s'exerce par la force . . . le créateur doit forcer le public. Et le public, tant qu'il n'est pas vaincu a raison de ne pas se laisser faire.'[18] Under this 'dictature' came, for example the section 'L'Art et le Sport', at the Salon d'Automne from 1941 onwards, 'Dessins d'enfants en hommage à Maréchal Pétain' at the Musée Galliera in January 1942, the 'concours-exposition' 'Fêtes de Jeunesse' there in March 1942, the 'Chantiers' exhibitions and the macabre offerings at the Salon du Prisonnier where pitiable cocks fashioned out of old tin cans attested to 'la pensée du Maréchal': 'Le travail des Français est la ressource suprème de la Patrie: il doit être sacré.'[19] Above all there was the Salon de l'Imagerie, where the 'Commissariat aux Sports, le Service d'Artisanat, le Service esthétique du Maréchal dirigé par Robert Lallemant, le Service du Cinema et même les écoles d'Art de Provence' collaborated to produce an imagery that was 'triomphante, aimable, gaie, fraîche, poétique, ingénieuse avec goût'.[20]

In the decorative arts, the Lyon silk industry produced metres of silk graced with the double-headed axe. The Manufactures Nationales at Sèvres and Beauvais were instantly geared to creating Pétainist propaganda, despite the fact that Beauvais tapestries take four or five years to weave – Gobelins three. By September 1943 the Orangeries welcomed a five month exhibition of tapestries and cartoons in honour of Pétain. The sculptor Alfred Janniot, responsible for the ornate reliefs on the façade of the Palais de Chaillot, the present Musée de la Ville de Paris, exhibited a voluptuously neo-classical cartoon entitled *La Renaissance de la France sous les auspices du Chef de l'Etat*, 'A la gloire du Maréchal Pétain*, a finished tapestry by one 'Charlemagne', woven at Aubusson was displayed.[21]

18. Jean de Beer: 'Notes sur l'Art Vivant', *Chantiers* 25 February 1943.

19. 'Exposition d'Art et d'Artisanat des Invalides de Guerre, Prisonniers Rapatriés', *Beaux-Arts* 20 July 1942.

20. *Beaux-Arts* , no. 134, 2 June 1944.

21. See Bertrand-Dorléac, 1986 illustrations between pp. 120–1. For Sèvres and Beauvais see 'La réorientation de Sèvres', and 'Nouveaux cartons pour les Manufactures Nationales de Tapisserie' in *Revue des Beaux-arts de France*, p. 95 and no. VII p. 33–9, and *Cartons et tapisseries modernes des Manufactures Nationales*, Musée de l'Orangerie, September 1943–February 1944.

Of course a permanent campaign was being waged on the walls of Paris with the hundreds of posters of all colours and sizes advocating Pétain and the Vichy government. From large, highly-finished images of Pétain as patriarch used on the façades of public buildings down to the simplest Imagerie d'Epinal this excercise in hagiography (with much crusader imagery, e.g. Pétain on his white palfrey joining Marianne and Jeanne d'Arc) took its place next to official administrative notices put up by the occupying forces, threats, lists of hostages, discriminatory and insulting posters on Jewish-owned shop fronts and so forth. In turn this propaganda was countered by the far less sophisticated handwritten or roneo-typed messages of the Gaullists or résistants.[22]

Graffiti or rips and tears to the German or Vichy posters ex-pressed a resistance which almost immediately became an offence punishable by fines. (This situation provided the stimulus, I believe, for Jean Dubuffet's poignant graffiti series *Messages*.) Finally, 1,368,420 postcards of Pétain in five different versions were handled by the postal service.

The return to medieval values, a new simplicity, humility and 'subjectivity' must be emphasised. Indeed the use of crusader imagery 'en contrabande' was used by the 'jeunes peintres de tradition française' who emerged in Paris during the Occupation, under the increasingly resistant auspices of Jeune France, initially a Vichy-based organisation. Works such as Charles Lapicque's *Saint Jeanne d'Arc traversant la Loire* 1940, and Jean Bazaine's similar *La Messe de l'homme armé* of 1944 (which was inspired by the music of Josquin des Prez and referred both to the crusaders leaving for Jerusalem and to the Allied landings) were patriotic, Catholic, and politically 'open' to various readings if the forms concealed in a hermetic abstraction based on a red-blue post-cubist armature were discerned. Adapting to the régime without subscribing to its ideology or its prescribed aesthetics, this art was nonetheless dubbed 'judéo-marxiste' and 'zazou' by the conservative, collaborationist press.[23] Jean Lurçat was working in the Communist Resist-

22. See Pierre Bourguet and Charles Lacretelle, *Sur les murs de Paris, 1940–1944*, Paris, 1959.
23. See Sarah Wilson, 'Les Jeunes Peintres de Tradition Française', in *Paris-Paris*, pp. 106–115, including 'Mosdyc', 'L'Art zazou: Douze fumistes d'aujourd 'hui', *Pilori*, 4 March 1943. Bertrand-Dorléac, 1986, chapter 4 discusses these painters extensively. See also Véronique Chabrol: *Jeune France, une experience de recherche et de decentralisation culturelle, novembre 1940– mars 1942*, 3eme cycle doctorate, Paris III, 1974.

ance at Aubusson at the time. The return to medieval craft attitudes and the cult of 'la vieille France' is very evident in his well-known works of the 1940s and 1950s. He would become the central figure in the renaissance of French tapestry after the war.

In the field of sculpture, however, the most laborious and expensive of the fine arts, there was little 'contrabande' or 'resistance' as such. Jean Fautrier's *Grand Tête Tragique* of 1942 and *Otage* of 1943, Picasso's dadaist 'bricolage' of bicycle saddle and handlebars used on the front of the resistant surrealist brochure *La Conquête du monde par l'image*, 1942, and his bronze skull, the *Tête de mort* of 1943, come most pertinently to mind. In contrast, René Letourneur's *La Sculpture Française Contemporaine*, April 1944, and Jacques Baschet's luxurious volume *Sculpteurs de ce Temps'*, 1946, show the prevailing idea of 'contemporary' masters after Maillol: Poisson, Despiau, Janniot, Gimond, etc. Baschet hails the 'salutaire retour aux disciplines du passé'. Many of these sculptors had worked on official state commissions for the 1937 Paris World Fair. By 10 April 1942, *Beaux Arts* published the maquette for the 'autostrade de l'Ouest' which was to be decorated with an Apollo by Paul Belmondo and tasteful nymphs by Henri Lagriffoul, in accordance with the Vichy arts programme.

Belmondo's bust of M. Louis Hautecoeur, Secrétaire-Général des Beaux Arts, exhibited at the Salon d'Automne in 1943, is in precisely the same cold, academic style as Arno Breker's bust of Hitler, printed as the frontispiece to Albert Buesche's catalogue brochure of 1942. More than any other single event during the period 1940–4, the exhibition of sculptures by Arno Breker at the Orangerie in 1942 was the very symbol of Occupation – and collaboration.

Over three months after the artistic tour of Germany, more advance propaganda appeared on the newsreels: 'Avant le départ d'une tournée artistique française pour l'Allemagne' was transmitted on 6 February 1942. A film of 10 April showed 'Des artistes français visitent l'Allemagne'. Breker's exhibition at the Orangerie opened to the public on 15 May.

Breker had come over to Paris to oversee the casting of his bronzes in Rudier's studio at Malakoff. Grand receptions for 'une nombreuse societé composée de peintres, de sculpteurs, d'écrivains, de musiciens' were held at the Ritz courtesy of the military command and the German Embassy often in the presence of Abel Bonnard, Ministre de l'Education Nationale. His German counterpart, Otto Abetz, whose wife incidentally was French, was described by Breker as 'le champion de l'entartete le plus en vue'. Hitler himself commented on the ambassador's stance towards Breker a year later, saying that 'Abetz had obviously manipulated him, wanting to use him as a pawn for his soft-line politics.'[24]

Breker's mobility within the artistic circles of occupied Paris was the fact that he had been trained in Montparnasse as just another member of the cosmopolitan 'Ecole de Paris' from 1924–33. The 'vieux montparno' had always been friendliest with the realist sculptors François Pompon, Paul Belmondo, Robert Wlerick – and above all his 'maître', Charles Despiau. In the tradition of Rodin, both specialised in the ideal form: muscled, naked, bronze Apollos and idealised, rounded women. How did Breker's brand of neo-classicism become 'Fascist' in 1942? In the late 1930s Breker's sculptures for the Berlin Olympics had taken as their models perfect physical specimens: 'Quant à la "Victoire", nous jetâmes notre dévolu sur une lanceuse de javelot dont le corps merveilleusement entraîné supportait la comparaison avec les sculptures grecques des grandes époques.'[25] The later work seen at the Orangerie, however, had developed both a specifically homoerotic content and a degree of stylisation that approached caricature. It was in fact in front of Michelangelo's David that Breker had first received a mystic call to work on a public scale. His 'reconstruction' of Michelangelo's Rondanini Pietà in 1933 had apparently marked a turning point in his work. In the original, Mary, standing, supports the exhausted body of Christ: the sculpture is moving in its both unfinished and eroded appearance. Breker's *Kameraden* of 1940, however, shows one naked warrior holding another. The sweet expression of David becomes the stylised snarl of a baroque Bellerophon in the upper figure. The exaggerated virility in Breker's later work reflects a disturbing, homoerotic aspect of Fascist ideology – the cult of the hero, the love of regalia, the comradeship of the barracks, whose most harmless manifestation perhaps was exemplified by the often distinctly homosexual flavour of high society receptions in Paris, where Breker's great friend Jean Cocteau popped his champagne corks while Parisians out in the cold gazed at inedible 'étalages factices'.

Giganticism, as well as this overdeveloped virility impressed the

24. Breker, *Paris, Hitler et moi* , p. 171, an extract from the diary of General Engel, 28 February, 1943.

25. *Arno Breker, 60 ans de sculpture*, Paris, 1981, copiously illustrated, with a biography by Volker G. Probst and complete Breker bibliography, p. XV.

spectators at the Orangeries with the strength and self-confidence of the Reich.

As it appeared in the collaborationist press, the private view was yet another high society occasion. The article in *Signal* for 1 August 1942, insisting on the fact that the exhibition took place under the patronage of the French government, not the occupying authorities claimed: 'Tous les artistes français qui portent un nom, de Derain à Cocteau, de Sacha Guitry à Cécile Sorel, sont venus.' Photographed at the Orangerie were Sacha Guitry in conversation with Madame Breker, Breker with the couturier Lucien Lelong, Cocteau, Despiau, Dunoyer de Segonzac, and Maillol and his wife listening to Abel Bonnard. Bonnard held a reception for artists in the Ritz and Robert Brasillach gave a lecture on Breker at the Théâtre Hébertot. The exhibition was filmed for the newsreels on 22 May 1942.

Propaganda aside, however, Breker recalled in his memoirs an initially less than enthusiastic reception, mulish guards, whose hearts were won over at the sight of his sculptures (and with cigarettes) and some press fury likewise tamed at a conference when Breker's 'montparno' record and Benoist-Méchin's invitation to exhibit were again the trump cards. When asked if there was such a thing as a National Socialist aesthetic, Breker replied: 'Avait-il appris quelque part que l'on pouvait opérer un caecum d'une façon catholique ou luthérienne?'[26] This ingenuous answer was belied by the German catalogue by Albert Buesche which had a plaster bust of Hitler as its frontispiece and proclaimed in a discourse on 'das neue Deutschland': 'Das große politische und völkische Drama der Gegenwart hat in diesen Plastiken ihre bekennende und bezeugende Form gefunden.' According to *Signal* Breker's success was due to the fact that 'des cercles de plus en plus larges sont prêts à reconnaître la nouvelle union européenne qui se forme sous l'égide de l'ésprit de paix et non par le glaive . . .' The 2,000 paying entries per day would have been a record in normal circumstances. Ten thousand French catalogues were produced by the Librairie Flammarion, and one of the young directors of the firm René d'Uckermann ghosted a monograph signed by Charles Despiau. A luxury book of colour plates by Charlotte Rohrbach was also produced. Buesche's handsome book used photographs by Marc Vaux for Breker's most recent works.[27] A German brochure, a simple list of

26. Breker, *Paris, Hitler et moi*, p. 146.
27. Charles Despiau, *Arno Breker*, Paris, 1942 – one of the 241 works published between June 1940 and July 1944 brought up at the investigation of the Libraire

works, described Breker's exhibition in the following words: 'Arno Breker, Ausstellung durch die Wehrmacht, Paris, Orangerie, 2–31 August 1942, Die Deutsche Arbeitsfront NSG "Kraft durch Freude" veranstaltet im Auftrage des Oberkommandos der Wehrmacht', suggesting that the exhibition was prolonged for another month. Celebrations were renewed at the 'Concert de clôture – sous la présidence de M. Jacques Benoist-Méchin, Secrétaire d'état auprès du chef de Gouvernement' where the pianist Alfred Cortot and others played Mozart, Fauré, Schumann, Strauss and Wolf.

During 1943, Breker busied himself with busts of Maillol, sculpted in Banyuls, and of Maurice de Vlaminck sculpted in the painter's studio at La Tourillièrie – 'a family event'. This was the year of Vlaminck's attack on Picasso in the newspaper *Comoedia*, when his pathological jealousy of Picasso (dating from the period when fauvism was usurped by Cubism, c. 1907–9) surfaced in a disgraceful, dangerous and racist article accusing the artist of having dragged French art into 'negation, impotence and death'.[28] According to Breker, Picasso was known to the German authorities as an active Communist who was fraudulently passing money to Russia via Denmark and Spain. All credit must be given to Breker for his intervention with the authorities which purportedly saved Picasso's life – as to the Gestapo the name 'Picasso' meant no more than 'Dupont' or 'Schmidt' (*sic*). Again, Breker's direct intervention saved the life of Dina Vierny, Maillol's much-loved and indispensable model described by Breker as 'une Russe de confession judaïque'. No wonder Maillol, well into his eighties, had made the lengthy journey from Banyuls to Breker's opening in May 1942, declaring Breker a modern Michelangelo – despite the fact that Albert Speer recalled seeing him at official receptions looking 'openly intimidated'.[29]

Flammarion at the Cour de Justice on 11 December 1946. See Pascal Fouché, *L'Edition francaise sous l'Occupation, 1940–1944*, Bibliothèque de Littérature française contemporaine, Paris, 1987, vol. 2, p. 229. Fouché, vol. 1, p. 263, cites a print run of 10,000 for the catalogue – but does not distinguish it from the monograph and, like Bertrand-Dorléac, does not suspect Despiau's authorship. See also *Arno Breker*, Lichtbilder von Charlotte Rohrbach, mit einer Einführung von Dr. Werner Rittich, ed. by Ewald König, n.d. (1942), and 'Arno Breker: Der Sieger' a review of the exhibition in the July 1942 number of the luxury monthly review with full colour plates.

28. Vlaminck: 'Opinions libres sur la peinture', *Comoedia*, June 1942, reprinted in *Paris-Paris*, pp. 101–2.

29. Breker, *Paris, Hitler et moi*, pp. 227–35, and Albert Speer, *Journal de Spandau*, Paris 1975, p. 172.

After Breker's return to Germany his memory was kept very much alive in *Signal* articles showing him at work not only on heroes but the busts of SS officers such as one Sepp Dietrich and even Göring's infant daughter. More pertinently, Breker was seen in the *Signal* number of August 1943 using trained French artists and sculptors released from their forced labour programme in Germany, the Service de Travail Obligatoire, to come and work at the 'state studio' at Jackelsbruch. Hitler had built this studio for Breker outside Berlin, so that monumental projects as big as the 260 metre long bas-relief for the main north-south Berlin axis could be achieved, working from the first sketches onwards in the correct scale. A typical reportage about this village of French artists and craftsmen at Jackelsbruch both insists on the harmony of Franco-German collaboration, the 'normalising' of everyday life and underlines the stability and inevitability of the situation: 'Il y a là du travail pour de longues années.' The sentimental focus on the daily lives of 'Maître Louis Poulain, agrandisseur' and 'Marius Renucci, mouleur' with their assistants begins: 'Ils avaient travaillé à Paris pour tous les grands sculpteurs des dernières décades: pour Rodin, Maillol, Despiau, Lejeune, Bouchard.' The French team are photographed at work on gigantic reliefs, in discussion with Breker, at lunchtime '. . . on se croirait à Paris . . .' looking at the garden and 'Après le travail: M et Mme Renucci chez eux. Les maîtres sont logés avec leurs familles dans de beaux apartments amenagés dans l'immeuble même des immenses ateliers . . .' The fate of other artists was not so fortunate: Boris Taslitzky in Buchenwald, Zoran Music in Dachau made clandestine drawings of the emaciated bodies of their fellow prisoners. The survival of these documents was miraculous.[30]

'1943=1918', the graffiti which appeared on the posters in Paris, heralded more atrocious reprisal killings, austerity measures, new affirmations of force which had their repercussions in the art world. On 27 May 1943, in the gardens of the Jeu de Paume museum, canvases by Masson, Miro, Picabia, Klee, Ernst, Léger, Picasso and others were slashed and then destroyed in flames. Within the museum the inventory stipulation was long dishonoured. Rose

---

30. 'La Voie d'Arno Breker' and 'L'atelier d'Etat', *Signal*, no. 23–4, December 1942; 'Les Maitres de Jackelsbruch', *Signal*, no. 15, August 1943. See also Zoran Music, 'Souvenirs des Camps' *Music*, Milan, 1980, pp. 23–7 reproduced with illustrations in *Paris-Paris*, p. 124, and Boris Taslitsky, *Cent et onze dessins de Buchenwald*, 1989.

Valland, who developed at night the negatives the Germans had taken by day was chiefly responsible for the eventual recuperation of the stolen works. Before the end of the war she had the names of all the 'Einsatzstab Reichsleiter Rosenberg' depots such as Neuschwanstein and Hohenschwangau. The ERR report for the 14 July 1944 listed 21,903 works inventoried since the beginning of operations, including 10,890 paintings, watercolours and drawings, and 583 sculptures, medallions, etc. 'Les chefs d'oeuvres des collections privées françaises retrouvés en Allemagne' were finally exhibited at the Orangerie in June 1946.[31]

Curiously, the 'Service artistique du Maréchal' directed by one Robert Lallemant did not appear until April 1944, 'la plus extravagante circulaire qu'ait produit une époque fertile en sottises'.[32] Georges Hilaire who took over from Louis Hautecoeur as Directeur-Général des Beaux-Arts in the same month wrote a circular letter on 26 May to various artists asking for their cooperation in restructuring artistic life after the war. On 5 August 1944 his 'Pour une politique des Beaux Arts' was published in *Comoedia* – over five full pages of proposals including the establishment of an 'office du goût': 'Je n'en reviens nullement à une manière de dirigisme artistique . . . Mais faut-il laisser dégénerer (cette) liberté en licence? . . .' In this article he insisted upon the 'normal' functioning of artistic life during the Occupation, quoting ten million francs spent by the state on artists each year between 1942 and 1944, including 244 painting commissions, 260 sculpture commissions, 68 tapestry cartoons, twenty million francs spent on furniture and objects of decorative art and the 'entretien' de la 'bonne main' des artisans, fifteen million francs in 1944.

Sixteen days later the Comité National de la Résistance, having occupied the Ministère de l'Education Nationale, appointed Joseph Billiet as Directeur-Général des Beaux Arts. Billiet had been involved since the 1920s with committed art and as a Communist had been responsible for negotiating the first exhibitions of Soviet painting of the Five Year Plan period in Paris in 1933. De Gaulle deposed Billiet brusquely in October 1944 in what was evidently an

31. Rose Valland, 1965, Chapter XX, 'Liquidation des tableaux d'art dégenéré'. See also *Les chefs d'oeuvre des collections privées françaises retrouvées en Allemagne par la Commission de Récuperation artistique et les Services Alliés*, Paris, 1946.
32. René Jean, 'L'Art de Vichy', *Arts de France*, no. 5, April, May, 1946. Bertrand-Dorléac who reproduces extracts as her Document no. 1 (p. 287) does not refer to Lallemant any time before April 1944.

anti-Communist move. The résistant Front National des Arts (FNA) and its organ *L'Art Français* were communist in inspiration; Picasso, who joined the party amidst much publicity on 4 October (two days before the Salon de la Libération opened), became the President of the Front National des Arts, and was thus nominally responsible for its 'Epuration' policy, although the instigator and driving force was the secretary André Fougeron.

The process of denunciation and 'Epuration' was quite as fraught and often as vindictive as that waged by the Comité National des Ecrivains (CNE). Arrest warrants for certain curators were sent out by the Secrétaire-Général de l'Education Nationale as early as 22 August. In certain cases jobs as well as exhibiting rights were lost. While the French workers co-opted for the Service de Travail Obligatoire who contributed not a little to Breker's still-existing statuary seem to have escaped the FNA's wrath, the campaign focused initially on the Comité d'Honneur d'Arno Breker, more or less those artists who in November 1941 had made the trip to Germany. 'Ceux du voyage' were immediately forbidden to exhibit at the Salon d'Automne of October 1944, the Salon de la Libération. On its opening day, 5 October 1944, they were publicly denounced in the press. The official FNA letter of denunciation of 3 October was later modified in view of certain testimonies such as Paul Landowski's, quoted above. Breker's retrospective declaration: 'il ne s'agissait pourtant que d'un voyage d'information dont les fins étaient exclusiviement artistique' should be treated sardonically. Even more worrying is the fact that the unfortunate Paul Belmondo, Othon Friesz and Jean-Marc Campagne were condemned for belonging to an artistic group 'Collaboration' run by Georges Grappe, a self-declared admirer of Germany based in the Musée Rodin, who had added their names to a list of members without consultation. The Front National des Arts subsequently retracted this accusation.[33] Alas, at the Salon de la Libération, where the 'Hommage à Picasso', the first tribute of this nature to a non-French painter, showed seventy-four bleak and uncompromising

33. Georges Hilaire, letter of 26 May 1944, reproduced in a version of 7 July in Bertrand-Dorléac, 1986, pp. 294–5. According to André Fougeron, in an interview of 31 December 1987, the group 'Collaboration' was set up to recruit French intellectuals by the Germans. It probably had ceased to exist by the Liberation after the death of Georges Grappe at an unspecified date. Bertrand-Dorléac mentions *Une année du groupe 'Collaboration', Septembre 1940–Septembre 1941* in her bibliography.

paintings and five sculptures; a crowd of youths crying 'Décrochez! Remboursez! Expliquez!' attacked and pulled down many canvases. The painter André Lhote who had predicted the violence in *Les Lettres Françaises* of 23 September, implicated the 'cinquième colonne de l'armée des Beaux Arts', abetted, one presumes, by the xenophobes, anti-modernists and failed salon painters who believed in deeds, not words. The response of the Front National des Arts was printed in the *LLF* for 21 October. 'Cet acte sans précédent en France perpétue l'interdiction d'exposer faite à un artiste par les envahisseurs, renouvelle les procédés de brutalité physique et d'intimidation qui sont ceux hitlériens contre la culture . . .'.

The Liberation unfortunately did not make a clean break with 'ceux contre la culture', while second-rate 'realisms' were perpetuated in the salons of the later 1940s. Ironically by 1948 the Salon d'Automne became the forum for the Socialist Realism debate waged by the Parti Communiste Français.

Breker was tried at Donauwörth in 1948. It took the authorities three years to collect the evidence of his work during the Berlin period and with his usual disingenuousness he escaped condemnation. The epigraph to his memoirs quotes Hitler: 'En politique, tous les artistes sont des innocents comme Parsifal' – omitting: 'C'est pourquoi ils sont dangereux' . . .'.[34]

At the time of the *Paris-Paris* exhibition at the Pompidou Centre in 1981, a vigorous press campaign and petition by French artists (mostly those omitted or 'under-represented' in the exhibition) managed to censure Breker from the show. The petition declared: 'le gangstérisme artistique devient un fait culturel entrant dans le cadre de la nostalgie et du renouveau nazis. Un autre "Nach Paris" d'Arno Breker provoquera de nombreux remous'. Under pressure the curators agreed to ban the three small works that had been selected as a token presence.[35]

---

34. Breker, *Paris, Hitler et moi*, General Engels' diary, epigraph and p. 171.

35. See P.C. (Pierre Cabanne), 'Arno Breker Rehabilité?', *Le Matin*, 13 March 1981: 'Coincidence sans doute, M. Gerhard Heller, grand maître de la censure allemande en France pendant l'Occupation, figure cette semaine à Apostrophes, et M. Albert Speer, l'architect de Hitler, publie L'Immoralité du pouvoir.' The petition signed by several well known School of Paris artists including Miro appeared in *Le Matin* on 18 March, and was reprinted in 'Controverse autour d'Arno Breker', *Le Monde*, 21 March 1981. In particular see the dramatic double spread: 'Arno Breker, le sculpteur de Hitler renonce à Beaubourg', *Le Quotidien de Paris*, no. 411, 24 March 1981, pp. 20–1.

The 'Museum Arno Breker – Sammlung europäische Kunst' opened in 1981 in the Schloß Nörvenich. Breker's recent portrait busts of Peter and Irene Ludwig, patrons of the massive new Ludwig Museum in Cologne, have already caused controversy and should provoke some reaction among historians of contemporary Germany, especially within the disturbing context of present 're-visionist' interpretations of the Nazi period.[36]

36. See Bazon Brock: 'Rhinegold – But Make It Figurative!', *Artscribe International*, no. 60, November-December 1986 (the busts are illustrated), and correspondence from Martin Weyl, director of the Israel Museum, Jerusalem, no. 64, Summer 1987.

8

CINEMA OF PARADOX: FRENCH FILM-MAKING DURING THE OCCUPATION

Roy Armes

The Occupation years form a controversial period in the history of French cinema, as in the history of France itself. The film work of the period was immediately documented by Roger Régent in a book completed in 1946, published two years later, and entitled simply *Cinéma de France*.[1] Then came almost thirty years of virtual neglect through to the end of the 1970s. By contrast, the 1980s have brought a welter of studies from very varying perspectives: critical and autobiographical, sociological and semiological. One thing that is clear – and emphasised in the most recent French-language study, by François Garçon – is that French cinema of the Occupation years did not produce its Célines, its Rebatets or even its Jouhandeaus. There is no Germanophilia equivalent to that of Jacques Chardonne, Drieu la Rochelle or Abel Bonnard.[2] But beyond this simple truth the picture that emerges from the various investigations is best summarised in the title of a recent study by Evelyn Ehrlich, which I have borrowed for this chapter, *Cinema of Paradox*.[3]

Before we look further at this paradox, we need to define exactly what we mean by 'French film-making during the Occupation'. The programming in the film theatres of the period comprised three ingredients: a newsreel, a short film (usually a documentary) and a feature film. The newsreel output of the period seems to have been largely ignored by film scholars, though the central propaganda

1. Roger Régent, *Cinéma de France*, Paris, 1948.
2. François Garçon, *De Blum à Pétain*, Paris, 1984, p. 198.
3. Evelyn Ehrlich, *Cinema of Paradox*, New York, 1985.

function of the newsreels is nowhere disputed, and several writers have drawn attention to the fact that the lights had to be left on in the auditorium to deter hostile audience reaction.[4]

Short film and documentary output owes much to specific interventions by the Vichy government (which I shall consider in greater detail later). These interventions led to an expansion of production, distribution and exhibition for documentaries. In many ways this is potentially the most interesting sector from a sociological point of view. It is here that we find the rare examples of overt Nazi propagandising – in films such as the anti-Semitic tract *Les Corrupteurs*, and the attack on Freemasonry *Forces occultes*. It is also an area in which the involvement of film-makers with the Pétainist ideology might usefully be probed. The paradoxes are immediately clear if we consider the case of the distinguished documentarist Georges Rouquier, who began his professional career in the early 1940s. During the Occupation he made a number of short studies of rural craftsmen, such as *Le Tonnelier* (1942) and *Le Charron* (1943). These could only be funded and produced because of the changes in film legislation brought about by the Vichy government. The subjects chosen were in no way calculated to disturb the Vichy censors. On the contrary, they would seem – at the very least – to owe much to ideas 'in the air' under the Pétain régime. Can we then not simply regard them as examples of a Vichy propaganda cinema? The problem is that, working with the same rural subject matter and a virtually identical visual style during the immediate postwar months, Rouquier completed the feature-length *Farrebique*, which is universally regarded as the forerunner of an (implicitly anti-Fascist) neo-realism which failed to take root in France.

Despite the interest of newsreel and documentary production, most film historians have so far focused their attention principally on the feature films of the Occupation years. Immediately, however, the question arises as to which specific feature films are to be considered. Virtually all studies are based on the celebrated list of 220 titles published in the magazine *Le Film* on 22 July 1944, but this list is unsatisfactory in several ways. It has a number of minor inaccuracies chronicled by Evelyn Ehrlich: it contains 219 titles, not 220 as is always claimed; it includes four films begun before 1940

4. See, for example, Jacques Siclier, *La France de Pétain et son cinéma*, Paris, 1978, p. 36.

and one which was never completed, while omitting one or two films whose production and release fall within the 1940–4 period.[5] It fails to distinguish between the thirty-five or so films completed in unoccupied France and the far greater number made in occupied Paris when film making was centralised there in 1942. Finally, and more fundamentally, it dates films by the beginning of shooting and not, as is customary, by release date.

This latter point might seem a quibble, but it has had enormous effect on the work of film historians by creating a corpus of films to be studied which has very significant omissions and inclusions. On the one hand, the list diverts attention away from those films begun in 1939 which were only completed and released in the 1940s. A key example is Jean Grémillon's *Remorques*, begun in July 1939 but not completed and released until 1941. This film, which has Charles Spaak as one of its co-scriptwriters and Jacques Prévert as author of its dialogue, was originally conceived very much as a continuation of the French 1930s style associated with Marcel Carné, Jean Renoir and Julien Duvivier. Both its stars, Jean Gabin and Michèle Morgan, went into exile in the United States and both were to have all their films subsequently banned for alleged anti-Fascist propaganda. Yet *Remorques* could still be completed and released in 1941, and a case history of its production would surely offer precise detail of the effect of the new pressures on film-makers in the Occupation years.

On the other hand, the accepted list of 22 July 1944 contains over twenty films which were not released until after the Liberation. These include some of the most successful and famous works of the 1940s. But can we expect Carné's *Les Enfants du paradis*, for example, to reflect solely the mood and atmosphere of the Occupation, when we know from Carné's memoirs that the film's production was deliberately slowed down after the Normandy landings so that it could be distributed as one of the first major releases of the post-war period?.[6]

Approaches to 'Vichy Cinema'

The failure to decide upon a rigorous definition of 'film making

5. Ehrlich, *Cinema of Paradox*, p. 193.
6. Marcel Carné, *La Vie à belles dents*, Paris, 1975, p. 235.

during the Occupation' is one reason for the disagreement among French critics and historians as to whether the films of the early 1940s constitute an entity which can justly be called 'Vichy cinema'. If, for Francis Courtade, 'l'expression "cinéma de Vichy" recouvre une réalité tangible'.[7] Jacques Siclier gives the first chapter of his study of the cinema of the period a dissenting title: 'Psychologie du spectateur, ou le cinéma de Vichy n'existait pas'.[8] For Evelyn Ehrlich too the rubric 'Vichy cinema' is misleading, since 'there were many changes during the period and Vichy was not an important factor after 1941'.[9] Nevertheless, virtually all writers on the cinema of the period see the films produced from 1940 to 1944 as forming a single entity, whether they refer to it as Vichy cinema, 'le cinéma entre deux républiques' or, simply, 'cinéma de France'. None has undertaken what might seem to be the essential step in clarifying the situation, namely seeking possible distinctions between the films made in the unoccupied zone up to mid-1942 and the much larger number made in Paris when production resumed after June 1941. Ehrlich, it is true, does devote a separate chapter to the thirty-five or so films made in Vichy itself between August 1940 and May 1942, but her conclusion that 'few of these films were important either artistically or commercially'[10] ignores all the key issues of ideological identity.

Equally, while it might seem that the period from June 1940 to August 1944 – the Occupation years – constitutes a complex entity with a very specific set of economic, social and cultural determinants, most film historians seem to want to extend the Vichy label. Several see an essential continuity with the 1930s. Thus, for Jean-Pierre Jeancolas, 'le cinéma de Vichy commence avant Vichy'[11] and he entitles his book on the period 1929 to 1944 *Quinze ans d'années trente*. This point is developed by François Garçon: 'Au cinéma, l'imagerie de la propagande attribuée ultérieurement au seul système pétainiste précède et de loin, la proclamation de la Révolution nationale.'[12] Conversely, other film historians have been keen to stress a continuity after 1944. Raymond Borde, for example, in his preface to Courtade's history, writes:

7. Francis Courtade, *Les Malédictions du cinéma français*, Paris, 1978, p. 221.
8. Siclier, *La France de Pétain*, p. 15.
9. Ehrlich, *Cinema of Paradox*, p. xiii.
10. Ibid., p. 37.
11. Jean-Pierre Jeancolas, *15 ans d'années trente*, Paris, 1983, p. 319.
12. Garçon, *De Blum à Pétain*, p. 196.

Je me demande même s'il ne faudrait pas, jusqu'en 1950, parler d'un cinéma post-vichyssois. A la surprise amère des militants clandestins, le Parti Communiste avait, dès la libération de Paris, repris à son compte les trois mots d' ordre du Maréchal: travail, famille, patrie. Cette politique pesa sur toute la vie intellectuelle du pays et la fadeur des films d'après-guerre lui est largement imputable.[13]

This view is supported by Evelyn Ehrlich, who sees the Occupation period as a 'moment of rupture' in the development of French cinema from the 1930s to the 1940s,[14] but stresses a continuity after Vichy which extends as far as 1960: 'What is remarkable about the Occupation period ... is that it gave birth to a new aesthetic which would dominate the French cinema for fifteen years after the Occupation ended.'[15] But perhaps the most extreme example of this approach to continuity is that of Jean-Pierre Jeancolas, who sees an unbroken uniformity before and after Vichy: 'Le cinéma de l'Etat français est un fleuve large et lent qui prend sa source dans le cinéma de la Troisième République et se jette dans celui de la Quatrième. Il ne connaît ni rupture ni discontinuité.'[16]

While historians are in general agreement in congratulating the film industry for abstaining from overt propaganda collaboration with the Nazis, the relations between French film-makers and German producers were complex and constitute a subject to which we shall need to return. Even more difficult to assess is the complicity between the cinema and the prevailing Pétainist ideology. At one extreme, Jacques Siclier claims to show that the films as a whole can be exonerated: 'même le contenu des films fut peu marqué par l'idéologie pétainiste',[17] a statement at variance with the declarations of film makers such as Louis Daquin who attempted to portray Resistance values. Siclier even launches a remarkable attack on those who wish to judge the films by criteria other than those inherent in their making: 'Ceux qui aujourd'hui scrutent le soi-disant 'cinéma de Vichy' à partir d'*a priori* politiques ou intellectuels ne se rendent pas compte qu'ils travaillent sur des éléments historiques dont ils ont eu une connaissance complète bien après coup.'[18] In this, Siclier is following the line established as early as 1948 by

13. Raymond Borde, preface to Courtade, *Les Malédictions*, p. 17.
14. Ehrlich, *Cinema of Paradox*, p. 94.
15. Ibid., p. 92.
16. Jeancolas, *15 ans d'années trente*, p. 298.
17. Siclier, *La France de Pétain*, p. 23.
18. Ibid., p. 23.

Roger Régent, whose position is made very clear at the beginning of his book:

> Si au cours de ce livre il nous arrive de juger durement parfois l'activité cinématographique de nos producteurs, nous devons en revanche rendre hommage à leur attitude nationale dans une conjoncture précaire . . . S'il nous arrive, dans les années qui viennent, de revoir quelques-unes des oeuvres médiocres conçues entre 1940 et 1944 et d'être encore douloureusement frappés de leur faiblesse, soyons fiers de n'avoir nul autre sujet de honte. Il est honorable qu'en cette épreuve le cinéma français n'ait à rougir que d'une forme inoffensive de la sottise.[19]

Other critics, more hesitant and less closely involved, attempt to salvage only a part of the total output of the Occupation years. Here we may cite Paul Léglise's defence of 'quality' production: 'Effectivement, la production française de cette époque marque une très nette distance avec la philosophie maréchaliste, du moins en ce qui touche les oeuvres de qualité.'[20] Elizabeth Grottle Strebel attempts a similar recuperation of the popular film:

> The most popular films of the Occupation period offered an escape into a largely agrarian, mythical past. As such, it is evident that they reflected more of the traditionalist, conservative ethos of Vichy than the radical, right wing approach of Doriot, Déat, or the German Reich itself. But we have also seen that the films are more complicated than a pure expression of Vichy consciousness.[21]

But there are some who take a harsher view, among them Jean-Pierre Bertin-Maghit: 'L'étude des films français de 1940 à 1944 montre que le cinéma sous Vichy a joué un rôle dans le soutien au régime dans le sens où il a cautionné sa politique.'[22]

I would argue that to understand the many paradoxes of the period we must indeed see the four years of the Occupation within the wider historical framework of the 1930s and 1940s. But we must be very careful to distinguish the differing levels of continuity and discontinuity with the pre- and post-Vichy periods. A further

19. Régent, *Cinéma de France*, p. 9.
20. Paul Léglise, *Histoire de la politique du cinéma français*, volume two, Paris, 1977, pp. 18–19.
21. Elizabeth Grottle Strebel, 'French Cinema, 1940–44, and its Socio-Psychological Significance: A Preliminary Probe' *Historical Journal of Film, Radio and Television*, vol. 1, no. 1, March 1981, p. 41.
22. Jean-Pierre Bertin-Maghit, *Le Cinéma français sous Vichy*, Paris, 1980, p. 138.

distinction, which needs to be made as far as the question of collaboration is concerned, is between collaboration with the Germans and with the aims and ideals of Vichy. Since the question has been answered with so much self-serving patriotic rhetoric by the film-makers themselves and by many French critics, the best starting point is not the presumed (and subsequently stated) attitudes and intentions of the film-makers, but the contemporary demands of the authorities. If we begin with the latter and ask what was actually required of the film-makers by the Germans and by Vichy, then the answers take on a rather different colouring, though the complexity and paradoxical nature of the issues is hardly lessened.

The Film-Makers and the German Authorities

The first set of paradoxes concerns the attitudes of the Germans. The approach of Josef Goebbels, who had ultimate control over the French film industry through the Propaganda Abteilung, can be seen from his diaries, as in this entry dated 19 May 1942:

> It isn't our job to supply the Frenchmen with good pictures and it is especially not our task to give them movies that are beyond reproach in their nationalistic tendency.
> If the French people on the whole are satisfied with light, corny stuff, we ought to make it our business to produce such cheap trash. It would be a case of lunacy for us to promote competition against ourselves. We must proceed in our movie policies as the Americans do in their policies toward the North and South American continents. We must become the dominating movie power on the European continent. In so far as pictures are produced in other countries they must be only of a local or limited character. It must be our aim to prevent so far as possible the founding of any new national film industry, and if necessary to hire for Berlin, Vienna or Munich such stars and technicians as might be in a position to help in this.[23]

At first German policy seemed to follow the line which Goebbels here advocates. The French film industry was closed down and many of the film theatres went out of business. British and American films were banned, and the first distributor allowed to operate again was the German-owned Alliance Cinématographique Euro-

23. Josef Goebbels, *Diaries 1942–1943*, New York, 1948, p. 221; quoted in Ehrlich, *Cinema of Paradox*, pp. 142–143.

péenne (ACE), which in the first summer of the Occupation achieved great success with a number of major German productions, including the infamous anti-Semitic *Jud Süß*. Only when this initial boom was over and it was clear that new French films would be needed to sustain audience levels, was production activity again permitted in Paris in the spring of 1941. But by this time a German-owned production company, Continental Film, was securely in place, and this company was able to play as dominating a role in the production sphere as ACE in distribution (eventually it was to produce some 30 of the 200 or so films of the Occupation years, far more than any other company).

The German control over censorship and this dominance in the spheres of distribution and production were actually exercised in a way very different from that envisaged by Goebbels. To begin with, censorship in occupied France was, if anything, less rigorous than in unoccupied Vichy and in some ways less ideologically motivated than in France as a whole during the phoney war under the Third Republic. Though steps were taken to exclude the work of 'non-Aryan' film-makers and actors from the screen, political censorship as such was not initially imposed. Though the French authorities in October 1939 had banned such films as *Quai des brumes*, *Hôtel du nord* and *La Bête humaine* as 'depressing, morbid, immoral or distressing to children',[24] the German authorities by contrast allowed the continuing distribution of films displaying Popular Front aspirations, such as *La Belle équipe* and *Le Crime de Monsieur Lange*. Moreover, far from down-grading French film output, the German authorities allowed it to grow and to surpass that of Germany itself. Thus, while there were 59 French feature films produced in 1941 as against 71 German productions, in 1942 the situation was reversed, with 77 features made in France and only 64 in Germany. Within this upsurge of French production (financially viable because film attendance tripled in relation to 1938 and French films captured around 80 per cent of this market), Continental Film played a key role with its 30 films. These were not the cheap trash advocated by Goebbels, but works distinguished from other French-produced films only by their greater production values. Indeed Evelyn Ehrlich even goes so far as to describe Continental as 'the MGM of French studios during the Occupation'.[25]

24. Ehrlich, *Cinema of Paradox*, pp. 2–3.
25. Ibid., p. 50.

From this it is clear that in practice the German imperative was commercial not ideological: to foster – or at least do nothing to hinder – the creation of a prosperous French film industry, reflecting French values, but within which German commercial interests would have a considerable share. To understand this German attitude we need to take into account the constant interaction during the 1930s when the French need for capital investment met up with the German search to earn foreign currency. It was this which led to the German producers' wartime conception of cinema in purely entertainment terms. The approach adopted in the 1930s had allowed even committed anti-Fascists like Jean Grémillon and his assistant Louis Daquin to work without qualms in the Berlin studios. Equally it had permitted René Clair and Jacques Feyder to create some of their most characteristic works thanks to German capital investment. Many leading figures in the French film industry saw nothing questionable about involvement with German finance – so long as it was profitable – and the advent of Hitler in 1933 did nothing to alter this. It was, moreover, by no means a marginal involvement. It has been estimated that in 1934 no less than 20 per cent of ostensibly 'French' production was the work of émigré teams with no roots in France (many of them refugees from Nazi Germany, intent on funding their passage to the United States) and a further 20 per cent was produced outside the French frontiers, largely in the German studios.[26]

The underlying reasons for this Franco-German involvement lie in the battle for control of world markets launched by the US companies RCA and Western Electric with the coming of sound. While they were able to colonise the British film industry effortlessly at the end of the 1920s, the US firms met a formidable rival in continental Europe: the Tobis company, which had taken over the valuable Tri-Ergon sound film patents previously owned by UFA and which was strengthened in 1929 by a merger with the Klangfilm company, a subsidiary of the German electrical giants, AEG and Siemens.[27] In true oligopolistic manner the US and German firms met together in Paris on a couple of occasions in an attempt to divide up the market profitably between them (with RCA even buying a sizeable stake in its rival, AEG). But meanwhile Tobis-Klangfilm had moved into France, setting up its own sound studio

26. Courtade, *Les Malédictions*, p. 106.
27. Douglas Gomery, 'Economic Struggle and Hollywood Imperialism: Europe Converts to Sound', *Yale French Studies*, no. 60, 1980, pp. 80–93.

at Epinay and equipping the French studios of Pathé and Eclair. At Epinay the emphasis was on prestige production, and it was here that René Clair in 1930–2 made the four sound films, beginning with *Sous les toits de Paris*, which put him in the forefront of European production.

Although the major films of the 1930s have a seemingly authentic French tone and atmosphere, much of the production finance came from Germany. Many of the major French stars of the period worked at some time or other in Berlin on French versions of German productions. Most of the actors and actresses who took part in the celebrated (or infamous) 1942 goodwill visit to Berlin were therefore simply renewing old acquaintances. A number of the directors who came to the fore during the Occupation years – Jean Grémillon and Henri Decoin, Henri-Georges Clouzot and Louis Daquin – had learned their craft in the Berlin studios. And although Jacques Feyder was later to refuse to work in Paris under German rule, his involvement with German finance was considerable in the 1930s. *La Kermesse héroïque* was directed in two separate language versions – French and German – by Feyder at the Tobis studio at Epinay, where Clair had earlier worked, and the two versions of *Les Gens du voyage* were in fact shot in Munich.

From 1934, a branch of UFA, the Alliance Cinématographique Européenne, specialised in producing French films under the supervision of Raoul Ploquin, later a key figure in the organisation of French production during the Occupation. From 1936 to 1939 in Berlin, UFA even produced a number of films exclusively in French, among them Grémillon's *Gueule d'amour* (1937) and Marcel L'Herbier's *Adrienne Lecouvreur* (1938). Even as quintessentially French a film as Marcel Carné's *Quai des brumes* started off as a UFA project. And it is indicative of the commercial, rather than ideological, imperatives that motivated the German film industry in its relations with France that when the project was discarded, the rights were sold to a German Jewish émigré producer, Gregor Rabinovitch.

Bearing in mind the fact that German demands during the occupation years were in essence no greater than those on the numerous film-makers – from Clair and Feyder to Grémillon and L'Herbier – who had worked for German-owned companies in the 1930s, how can we evaluate the issue of collaboration? French critics concerned to give their national cinema a clean bill of health for the years 1940–4 have stressed that no French film-maker worked in the

German studios, no adaptation of any work of German literature was undertaken, that publicity visits to Berlin were rare and films with explicit pro-German sympathies non-existent. All this is true, but it has to be said also that there is no evidence of pressure on film-makers to work in Berlin or to adapt German source material, and little compulsion to undertake propaganda visits or to display pro-German views in their films.

If we ask why it was that the French did not collaborate at this level, then one answer must be that they were never required to do so by the Germans. But from the outside it is possible to pose the question of collaboration rather differently. If to fulfil the aims set by the Germans, to enrich German production and distribution companies and to allow films to be shown in cinemas confiscated from their Jewish owners is to collaborate, then French film-makers must take their share of guilt. Evelyn Ehrlich puts this decidedly non-French view very forcefully: 'What the French cinema accomplished during the Occupation was not the upholding of French culture, but the glorification of the new Europe. Had Germany won the war, these film-makers' defence of the national film industry would have been turned against them, used to drive a wedge into foreign markets in order to sell the Germans' own products.'[28]

The Film-Makers and Vichy Ideology

The situation is if anything even more paradoxical when we consider the relationship between the film-makers and the state during the late 1930s and the Occupation years. In view of the international reputation acquired by French cinema in the late 1930s, it is perhaps surprising to discover that the industry was totally disorganised, with hundreds of tiny underfinanced production companies and dozens of distributors, each handling no more than a handful of films.[29] The small number of striking instances of left-wing political commitment to which every film historian refers are in fact virtually the only instances of such attitudes in a national output which is fundamentally reactionary and xenophobic. The connections between the cinema and the Popular Front government also turn out to be a myth. The politicians gave little or no support to film-makers

28. Ehrlich, *Cinema of Paradox*, pp. 156–157.
29. For a fuller account of the film-making of the period, see Roy Armes, *French Cinema*, London, 1985, pp. 86–108.

who advocated Popular Front policies and seem to have been unaware of, or indifferent to, the propaganda potential of cinema. The left-wing coalition raised taxes on cinema, yet offered no aid to quality production or support for moves aimed at a degree of nationalisation for the industry. Instead, the Popular Front government gave assistance to the ruined Gaumont company (controlled by an opposition parliamentarian, Louis Aubert), confirmed the ban of Jean Vigo's *Zéro de conduite*, and even introduced for the first time into French film production the idea of pre-censorship (in a circular distributed by Edmond Sée in 1937).

Against this chronicle of neglect the actions of the Vichy government can only be seen as highly positive. Anxious to protect the film industry from total domination by the Germans, the Vichy government involved itself in the affairs of the industry to a quite unprecedented degree. Some of the new regulations – such as those requiring professional accreditation for all engaged in the film industry – were clearly not simply designed to assist production, since they formed part of the legislation undertaken by the Vichy government to eliminate Jews from all walks of life. But by setting up the Comité d'Organisation de l'Industrie Cinématographique (COIC) in November 1940 – initially under Guy de Carmoy and using his structure devised for (and rejected by) the Popular Front government of the mid-1930s – it allowed the re-establishment of a commercially healthy French film industry and, incidentally, concentrated power (and hence profit) in the hands of a small number of individuals and groups.

Many of the other measures which were to shape French cinema after the Liberation also have their origins during the Occupation years. It was the Vichy government which established censorship to protect viewers under the age of sixteen and eliminated the double bill system of exhibition, thereby making feature film production more profitable, while at the same time fostering short and documentary production. To encourage quality production it established a Grand Prix du Film d'Art Français, and though the notorious Lucien Rebatet was one of the judges, the choice of films during the Vichy years was impeccable: *Les Visiteurs du soir* in 1942 and *Les Anges du péché* in 1943. The Vichy government also founded the national film school, the Institut des Hautes Etudes Cinématographiques (IDHEC), and granted aid to Henri Langlois's film archive, the Cinémathèque Française.

In view of these very positive measures and the French cinema's strong currents of right-wing nationalism in the 1930s, one might expect the film industry to collaborate fully in the propagation of the Vichy ideology. In fact the actual situation is somewhat different. François Garçon has demonstrated through numerous detailed examples that, as far as the classic themes of work, fatherland and family are concerned, there is indeed a continuity with the 1930s: 'Le discours du Maréchal, pour une grande partie de ses thèmes tout au moins, est déjà cinématographiqement inventé avant 1940. Qui plus est, les cinéastes de l'Occupation ne font qu'accentuer des tendances déjà inscrites dans ce mode d'expression.'[30] But if the positive side of the Pétainist ideology thus finds its reflection on the screen, the negative anti-Semitism and xenophobia of the period is entirely missing. To quote François Garçon once more:

> L'observateur attentif note l'infidélité des cinéastes français vis-à-vis des prescriptions antimaçonnes, antisémites, anglophobes et anti-communistes professées en haut lieu et qui susciteront les abjections que l'on sait. Il remarque aussi l'infidélité des mêmes créateurs à l'égard de ces millions de Français que le doute civique n'assaille guère à l'écoute des péroraisons vichystes et parisiennes aux désastreuses conséquences. Refusant d'être solidaire de la parole étatique et du joug commun, le cinéma de fiction, rompant avec ses habitudes antérieures, n'a rien dit de l'Angleterre ni des Juifs; or il se complaisait anecdotiquement mais perfidement aussi dans ces thèmes auparavant, avant que l'histoire ne les légitime et ne les propulse comme sujets de propagande.[31]

This refusal of immediacy is one of the more striking aspects of a style of film-making characterised by a retreat into the past, into allegory or into a kind of timeless version of the present which Jean-Pierre Jeancolas has aptly termed 'le contemporain vague'.[32] In the characteristic films of the Occupation period, there is to be found, too, a certain coldness, a concern with formal perfection and a resultant gap between the film-maker and his work. The lack of detail linking the films either to contemporary actuality or directly to the film-maker's personality leads to the creation of narratives which are extremely ambiguous in meaning, unless we take the overall context into account. For example, Jean Delannoy's historical study, *Pontcarral* (1942), is frequently seen by French critics

30. Garçon, *De Blum à Pétain*, p. 196.
31. Ibid., p. 197.
32. Jeancolas, *15 ans d'années trente*, p. 321.

as an anti-German work – Francis Courtade describes it as the only 'authentic Resistance film' of the Vichy period.[33] Yet Delannoy's version of Jean Cocteau's mythically inspired *L'Eternel retour*, made just a year later, can equally easily be seen as the work of an Aryan apologist – when it was shown in London in 1945 Richard Winnington, for example, called it 'a pleasure for the Nazis'.[34] But if we consider the director's whole career as a skilled but routine director without a deeply felt range of subject matter, this shift becomes more easily understood, and the superficiality of both ideological approaches becomes apparent.

The difficulty of evaluating the ideological stance of the films of the period is increased by the inability of contemporary Resistance critics to distance themselves from the all-persuasive Pétainist ideology. While we can hardly expect anti-Fascist critics to refute the slogan 'Work, Fatherland and Family' by urging the people to be idle, unpatriotic and adulterous, there is a striking and worrying convergence of opinion between the clandestine Resistance paper *L'Ecran Français* and the apologists of Vichy. Thus, Jean Grémillon's *Le Ciel est à vous*, which was given a special première attended by the Maréchal himself, was praised in *L'Ecran Français* on the grounds that it offered characters who were full of French vigour, authentic courage, moral health and was a film in which was found again that national truth which cannot and will not die.[35] Conversely, Henri-Georges Clouzot's *Le Corbeau* was attacked as anti-French, not only by Vichy officials and the Catholic church, but also by *L'Ecran Français* which criticized Clouzot's 'servile imagination', claiming that the characters were made up as if under Nazi orders.[36] Thus a film which caused Continental to terminate its contract with the director and was rejected by UFA for distribution in Germany because it was too morbid,[37] also resulted in Clouzot being banned from his profession in France for two years after the Liberation. Both Vichy and the Resistance wanted, it would seem, to claim a monopoly of virtue. Neither was prepared to admit the existence of a France in which people sent anonymous letters to harm their neighbours, despite the fact that the film was based on a real incident in Tulle in the 1920s and anonymous

33. Courtade, *Les Malédictions*, p. 209.
34. Richard Winnington, *Drawn and Quartered*, London, n.d., p. 46.
35. Ehrlich, *Cinema of Paradox*, p. 122.
36. Ibid., p. 122.
37. Ibid., p. 183.

denunciatory letters were known to be a valuable aid to the German authorities in their battle with their opponents in occupied France.

Conclusions

Though the recent work of such historians as François Garçon and Evelyn Ehrlich can help us resolve many of the ambiguities of film-making in France during the Occupation, we are still left with the problem of how to explain that the fiction film could remain so free from the propaganda prevalent in the other mass media. Film-makers – like everyone else – were undoubtedly influenced by the dominant mood and by attitudes in occupied Paris. Louis Daquin, for example, who joined the Communist Party in 1941 and was active in the Resistance, tried to express his own views and values in a 1944 film *Premier de cordée*, a mountaineering film that took him out of the studios and away from Paris. The result did not live up to his expectations, however, as he himself has explained: 'Apart from the storm scene, the whole film was made in the mountains in unbelievably difficult conditions. But looking back on it, I realise how much the dominant ideology can influence you . . . the idea of going back to the land, returning to nature. You can feel the influence of a Pétainist ideology in that film.'[38] How was it then that the films as a whole could be so free of a collaborationist taint?

Part of the answer lies in the historical identity of the film medium, which was born into a world of late-nineteenth-century laissez-faire capitalism and has never had the same close links with the state as those which have universally characterised the twentieth century broadcast media of radio and television. Moreover the fiction films of the Occupation period were seen by all – the German occupiers, the Vichy government and the film-makers themselves – purely as entertainment. The popular entertainment film, in Hollywood as elsewhere, has always avoided too close an involvement in national politics or issues of the moment. It is par excellence a form designed for a universal audience, as Victor Perkins makes clear. Popular movies, he notes, are:

> most readily linked by what they are *not*. None of them makes extensive demands on the spectator's intellect. The dialogue and action of each of

38. Louis Daquin, Interview, *Film Dope*, no. 9, April 1976, p. 5.

them is fully understandable without specialized knowledge of political mechanisms, sociological jargon, philosophical concepts or historical facts . . . Where a particular knowledge is required – then it is part of the common knowledge of common man.[39]

Too close an involvement with contemporary political attitudes would also be discouraged by two aspects of film production. Firstly, film-making is a collective operation, involving dozens of people with widely differing views and opinions, and, secondly, a single film may well take a year or more to move from conception to first-run release. Moreover, film-making in the 1940s was still basically a studio-based art, and since the world of ostensible reality was all constructed, not recorded directly, there was no need to include reference to displeasing or upsetting aspects of contemporary life outside the studio. In addition, many of the producers and directors involved in film-making during the Occupation had previously worked on French-language films that were in fact shot in Germany and so would be used to creating a largely mythical portrait of France and French reality. Some of the silences which François Garçon details can be put down to prudence, or cowardice, on the part of the film-makers concerned, but the lack of opportunistic references pleasing to German and Vichy authorities is still puzzling. There still remains a discrepancy which has yet to be fully accounted for, an apparent autonomy from the mood of the times which cannot be fully explained. The Cinema of Paradox represented by French film-making during the Occupation has not yet given up all its secrets.

39. V.F. Perkins, *Film as Film*, Harmondsworth, 1972, p. 162.

9

THE THEATRE: COMPROMISE OR COLLABORATION?

Patrick Marsh

During the German Occupation the theatres enjoyed 'une espèce d'âge d'or'[1] – attendance had never been so great; shortly after the war ended Armand Salcrou wrote: 'C'est un fait que pendant l'occupation nazie, les théâtres furent pleins.'[2] Even at a time of national humiliation and defeat the French still needed amusement, distraction and stimulation; many traditional leisure-time activities were necessarily curtailed by the war and occupation: dinner parties, excursions in the car, weekends at the sea were things of the past. Henri Amouroux in *La vie des français sous l'occupation* comments on the plight of the French:

> Pour oublier le trop triste aujourd'hui, pour oublier, pendant quelques heures l'occupation, le marché noir, les incertitudes de la guerre, les Français qui n'ont plus d'essence pour leurs voitures et réservent les pneus de vélos aux raids de ravitaillement, les Français disposent du théâtre, des cinémas, des champs de course, des bibliothèques, des stades.[3]

But not all the amusements that Amouroux lists here were readily available; although racecourses still functioned it was on an uncertain and somewhat ad hoc basis; books were in short supply as the lack of paper made it more and more difficult for the publishers to satisfy the public's demands, and although the cinema produced

---

1. Alain Laubreaux, *Je suis partout*, 14 January 1944.
2. Armand Salacrou, 'Un auteur français et son public', *La Revue Internationale de Théâtre*, vol. 1, 1947, pp. 48–50.
3. Henri Amouroux, *La vie des Français sous l'occupation*, Paris, 1961, p. 40.

some masterpieces during the war, foreign films and many French films were banned – a film based on *L'Arlésienne*, for example, was refused a visa on the grounds that no Frenchman, in the Germans' view, was capable of dying for love; a large number of the films shown were of German inspiration or origin and were unacceptable to most Frenchmen. Simone de Beauvoir remarked bitterly: 'Ce dont j'ai bien envie, c'est de cinéma, mais on ne joue que des films impossibles.'[4]

The theatre had a strong appeal for many reasons: the most important was, perhaps, that on entering the theatre, one was among Frenchmen taking part in an essentially French experience which the horrors of war could not, temporarily at least, affect. The theatre was a means of escape from harsh reality, an escape into antiquity, heroic legend, an unreal world where France and Frenchmen could be great once again. In an article published in 1943, Giorgio de Chirico described the theatre as 'un monde où il y a tout, sauf la réalité';[5] the theatre, he wrote, showed a man things which 'le passionnent, qui l'absorbent complètement, lui permettant de s'évader de sa propre vie, tout au moins pendant quelques instants'.

One of the first aims of the Germans after the beginning of the Occupation was to restore as far as possible an air of normality to the capital; high on the list of priorities was the reopening of the theatres and the re-establishment of programmes in as many places of public entertainment as possible. The first of these to open (and this is historical fact rather than historical legend) was the Folies-Bergère at the beginning of July 1940, barely two weeks after the fall of Paris. That the Germans preferred unintellectual entertainment is made clear by the fact that it was mostly the music-halls which reopened quickly – on 4 July the ABC opened, as did the Pigalle the following day.

On 6 July the first theatre opened – ironically enough it was the George VI which was hastily renamed and became the Edouard VII . . . much to the fury of the Fascist press. On 15 and 16 July there were performances of the Ballets Russes (as yet not renamed) at the Salle Pleyel and on 2 August the first of the state theatres reopened – this was the Opéra-Comique which staged *Carmen* while the Opéra staged the *Damnation de Faust* on the 24th. The Comédie-Française opened with *Un Caprice* and *Le Misanthrope* on 8 August and the

---

4. Simone de Beauvoir, *La Force de l'Age*, Paris, 1960, p. 470.
5. Article in *Panorama*, 9 December 1943.

Odéon reopened a week later.

By the middle of September theatrical activity was returning to normal – Jean Marais was rehearsing *Les Parents Terribles* at the Théâtre de la Michodière and Jouvet was preparing a production of *L'Ecole des Femmes* at the Athénée. Gaston Baty returned to Paris on 12 September while, the next day, Serge Lifar put on an evening of ballets at the Opéra which included *L'Après-Midi d'un Faune*. Later in the month Edith Piaf returned to the capital after a tour in the provinces and, at the end of September, at the Renaissance cabaret, Georgius was already singing songs which had such risqué titles as *Méfie-toi de la Patrouille* and *Elle a un Stock*. By the beginning of December the Cirque du Médrano was functioning again and André Castelot, drama critic of *La Gerbe*, had warm praise for the evening's entertainment.

At the end of 1940 thirty-four theatres, fourteen music-halls, two circuses (the Cirque d'Hiver and the Cirque Médrano), six cabarets and about thirty cinemas were open. If the theatres were eager to reopen, the audiences were equally eager to return despite the difficulties of transport and the risk of spending the night in a police station for being out on the streets after curfew; one of the main problems to be faced was that of the métro which stopped running at eleven o'clock – this obliged theatres to finish their performances in time for the audiences to get home: many theatres opened at eight-thirty to close at ten forty-five, which gave theatre-goers little enough time, considering how unreliable the métro could be.

But it was not just the problem of getting home in the dark and on time that confronted the would-be theatre-goer; the biggest hazard of all was that of the air-raids. When the war started, Parisians soon became accustomed to the sound of the sirens, and by the time the Armistice had been signed audiences had become completely used to the procedure required: when the alert sounded the safety curtain was lowered and the usherettes showed the audiences to the shelters used by the theatre which were often quite comfortably furnished.

If theatres were to open and to function in a reasonably normal manner, then their owners and directors were obliged to collaborate with the German authorities. The administration of theatres was the responsibility of the Propagandastaffel which appointed Robert Trébor as link-man between the theatres and the occupying authorities; Trebor held this position until January 1941 when he was replaced by the triumvirate of Charles Dullin, Gaston Baty and

Pierre Renoir. On the Germans' side a Lieutenant Baumann was the man delegated by the Propagandastaffel to be responsible for the theatre. Although in theory Vichy had jurisdiction over the state theatres, in reality it was always the Germans who had the final word in any controversy – as, for instance, when Copeau was replaced as Administrateur-Général of the Comédie-Française despite the opposition of Pétain's government. Private theatres came directly under German jurisdiction and usually co-operated fully with the occupying authorities in order to open, or to remain open.

The organisation of the theatre in the first period of the occupation was not particularly satisfactory, and was often criticised in the press, but a change was heralded at a press conference given in early 1941 by Lieutenant Baumann and André Barsacq, who at that time was director of the Théâtre des Quatre Saisons at the Atelier and who was shortly to succeed Dullin as director of the whole theatre – Dullin himself was to move to the Théâtre Sarah Bernhardt which was soon to be renamed the Théâtre de la Cité for racial reasons. At the press conference Baumann's remarks made it clear that the Germans were going to take over, as far as possible, not only the French material wealth but their spiritual wealth as well; he spoke of the theatre as a 'moyen supérieur de compréhension entre les peuples'[6] and mentioned the 'nombreuses éliminations de personnages tarés du théâtre qui ont eu lieu sous l'impulsion des autorités occupantes' – Sarah Bernhardt was not the only Jew to be forced off the stage. He finished his speech by emphasising 'l'intérêt et la sympathie avec lesquels les autorités allemandes suivent l'activité théâtrale à Paris' – an interest which, obviously, cut both ways. Following Baumann, Barsacq laid the blame for the poor state of the theatre at the door of the government which, during the closing years of the Third Republic, had never ceased to regard the theatre as 'une industrie de luxe, la moins nécessaire des industries de luxe, et de lui dénier toute importance sociale'. Barsacq finished his address by hoping that 'les répercussions de la révolution nationale parviennent jusqu' au théâtre, et notamment que des mesures rigoureuses soient prises pour créer une fédération corporative du spectacle qui règle, par exemple, les conditions dans lesquelles peut avoir lieu la nomination d'un directeur de théâtre'.

How disorganised the situation of the theatrical world was in the period leading up to the invasion of France is a matter of opinion;

---

6. *Les Nouveaux Temps*, 9 January 1941.

the pro-German Fascist press, and particularly papers such as *La Gerbe*, took a delight in castigating the mores of the decadent French of the inter-war years, and also of ridiculing any attempts Vichy might have made to put things on a better footing. No doubt there was bad management, inefficient control, corruption, but the Comité d'Organisation des Entreprises de Spectacle (COES) which was set up on 7 July 1941 – a brain-child of the champions of the 'Révolution Nationale' – although helping to rectify certain abuses, no doubt made the running of a theatre infinitely more complicated because of the mass of laws, controls and restrictions that it imposed on the theatrical world. A theatre director had no option but to co-operate with the COES if he wished to do business.

Along with the COES (under the direction of René Rocher, who was also the director of the Odéon during the war) were the Comités d'Organisation des Auteurs, Compositeurs et Editeurs de Musique under Henri Rabaud, the Comité d'Organisation pro-fessionelle des Industries et Commerces de la Musique under René Dommange, the Comité d'Organisation professionelle de la mu-sique under Alfred Cortot, and a Comité d'Organisation de l'In-dustrie Cinématographique under the joint direction of Marcel Achard, André Debrie and Roger Richebé.

Rocher, comparing this new system of organisation with the state of affairs which existed before the war, explained that not merely was membership of a union or professional body voluntary then, but that these unions and professional bodies had no authority over their members: 'La situation créée par ce manque de construc-tion était voisine du désordre, voire de l'anarchie'. All this was to change – the new slogan of a renascent theatre was to be:

> Responsabilité, Autorité, Discipline qui s'avèrent indispensables au maintien de la conservation de l'économie.
> Le recensement de la profession, s'établissant sur des bases stables et dans des cadres solides en est le préliminaire obligatoire. La profession organisée sera la pierre de base de l'ordre nouveau.[7]

This so-called independent organisation had absolute control over all theatrical activity in Paris and the provinces from the middle of 1941 until the end of the occupation. Commenting on the activities of the COES, *La Scène Française* (a clandestine journal

7. René Rocher, in *L'Officiel du Spectacle*, II, 7 October 1942.

devoted to the theatre, only one number of which appeared during the Occupation) attacked Rocher in the following terms:

> Investi d'une souveraine autorité, René Rocher juge, tranche, taille, rogne, interdit, ordonne. Nulle intention n'est valable si elle n'émane de M Rocher, nulle initiative permise si elle échappe à son contrôle.
>
> Un théâtre ne peut ouvrir ses portes sans le consentement de M Rocher; une troupe ne peut se grouper sans l'assentiment de M Rocher; un artiste ne peut exercer sa profession sans l'agrément de M Rocher, M Rocher, M Rocher, M Rocher.
>
> L'on aurait tort toutefois, de croire que M Rocher agisse à sa fantaisie: la raison de ses actes est la raison allemande, que sa raison n'ignore pas.[8]

As the article stated, Rocher's independence was relative in so far as the Germans could ultimately change any decision he took, and they could impose any policy of their choosing on the theatre through this committee. It is quite clear that Rocher must have consciously chosen to espouse the cause of Vichy and the 'new order' to have accepted a post which was as compromising as this, for it was through the COES that the Germans were able to put a great deal of pressure on the way in which the theatre was organised and the way in which policies were made.

The most infamous policy that the Germans imposed on the French theatre by means of the COES was that concerned with their anti-Jewish legislation. On 6 June 1942 the following law 'réglementant en ce qui concerne les Juifs, les professions d'artiste dramatique, cinématographique et lyrique' came into force:

> Article Premier – Les Juifs ne peuvent tenir un emploi artistique dans les représentations théâtrales, dans des films cinématographiques ou dans des spectacles quelconques, ou donner des concerts vocaux ou instrumentaux ou y participer que s'ils satisfont à l'une des conditions prévues à l'article 3 de la loi du 2 juin 1941 ou s'ils y ont été autorisés en raison de leurs mérites artistiques ou professionnels par un arrêté motivé du secrétaire d'Etat intéressé, pris sur la proposition du Commissaire général aux questions juives et, en outre, dans le cas où le ministre secrétaire d'Etat à l'Education nationale n'est pas compétent pour donner lui-même l'autorisation d'exercer la profession, sur l'avis dudit secrétaire d'Etat.
>
> Article 2 – Les Juifs atteints par l'interdiction résultant de l'article

8. *La Scène Française*, no. 1, December 1943.

précédant devront, dans le délai de deux mois à partir de la publication du présent décret cesser d'exercer la profession qui leur est interdite.[9]

The laws enforced by the COES did not affect just the Jews – Negroes and other coloured people were also subject to a number of restrictions codified by the *Officiel du Spectacle*:

Engagement des Nègres

Des différences d'interprétation ayant pu avoir lieu, en ce qui concerne l'engagement des nègres dans les Etablissements de Spectacle, nous tenons à préciser l'état de la question à ce jour.

Les gens de couleur, des colonies françaises, porteurs de passeport français, sont considérés par les Autorités allemandes comme citoyens français.

Rien ne s'oppose donc à leur production sur scène.

L'engagement des nègres (sujets français) pour la scène est donc autorisé à la seule condition que la représentation garde un caractère civilisé.

Il est préférable de ne pas abuser de cette autorisation; le personnel nègre doit être réduit au strict minimum, particulièrement dans les Entreprises que fréquentent, presque exclusivement, les représentants de l'Armée allemande.[10]

Managers of any establishment of public entertainment had to fulfil a large number of requirements, among which were the following:

1) Etre de nationalité française.
2) Etre majeur.
3) Ne pas être frappé des interdictions édictées par la loi du 2 juin 1941.
4) Ne pas avoir été condamné à une peine afflictive et infamante, à une peine prononcée pour vol, escroquerie, abus de confiance, émission de chèques sans provisions, etc. . . .
5) Ne pas être failli réhabilité.
6) Etre muni d'un certificat de bonne vie et moeurs.
7) Etre titulaire d'une licence d'exploitation . . . etc., etc.

Not only were Jewish actors and playwrights officially banned from theatres and other places of entertainment, but they were also subjected to an extremely unpleasant form of harassment in the

9. 'Décret du 6 juin 1942', *Annuaire général du spectacle 1942–1943*, p. 334.
10. *L'Officiel du Spectacle*, no. 11, 15 July 1943.

press; Michel Lapierre writing in *La Gerbe*, for example, decided that the job of the music hall artist was not an easy one: 'Que peut-on ridiculiser aujourd'hui, que peut-on stigmatiser?' she asked.[11] It was difficult, she decided, to make jokes about the Germans, but luckily 'on reprend la "blague" de notre bienfaiteur à tous, j'ai nommé l'inénarrable Léon, le Blum des familles, l'illustre représentant d'une race entre toutes sacrées: griffes pointues et long nez'. Quite apart from this, concluded the same writer, there was another sign of 'une époque meilleure' which was that there was no 'critique sur le chef de l'Etat'.

At the press conference given by Lieutenant Baumann and André Barsacq in 1941 Baumann explained to the audience that it was the Germans' duty to rid the French institutions – including the French theatre and its repertoire of all Jewish influence; he revealed some somewhat surprising statistics to the audience:

> Dans le répertoire juif nous avons trouvé un nombre impressionnant de scénarios équivoques:
> 310 assasinats
> 104 attaques à main armée
> 74 chantages
> 405 adultères
> 642 cas de vols
> Voilà ce qui explique notre attitude exclusive à l'égard des Juifs du théâtre; d'où exclusion totale pour obtenir l'extension de la sincérité et de la vérité artistiques.[12]

Throughout the Occupation a system of censorship carefully vetted all plays that were to appear in Parisian theatres; texts were first read by the Vichy censor and then sent on to the German censor at the Propagandastaffel. Texts had to be sent to the censor well in advance so that the authorities would have ample time to give their decision about the suitability of any particular work. The plays of authors who were suspect for racial or other reasons were automatically banned – they included plays by Tristran Bernard, Edmond Sée, Georges de Porto-Riche, Romain Coölus, Jean Jacques Bernard and Henry Bernstein. Not merely were original works by Jewish authors banned, but so also were translations made by Jews – the plays of Pirandello translated by Benjamin Crémieux

11. *La Gerbe*, 1 May 1941.
12. René Saint-Serge, report in *La France au Travail*, 10 January 1941.

did not appear, nor did *Hamlet* in the translation by Eugène Morand and Marcel Schwob. *Athalie* and *Esther* were banned because of their subject matter, as was *Judith* by Jean Giraudoux.

A number of plays were rejected for other reasons: *Le Soir d'Austerlitz* by Sacha Guitry had to be renamed *Vive l'Empereur!* before it could be put on. A revival of the plays *Crime et Châtiment* and *Anna Karénine* by Marcelle Maurette were banned because of their Russian associations. *Amants* by Maurice Donnay and *Boudu sauvé des eaux* by René Fauchois were not permitted because they are concerned with adultery.

The Germans exploited the climate of dissatisfaction created by the Vichy censor to sow discord between Paris and Vichy; articles appeared in *La Gerbe* strongly attacking the bans imposed by the French government, a large number of these articles being written by H.-R. Lenormand whose attitude, however, showed a certain ambivalence: at the beginning of 1941 Lenormand was worried because he felt that the French theatre was not producing the sort of plays that would present a good image to the rest of the world – he wanted the theatre to be taken out of the control of the bourgeois capitalists, and real reforms to take place; he explained that 'l'extirpation des vices esthétiques de la bourgeoisie ne s'accomplira que par la force'.[13] Later in the same year when some of the measures he called for were applied to his own works, his tune changed somewhat; in an article published in November 1941 in *Comoedia* under the title of *La Terreur Puritaine* he violently attacked the measures taken by Vichy:

> Au sang généreux qui coule encore, malgré la défaite, dans les veines de l'écrivain français, on s'efforce de substituer un fade et rosâtre liquide. Un grand éditeur se voit obligé de retirer 700,000 volumes de la circulation. Le substantif 'fesse' n'est plus imprimable. Un ouvrage d'éthnographie africaine est mis au pilori parce qu'il contient la photographe d'un indigène 'in naturabilis'.. On dresse déjà la liste des auteurs dramatiques censurés. Y figurent dans un voisinage incohérent, Maurice Donnay, Paul Raynal, René Fauchois, Jean Cocteau et le signataire de ces lignes.
>
> Pour comble d'humiliation, aucune de ces mesures n'est imputable aux Allemands. Elles émanent toutes de certains puritains de Vichy.

13. *L'Oeuvre*, 21 February 1941.

The words 'zazou' and 'swing' were also banned; an announcement in L'Officiel du Spectacle for 15 September 1943 ran as follows: 'A MM. les Directeurs d'Enterprises de Spectacles: la propaganda Abteilung nous a chargés d'informer tous les Directeurs d'avoir à bannir les termes 'swing' et 'zazou' de toute texte, qu'il s'agisse de paroles proncées sur scène ou de titres publicitaires reproduits sur les affiches, programmes, etc.'

In another article published soon afterwards in *La Gerbe*,[14] Lenormand did not confine himself to the measures passed concerning the theatre – he also criticised those measures relating to the cinema; he quoted the example of a law, recently passed, which had banned 'tous les films pouvant exercer une influence pernicieuse ou démoralisante sur la jeunesse, ou qui pourraient jeter une fausse lumière sur la France'. With such a law, argued Lenormand, most classics could be banned – *Tartuffe, Dom Juan, Lorenzaccio* and the plays of most contemporary writers. 'Il est douloureux de voir confondre ainsi', he continued, 'les règles morales indispensables au relèvement social du pays et celles dont peut s'accommoder la création artistique.'

La Gerbe began a public debate on censorship by publishing a number of articles by writers such as Jean Anouilh who wrote: 'Mon Dieu, je me réjouis de l'activité de cette censure. Elle va provoquer la naissance de *Lettres Persanes* dont nous n'aurons pas à rougir.'[15] Neither Baty, Guitry, or Jean-Louis Vaudoyer was in favour of censorship, but René Rocher, not surprisingly, was very much in favour of such a move, providing that those responsible for this censorship were men of quality and disinterested.

The theatre was a place where French men and women could, to some extent, rediscover their self-respect, a place where the man in the street could even enjoy moments of spiritual and intellectual resistance in innumerable and often totally unexpected ways which often escaped the vigilance of the German censor; Béatrix Dussane, in her *Notes de Théâtre*, asks the question: 'Fera-t-on jamais une histoire de la vie du spectacle pendant les années d'occupation? Il y faudrait les archives, sans doute disparues, des services de censure et de police allemande . . .'[16]

These records have indeed disappeared, as the Germans destroyed the archives of the Propagandastaffel before they were

14. *La Gerbe*, 27 November 1940.
15. Ibid.
16. Béatrix Dussane, *Notes de Théâtre 1940–1950*, Paris, 1951, p. 32.

driven from Paris; nor are there any records in the French public archives of plays censored during the German Occupation. What does exist, however, are the prompt copies used at the Comédie-Française during the war. A study of the censored passages reveals that it was often the very unlikely and seemingly trivial remarks that, for the reason that they aroused some sort of feeling of resistance in the audience, the occupiers felt had to be cut out. Marcel Thiébaut, commenting on audience reaction during the war, wrote: 'On retourna au théâtre: ce fut d'abord pour y guetter les moindres allusions qui, d'un coup, auraient rendu toute la salle hostile ou complice. On épiait les sous-entendus.'[17]

The cuts show that the Germans were liable to censor in two different ways; firstly they were sensitive to passages which were likely to arouse feelings of patriotism and, secondly, they suppressed all remarks that could have been interpreted in a way likely to ridicule the contemporary situation. A seemingly inoffensive play contained lines the explosive import of which would often be hard to interpret if one did not keep in mind the hardships of occupied France; for example, this apparently innocent remark of Camargo in scene VI of *Les Marrons du Feu* was struck through with the blue pencil:

> Approchez un peu. – J'ai
> Depuis le mois dernier, bien pâli, bien changé,
> N'est-ce pas?

In another of Musset's plays, *André del Sarto*, which opened on 19 May 1941, it is André del Sarto himself, in Act I sc. 3, who is guilty of a certain indiscretion when he asks Lucrèce: 'Dites-moi, Lucrèce, cette maison vous plaît-elle? Etes-vous invitée? L'hiver vous paraît-il agréable cette année?'

All references to England and things English were censored – unless they were pejorative; similarly, all references to Germany were cut: for example André del Sarto makes this unacceptable remark to Lucrèce about Cordiani:

> *André*: Cordiani est parti pour l'Allemagne.
> *Lucrèce*: Parti! Cordiani?
> *André*: Oui, pour l'Allemagne. Que Dieu le conduise!

17. Marcel Thiébaut, 'Le théâtre à Paris pendant la guerre', *Cornhill Magazine*, no. 964, April 1945, pp. 334–8.

The following lines of Arcas in *Iphigénie en Tauride*, duly censored of course, would have alluded to another side of the same situation:

> Qui donc a si souvent renvoyé dans leur patrie
> Les captifs arrachés à une mort certaine?

A passage from a play by Labiche had to be changed when an allusion to a certain German personality was too striking; in *29 degres à l'ombre* the line: '. . . et qui est-ce que je vois dans le vestibule? M. Adolphe, l'ignoble Adolphe! . . .,' caused an uproar at the Comédie-Française; for the next performance Adolphe was rechristened Alfred.

Perhaps the strangest case of censorship was that which concerned a projected production of Rostand's *L'Aiglon* at the time when Jean-Louis Vaudoyer was Administrateur-Général of the Comédie-Française. When Vaudoyer was approached by an anonymous but high-ranking German official – apparently the personal emissary of Hitler himself – there was, for good reason, considerable dismay at the Théâtre Français. This emissary had 'prétentions à la compétence théâtrale, et ses idées particulières sur un nombre de pièces et d'acteurs', wrote Béatrix Dussane,[18] and one of his most admired authors was Edmond Rostand – and he wanted *L'Aiglon* put on in the middle of the Occupation! He may have thought it appropriate at a moment when the ashes of the Duc de Reichstadt were being brought back to Paris. Despite the considerable reluctance of the Comédiens Français, the emissary insisted and, after making very considerable cuts ('Le peu de texte qui restait faisait encore trembler les gens circonspects', recounts Dussane), everything was ready in just a few weeks. A few days before the 'répétition générale', the performance of the play was announced; the German censor who, up to that moment had not been consulted at all, expressed polite astonishment, and advised the Comédie-Française that no permit had been given for this play. The Comédie-Française, in turn, retorted that the idea was not theirs, and mentioned the special emissary who had by then, of course, disappeared.

The official reaction of the Comédie-Française is to be found in the minutes of the Comité d'Administration of Thursday 18 De-

18. Béatrix Dussane, *Notes de Théâtre 1940–1950*, p. 35.

cember 1941, the day before the gala opening of *L'Aiglon* was due to take place:

> Au début de la séance, M. l'Administrateur informe le Comité que la question de *L'Aiglon* se posede la manière suivante:
>
> Il semble qu'aucune autorité occupante officielle n'ait demandé les représentations de *L'Aiglon* à la Comédie-Française à l'occasion de l'anniversaire du retour des cendres du Duc de Reichstadt.
>
> Les autorités occupantes ne sont pas disposées à autoriser les représentations dans les circonstances actuelles.
>
> Une répétition a été donnée le mercredi 17 decembre pour présenter le spectacle à une commission où étaient représentés du côté des autorités occupantes: l'Ambassade de l'Allemagne, la Propagandastaffel et l'Institut Allemand. D'autre part, du côté des autorités françaises, étaient présents: S.S.M. de Brinon, Ambassadeur de France, délégué du gouvernement pour les territoires occupés; M. Verrier, directeur du Cabinet de M. le Secrétaire d'Etat à l'Education Nationale et à la Jeunesse; et M. Lamblin, directeur des Beaux-Arts, représentant M. le Secretaire Général des Beaux-Arts.
>
> Une décision sera prise à la suite de cette représentation.

The German censor agreed to watch the 'répétition des couturières' in order to judge the play by seeing it, rather than by reading it. Béatrix Dussane takes over the story:

> Les évocations de la Grande Armée dans cette atmosphere participaient de l'incohérence risible propre à certains cauchemars. C'est pour ma part un des jours ou j'ai le mieux mâché la saveur de la défaite. Bien entendu, le spectacle terminé – sans un accroc, sans une défaillance – les fonctionnaires prodiguèrent les compliments . . . et ajournèrent l'autorisation, qui finalement ne fut jamais accordée.[19]

The whole incident serves to illustrate the almost impossible position the Comédie-Française was in when presenting plays which could in any way be held to be 'pièces de résistance', and emphasises the fact that the Comédie-Française was not an independent body, but one which was forced to co-operate with the occupying authorities.

Within a few days of the German Occupation of Paris newspapers began to reappear; in general, they tended to adopt either a pro-Vichy, or anti-Vichy pro-German line.

19. Ibid., p. 36.

The first papers to be printed were the *Victoire* on 17 June and *Le Matin*, also on 17 June which appeared on just two sheets, and on 22 June *Paris-Soir* reappeared. Virtually all news, both foreign and domestic, was filtered through the Agence Française d'Information, which was organised and came under the control of the Propagandastaffel. Newspapers were subject to the Propagandastaffel not only for what they published, but also for such details as the lay-out of the paper, the number of columns per page and even the characters to be used. Thus newspapers were completely controlled throughout the war, both at source and distribution levels.

Apart from *Le Matin*, papers such as *Paris-Soir*, *La France au Travail* and *Le Cri du Peuple* supported Pétain's government; on 3 October 1940 *La France au Travail* stated that the policies of Vichy were 'l'unique moyen que l'on ait de rappeler l'Etat à ses devoirs élémentaires'. *Le Cri du Peuple,* a weekly which appeared for the first time on 19 October 1940, managed to receive subsidies from Vichy, the Germans and Fascist Italy, and had the somewhat dubious distinction of having Jacques Doriot as its director; many of its contributors were distinguished if notorious: they included, among others, Drieu la Rochelle, Ramon Fernandez and Robert Brasillach.

Of the papers which supported Vichy, *Le Cri du Peuple* was the only one that had a drama critic of any distinction; this was Alain Laubreaux who also wrote for *Je suis partout* and *Le Petit Parisien*. Laubreaux was an arch-collaborator, and wrote reviews which were often vindictive, frequently unfair, violently anti-Semitic and wildly prejudiced – nevertheless he must be regarded as one of the most influential drama critics of the war. Many of Laubreaux's friends wrote for *Le Petit Parisien*, notably Robert Brasillach, who was the book critic; other contributors included Colette, Sacha Guitry and Georges Simenon.

La Gerbe, a weekly paper which was hostile to Pétain and Vichy, was directed by Alphonse de Chateaubriant, a fervent Nazi, a champion of collaboration and an admirer of Hitler. The theatre critic of the paper was André Castelot and during the Occupation the paper ran a series of debates on the arts and the theatre; among the contributors to these debates were Charles Dullin, Sacha Guitry, H.-R. Lenormand, Henry de Montherlant and Jean Sarment.

Comoedia, first published on 21 June 1941, was a weekly paper devoted entirely to the arts; it dealt with cultural activities not only in France, but also informed readers about the arts and theatre in Germany and in German occupied countries in its page entitled 'Connaître l'Europe'. An article which appeared in *Les Lettres Françaises Clandestines* accused *Comoedia* of appearing merely to publish this page of Nazi propaganda.

For Vichy and the Nazi symphathisers it was an accepted fact that the defeat of the French was a result of the rife corruption of the Third Republic during its closing years – the champions of the 'Révolution Nationale' asserted throughout the whole period of the war that this corruption had spread to the theatre, the cinema and even the opera. Not merely had these art forms become corrupted but they, in their turn, had become corrupting influences. These critics were particularly hostile to experiment and innovation in the theatre (there were, for example, violent attacks against Cocteau who represented the 'decadent' surrealist movement) and plays which appeared to be immoral in any way – for many critics the theme of the husband, the wife and the lover still played a disproportionately large role in too many plays, although in 1943 Bertrand Durieu, drama critic of *Semaine à Paris*, noted with satisfaction that more dramatists seemed to be making an effort to include the themes of 'la famille et même le retour à la terre' in their plays.[20] Critics demanded that the ideals of the 'Révolution Nationale' should be extolled in the theatre – not only 'le retour à la terre' but 'patrie, travail, famille' were the themes that they demanded should form the basis of a new and morally healthy theatre. In August 1940 Jean Sarment stated that Frenchmen had become 'avilis' and 'abâtardis' and recent theatre depicted his countrymen as they had become: 'Egoïstes oisifs . . . badauds épris de criaillerie et de politicaille.'[21] This had to stop, Sarment wrote, the standards of playwrighting had to be improved, the public re-educated and, above all, the theatres had to be put in the hands of people who knew their trade – not left to the evil influences of money makers.

Comoedia stated[22] that it was the duty of Vichy to make the theatre a fit part of the 'Révolution Nationale', to rid it of all partisan ideology and bourgeois ideas, 'de l'assainir sans l'affadir, de le purifier sans le déviriliser'.

In the orgies of breast-beating that took place time and time again in the pages of the daily press, the superiority of the German theatre

20. *Semaine à Paris*, 15–23 January 1943.
21. *La Gerbe*, 8 August 1940.
22. *Comoedia*, 13 November 1941.

and its other arts was thrust upon the reader. Louis Thomas reminded the readers of *Les Nouveaux Temps* [23] that it was blind prejudice which led the French to think that they had 'le monopole de l'esprit, de la civilisation, des beaux-arts, du goût et de la culture intellectuelle'. The fact that his compatriots thought that they lived in the only country to have true artists, writers, sculptors, actors and producers was 'un acte d'ignorance catastrophique et brutal'. The theatre in Germany, he continued, was undoubtedly better than that in France; although it could boast a Dullin or a Baty, the French theatre was generally of a level to appeal only to the ignorant. Louis Thomas includes in his article an impressive list of plays and operas put on in Berlin during September 1940 when the Battle of Britain was at its height; the list includes *Hamlet, As you like it* and *A Midsummer Night's Dream* – 'Ce qui faisait que l'on donnait trois oeuvres de Shakespeare à Berlin en plein combat contre l'Angleterre!'

During the Occupation a number of plays were written and staged which, to varying extents, mirrored the ideals of the new order. It is worth examining two of these plays in some detail – *800 mètres* by Andre Obey and *Les Pirates de Paris* by Michel Daxiat. *800 mètres* was staged during July 1941 at the Stade Roland Garros – the 'spectacle' consisted of a number of actors running slowly round the track of the stadium, stopping from time to time to allow Fernand Ledoux to read various passages from the text over the public address system; as the race progressed, so the text progressed and the order of the 'runners' changed.

800 mètres was part of what was called a 'représentation exceptionnelle' in the publicity printed in *Comoedia*, the paper that championed this open-air production; there were two of these 'représentations exceptionnelles' which included a presentation of *Les Suppliantes* by Aeschylus with music by Arthur Honegger who also wrote a 'commentaire musical' for *800 mètres*.

This somewhat unusual theatrical event must be considered as having a clear affinity with the cult of the body beautiful which the Nazi propagandists promoted through the pages of the daily press; the publicity for the play in *Comoedia* was surrounded by a series of statements written by none other than Jean Giraudoux: 'Qui néglige l'entraînement de son corps, néglige la santé de son pays . . . Il n'est pas un héros de Racine qui ne soit sportif . . . Les

23. *Les Nouveaux Temps*, 2 March 1941.

peuples qui ont le pourcentage le plus considérable de revues d'art sont ceux qui comptent le pourcentage le plus fort de gymnastes: l'Allemagne et la Finlande.'

The performances were preceded by a number of articles in *Comoedia* written by Barrault and Obey. In one of these articles[24] Barrault praised the virtues of 'la joie de l'effort' while elsewhere Obey[25] recounts that, when Barrault asked him for something for 'le plein air et, éventuellement, le soleil', Obey wrote the tragedy *800 mètres*; tragedy because the 'luttes de stade étaient des tragédies'. The play was inspired, he tells the reader, by an account of the eight hundred metres final at the Olympic games held at Colombes in 1924, recounted to Obey by 'un grand et bel athlète suisse, le charmant, le loyal, le blond Paul Martin', who had come second in the race after very nearly winning it.

The event received a mixed reception from the press. Armory writing in *Les Nouveaux Temps*[26] admired the splendid physique of Jean Marais; however, he admired less the 'beaucoup plus contest-able' figure of Barrault who was 'chargé paradoxalement d'incarner le vainqueur'. Maurice Rostand praised the 'majesté du spectacle' but a critic writing in *La Gerbe* found the text of the commentary 'creux... prétentieux, saupoudré de métaphysique sportive'.[27] Jacques Berland, writing in *Paris-Soir*,[28] more prudently perhaps, described the performance as 'une initiative fort intéressante'.

Les Pirates de Paris – which had the subtitle *L'Affaire Stavisky* – another play inspired by the spirit of the new order – was written by Michel Daxiat, who was none other than Alain Laubreaux. The play was based, as the subtitle indicates, on the Stavisky affair, which was the scandal of France in the early 1930s. Alexander Stavisky, a Russian Jew, organised an immense fraud by selling bonds in the name of the 'Crédit Municipal de Bayonne' which were guaranteed by jewels that were either stolen or false; the scandal which resulted when the affair was unearthed contributed to the fall of the Chautemps ministry, and to the events of 6 February 1934.

The subject gave Laubreaux the opportunity to attack both the Jews and the Third Republic. The plot of the play is weak and loosely episodic. The story begins in 1899, at the house of Stavisky's

24. Jean-Louis Barrault, 'Nécessité de l'effort', *Comoedia*, 21 June 1941.
25. *Comoedia*, 28 June 1941.
26. *Les Nouveaux Temps*, 11 July 1941.
27. *La Gerbe*, 10 July 1941.
28. *Paris-Soir*, 12 July 1941.

parents; the future swindler is twelve years old, and we see him already a thief – he steals a watch chain from a school friend called Laurent who, having turned thief himself, eventually reforms and becomes an inspector at the Sûreté Générale and is later to play a role in putting an end to Stavisky's activities. Next we see Stavisky at the age of forty, bouncing cheques and forging money; he organises the loan on the stolen jewels and is arrested at Marly and imprisoned. However, under pressure from a friendly minister, he is set free, and in the second act we find that he has changed his name and become Serge Alexandre. The dreadful exploits begin again; he becomes an important financier, he calls députés 'tu' and he rubs shoulders with members of the government. But – coup de théâtre – everything is discovered and Stavisky flees to Chamonix where he dies.

The play was given a considerable build-up in *Le Petit Parisien*, a paper to which Laubreaux regularly contributed, and of which he was a director. An interim critic of *La Petit Parisien*, Morvan Lebesque, interviewed the author of the play at the Théâtre de l'Ambigu where the play opened on 10 March 1942; the author described the Stavisky affair as a 'vraie pièce de théâtre'[29] with all its 'rebondissements' and drama. Another critic writing in the same paper maintained that it was important that the story should be given a public airing, and that the French public should not forget about 'la corruption juive introduite dans l'organisme social français'; for Georges Blond *Les Pirates de Paris* offered the French public a timely moral tonic.

Despite the considerable support and publicity that the play received from *Le Petit Parisien*, it is to the credit of most other critics that the play received an overwhelmingly hostile reception in the press. Writing in *Paris-Soir*, Jacques Berland[30] asked the question: 'Mait était-ce vraiment nécessaire de vouloir replonger le public dans un cloaque qu'on cherche précisément aujourd'hui à assécher?'

Writing in *Comoedia*, Roland Purnal wanted to know whether 'semblable' évocation est-elle ou non salubre, utile et souhaitable'[31] while Georges Ricou in *La France Socialiste* came to the conclusion that there are 'des sujets qui ont causé trop de ravages dans notre

---

29. *Le Petit Parisien*, 28 February 1942.
30. *Paris-Soir*, 13 March 1942.
31. *Comoedia*, 21 March 1942.

pays, entretenu trop de discordes'.[32]

The only critics who held any brief for the play were Maurice Rostand, Armory and Morvan Lebesque. Rostand's appreciation was rather lukewarm: he found the first part rather 'anodine,'[33] but from the beginning of the second half 'le ton s'élève', and the final three tableaux 's'écoutent avec intérêt et sont assez sobrement mélodramatiques'. Paul Oettly was a Stavisky 'plein d' autorité', Maurice Rémy as a policeman 'joue avec une étonnante canaillerie', and Alice Field was 'adroite et belle'. Armory wrote that he understood the idea of Michel Daxiat very well: 'rappeler par l'histoire du personnage la pourriture des moeurs, prémisses de notre défaite, justification d'une réforme totale à accomplir'.[34] The critic of *La Gerbe*, understandably, was full of praise for both the play and the acting; Michel Daxiat had 'réussi dans son entreprise'[35] and the article ended by pointing out that: 'il sera curieux de noter la réaction du public populaire devant cette formule nouvelle du mélodrame'.

If there was any notable reaction from the public, it was not one of curiosity, and the play was taken off in the middle of March giving a run of less than a month, despite the article that Alain Laubreaux wrote in *Je suis partout*:

Je pense à l'article que j'écrirais sur le spectacle de l'Ambigu si je n'étais pas l'ami de Michel Daxiat. C'est bien simple, je fulminerais. Je demanderais à l'auteur et à son théâtre s'ils sont fous, ayant entre les mains l'instrument qu'ils possèdent, d'être demeuré en deçà de l'effort qu'ils pouvaient fournir. Sur l'oeuvre lui-même, je n'ai rien à dire que ne pense l'auteur [. . .] C'est un mélo, consciencieusement construit et écrit sur la demande qu'il en a reçu, dans la forme même et dans la moule que cette demande lui fixait . . .

Durant tant d'années, on n'a montré que des pièces de confection ou d'inspiration juives, ou les Chrétiens étaient honteusement représentés, des comédies à adultères, à coucheries, qui diffamaient la famille française, peinte aux couleurs les plus abjectes, pour la première fois on lui offre une pièce où on appelle un Juif un Juif, ou le Juif apparaît en clair sur le fond d'un régime d'ordure et de décadence.[36]

32. *La France Socialiste*, 14 March 1942.
33. *Paris-Midi*, 13 March 1942.
34. *Les Nouveaux Temps*, 17 March 1942.
35. *La Gerbe*, 15 March 1942.
36. *Je suis partout*, 14 March 1942.

It is interesting to note that despite the fact that *800 mètres* and *Les Pirates de Paris,* in different ways, supported the ideals of the Germans and Vichy, dramatic critics on the whole were unimpressed by the 'philosophy' of the two plays and retained a certain independence of judgement when reviewing the two plays; the more moderate critics tended to review them on their dramatic merits rather than on anything else.

Various critics adopted various political attitudes according to the political stance of the newspaper for which they were writing. Some critics were very outspoken and allowed their criticisms to be affected by these beliefs; others, to their credit, remained reasonably independent of political circumstances. But it is very rare to find a man who, during the Occupation years, never allowed a personal attitude or political bias to colour in some way his activities in the theatre.

From all parts of the political spectrum came opinions as to what the theatre should do and what the theatre should be; from the example preached by a Fascist dictator, to those people who held more reasonable views. Yet many of those people who wished to adopt an apolitical attitude must, to some extent, be guilty of bowing to the pressure of Vichy and the Nazi collaborators. For Dullin to write in such a violently Fascist paper as *La Gerbe* indicated that he, in some way, allowed himself to be identified with the philosophy of the 'New France'. Capable as Barrault may have been as a theatrical 'animateur', he nevertheless fostered the cult of the body and the stadium; writers such as Obey and Giraudoux expressed attitudes and opinions which, in the rapidly changing circumstances, they might have kept to themselves if they had known how their writings were to be interpreted.

10

THE IMPLICATIONS OF LEGALISED PUBLICATION

Robert Pickering

One of the most potent and intellectually seductive legacies of post-Liberation and Gaullist views of French experience during the Second World War has, without doubt, been a propensity for clear-cut definitions and sharp ideological contrasts, awakening in us expectations of clearly defined and articulated hierarchies of values. As a whole, de Gaulle's own *Mémoires de Guerre* are exemplary in this regard: the possibility of problematic qualifications or discordant nuances in de Gaulle's own appreciation of the war tends to be conspicuous by its absence, the writing being permeated with a unilinear consciousness of personal destiny, and of collective identification with an inviolable sovereignty.

It is this tendency towards the sharp definition of criteria and conceptual parameters which has, of course, been increasingly scrutinised in recent years. Works which can now be seen as seminal in the reappraisal of French experience, such as Ophuls's *Le Chagrin et la pitié*, or, much earlier, Jean-Louis Curtis's *Les Forêts de la nuit*, with its courageous espousal in 1946 of the unthinkable, a call for closer examination of notions of integrity or collective response in resistance to occupation, have ushered in a tendency towards the relativisation, or at the very least a neutralisation, of the most outspoken generalisations or tendentious interpretations of what is increasingly being shown to have been a deeply problematic attitude. The dividing line here, as in so many other ideologically orientated aspects of French experience at this time, between the blunting of the sharpest edges of postwar claims to an unadulterated, inviolate French identity, maintained intact throughout the war years, and a much more concerted and dubious attempt at the rehabilitation of elements of the Fascist ideology in an apologetic, justificatory context (the so-called 'mode rétro'), is a further source of complexity and dilemma. If some recent research may, on occasion, have gone rather too far in denouncing the Gaullist 'myth'[1] – myth it may have been in some respects, but at the same time one might wonder how it could have imposed itself as securely as it did in political and ideological terms, without a real and lasting foundation in French social and political reality – it is nevertheless true that the conceptual touchstone in appraising this period has tended increasingly to devolve from interpretations of ambivalence or ambiguity. H.R. Kedward, speaking of the lack of consensus in judging the ideological resonance of the simple act of keeping the country running in a situation of foreign occupation, touches the quick of an interpretative dilemma which claims of inviolable national consciousness have not succeeded in dispelling:

> ... the same details of everyday life can be used to suggest *either* an almost treasonable indifference to the occupation *or*, on the contrary, a heroic determination to maintain French life and vitality in the face of the occupiers.... In France, ..., the severe divisions caused by the defeat and occupation ensured that no ... consensus emerged either at the time or since.[2]

It might indeed be claimed that it was de Gaulle himself, with his paradoxically sybilline suggestions of a nuanced attitude towards Pétain,[3] who first gave lasting voice, perhaps unwittingly, to an awareness of the possibility of divergence or ambivalence. This awareness is at its most polemical in the domain of political legitimacy or in that of claims to national representativeness. Studies here usually assume legitimacy to be self-evident, in whatever perspective of the ideological spectrum they are situated.

In recent years, however, other aspects or fields of legitimacy

1. Alan Morris, 'Attacks on the Gaullist "Myth" in French Literature since 1969', in Ian Higgins (ed.), *The Second World War in Literature*, Edinburgh, 1986 (reprinted from *Forum for Modern Language Studies*, volume XXI, No. 1), pp. 71–83.
2. R. Kedward, *Occupied France: Collaboration and Resistance 1940–1944*, Oxford, 1985, pp. 13–14.
3. Charles de Gaulle, *Mémoires de guerre*, Paris, 1959 (3 vols.; vol. 3, 'Le Salut 1944–1946', p. 250): 'En se taisant, [Pétain] accorda comme un ultime ménagement à la dignité militaire dont l'avaient revêtu ses grands services d'autrefois.... le Maréchal n'était qu'une proie offerte aux intrigues serviles ou menaçantes. La Cour prononça la peine capitale mais, en même temps, exprima le voeu qu'il n'y eût point exécution. J'étais, d'ailleurs, décidé à signer la grâce, en tout cas. D'autre part, j'avais fait prendre les dispositions voulues pour soustraire le Maréchal aux injures qui risquaient de l'assaillir.... Mon intention était, qu'après avoir été détenu deux ans dans une enceinte fortifiée, il allât terminer sa vie, retiré chez lui, près d'Antibe.'

have been subjected to serious research. Foremost amongst these, for the literary specialist, has been the situation of French writing in relation to Fascist-inspired calls for the 'Europeanisation' of creative literary output during the Second World War. Gérard Loiseaux's *La Littérature de la défaite et de la collaboration*,[4] has given invaluable impetus to research in this area. When considered in conjunction with the specific directives of conservative ideology emanating from Vichy, its translation of Bernhard Payr's *Phönix oder Asche?* has added a major contribution to our understanding of what might be termed the prescriptive code of literary and artistic directives, and can usefully be supplemented by recourse to major organs of Fascist propaganda in wide circulation throughout France at this time, such as the magazine *Signal,* the French-language version of the *Berliner Illustrierte Zeitung.* What might, on the other hand, be termed the proscriptive code of ideological taboos is also well documented: Philippe Amaury's *De l'Information et de la propagande d'Etat – les deux premières expériences d'un 'Ministère de l'Information' en France*[5] has added another fundamental dimension to research into the background against which French writers had to function during the Occupation.

When considered in relation to such works, which delimit the parameters of prescriptive and proscriptive directives regarding ideological conformity or deviation, French writing of the Occupation tends frequently to be construed in terms of sharp ideological discrepancies, which are at their most trenchant in the divide between collaborationist and resistant persuasion. Recently there have been signs of a move in interest away from works of Resistance and collaboration towards the obvious but hitherto neglected corpus of literature whose only ostensible link with the period of the Occupation is its date of publication. It is only possible here to introduce this field, and to attempt to pinpoint some of the most salient points in the problematic dimension which it proposes. 'Implications of legalised publication' may need some elucidation, both in terms of what it potentially includes, but also rejects, as possible means of approach and methodology. The title obviously does not suggest treatment along the lines of the 'consequences of legalised publication'. The vagaries of sanction, censure or retribution in the immediate post-Liberation period constitute a possible

4. Paris, 1984.
5. Paris, 1969.

extension of the question as a whole. The situation of French intellectuals generally has been analysed, however schematically, by Pierre Assouline in his *L'Epuration des intellectuels*,[6] which bears upon the ultimate moral responsibility of certain writers and publishers in respect of works of this period. But such analysis cannot throw light on the specific ideological situation of such writing, understood here less in terms of overt statements or attitudes than in terms of the structural mechanisms of its internal functioning, and the way these relate to the artistic dictates of the dominant conceptual or ideological scale of values.

It would, in effect, seem imperative to take our distance from the kind of ideological condemnation en masse formulated by a writer such as Georges Politzer, however altruistic may have been his motivation in dismissing all legalised publications during the Occupation as being irremediably compromised by an insidious capitulation to a discredited and degrading ideological system ('Aujourd'hui, en France, littérature légale veut dire: littérature de trahison').[7] The gist of this appraisal has all the appeal of the clearly delimited generalisation and is used effectively by Reboul, Commissaire du Gouvernement in the trial of Robert Brasillach, to reassert the advantages of democratic republicanism and of the right to free speech guaranteed by the Republican constitution. Under a totalitarian state there can be no question of 'the right to dissent'; the consequences of such dissension are clear-cut in their intolerant brutality: 'la question ne se pose que sous un régime de liberté. Sous un de ces régimes fascistes chers à l'accusé, la question n'a aucun sens car: ou l'intéressé parle conformément au régime, et alors il n'a aucun mérite, ou il se dresse contre, et alors, seul, le bourreau lui répond'.[8] The untroubled simplicity of perspective which such an attitude bespeaks is further comforted by the stance of a number of well-known literary figures, also notable Résistants, who refuse to contemplate publication under the Occupation on the grounds that it is intrinsically and ethically wrong. For a René Char or a Pierre Reverdy, to publish legally is to acquiesce in an imposed ideological and political situation, and hence to lend it respectability, in however indirect a way. Char, writing in 1941, differentiates between

---

6. Brussels, 1985.
7. Quoted in L.-A. Maugendre, *Alphonse de Châteaubriant 1877–1951*, n.p., 1977, p. 337 (quotation from Pierre Daix, *Aragon: une vie à changer*, Paris, 1975, p. 319).
8. Jacques Isorni, *Le Procès de Robert Brasillach*, Paris, 1946, p. 128.

writing and publication ('. . . il faut écrire des poèmes, tracer avec de l'encre *silencieuse*[9] la fureur et les sanglots de notre humeur mortelle . . . ').[10] Actively to seek publication is, by implication, too fraught with ideological danger for it to be a serious option. Such attitudes imply certain ideological presuppositions and take no account of a number of complex and problematic factors: the process of ideological and conceptual 'récupération' by the Vichy authorities of all literary elements which, in context or out of it, might lend themselves to the justification or legitimisation of the principles of the Révolution Nationale (the promotion under Vichy of a certain tradition in French Classicism, particularly of Corneille, as also, for example, of the writing of Giono or of 'pure poetry', are particularly interesting cases of this literary manipulation). Again, in a wider context, a similar 'récupération' by elements of German propaganda of any attitudes appearing to authorise social and political regeneration, and the institution of a 'new order' in Europe. Finally, and perhaps most importantly, there is the play of the literary imagination itself, its transformational propensities in respect of reality or the dictates of a specific ideological context.

Aspects such as these, each of which calls for an independent treatment which the limits of the present context do not allow, tend to be diminished in favour of the kind of ideological unilateralism naturally devolving from that clear-cut political and moral stance which the circumstances of political expediency and unification have tended to highlight in postwar France. Inasmuch as the fact of publication, as also of publishing, presupposes prior validation through the scrutiny of a complex system of censorship approval subservient to the dominant ideological ethos, it is thereby construed as the mere conformity to various constraints in a situation of duress, as an act of compliance, of resignation or acceptance. At the same time, legalised publication in the France of the war years is also more than this: each published work could itself be seen to legitimise the status of the constraints against which it is situated. In this respect, a two-way relationship could be seen to be instituted, conferring a retrospective legitimacy on the legitimising process itself.

Analysis of the implications of legalised publication transcends consideration of effects or consequences, based on conceptions of

9. Author's emphasis.
10. Quoted in Ian Higgins (ed.), *Anthology of Second World War French Poetry*, London, 1982, p. 192.

the ultimate representativeness, the sovereign status or otherwise, of the legitimising authorities, and activates a deeper level of investigation, that which concerns the status of writing itself in a fraught situation of ideological claim and counter-claim. It also raises questions of the relationship of such writing to the reality it purports to represent. Such an approach to the literature of this troubled period has the advantage of suggesting the broad outlines of a methodology which does not confine itself to a series of value judgements based on ideological preferences, a methodology which would enable us to home in on the reflective nature, or the greater or lesser transformational virtue of any given text, in its relationship to the reality from which it arises.[11] The question of the legitimacy or otherwise of the French state, of its constitution and of its institutions, is one which is so vexed that it would seem appropriate to leave it to the domain of historians and jurists. It cannot, in any case, assist us a great deal in analysing the peculiar complexity surrounding, for example, 'littérature de contrebande' – published legally but containing an ambiguity of message or of ideological motivation which places it in problematic status with the very legality of its dissemination.

The same can be said of the legitimising authorities themselves: clear-cut definitions of legality or illegality have been further obfuscated in their relation to publication under the Occupation by the autobiographical revelations of Gerhard Heller,[12] who, in his capacity as Director of the censorship services of the Paris-based Propagandastaffel has claimed to have aided and abetted the publication of French authors, as a result of personal convictions and humanistically inspired francophilia. If criticism has been voiced concerning the good faith of such revelations, they cannot be neglected totally as delineating a further level of complexity in any attempt to sound the implications of legalised publication in France at this period.

Whatever opinion one may have of such claims, and of Heller's own good faith, it would seem essential to situate them in relation to what we know of the facts of published works during this troubled time. If we do so, generalisations rejecting such publications as arising necessarily from some kind of insidious capitulation or

11. For further reflection on this topic, see my essay, *Writing against the Grain: Some French Literary Responses during the Second World War*, Cork, 1986 (Inaugural Lecture Series No. 3).
12. *Un Allemand à Paris 1940–1944*, Paris, 1981.

contamination of the writer in the face of strict guidelines and the pressure of circumstances, encounter objections which, on this level alone, they cannot accommodate. For example, Heller claims to have championed Camus's *L'Etranger*, published in June 1942 by Gallimard. The work contains no overtly polemical or critical perspective, relative to political realities of the war, and could therefore be interpreted, on a superficial level, as embodying a policy of conformity and of ideological subservience. Such an interpretation, however, runs spectacularly counter to both the conceptual thrust and literary functioning of the work, to its radical rejection of conventions and absolutes, as also to the disjunctive, discontinuous relationship it institutes between language and reality, through a highly innovatory style. Few texts published officially, with the full assent of the authorities presiding over ideological legitimacy, stand in as transgressive a relationship with those principles. The conceptual and metaphysical connotations of 'absurdity' cannot but intermesh with the specific circumstances pertaining to the catastrophe of national collapse. The sweeping away of a whole political, military and social system, which had survived the First World War seemingly intact, added to the destabilisation of an entire psychology based on a belief in the durability of that system, and the vacuum subsequent to the apparent bankruptcy of Republican principles, all foster a state of dilemma containing multiple ramifications. *L'Etranger*, deeply committed to a generative dynamic turned towards the rejection of distorting social and judicial conventions, projects this state of vacuum, and through the radical peripheralisation of the protagonist, makes an unequivocal statement in the direction of non-conformity, or a questioning of such constraints and conventions. Portrayal of the individual's meaningfulness in the widest experiential context invites a parallel questioning of the individual's place in a discredited social and political system, and states the value of the act of defiance in relation to both.

L'Etranger provides an exemplary model of transgressive writing, published during the Occupation period, and standing impenitently beyond the guidelines of ideological orthodoxy. But before proceeding further to outline some of the problematic forms which legalised publication can take, it is imperative to consider the theoretical status of writing in relation to such ideological orthodoxy. To this end, I should like to consider briefly a number of significant texts, each published in full conformity with the dominant ideological ethos, and contributing towards the circumscription of the writer's role in the context of the specific problematics arising from foreign occupation.

The first of these, an article entitled 'Littérature 1941' by Adolphe de Falgairolle, is situated not only in the mainstream of Vichy orthodoxy, by virtue of its very publication as part of the official almanac of that year (*Agenda de la France Nouvelle 1941*), but also in that of a certain simplistic conservatism which, despite its obvious conceptual banality, at least has the virtue of delineating a working model of literary acceptability. At the beginning of the article, the author is concerned to highlight what is conceived as constituting a certain decadence in the literature of the inter-war period, the caricatural representation of family life and manual labour, associated essentially with the peasantry. Over and above such generalities, however, the author pinpoints a theoretical or abstracting tendency in the literature of the time, as being particularly destructive of traditional values:

> Tous ces romans qui ne dépeignaient que des héros malades, des femmes aux sentiments monstrueux, qui se complaisaient dans la description salissante du métier, dans l'avilissement du travail quotidien, nous n'en voulons plus. Et cette autre littérature dite paysanne où M. l'écrivain, d'ailleurs citadin, nous décrivait toujours une certaine caricature de terrien sale, égoïste, brutal et incapable d'admirer un rayon de soleil sur une meule de blé, on n'en veut plus. Et cette poésie qui ramenait le plus beau paysage à des comparaisons abstraites avec ce que le travail à la chaîne peut avoir de plus ennuyeux, on n'en veut plus.[13]

It is not difficult to distinguish in such criticism, inspired by the sacrosanct trilogy of Vichy's moral and patriotic code, veiled references to a certain psychological strain in French literature, in which analysis of feeling can assume a morally transgressive or subversive character: for example, in the work of Gide and Proust, fair game for reactionary criticism, but also in Romain Rolland,[14] Raymond Radiguet or the Mauriac of *Thérèse Desqueyroux*.[15] There are

13. 'Littérature 1941', in *Agenda de la France Nouvelle 1941*, Toulouse, Edition des Services d'Information, Vice-Présidence du Conseil, p. 119.
14. Rolland's *Jean-Christophe* and *Quinze ans de combat* are cited in two documents held at the Bibliothèque des Archives Départementales in Clermont-Ferrand ('2ème Liste d'ouvrages exclus des bibliothèques scolaires et post-scolaires du Département', and 'Liste des ouvrages de la Bibliothèque de Roanne dont le retrait a été prononcé par la Commission interministérielle').
15. Gerhard Heller, in *Un Allemand à Paris 1940–1944* (pp. 144–5), gives an

critical echos also of a certain view of French provincialdom, of which salient examples are to be found in Flaubert and Zola[16] and rejection, in the reference to 'abstract comparisons', of certain tendencies common to both symbolist and surrealist poetry. In opposition to such distortion or marginality, the article continues: 'Le paysan a droit pour son coin du feu, à des livres qui dégagent la poésie du labour, la noblesse dè sa famille qui depuis des siècles fait s'épanouir sur notre sol le chou que le sculpteur a immortalisé dans le gothique de nos cathédrales.'[17] The civil servant should expect literature to exalt ' . . . l'amour qu'il apporte, lui rouage minuscule et capital, à prendre des initiatives de fonctionnaire . . .' Woman has a right to edifying works directed towards consolidating a state of unmitigated drudgery ('Et la femme . . . a droit aussi à ne pas être découragée de son dur et anonyme labeur au foyer, par ces littérateurs, millionnaires, qui décrivent la révolte du pauvre . . . dont ils vivent le plus loin possible'). Literature thus regenerated would change from being a source of extravagant imagining, and would assume its traditional, exalted status of soporific gratification: 'Le livre sera de nouveau l'optimiste marchand-de-sable qui, quand notre journée est faite, nous apporte de beaux songes et non plus le fantôme de malédiction et de cafard.' De Falgairolle concludes, 'Demain notre littérature redeviendra terrienne, française': only in this way, according to the author, can the state of French letters be purified of what is patently held to be its parasitic and debilitating perversions.

Platitudinous and humorous though such comments may appear to be, they nevertheless have the virtue of sketching a certain conceptual and ideological background, which delineates in its own very limited way certain principles of orthodoxy and of deviation. The apology of literary transparency, of the representation of dominant social and ideological conventions, reflect back to a reality which is perceived to be fixed and immutable, to a belief in the status quo, from which would devolve a literature of certainty and of unreflecting acceptance. When de Falgairolle shifts from

account of the prejudiced view of psychological literature directed at Mauriac's *La Pharisienne* (published 1941) by Karl Epting, Director of the German Institute in Paris.

16. Zola's *La Terre, Nana* and *Pot Bouille* are cited in documents held at the Bibliothèque des Archives Départementales in Clermont-Ferrand ('Livres radiés des bibliothèques scolaires du Département du Puy-de-Dôme – lère liste').

17. Adolphe de Falgairolle, 'Litterature 1941', p. 120.

literary exhortation to literary practice, all the potential defects of such a view of the function of literature become evident: a poem entitled 'Quatre Saisons au bassin d'Arcachon', published rather surprisingly in *Confluences*,[18] the literary review edited by René Tavernier, of courageously open-minded and sometimes outspoken patriotic conviction, is almost entirely composed of well-worn pastoral and classical clichés ('En ru au ciel marin un olympien bélier/Mène un troupeau de nuages en transhumance'), which tend naturally towards that disparaging portrayal of the French peasant which de Falgairolle is elsewhere anxious to modify ('Un "grain" proche a gonflé le ciel trop diaphane;/La voix du large étonne un craintif cul-terreux').

A rather more intelligent approach to the topic is to be found in two articles by Léon Daudet, both published as editorials in *L'Action Française*. The first, entitled 'La littérature de demain' (dimanche 15 septembre 1940, p. 1), is pitched at a considerably higher level of conceptual awareness: it is significant that, despite the otherwise dogmatic nature of much of the writing in *L'Action Française*, and in stark contrast with the strongly polemical tone of de Falgairolle's article, the dominant mode of the commentary is one of hypothesis and of uncertainty ('Certains de nos confrères commencent à se demander, ce que sera la littérature française de demain. Si elle sera libre et prête à user de la liberté . . ., si elle subira des ordres ou des influences, dans quelles directions? Si elle demeurera indépendante, au milieu des contacts nouveaux et des imprégnations difficiles à prévoir . . .; si une forte personnalité s'imposera . . .'). If, as we would expect from an organ of uncompromising conservative convictions the commentary does not succeed in considering the status of literature under the Occupation above and beyond a discourse implacably highlighting Republican responsibility for present misfortunes, its abiding characteristic is an absence of conceptual closure or of artistic bias: Péguy, Claudel, Saint-Exupéry (' . . . un genre mêlé de science, de désespoir et de poésie, tel qu'on peut l'attendre par exemple de l'aviation'), and astonishingly Proust ('Marcel Proust, qui nous avait apporté un art minutieux et savant, habile à sonder les cryptes inconnues'), are advanced as the possible literary models of the future generation. Daudet's second article, 'L'Avenir des lettres et la critique' (*L'Action Française*, vendredi 18 octobre 1940, p. 1), goes even further

18. *Confluences*, no. 18, March 1943, p. 367.

along this adventurous and independently minded path by quoting from the 'journal' of Gide, extolling it as a source of enlightened reflection on the destiny of French literature ('un journal où abondaient les réflexions judicieuses sur notre métier d'écrivain et les services qu'il peut rendre dans une société assez mal en point'). If both articles are by definition very schematic in their proposals for future literary development, they nevertheless stand out by their independence of tone and of conviction; most importantly, they are resonant with a sense of dilemma, a deep strain of uncertainty, which stands in stark contrast to de Falgairolle's rather blinkered pronouncements as the official spokesman on literary matters of Vichy orthodoxy.

The texts mentioned above of Adolphe de Falgairolle and of Léon Daudet formulate certain principles of literary production and reception, which can be seen to be at work on a large scale in the implications of legalised publication. Before turning, however, to brief consideration of some interesting works published during the Occupation, and which project or prolong those principles, I should like to consider a third author whose theoretical writing on the status of literature should be given some weight in the present context. Such writing is, in effect, all the more significant since it emanates from the pen of one of the signatories to the 'Otto list', the Parisian publisher, Bernard Grasset. In *A la Recherche de la France – notes à leur date* (1940), Grasset is essentially concerned, as the title suggests, to make the case for the constitution of a coherent French identity, but he also poses with a lucid awareness the essence of the writer's problematic situation: 'Ayant en effet pour objet tout ce qui est pensé et projeté dans le monde, le métier d'éditeur – comme, au reste, l'écriture – risque, à chaque tournant, de croiser les points les plus susceptibles de la pensée et des projets de l'occupant'.[19] From this focal nexus of writing, publication and externally imposed directives in a situation of duress, Grasset articulates a procedural principle which smacks perilously of what Sartre has defined as one of the guiding motivations in collaborationist psychology, that of realism:

> Pour moi, je suis bien décidé, quant à la chose française, à prendre toute la place qu'on m'y laissera. J'entends que je soumettrai à la censure de l'occupant les textes les plus français d'inspiration et de manières. Qu'ils

19. *A la Recherche de la France – notes à leur date*, Paris, 1940, pp. 15–16.

soient de moi ou de tel autre. Je ne connaîtrai d'autres limites que celles qu'on m'imposera. D'un mot, je reprendrai toute l'existence qui me sera possible, persuadé que l'existence française est subordonnée à toutes ces existences reprises.[20]

As the essay continues, however, it becomes clear that this attitude of apparently realistic acceptance is not based on outright capitulation, but on a singularly problematic middle course, fraught with tensions and potential danger. The ideal publication is envisaged as testing the very limits of a precarious middle ground, and as necessarily acquiring greater intensity, density and efficacy because of it. Nor, does Grasset claim, is it simply the contingencies of present circumstances which dictate such a course: constraints and difficulties are indispensable if French writing is to aspire to any valid degree of sovereign status: ' . . . je me disais . . . : "Quelle chose publier qui soit d'une part correcte envers l'occupant et d'autre part vraiment française?" Et je songeais à une sorte d'album de photographies, accompagné d'un texte dans les deux langues, portant comme titre: "Horizons français." Je sentais bien qu'avant tout, c'était la "chose française" qu'il fallait maintenir.'[21] The perils of such a balancing act are outlined in a chapter entitled 'Ecrire dangereusement', dated 11 September 1940: the call for the expression of the truth of French nationalism necessarily implies forms of literature in which inner value can only be judged in terms of the testing to the extreme of limits of acceptability. Such, according to Grasset, is not the case, at least in the France of 1940:

Si vraiment une France nouvelle était près de surgir, elle apparaîtrait déjà dans les écrits des Français. Dans un certain danger couru, dans un risque accepté. Une révolution, même de l'esprit, ne pouvant aller sans dangers ni risques. Or il semble que le premier souci des Français, qui écrivent présentement, soit de le faire sans risques. . . . Ils évitent les uns et les autres tous les sujets dangereux. C'est-à-dire tout ce qui importe.[22]

Were such sentiments to be penned by anyone other than a publisher, there might be a tendency to dismiss them as eccentric, as 'unrealistic', precisely, in their apparently limited applicability. But we are dealing here with one of the disseminators of the written

20. Ibid., p. 16.
21. Ibid., p. 20.
22. Ibid., p. 23.

word: to this extent, Grasset's apparent espousal of a doctrine of acceptance or of 'realism' assumes the character of paradox. If it is in the interests of France and of its regeneration to test, but also to respect, the limits of German validation, so too is it ultimately in German interests to allow the untrammelled expression of such nationalism. Sovereignty must ultimately depend on subjugation, and vice versa: it is the vocation of literature to give expression to this potential overlap of apparently conflictive forces, to embody the interpenetration of divergent tendencies and interests. To write is to measure one's words, with all that this phrase implies of ambiguity, to give full force to feeling and belief, all the while carefully measuring the distance between acceptable limits of personal or collective expression, and censure: 'Certes, je prendrai garde à tous mes mots. D'abord pour qu'ils soient exactement conformes à ce que je sens. Ensuite pour qu'ils ne heurtent pas l'occupant. Mais je conjure les censeurs allemands de ne m'en supprimer aucun. Je pense qu'ils tiennent à notre totale sincérité'.[23] We may be tempted to reject this as wishful thinking, as a camouflaged language of collaboration, impregnated with a suspect ideology, but Grasset confounds any such reaction by rehabilitating at the end the notion of discrepancy, of the right to dissent and to displease:

> L'intérêt d'un pays ne peut exactement se confondre avec l'intérêt d'aucun autre pays. . . . D'où . . ., quand on écrit sur la France, en pays occupé, il n'est pas possible de plaire intégralement à l'occupant, même si l'on reste totalement correct envers lui, et même si l'on est entièrement d'accord avec lui sur la forme souhaitable de l'autorité en France. D'où l'on doit s'exposer à lui déplaire en partie.

Grasset's other significant publication in this area, *Les Chemins de l'écriture*, is a collection of essays which, although published in 1942, dates from the inter-war years. The essays are therefore totally devoid of reference to the political and ideological realities of the Occupation, with the exception of occasional brief introductions or footnotes. Yet it is revelatory that these essays, which explore the motivations generating an imperative 'besoin d'écrire' ('Préface', p. 13), and propose to enlighten the 'sources de l'écriture', should appear at a time when creative impulses must cope with unprecedented constraints and prescriptive procedures. In this respect, the

23. Ibid., p. 24.

return to the very sources of the creative literary act, and a questioning of the latter's inherent sincerity or authenticity, transcend the avowedly personal nature of the analysis, and progressively assume the status of a particularly eloquent sign of the times.

Of the numerous aspects of the implications and motivations underlying literary production, some of which, it must be said, are characterised less by their originality than by their conventionalism, two are of special significance. Developing thoughts of the Italian poet Leopardi, in which the latter places action higher than the practice of literature in those values which have right of city, Grasset modifies this assertion by emphasising not the subservience of writing, but its status as an alternative to action; if such be the case, Grasset continues, it can only be so if writing is impregnated with an autonomous power at least the equivalent of a creative potency which might be channelled in other directions:

> Ici c'est le mot 'force' qu'il faut retenir. L'écriture ne vaut que dans la mesure où elle est l'emploi d'une force. Le besoin de créer, dans l'ordre de l'esprit, comme en tout autre, n'est qu'une des formes de ce besoin d'affirmer sa personne, de dépenser sa force, qui est naturel à l'homme. . . . Je ne crois pas que l'homme songe d'abord à employer sa force dans l'écriture. . . . affirmer que le premier besoin de l'homme est d'agir, ce n'est pas diminuer l'écriture. C'est seulement dire que l'écriture vaut dans la mesure où elle est le témoignage d'une force qui aurait pu être employée ailleurs.[24]

It is easy to recognise in this dialectic of literature and action one of the conceptual constants not just of the war years (it is given particular urgency in the writing of Drieu la Rochelle, for example), but also of the inter-war period. It assumes, however, an equal if not greater prominence in the implications of legalised publication under the Occupation, and intermeshes with Grasset's thoughts on the status of writing in *A la Recherche de la France*, both in terms of conceptual coherence, and also in terms of chronology. In effect, both works, the one a collection of personal convictions, of arguably limited resonance, the other a work which might more adequately be described as a pamphlet or a work of circumstance, cross-fertilise, and add a valuable additional dimension to our expectations of the works published at this time. To write 'dangerously', such as Grasset defines it, merges with an imperative of

24. *Les Chemins de l'écriture*, Paris, 1942, pp. 148–9.

175

literary dynamism and power, to create an important new yardstick of literary legitimacy: it could with profit be applied to the works of Drieu la Rochelle or of Céline, as an expression of intellectual and artistic independence, rather than of servile conformity with alienating ideological pressures.

Another important aspect of Grasset's analysis deserves mention. It occurs primarily in one of the chapters of *A la Recherche de la France*, entitled 'Loyalisme et servilité', which examines the relationship between journalism and the full representation of a problematic reality. In Grasset's view, the servile acquiescence on the part of French newpapers in the occupied zone to German-slanted views of events, tells a great deal more concerning the lack of moral fibre of the newspaper concerned than it does of external pressures and censorship:

> Il faut une fois pour toutes, que tous les Français sachent, que si, en zone occupée, tel journal français ne semble fait que de communiqués de l'occupant, c'est la faute de ce journal, et non de l'Allemagne. . . . Pour tout dire, si un journal donne l'apparence d'être uniquement fait de communiqués de l'occupant, c'est que ce journal n'avait rien à dire touchant la France. Ou qu'il ne tenait pas à le dire.[25]

Either way, the condemnation of what Grasset sees as a certain dereliction of duty, both towards oneself and in relation to one's national responsibilities, is forcefully affirmed; it is the condemnation of an escapism of attitude, a strong element of which is frequently to be found in artistic expression over a wide scale, during the war years. Responsibility is seen to lie ultimately with the source of literary production, as indeed it also does with the focus of reception, the reading public itself, who can choose either actively to probe, and draw the conclusions from, such an abdication, or to participate itself in a kind of collective oblivion. If such is the case, not even the most ideologically or artistically subversive work can have any meaningful efficacy: as Grasset had stated in an observation of 1937, 'Lire', published in 1942 in *Les Chemins de l'écriture*, thereby acquiring a particular potency and relevance, ' . . . il est deux façons de lire. On peut lire pour se chercher, et, tout à l'inverse, pour s'oublier. . . . Quant à moi, j'aurais là mauvaise grâce à railler. Sans le vaste public de ceux qui lisent sans profit, le métier d'éditeur serait-il possible?'.[26]

25. Ibid., p. 43.
26. Ibid., p. 155.

We should not, in my view, read cynicism into such a statement. As part of a coherent overall approach to a singularly tension-ridden context of textual production and reception, the theory of a kind of conspiracy of silence between point of origin and point of consumption is not far-fetched. Grasset's attitude is critical, but at the same time it remains closely attuned to the peculiar problematics of the situation. If the escapist, or predominantly conformist text is to be condemned, it should be on the grounds of its own internal integrity, those of its adherence to, or departure from, certain principles which should link it in a valid way to reality, whatever may be the specific historical or ideological circumstances in which it is engendered. The interest or significance of what a text has to say can be judged in relation to its inherent experiential or existential depth, and not necessarily just in relation to prescriptive or proscriptive pressures. The 'silence' of a text, Grasset's 'n'avoir rien à dire', depends on context, and in any case is open to interpretative ambiguity. If Grasset's view is to be criticised or qualified, we might conveniently start at this point: Sartre has highlighted the divergencies of interpretation which focused on the silence of the two protagonists in a text as totally above suspicion as Vercors's *Le Silence de la mer* – generally maligned by the population of French expatriates, yet greeted with acclaim as an effective expression of the realities of political subjugation by those subjected to it.[27]

At this point, we return to consideration of the potentially ambiguous text, to a discourse of uncertainty, the significance of which, if rejected by de Falgairolle, is nevertheless implicitly reinstated by Daudet, and is a natural consequence of Grasset's 'writing dangerously'. One of the most interesting cases in this respect with which the legalising authorities have to cope, is that of Saint-Exupéry's *Pilote de guerre*, interesting both for the fact that it reveals the limitations of such authorities when faced with an eminently problematic discourse, and also for the fact that it should warn us again against any hasty assimilation of such works with overtones of collaboration or ideological capitulation. In effect, *Pilote de guerre* receives the censor's imprimatur, is printed by

27. J.-P. Sartre, *Qu'est-ce que la littérature?*, Paris, 1948, pp. 92–93: ' . . . il est frappant que le *Silence de la Mer*, ouvrage qui fut écrit par un résistant de la première heure et dont le but est manifeste à nos yeux, n'ait rencontré que de l'hostilité dans les milieux émigrés de New York, de Londres, parfois même d'Alger et qu'on ait été jusqu'à taxer son auteur de collaborationnisme. C'est que Vercors ne visait pas *ce public-là*. Dans la zone occupée, au contraire, personne n'a douté des intentions de l'auteur ni de l'efficacité de son écrit: il écrivait pour nous'.

Gallimard, and is listed officially as from 27 November 1942; it is then banned on 5 February 1943 by the very same Propagandaabteilung which issued the authority to publish in the first place, and the 21,000 copies printed are seized. Heller refers in passing to this fiasco in his autobiographical work:[28] if we accept his own explanation for it – recognition of the work's literary merit, dictated by his attitude of integrity towards French literature and French culture – the banning of the book could be seen as resulting quite simply from the action of Heller's superiors, obliged to act on receipt of letters of criticism and denunciation. Such an interpretation, however, would seem simplistic in relation to the problematic directions of the book's discourse and conceptual framework. The latter have been studied with considerable finesse by Beynon John;[29] a systematic study, however, remains to be written of the ways in which various textual elements confusingly intermingle and interpenetrate – the significance, for example, of Christian imagery, consistently developed, merging with the themes of self-sacrifice and of the necessity within the individual of increased awareness of his responsibility in collective terms ('Chacun est seul responsable de tous').[30] The 'all for one, one for all' philosophy merges disconcertingly with certain directions of Pétainist self-justification, particularly with the identification of self and nation (Appel du 16 juin 1940 : ' . . . je fais à la France le don de ma personne pour atténuer son malheur'); and the text's systematic criticism of democracy, as also of rabid individualism, situates the writing further in the mainstream of Vichy orthodoxy. At the same time, however, the preoccupation with considerations of justice, injustice and the Rights of Man, reads as a potential clarion call to arms, to deliverance from alienating and oppressive forces (' . . . il est équitable que mille meurent pour délivrer un seul de la prison de l'injustice').[31] Again, the apology of a corporate intermeshing of qualities and of strength, which is centred in the final chapters on the image of the cathedral, would appear to situate the writing squarely in one of Vichy's central precepts: but other discordant voices destabilise

28. Heller, *Un Allemand à Paris 1940–1944*, p. 134.

29. See particularly S.B. John, 'Vichy France, 1940–1944: The Literary Image', in J. Cruickshank (ed.), *French Literature and its Background*, Oxford, 1970, volume 6, pp. 205–225; and his article, 'Saint-Exupéry's *Pilote de guerre*: Testimony, Art and Ideology', in R. Kedward and R. Austin (eds.), *Vichy France and the Resistance: Culture and Ideology*, London, 1985, pp. 91–105.

30. *Pilote de guerre*, Paris, 1942, p. 213.

31. Ibid., p. 234.

such sentiments, implicitly criticising ill-founded 'religions de l'Etat ou de la Masse', or reasserting a state's dependence on a collective delegacy ('D'autres se sont emparés de ces pierres sans pouvoir et, de cette somme, ont fait un Etat. Un tel Etat ne transcende pas non plus les hommes. Il est également l'expression d'une somme').[32]

It is scarcely surprising, therefore, that Saint-Exupéry's overall credo should propose a singularly slippery combination of potentially conflictual elements, roundly criticising on the one hand, the trilogy of virtues in the erstwhile Republican ethos, yet on the other singling out the state as a possible cause of distortion, whereby 'l'unité de l'Etre',[33] the cathedral's interlocking structural coherence, is denied rather than affirmed. So too the individual, whose anarchic independence must be tamed, or actively combatted: 'Je combattrai donc quiconque prétendra imposer une coutume particulière aux autres coutumes, un peuple particulier aux autres peuples, une race particulière aux autres races, une pensée particulière aux autres pensées'.[34] Such an intermingling of concepts may be vibrant with its own inner coherence, but when placed in relation to the specific ideological forces at play, it cannot but foster a problematic response. If it is difficult to see Saint-Exupéry as a proto-Fascist, there is nevertheless a conservative strain to the writing which places it in the lineage of a certain patriotic or nationalistic tradition, claimed by Vichy apologists as a source of the régime's legitimacy. Few texts are as difficult to situate in ideological terms, and the vagaries of its publication bear eloquent witness to its singularly polyvalent potentialities.

If Grasset's 'dangerous writing' here tips the balance, and results in official sanction, blurring in exemplary fashion expectations and presuppositions in respect of the implications of legalised publication, the same can be said of a multitude of works which, in a less spectacular way, receive the censor's imprimatur, and keep it. Space admits only of the most general outline of some major categories in theme and genre. A strain of writing in the pastoral vein, official advocacy of which figures prominently in de Falgairolle's view of what literature ought to be in the context of the National Revolution, emerges as a favoured thematic focus, and it is scarcely surprising that writers who follow this direction should be

32. Ibid., p. 239.
33. Ibid., p. 232.
34. Ibid., p. 243.

appropriated by the Vichy authorities as an eminent source of artistic and ideological justification. I have studied elsewhere the case of Giono, who is frequently subjected to ideological 'récupération' of a particularly blatant kind.[35] The same could be said of Henri Pourrat, master chronicler of rustic life in Auvergne, and because of this geographical and ideological proximity, an even more obvious candidate for promotion by Vichy apologists: his novel *Vent de Mars*, depicting the hardships but also the nobility of rustic life, is awarded the Prix Goncourt in 1941. Here, too, the implications of legalised publication run deep, and are not easy to live down, compounded by the additional stigma devolving from the official consecration of a literary distinction: contemporary appreciations of this novel still feel obliged to talk of it in apologetic terms, as something of an embarrassing liability.[36] Yet the conceptual thrust of the work is not unilateral in its espousal of the attitudinal precepts which the Vichy authorities promulgate, nor is the evocation of the peasantry of Auvergne totally devoid of discordant resonance. The paean to rustic values and pastoral morality places the writing in the mainstream of officially promulgated ideas: arguments in favour of 'revolution' or of 'rebuilding' ('. . . on refera tous ensemble une France')[37] strike a familiar note, and calls for changes of an administrative or political nature, rehabilitating, for example, the historical 'provinces' as opposed to the artificially imposed 'départements', conform to the fundamentally anachronistic terminology of Vichy France. But the apparently Pétainist-inscribed injunctions and exhortations are presented as growing organically from the paean to the peasantry, which constitutes the subject of the book in any case, and hence are not prompted by circumstances, tending to remain independent from specific references to the war context. Continuing allusions, also, to the semantically loaded and ideologically ambiguous concept of unification or of national accord, foster within the writing a vision of synthesis

35. See my article, 'Writing under Vichy: Valéry's *Mauvaises Pensées et autres*', *The Modern Language Review*, Jan. 1988 (vol. 83, no. 1), pp. 40–55.
36. The abiding uneasiness with which such official consecration during the Occupation is still met, is eloquently expressed in an article on Pourrat's *Gaspard des Montagnes*, published in the newspaper *La Montagne/Centre-France* (Clermont-Ferrand), in 1986 (Sunday 24 August 1986, p. 16). A caption under a photograph of Pourrat reads: 'Henri Pourrat eut le prix Goncourt en 1941 pour *Vent de Mars*, à une époque où le mot d'ordre était justement celui du retour à la terre'. The hint of embarrassed apology beneath what is otherwise presented as simple explanation is of the greatest significance in pinpointing the problematic status of the work.
37. *Vent de Mars*, Paris, 1941, p. 173.

which, in the context of the France of 1941, with its various zones and demarcation line, cannot but have problematic overtones: ' . . . cette terre qui marie Nord et Midi, plaine et montagne, rudesse et douceur, largeur et finesse . . .'.[38] Certain tendencies in stylistic functioning also echo this movement towards a global, rather than a piece-meal view, of a durable French identity, which changes of the moment cannot modify: the writing can juxtapose visions of the country which are bent both towards recreation of the organisation of the land in the past, and towards a constructive dynamic which projects the future: 'Les hommes ont eu des prairies . . . . Ils se sont fixés, ils ont fondé les villages . . . , ils ont aménagé le terroir et ont commencé le grand labourage./ Au Nord et à l'Est, en France, ce sera une organisation de plaine . . . il faudra lever les récoltes ensemble . . .'.[39]

Such indirect portrayal of the events and effects of the war can shift towards a vein of writing in which the latter tend to disappear from sight altogether, or retain only a token presence as the catalysts for an affirmation of the continuity of values and ways of life, which is advanced as an implicit guarantee of the permanence of a French identity. A particularly interesting instance of this tendency can be found in a collection of short essays and articles, liberally illustrated with sketches, lithographs and paintings, entitled *Paris 1943 – Arts, Lettres*, published by the Presses Universitaires de France, under the aegis of the 'Ville de Paris, Inspection Générale des Beaux-Arts' ('autorisation N° 12.584'). As the title implies, the work is a celebration of Paris in all its diversity, and reads as something of a public relations exercise in the direction of bolstering the capital's claim to capital status. This very fact situates it squarely in that nexus of ambiguous interpretations emphasised by Kedward: unpatriotic escapist peripherality, or the courageous affirmation of the inviolability and irreplaceability of a proud cultural and artistic heritage, which the publication demonstrably aims to show is still very much alive? In a review entitled 'La Vie musicale à Paris, ou beaucoup de bruit . . . pour quelque chose', the range and diversity of musical activity in all spheres is extolled as a source of pride for posterity ('Votre plaisir passé, que vous importe, ô lecteur égoïste; il en restera tout de même bien assez, pensez-vous, pour que puisse s'ébahir la Postérité, comme elle le fit en étudiant

38. Ibid., p. 189.
39. Ibid., p. 183.

les temps de la chute de l'Empire romain, sur la richesse et la variété des oeuvres musicales nées pendant l'Incendie'),[40] as a patriotic gesture of faith in the capital's timeless vocation as an unequalled source of artistic creativity. At the same time, however, the text reminds us, such creativity cannot be expected to flourish unassisted; if Paris is something of a world centre in artistic terms, it is largely because the 'gouvernement du Maréchal' wishes it to be:

> Les puissances officielles donnent le branle et terrassent les difficultés de l'heure. C'est ainsi que, malgré la dispersion du personnel technique et artistique, les restrictions textiles, électriques, calorifiques, – ah! la belle kyrielle! – ... les théâtres lyriques subventionnés, supportent assez gaillardement le poids du Cahier des Charges. ... Le gouvernement du Maréchal ne lésine pas sur le chapitre des subventions musicales et si quelques restrictions ont risqué de stériliser certains efforts, ... les associations symphoniques, elles, grâce à lui, ont pu inscrire à leurs programmes un nombre appréciable de premières auditions'.[41]

A number of the texts emerge from echoes of the war's presence – a short story, 'Confidences', of Marcel Aymé, turns on the status of prisoners of war, and an article by Georges Bastien, 'Les Prisonniers et l'art', goes directly to the heart of the prisoner-of-war experience, including a number of sketches and a lithograph from prisoners themselves – but that presence is muted, made subservient to a celebration of a continuing artistic tradition. The volume's problematic status, however, is reasserted in an ideologically loaded appreciation, by Yves Gandon, of 'Ce que lisent les jeunes'. Gide and the philosophy of the *Nourritures terrestres* are roundly rejected ('A ma ville, à ma famille, je sais ce que je dois. ... Je me sens solidaire de ma cité, de mes compagnons, de mon pays');[42] Proust ('Il m'aide à comprendre les hommes, certains hommes. Cela ne suffit pas pour aider à vivre') and Valéry[43] (' ... un grand écrivain', ' ... mais ni l'un ni l'autre n'en ont voulu dire davantage') are damned with faint

40. *Paris 1943 – Arts, Lettres*, Paris, 1943, p. 23.
41. Ibid., pp. 20–1.
42. Ibid., p. 188.
43. The nature of Valéry's problematic situation in respect of the ideology of Vichy France and of the Occupation is studied in an article by the present author, 'Ecrire sous l'Occupation: les *Mauvaises Pensées et Autres* de Valéry' (*Revue d'Histoire Littéraire de la France* 88ᵉ année, no. 6, pp. 1076–95). Valéry's well known 'Présence de Paris' (*Oeuvres*, II, pp. 1011–15, Gallimard, 'Bibliotheque de la Pléiade') is conspicuously absent from a volume whose centralising point of reference is a celebration of the capital's focal significance in cultural and artistic terms.

praise; Mauriac and Giraudoux implicitly stated as suspect by virtue of the controversy they provoke. The coming generation is stated to turn towards Péguy and his *Présentation de la Beauce à Notre-Dame de Chartres* ('Il y a dans ces vers pleins et fermes, comme malaxés dans de bonne argile, toute la solidité paysanne, tout le mysticisme profondément national dont j'éprouve le besoin. . . . Voilà un homme de chez nous'),[44] or to Claudel, whose work is seen to be of abiding national relevance (' . . . c'est un poète pour tous, je veux dire pour tous les Français, comme Péguy, parce qu'il est un poète de son terroir, un cher grand paysan champenois'), and the article concludes: 'Il semble, au total, que les jeunes gens d'aujourd'hui se détournent visiblement des stériles virtuoses de la pensée, des rhéteurs superficiels et de toute espèce de jeux gratuits pour chercher des enseignements et des mots d'ordre chez les écrivains dont la forte conscience terrienne leur livre une leçon d'énergie et de grandeur d'âme'.

Such sentiments bear a marked resemblence to those of de Falgairolle's article in the Vichy Almanac for 1941. Yet we should be wary of ascribing too great a degree of transparency to the text's relationship with the fact of its publication, as with that of its status as the official organ of a governmental institution. Discordant voices, charged with the prestige of what we now know to have been an attitude of unimpeachable national dignity and irreproachable patriotic conviction, such as that of Robert Desnos, whose typically symbolistic piece, 'Voici des fleurs', ends with a vision of coming regeneration (' . . . les roses . . . l'attente nocturne de la rosée et de l'aurore qui viendra laver ses doigts dans leurs ondes parfumées'), cut across impressions which we may have of a predominantly unilinear ideological discourse, and point to the potentially divergent interpretations which the volume's publication inherently solicits.

The status of novels or of extended recreations bearing on actual events during the period of hostilities between the outbreak of war and the Armistice, is also highly problematic, since it brings the ambiguity of effect which is generated by the statement of French national consciousness into contact with the implications of hostility, and a subsequent designation of 'the enemy'. As we have seen, the implications of legalised publication could be seen, on a primary level, to be necessarily dependent on a recognition, by the writer, of

44. *Paris 1943 – Arts, Lettres*, p. 189.

the political status quo, yet the very theme of open hostilities, so fresh in the national consciousness, proposes a conceptual background which tends naturally to negate that status quo. It is surprising, therefore, that this particularly fraught subject should not be one which is neglected: on the contrary, it becomes the fulcrum for explorations of self, community and nation, the ideal testing-ground for that vocation of risk, of potential transgression, or at the very least, of serried and intense debate with the occupying power, advocated by Grasset. Examples here are legion: some particularly pregnant texts which might be advanced as test cases or models of a problematic literary and ideological discourse, are François Reuter's *Le Chemin du stalag* (Marseille, Jean Vigneau, 1943, N° d'autorisation 1.655);[45] Robert Gaillard's *Les Liens de chaîne . . .* (Paris, Editions Colbert, 1942, Autorisation N° 15.937); Maurice Guierre's *Marine-Dunkerque* (Paris, Flammarion, 1942, Autorisation N° 11.068); or Capitaine Accart, *On s'est battu dans le ciel* (Paris, Arthaud, 1942 (N°ˢ de visa (illustrations) Q.o. 23731 à Q.o. 23748).

Such texts tend to follow either one or another of two possible experiential trajectories. The dramatic portrayal of war events, before defeat and Armistice, provides the novelist with fertile ground for the depiction of a state of catastrophe, of physical and psychological disarray, but the constant threat from elements of disorientation is forcefully counteracted by a still valid sense of national unity. The emphasis changes in texts devoted to a depiction of French experience subsequent to the Armistice: the erstwhile sense of unity becomes a nostalgia, attenuated by elements of physical (the Demarcation Line) or psychological division (separation from loved ones and traditional community), but fuelled at the same time by themes of hope and national regeneration, open to appropriation by both Vichy orthodoxy and Resistance ideologists. In both these cases, the writing treads a tightrope of acceptability, imbuing it with a particular urgency and resonance. The latter may also be seen as generated by proximity in time to the events described; with the passage of time, there comes a sense of distance, which can confer on the depiction of institutions presented earlier as sources of pride, a note of scepticism or of irony. This is particularly the case with the French military tradition: an ironic appreciation of army life by Jean Fougère, *Les Bovidés* (Paris, Editions du Pavois),

45. I have analysed this briefly in 'Writing under Vichy: Ambiguity and Literary Imagination in the Non-Occupied Zone', in R. Kedward and R. Austin (eds.), *Occupied France: Collaboration and Resistance 1940–1944*, pp. 260–64.

published in 1944 before the Liberation (Autorisation N° 19.872), is awarded the Prix Courteline for that year. The projection of the army type into the bovine species acts as a springboard for some highly imaginative and occasionally savage caricature, enhanced by the illustrations of Jo Merry; a concluding 'Eloge', however, converts the irony into a bantering tenderness, and transforms all that precedes by the context of uncomplaining self-sacrifice in death. It is interesting to note that the text, although published only in 1944, is ostensibly dated 'Juillet–Décembre 1940': the lapse in time between composition and publication would tend to suggest that the traumatic circumstances of defeat and occupation probably precluded satire of the army itself, if they did not preclude scarifying satire of those held to be politically responsible for the army's discomfiture. In effect, by 1944 the implications of legalised publication which had held true previously, are no longer operative. With the imminent reassertion of Republican values, de Falgairolle's advocacy of conservatism in theme and mimetic transparence in representation is shown to be anachronistic, the extension of a set of deeply compromised doctrines, which are on the point of being replaced; gone, too, are the circumstances favouring Daudet's uncertainty, or generating Grasset's espousal of a kind of writing which would be situated permanently on the knife-edge of political and ideological acceptability. By then, for some,[46] implications will have become consequences, and later, national degradation or outright retribution; for the many other authors, there will remain the unpredictable but abiding stigma of publication during the Occupation.

A final point, to be found recurring with significant insistency in the writing of this time, both legal and clandestine, provides my concluding comment, and a source, perhaps, of further reflection. It is the frequency of reference to the theme of absurdity, understood in the Camusian sense of the absence of signifying, meaningful parameters to experience, and traversing apparently incompatible ideological divides. Apart from *L'Etranger* itself, which proposes an

46. Loiseaux's lists of authors (*La littérature de la défaite et de la collaboration*, Paris, 1984, pp. 513–524), designated by the German authorities as either ideologically suspect (the 'Liste Bernhard') or sound (the 'Gesamtliste des fördernswerten Schrifttums bis zum 31–12–1942'), can usefully be complemented by lists of authors designated by the Comité National des Ecrivains as politically and ideologically undesirable (one such list can be consulted at the Bibliothèque des Archives Départementales, Clermont-Ferrand, document no. M.06116). As the present article aims to show, however, the implications of legalised publication at this time are just as significant for lesser known or less ideologically committed writers, as they are for writing which can be situated unequivocally in a specific ideological context.

unparalleled literary model in terms both of the articulation of
concepts and of narrative functioning, traces of one and the same
preoccupation can be perceived across a wide range of writing:
Saint-Exupéry, whose *Pilote de guerre* is fundamentally concerned
to revivify language and the concepts for which it acts as vehicle
('Notre vocabulaire semblait presque intact, mais nos mots, qui
s'étaient vidés de substance réelle, nous conduisaient, si nous
prétendions en user, vers des contradictions sans issue'),[47] in the
face of an experience of war which is repeatedly held to be devoid of
meaning ('Mais il est une impression qui domine toutes les autres au
cours de cette fin de guerre. C'est celle de l'absurde. Tout craque
autour de nous. Tout s'éboule. C'est si total que la mort elle-même
paraît absurde');[48] Brasillach, whose *Journal d'un homme occupé* is
redolent with a sense of radical disorientation, of a quest for a
generative kernel of meaningfulness (' . . . les plus enclins à ce genre
de sottises [illusions] ne parlaient point de l'avenir, faisaient
décemment leur métier, souvent absurde . . .';[49] 'Ces allées et ven-
ues, ces départs dans la nuit, alors que nous ne savions rien de
l'avance ennemie, donnent à ces journées une couleur absurde et
fantomatique',[50] ' . . . nous savions seulement que la retraite absurde pour nous était finie . . .')[51]; Anouilh, whose Créon in *Antigone*, first performed in February 1944, is incredulous at Antigone's
uncompromising rectitude in the face of what he sees as the respect
of a minor convention ('Et tu risques la mort maintenant parce que
j'ai refusé à ton frère ce passeport dérisoire, . . ., cette pantomime
dont tu aurais été la première à avoir honte. . . . C'est absurde!');[52]
Cassou's 'refus absurde' of the temptation of acquiscence;[53] Maurice Guierre's *Marine-Dunkerque*, where the writing is invested with
a permanent sense of the precarious and a thrust towards understanding, no less permanently denied (' . . . devant tant de jeunesse
fauchée, nous avons le coeur serré et nous cherchons vainement à
comprendre . . .');[54] and Vercors's narrator in *Le Silence de la mer*,
keenly aware of meaninglessness and of discrepancy (' . . . je me

47. Saint-Exupéry, *Pilote de guerre*, p. 238.
48. Ibid., p. 9.
49. Robert Brasillach, *Journal d'un homme occupé*, in Maurice Bardèche (ed.),
Oeuvres complètes de Robert Brasillach, Paris, p. 379.
50. Ibid., p. 391.
51. Ibid., p. 394.
52. Jean Anouilh, *Antigone*, London, 1954 (edited by W.M. Landers), p. 72.
53. Quoted by Kedward, *Occupied France*, p. 47.
54. Maurice Guierre, *Marine-Dunkerque*, Paris, 1942, p. 68.

sentis soulevé par une absurde colère: la colère d'être absurde et d'avoir une nièce absurde'),[55] which are consciously assumed as a source of refuge ('ce travail absurde était le seul sans doute qui pût encore s'accorder à son attention abolie, – et lui épargner la honte').[56]

The theme recurs with a haunting consistency across a very wide range of writing. Perhaps no other single element conspires as eloquently to defeat conditioned responses to the implications of legalised publication than this: the vision of absurdity, whatever its ideological context, strikes at the very roots of officially promulgated doctrines, aimed at the reinstatement of meaning and signifying patterns, or at justification and apology. The urgency of calls from Resistance writers, for a cleansing and affirmation of the French language in the face of foreign infiltration, acutely analysed by Ian Higgins,[57] is an aspect of this tendency: but there is undeniable evidence of a much more widespread dissatisfaction with language's ability to cope with reality, with the complex problems and pressures of French experience. Such statements of unease, to which Paulhan's postwar *Les Incertitudes du langage* is a significant pointer, are set in radically destabilising counterpoint to official voices which proclaim the regenerative virtues of traditional values and ways of life. A sense of pointlessness is seen to permeate all levels of existence, to corrode action and to paralyse initiative: the de facto recognition of such views through official publication and dissemination would tend to suggest incompetence or connivence in censorship, or a text so cleverly camouflaged that the deviant elements with which it is imbued are overshadowed by its surface adherence to orthodoxy. To publish legally in this context equates not to an act of betrayal or of unscrupulous opportunism, but to the expression of a deep despair, of experience adrift and uncontrollable; more, it could be seen as an attempt, conscious or unwitting, to neutralise or negate such absurdity, by its very formulation, in a way which appears to stand beyond the prescriptions of a specific set of beliefs or directives. The text could thus be seen to nurture within it the seeds of a deep autonomy, in respect of the conceptual

55. *Le Silence de la mer.* Paris, 1951, p. 48.
56. Ibid., p. 52.
57. See, *inter alia*, 'France, Soil and Language: Some Resistance Poems by Luc Bérimont and Jean Marcenac', in R. Kedward and R. Austin (eds.), *Occupied France*, pp. 206–21; and 'Tradition and Myth in French Resistance Poetry', in I. Higgins (ed.), *The Second World War in Literature*, pp. 45–58.

restraints which circumscribe it. But that autonomy can itself, in a final irony, be both deceptive and ambiguous: deceptive if one gives credence to the Barthian concept of a symbolic, ideologically motivated order, which 'writes the writer'; and ambiguous inasmuch as autonomy can only be defined in relation to the forces which engender it, and on which it is ultimately dependent for its own valid self-definition and self-designation; ambiguous, too, in so far as modern literary criticism has demonstrated how the text can acquire autonomy over its very author, once it is completed and disseminated in the intricacies of reader reception.

Such a process might help to explain, for example, how the works of Romain Rolland can be taken to task as undesirable both *during* the Second World War and *after* it: *during* the war, for the defeatist attitudes which Rolland's vision of a Franco-German empathy tends to foster; *after* the war, for his sometimes explicit elevation of German cultural and social achievement, or for what is perceived to be his betrayal of the French cause by the very notion of confraternity and a shared mystical communion, soured deeply by the bitter realities of collaboration, and criticised by Jean Paulhan[58] in defiance of Rolland's rehabilitation by the Comité National des Ecrivains. Such vagaries of reception, whatever may be their intrinsic validity, suggest that the destiny of texts might simply be the plaything of oscillating ideological trends, or worse, of snobby fads, an interpretation which has been given effective and ironic voice in Nathalie Sarraute's *Les Fruits d'or*. Some writers, perhaps more acute or self-aware than others, remain attuned to the perils, yet also the potentialities, of the writer–reader interface. An observation by Paul Valéry, written in 1898 in the secure privacy of his 'cahiers', addresses the focal point of a problem which will resurface for him in September 1942, with the publication of his *Mauvaises Pensées et*

---

58. Jean Paulhan, *De la paille et du grain*, Paris, 1948, pp. 79–80: 'Vous avez reconnu les deux thèmes de la propagande pan-germaniste, qu'allait reprendre bientôt la propagande hitlérienne: l'Allemagne a été attaquée, l'Allemagne est le pays de la droiture et du travail, que l'Europe jalouse. Vous paraît-il cette fois injuste ou inexact de dire que Romain Rolland, Français lui-même, trahit ce faisant la cause de la France?'; p. 138: ' . . . Rolland, lui, s'est fixé en Suisse, d'où il nous dit, nous écrit, nous laisse entendre de mille manières que notre cause à nous Français ne vaut pas mieux que la cause d'en face – et même vaut un peu moins. Est-ce là trahir la France? Est-ce mener une intrigue avec l'ennemi? Non. C'est très simplement trahir la *cause* de la France. En doutez-vous un instant? Imaginez donc Châteaubriant publiant à Genève, en pleine guerre, son *Au-dessus de la mêlée*: jetant au même sac Hitler avec Daladier, Churchill avec Goering. Qu'est-ce qu'on aurait dit? Qu'est-ce qu'on n'aurait pas dit? Bien sûr que "trahir la cause" eût paru mille fois trop faible.'

autres by Gallimard: 'Un auteur doit trembler en songeant aux motifs que tout lecteur de bon sens peut attribuer à son acte d'écrire' (*Cahiers*, C.N.R.S., volume I, p. 287). Beyond this aleatory, variable nature of the significance of writing and publication, there remains nevertheless the possibility of a given discourse's capacity to disconcert and to transgress the barrage of receptive phenomena to which it is necessarily subjected, to evoke in us, over and above the shifting displacements and permutations of ideological stance, a nostalgia for greater stability, which in old-fashioned terms might be called an ethical or moral awareness – a nostalgia which paradoxically resurfaces behind the initially cynical reply of the occupying authorities to Valéry's request for the paper necessary to publish the *Mauvaises Pensées*, eventually, indeed, to be published, with the full weight of censorship approval: 'Pourquoi n'écrit-il pas les Bonnes?. . .'.[59]

59. Paul Valéry, *Oeuvres*, Paris, 1957, vol. I, p. 67 ('Bibliothèque de la Pléiade').

11

CÉLINE

Colin Nettelbeck

> I get a splitting headache every time I try to write about
> Céline.
>
> Kurt Vonnegut Jr.

With the publication of *Voyage au bout de la nuit* in 1932, Louis
Ferdinand Céline (born L.F. Destouches in 1894) swept into French
literary history with rare and irresistible authority. In *Voyage*, the
delirious adventures of the anti-hero Bardamu serve as the base for a
hilarious and bitter satire of war, colonialism, the economic dreams
of the New World, and the decaying values of French society.
Above all, Céline introduced a new style of writing, creating,
through an amalgam of an immense range of verbal registers that
draw particularly on the structures and vocabulary of popular
speech, a language of staggering emotive power. Since then, he has
often been paired with Marcel Proust as the greatest of French
novelists of this century. Certainly, he is a larger-than-life figure,
and of all the French writers who espoused collaborationist ideas
under the German Occupation, he is probably the only one with
lasting claim to genius. His work has been translated into many
languages, and recognition of his importance, which might have
been expected to be difficult with one so compromised both politically and morally, has continued to increase with the passage of
time. The description coined by the early American critic Milton
Hindus remains apt: Céline is a 'crippled giant'.[1]
   The complicated individual case has been made even thornier by
numerous scholarly and critical studies demonstrating profound
symbolic links between Céline and his society, and showing in
particular that his virulent anti-Semitism and other pro-Nazi sym-

1. Milton Hindus, *The Crippled Giant*, New York, 1950.

pathies reflect values often quite generally shared by the French population at the time. In short, his attitudes were far from atypical, and any approach to this part of Céline's opus sooner or later engages one in the question of how France as a whole came, during the Occupation, to commit itself so fully and willingly to economic, political, intellectual and moral collaboration with the Hitlerian régime.

Only very recently has it become possible to coax apart some of the tangled strands of the Céline–Occupation nexus. The reasons for this are twofold. On the one hand, Céline's own biography remained for a long time frustratingly blurred. Although he had been tried and found guilty of collaboration in 1950, much of the detail of his wartime activities did not surface at the trial, and indeed, the trial itself was quickly forgotten after his amnesty and return from his Danish exile in 1951. Following the rebirth of wide public interest in his writing, which occurred in 1957 with the appearance of *D'Un Château l'autre*, it was only gradually that scholars and critics, working backwards from the postwar novels, and forwards from the early ones, started to research systematically the dark middle years. Only slowly, too, were essential documents – the correspondence, the newspaper articles, the archival material – uncovered and published. On the other hand, and analogously, the Occupation period in France has not easily yielded its secrets. Of course, if so much remained hidden for so long, it was because there was much to hide, from the personal shame or pain of individuals to the calculated obfuscations of political ambition. It is now clear, however, that the Occupation was a crucible in which fundamental and permanent change was wrought in all aspects of French society. It is also clear that Céline is a significant key to understanding a number of facets of that change, of which he was simultaneously victim, chronicler, and – somewhat paradoxically – one of its important agents.

When the Second World War broke out, Céline's situation had been less than stable for some time. Although the instant notoriety, and considerable fortune, that *Voyage au bout de la nuit* had brought him in 1932 might have suggested an assured and steady development of his literary career, his path had in fact proven erratic. The publication of his early and mediocre play, *L'Eglise* (1933), was an obvious attempt by his publisher Denoël to capitalise on the success of *Voyage*, and had added little, if anything, to the author's reputation. The polemical attack on the Soviet system that followed his trip to Russia, *Mea Culpa* (1936), which was joined in a single volume with his medical thesis on Semmelweis, was similarly anticlimactic. Both these texts, as well as being informative about their subject matter, would prove, in retrospect, to offer rich insight into some of Céline's artistic and ideological motivations. The deep uncertainties in his private life, as well as his confused reactions to the political and social ferment in France, also find their way into the prologue of his second novel, *Mort à crédit* (1936). The relatively unenthusiastic reception of this work devastated Céline. He had exhausted himself mentally and physically in its creation, and believed that, beyond the epic portrayal of life in turn-of-century France, he had achieved an unparalleled revitalisation of the French language. Dogged by accusations of obscenity which resulted in the book appearing with whole sections of the text truncated, and by general critical misunderstanding, he had to suffer the further humiliation of Denoël publishing a defence of the novel. Although he had begun *Casse-pipe*, the second volume of what was to be a saga about the apprenticeship in life of his protagonist Ferdinand, it was evident that serious and dangerous imbalance had emerged.

It is reasonable to consider 1937 as the turning-point, the beginning of what was to be a decade of disasters for Céline – disasters brought upon him by errors of judgement and by the stubborn wrong-headedness of his ideological choices, and compounded by the eruption of a latent persecution complex and an obsessional concern with material security. Well before the publication of *Bagatelles pour un massacre* at the end of that year, Céline's correspondence shows him building up towards the unbridled anti-Semitic outbursts contained in that pamphlet and its 1938 sequel, *L'Ecole des cadavres*. For those who recognise and enjoy the power of Céline's literary work, there is a temptation to try and diminish the importance of these pamphlets, by stressing their pacifist motivations, and by asserting that their chief target is less the Jews than French decadence. Such interpretations are not without basis, but it would require a particularly selective reading to avoid the conclusion that the mainspring of the works is a racist hatred that seeks intellectual justification in the combined theories of biological hierarchy (some races are 'purer' than others) and of world-power conspiracy (the Jews control the world). Anti-American and anti-English sentiment is explained in terms of the US and Britain being corrupted and dominated by the Jews, and opens the way to numerous expressions of pro-German – and explicity pro-Hitlerian – ideas. With these works, Céline set a course from which he would not deviate for several years, a course which was to coincide broadly with many of the policies of Vichy France, and with the ideology of the French Fascists of occupied Paris.

The publication of the pamphlets had negative consequences for Céline that both intensified his rage and confirmed his sense of paranoia. At the end of 1937, he was obliged to resign from the Clichy medical clinic where he had worked regularly since 1929, and also lost another medical position as adviser to a pharmaceutical laboratory. In both cases, the doctors in charge were Jewish, which fed Céline's fantasies of persecution. A defamation suit was brought against him in 1939 by a man he had – wrongly – accused of being Jewish, which led to a (modest) fine, and more importantly to the decision to withdraw both *Bagatelles* and *L'Ecole* from circulation. Céline's state of mind, and his astonishing thoughtlessness, can be gauged from a letter written in 1939 to a Jewish ex-friend who had informed him that her husband had died in a concentration camp:

> De mon côté mes petits drames ne sont rien comparés aux vôtres (pour le moment) mais cependant la tragédie est là . . .
> A la suite de mon attitude antisémitique j'ai perdu tous mes emplois (Clichy etc . . .) et je passe au Tribunal le 8 mars. Vous voyez que les Juifs aussi persécutent . . . hélas! Ici vous savez nous sommes littéralement envahis et de plus ils nous poussent ouvertement à la guerre. Je dois dire que toute la France est philosémite – sauf moi je crois – aussi évidemment j'ai perdu![2]

Céline's French biographer, François Gibault,[3] while consistently seeking to attenuate their impact, has brought to light a large number of vital – and very damaging – documents about Céline's wartime activities. For example, the writer's often repeated claim that when war broke out he volunteered for service is demonstrably spurious. His brief time as a ship's doctor on the *Chella*, a merchant ship later taken over by the navy, did lead to a temporary military rank, but there can be no doubt that he had taken the position at least as much for pecuniary as for patriotic reasons. When the *Chella* was put out of action by a collision with a British ship,

2. Colin Nettelbeck (ed.), *Cahiers Céline 5: Lettres à des amies*, Paris, 1979, p. 144.
3. François Gibault, *Céline*, vol. 2, '1932–1944: Délires et persécutions', Paris, 1985, passim.

Céline declined another offer from the same firm, and went back to work in suburban medical clinics.

Again, at the time of his trial, Céline declared that he had done nothing reprehensible during the war, and that if he did know some of the German authorities and French collaborationists, it was only in the most casual manner. In fact, the Gibault biography leads inexorably to the picture of a man most deeply involved. Already before the war, although his anarchistic spirit steered him away from membership in any organisations, Céline shared the ideology of a number of Fascist or proto-Fascist groups. He also knew personally and regularly frequented people like Marcel Déat, Alphonse de Châteaubriant, Lucien Rebatet and Robert Brasillach, who all became arch-collaborationists in occupied Paris. And during the Occupation, he dined often at the German Institute, whose director, Karl Epting, was both a close friend and a valued contact – among other things, Céline used him to obtain paper, a scarce commodity, for the printing of new editions of his anti-Semitic pamphlets. He was also close to Hermann Bickler, director of German political intelligence for Western Europe. It is unlikely that Céline, as some of his enemies claimed, was a Gestapo spy. But there is no doubt that he used his highly-placed German connections to obtain favours – for himself in the form of trips around occupied Europe or regular holidays in the restricted military zone on the coast of Brittany, or occasionally for others by obtaining the release of arrested friends or false papers to enable acquaintances to avoid the Obligatory Labour Service in Germany. At one stage, he was a serious contender for the position of head of the Commissariat générale aux questions juives – a position taken by Xavier Vallat, and then Darquier de Pellepoix. He corresponded with Captain Sézille, director of the Institut d'étude des questions juives, and indeed with most of the leading collaborationist journalists, and his letters were published across the whole range of the collaborationist press. He attended political meetings – including the 1942 demonstration in favour of the Légion des Volontaires Français. He gave speeches, and he wrote in support of Doriot and the Parti Populaire Français. In short his public – and collaborationist – profile was quite high. If he was clearly not as committed as a Brasillach or an Alain Laubreaux, he was just as clearly much more so than many other writers who continued to be active under the Occupation – the Gionos, Marcel Aymés, or Jean Anouilhs. Moreover, in his 1942 preface to the new edition of *L'Ecole des cadavres*, he lays explicit claim to his position. His pamphlet, he says, was 'the only text of the period (newspaper or book) *at one and the same time*: anti-Semitic, *racist*, collaborationist (before the word was invented) to the point of demanding an immediate military alliance, anti-English, anti-freemason, and predicting absolute catastrophe in the event of conflict.'[4]

There is no evidence that Céline was guilty of denouncing individuals – Jewish, Gaullist, or Communist – and indeed, he would appear at times to have helped such people.[5] Certainly he carried out his medical duties with the spirit of conscientious service that characterises his career as a doctor – treating the sick with a combination of compassion and the despairing conviction that humanity itself was some kind of incurable disease. But if such behaviour serves to underline the contradictions of his character, it is hardly cause for exoneration, the less so in that even when – towards the end of the Occupation – he backs away from some of his more violent expressions, there is no sign of any real change of heart. Gibault's remark[6] that he shocked some Germans by his outspoken eccentricity, sloppy clothing or lack of personal hygiene seems of marginal relevance to his general stance, and it is not surprising that his name was on the lists of those who, at the Liberation, would have to answer for their behaviour.

In his critical biography of Céline, Patrick McCarthy makes the point that had Céline been brought to justice closer to the Liberation, he would probably have received a sentence much stiffer than the one handed down at the 1950 trial.[7] It is very possible, however, that had he remained longer in Paris, he might simply have been assassinated, like his colleague in racism Georges Montandon. That is certainly what he feared – on the basis of a steady flow of threats received at his Montmartre home and on the Resistance radio – and in undertaking the flight that would lead him, his wife Lucette and his cat Bébert across the ruins of Germany to Denmark, he had no doubt that his life was at stake.

That journey, and Céline's subsequent exile, exacted a heavy toll. The fourteen months he spent in a Danish prison as an illegal immigrant kept him from the more threatening clutches of French justice, but they also contributed to the ruin of his health. The

---

4. *L'Ecole des cadavres*, Paris, 1942, p. 12 (Céline's italics, my translation.)
5. C.f. Gibault, *Céline*, pp. 270–2, 336–7.
6. Ibid., pp. 254–5.
7. Patrick McCarthy, *Céline: A Critical Biography*, London, 1975, p. 216.

protracted legal battles, as well as causing mental stress, also ate away much of the nest-egg he had put away in Denmark before the war. Back in France, the sale of his books was banned, so that, although a group of faithful admirers and friends – such as Nimier, Paulhan, Paraz and Aymé – were working up a momentum for his rehabilitation, he was subjected to pressures that would eventually rob him of any vestiges of dignity. It is thus fair to say that in personal terms, Céline received, albeit by chance rather than by design, a fairly harsh punishment for his collaborationist activities. If he fared better than other literati, like Brasillach or Luchaire, who were executed during the 'Epuration', he suffered more than many, including more flagrant cases than his own, like Alain Laubreaux or Darquier de Pellepoix, who enjoyed long and untroubled postwar 'retirements' in Spain.

In the light of these circumstances, Céline's phoenix-like postwar revival is especially striking. The more so, in that beyond the successful relaunching of *Voyage au bout de la nuit* and *Mort à crédit*, he created a whole new dimension of his opus. With *Féerie pour une autre fois* (1952, 1954), *D'Un Château l'autre* (1957), *Nord* (1960), and *Rigodon* (posthumous, 1969), despite various continuities with his pre-war literary production, Céline synthesised a visionary portrayal of the French experience of the Second World War, and in the process, advanced his stylistic invention to such an extent that these works stand out in a category of their own.

Underlying this renewal are two factors, one dependent on Céline's own inner disposition, the other on the change of perspective afforded by the Danish exile. In respect to the first, it is possible to argue, if not demonstrate, that Céline's commitment to his art remained a deeper, and stronger motivating force than his racist ideological beliefs. This is not to suggest that the latter were in any way marginal, simply that, in the extreme 'survival' situation he found himself in at the end of the war, he opted to sacrifice his ideology in order to save his art. There is a telling symbolic illustration of this choice in a recently published early version of *Féerie pour une autre fois*,[8] in which the narrator, on the day after the allied bombing of Montmartre, is depicted in the desperate position of an accused collaborationist looking for a way out. More significant than the distinction drawn between the narrator and a 'real' collaborationist – the *Je suis partout* cartoonist, Ralph Sou-

---

8. *Maudits soupirs pour une autre fois*, ed. by Henri Godard, Paris, 1985, passim.

pault, who is pictured as a comic bandit, armed to the teeth and ready to defend his ideas to the finish – is the fact that the narrator's main concern, and the principle guiding all his actions, is to find a safe place for his literary masterpieces. It is possible, of course, to see this text, which was written well after the event, in Denmark, as a more or less contrived self-portrait, by which the author might persuade others of the primacy of his artistic motivations. Although such manipulation was certainly not beyond Céline, it seems more reasonable to interpret it as an attempt by the writer to reassert and redefine his identity as a writer, in the wake of the upheavals experienced during the war. This is a complex matter, involving coming to terms both with the consequences of his own public ideological stance, and with a more general vision of the historical significance of events.

The tension between ideological and artistic commitments can readily be seen in the two major works that Céline actually wrote and published during the Occupation: *Les Beaux Draps* (1941) and the first volume of *Guignol's Band* (1944). The former continues the line of the political pamphlets; the latter opens the third part of the novel cycle he had begun with *Mort à crédit*. The account of the 'débâcle' in each of these works shows how differently the ideologue and the novelist approach the same material. In *Les Beaux Draps*, the narrative underlines the speed of the defeat, the collapse and rout of the French army, and the author exploits this image as a symbol of the generalised national decay which will become the main theme of the book. The humour – 'J'ai pourchassé l'Armée française de Bezons jusqu'à la Rochelle, j'ai jamais pu la rattraper'[9] – is tinged with a dark mixture of nostalgia and despair: 'Tout de même y a une grosse différence entre 14 et aujourd'hui. L'homme il était encore nature, à présent c'est un tout retors. Le troufion à moustagache, il y allait "comptant bon argent" maintenant il est roué comme potence, rusé pitre et sournois et vache . . .'[10] The perception of reality, and particularly of time, is entropic: 'Aux cendres le calendrier! Plus rien ne pèse! plumes d'envol! Au diable lourds cadrans et lunes!'[11] And throughout, the narrator's position if that of judge, rather than witness, of the situation portrayed.

In the opening of *Guignol's Band*, on the other hand, where the exodus of 1940 is again evoked, the narrator is in the midst of the

9. *Les Beaux Draps*, Paris, 1941, p. 11.
10. Ibid., p. 20.
11. Ibid., pp. 220–1.

action, and on the same level as everyone else, a part of, and not apart from the experience of history. This is the first manifestation of what will become a major element of the formal organisation of Céline's postwar novels – the creation of a narrator-chronicler whose eye-witness involvement in historical events is integral to the novelist's creation of a poetic vision of the dynamics of history. At the same time, it marks a significant shift from the nihilism of *Les Beaux Draps*, where the historical dilemma was presented as an end in itself, without anything to counterbalance it. In *Guignol's Band*, although the theme of the end of a certain France is still strongly present, it is used, structurally, as the way of beginning the novel. This opening section combines in fact all the major elements of composition of the post-war novels: the historico-mythical dimension, the narrator-chronicler, and the 'telegraphic' writing. The language owes much to the pamphlets, where Céline had forged a style principally designed as an offensive ideological weapon, and hence capable of being targeted onto a wide range of experience, collective as well as individual. Abstracted from its original function, it will remain a powerful tool, capable of rendering the scope of a major historical change.

But *Guignol's Band* as a whole is not integrated with its 'prologue'. The experiences recounted, which centre around the coming to manhood of the protagonist Ferdinand in the London of the First World War, although thematically and symbolically related to the Second World War events of the prologue, are very much retrospective, still belonging to the *Mort à crédit* cycle: that is, to an ethos and a vision elaborated before what Céline would come to call the 'Deluge'. It is surely no accident that once in Denmark, the novelist should abandon *Guignol's Band*, whose second volume was already virtually completed, in order to devote himself to *Féerie pour une autre fois* and the last novel sequence. The direct experience of the Montmartre bombing and the physical flight across war-torn Europe had provided him not only with new material, but with a radical shift of viewpoint. From being inside France, a prisoner of a particular set of historical circumstances, he is projected outside, into a wider sense of history, and to a distance such that the specifically French experience diminishes in importance. And in addition, the point of observation of the Deluge is post-diluvian, presupposing the actual survival of the world whose destruction had been feared. It is the move from absolute imprisonment to relative freedom, from apocalypse to a modest sense of continuation that shapes the development of the last novels.

Within the framework of Céline's own opus, the narrative from *Féerie* to *Rigodon* traces both a personal liberation and the affirmation of a liberating aesthetic. The personal liberation is evident in terms of the most basic experience portrayed: in *Féerie*, the author describes his imprisonment in Denmark, and the constantly renewed threats of death – either from the bombing, or from those who have branded him as a traitor; in *Rigodon*, on the other hand, he gathers the more positive motifs of the intervening novels, and presents his protagonists finding their way to a Denmark representing safety and survival, if not serenity. But the theme of liberation has a more extensive sense. In the symbolic images[12] of a collapsing France (*Féerie*), of the ridiculous and dramatic shrinking of French power in Sigmaringen (*D'Un Château l'autre*), of the fall of the New Europe (*Nord*), and of the future being, if at all, in the hands of a band of mentally defective youths (*Rigodon*), there is a kind of perverse, and subversive, delight. For the civilisation that Céline shows in its unravelling is precisely the one that he attacked so vehemently in his early novels, and in his pamphlets, for its hypocritical values, its absurd and bellicose nationalism, its materialistic ruthlessness, its brutal injustices. If, in his post-war novels, he is able to leave both his pamphlets and his early novels behind, it is because he sees the war itself as having completed much of the task of 'decomposition' he had set himself.[13]

From an aesthetic point of view, the choice of a resolutely comic mode ensures that the thematic transformations – prison/freedom, death/life – do not suffer from any facile sentimentality. In his prewar novels, and in his pamphlets, Céline's humour was unremittingly black, and subordinated to a vision of tragic futility: his protagonists, caught in hopeless situations, were obliged to struggle, but for no purpose. In the later novels, the futility and hopelessness are still there, but not the frustration. Whether one considers the narrator-in-the-present, roaring his abuse at the post-war world from his Danish prison or his Meudon villa, or the chronicler

12. C.f. Colin Nettelbeck, 'Un Art conscient: structures, symboles et significations dans les derniers romans', in *L.-F. Céline 2*, Revue des lettres modernes, 1976, pp. 99–119.
13. See his letters to Elie Faure in *L.-F. Céline*, ed. de l'Herne, 1972, pp. 69–78. Especially: 'Nous sommes tous en fait absolument dépendants de notre société. C'est elle qui décide notre destin – Pourrie, agonisante est la nôtre . . . Hâter cette décomposition, voici l'oeuvre – Et qu'on n'en parle plus!' (p. 73).

leading the reader on a rickety and often broken journey through the past, the sense of history which emerges is one in which human intervention seems trivial and theatrical, utterly without moment. Against the dark vestiges of realism that are important elements in the early work, the novelist pushes towards an ever greater blurring of edges, chronological, psychological, and in his telling of events, in order to produce effects that are both emotionally powerful and strongly cathartic. Questions of particular comportment, of guilt or of innocence, of collaborationism or not, etc, are raised in the texts, but in a context which dissolves their significance. As an example, one has only to consider the treatment of the town of Sigmaringen in *D'Un Château l'autre*, where the particular adventures of the collaborationist rump are distended and merged into a sweeping vision of European history since the Renaissance; and where the castle, the hotel, and the railway station are transformed into microcosmic symbols of a world in ferment. Within this context, Céline's acts or attitudes during the Occupation do not disappear, but they become signally less preoccupying.

Céline's contribution to the postwar ethos in France is two-fold. On the one hand, by re-establishing himself, a convicted collaborationist, in a position of eminence as a novelist, he is not unlike Jean Genet, a constant source of disturbance and questioning, who obliges the public to confront an experience that is both abhorrent and undeniably authentic. It is of course possible to read Céline's work as being essentially autobiographical, and to see one of its major achievements as being the account it gives of a whole, but individual, existence.[14] In embracing so explicitly the times and places where personal experience intersects with the great turmoils of the war and its aftermath, however, the narratives from *Féerie* to *Rigodon* invite a wider interpretation. Céline is quite different from Genet in that he lays claim to being something of a historical seer,[15] and even when he fragments the history of the war, it is in the interests of another version, another vision of history, which by pouring derision on any simplistic account of French behaviour during the Occupation, becomes a permanent cautionary presence.

On the other hand, and ultimately more importantly, there is Céline's linguistic and literary legacy. In this area, his work on the

14. This is the view espoused by Henri Godard, in his *Poétique de Céline*, Paris, 1985.

15. See, for example, *Nord*, in *Romans 2*, Paris, 1974, p. 525: 'Je peux dire, sans me vanter, que le fil de l'Histoire me passe part en part, des nuages à ma tête, á l'anu . . .'

novel as genre has received extensive attention, as has his revolutionising of French literary language. In respect to language, he is of course not alone. Since the mid-nineteenth century, a broadening movement – which must include the major manifestations of the literary avant-garde from Rimbaud and Mallarmé, Jarry and the birth of 'pataphysics, to Apollinaire and the surrealists, Queneau, Boris Vian and the Oulipo group – has sought to break open the fixed forms in which the French written language had, over the centuries, progressively been enclosed. Céline recognised the influence of Henri Barbusse – for his use of the spoken idiom – and Paul Morand – 'le premier de nos écrivains qui ait *jazzé* la langue française'[16] – but they too are part of a wider thrust to free syntax and lexicon from their classical constraints, and to create a language more adapted to the experience of an immensely changed world. If, in this long resurgence of the collective imagination, Céline stands out, it is partly because of the sheer scope of his production, and partly because of the intensity of energy he managed to maintain, right to his last work. It would not seem exaggerated to say that with Céline, the linguistic revolution ceases to be a marginal or avant-garde phenomenon, and is integrated into the mainstream of the ongoing French literary tradition as a permanent landmark, for among many others, writers as different from him (and from each other) as Alain Robbe-Grillet, Jean-Marie Leclézio or Patrick Modiano, in seeking to define their own identities and purpose as writers, use his example of stylistic renewal as their most significant point of reference.

In terms of his more general contribution to the novel, there is simply no post-Proustian French writer of his stature. If comparisons are to be made, it has to be with Joyce, Heller, Pynchon, Grass, Márquez – with those novelists who, whatever their personal driving-force or vision, have been able to create new fictional forms, and open new imaginative possibilities for the western novel. That Céline should have been an artistic revolutionary does not, of course, excuse his reactionary and racist political stance, and one does not forgive Céline his anti-Semitism simply because he is a great writer. Nor can one merely take the novels for what they are and ignore the rest, since the novels – and particularly the last ones – are inextricably tied in with the wartime experience. Indeed, when one considers the degree to which the language of the racist pam-

---

16. Letter to Milton Hindus, in *L.-F. Céline*, l'Herne, pp. 114–15.

phlets had contributed to the novelist's stylistic evolution, one is drawn to speculate – though it is impossible to verify – that his xenophobia may have been part of the same energy pattern guiding his linguistic innovation, the defence of the French language being fused with a defence of some deeper sense of French identity ... In the end, the price of reading Céline is concomitant with the rewards: to enjoy the vision, the humour, the revolutionary vitality of the language – all the elements that compose such an original and striking style – is also to suffer the discomfort of recognising the more shameful dimensions of the author's work. Perhaps it is not unreasonable to follow Sartre's sanguine tightrope walk: before the war, Sartre had had no qualms about choosing as an epigraph for his own first novel (*La Nausée*, 1938), a text from Céline's *L'Eglise*, though one of the acts of the play is blatantly anti-Semitic; in his immediate postwar 'Portrait de l'Antisémite' (1945),[17] he accuses Céline of being in the pay of the Germans – an accusation of treason which at the time could have had lethal consequences; a few years later, still in the context of his 'littérature engagée' crusade, he makes a remarkable concession: 'Peut-être Céline demeurera seul de nous tous.'[18]

17. In *Les Temps modernes*, 3, 1 Dec. 1945. Reprinted in *Réflexions sur la question juive*, Paris, 1947.
18. In *Les Temps modernes*, 33 Jun., 1948, p. 2121.

12

MARCEL AYMÉ AND THE
DARK NIGHT OF THE OCCUPATION

Nicholas Hewitt

A significant feature of French postwar politics has been the way in which all major political parties, of the Right and Left, established their legitimacy in a particular view of the Occupation, the Resistance and the Liberation. That view is summed up by Colin Nettelbeck in Chapter 15 (esp. p. 256) on the rectification of what he terms the 'Gaullian' myth of the period, but which is, in reality, a general concensus perception of the events adhered to by all parties. As Nettelbeck shows, the death of de Gaulle in 1970 acted as a release which enabled the unsayable to be articulated at last: novelists like Modiano and Tournier and film-makers such as Marcel Ophuls and Louis Malle began to show a much more complex and more unflattering view of the behaviour of the French during the Occupation, albeit at the cost of establishing a politically dubious 'mode rétro'.

In fact, as Nettelbeck himself suggests, it was the Fourth Republic gradually and then the Fifth Republic which imposed this orthodox perception of the period: at the very beginning of the post-Liberation era, novelists, often with impeccable Resistance credentials, were more than willing to point to the complexity and ambiguity of the entire experience. Thus, Jean-Louis Bory, in *Mon Village à l'heure allemande*, of 1945, gives a painfully complete picture of the behaviour of an entire community under the Occupation, while Jacques Perret, in *Bande à part* (1946), emphasises the almost absurd gratuitousness of Resistance activity. Finally, the very title of Roger Vailland's Resistance-novel, *Drôle de jeu* (1945) and its highlighting of the Don Juanesque comportment of its hero, hardly coincides with the orthodox Communist celebration of the FTP, the 'Parti des fusillés' and its martyrs, Gabriel Péri and Colonel Fabien. Similarly, the ambiguities of the Occupation experience were played upon by the novelists of the New Right, particularly the 'Hussards' group of Jacques Laurent and Roger Nimier, who chose, in novels like Laurent's *Le Petit canard* of 1954, and Nimier's *Les Epées*, of 1948, and *Le Hussard bleu*, of 1950, to counter the orthodox myth with emphasis on the complexity of personal experience and the arbitrary nature of commitment.

Yet these writers, of the Right and the Left, had one distinguished precursor who, even during the Occupation itself, was acutely aware of the bewildering *obscurity* of life under the Germans. In a number of short stories and novels published under the Occupation and in its immediate aftermath, Marcel Aymé established as his own a particular area of ambiguity which subsequent novelists would then explore: the inherent difficulty in perceiving events and motivations from the midst of a historical situation and, especially, the unique weakness of the French bourgeoisie and its dominant philosophy of liberal humanism to come to terms with an historical reality which challenged it at its very base. In this sense, whereas for other commentators, like the liberal Jean Guéhenno, the Occupation constituted a succession of 'années noires',[1] a period of moral and political gloom and shame, Aymé uses the metaphor of darkness to characterise the period from 1940 onwards, but in a much more literal and perceptual sense, denoting confusion, bewilderment and, ultimately, the dark recesses of the human personality itself.

Marcel Aymé was born in Joigny in the Department of the Yonne in 1902, but his childhood was spent in his father's native province of the Jura which was to become the setting of so much of his later fiction. After his military service in Occupied Germany in the years 1922 and 1923, he moved to Paris where he worked as a journalist in a news agency. His ambition to become an engineer was cut short by a serious illness and it was at this time that his literary career began. As he recalls in one of his rare autobiographical statements: 'En 1925, comme j'étais tombé malade, j'ai profité de ma convalescence pour écrire un premier roman intitulé *Brûlebois*'.[2] The success of this first novel led to his being taken up by the publishing house of Gallimards, with the help of Pierre Bost and Germaine Paulhan,[3] and thereafter, until his death in 1967, Aymé pursued an

1. Jean Guéhenno, *Journal des années noires*, Paris, 1947.
2. Marcel Aymé, 'Les Jours', in Pol Vandromme, *Aymé*, Paris, 1960, p. 44.
3. See ibid., p. 44.

uninterrupted career as a professional writer, producing a massive amount of writing in the form of novels, short stories, essays and plays. Yet, whilst this writing brought him early success and later prestige, it never led to serious critical appraisal: few major writers of the period are so little explored and critically valued. Clearly, one reason for this lack of critical attention is political: Aymé was a right-wing writer who published in the collaborationist press during the Occupation and who suffered the subsequent critical neglect of his work in the post-war period which was the fate of all collaborationist writers, albeit for an unequal and arbitrarily-determined period. Nor has Aymé's reputation been particularly helped by the enthusiastic support of right-wing literary critics such as Pol Vandromme, in spite of his attempt to render the Right more cosy and appealing by calling it 'la droite buissonnière'.[4] Undoubtedly, in the period 1940–4, Marcel Aymé sailed very close to the wind indeed: his novel *Travelingue*, which appeared to be a biting denunciation of the Front Populaire, was published in 1942, after having been serialised in Brasillach's *Je suis partout*, and throughout the period of the Occupation, Aymé published a stream of short stories and novels in serial form in *Je suis partout* and Alphonse de Châteaubriant's *La Gerbe*,[5] right up until the Allied landings of June 1944. As Aymé himself admitted later, this literary Collaboration could have had far more serious consequences at the Liberation: 'Pendant l'Occupation, je donnai des romans et des nouvelles à *Je suis partout* et à *La Gerbe*. A la Libération, j'ai eu de la chance qu'on ne me mette pas en prison et qu'on se contente de me maltraiter dans les journaux.'[6]

Nevertheless, there is some considerable ambiguity in Aymé's

4. See Pol Vandromme, 'Le Géomètre de l'absurde', in *La Droite buissonnière*, Paris, 1960, pp. 129-40.

5. Aymé's contributions to *La Gerbe* and *Je suis partout* in the period 1940–4 were as follows: *La Gerbe*: 'La Carte, extraits du journal de Jules Flegman. Nouvelle inédite de Marcel Aymé' (2 April 1942); serialisation of *La Vouivre* (22 July 1943 to 9 December 1943); reply to the questionnaire: 'Les Elites françaises devant le sacage de la France' (13 July 1944). *Je suis partout*: Serialisation of *Travelingue* (20 September 1941 to 17 January 1942); 'Chas-Laborde illustrateur'(31 July 1942); 'Brillat-Savarin illustré par Ralph Soupault' (21 August 1942); 'Légende Poldève. Nouvelle inédite de Marcel Aymé' (2 October 1942); 'Les Danseuses de Jodelet. Nouvelle inédite de Marcel Aymé' (20 November 1942); serialisation of 'Les Sabines'. Nouvelle inédite de Marcel Aymé' (8 January 1943–22 January 1943); 'La Patte de chat. Nouvelle inédite de Marcel Aymé' (28 May 1943); 'Avenue Junot. Nouvelle inédite de Marcel Aymé' (13 August 1943); 'Trois illustrateurs montmartrois, par Marcel Aymé' (25 November 1943); 'Grace. Nouvelle inédite de Marcel Aymé' (2 June 1944).

6. Marcel Aymé, 'Les Jours', p. 44.

activity during the Occupation which makes it difficult to use political criteria alone as a reason for his subsequent eclipse. In the first place, the leaders of the literary Resistance after the war appear to have been uncertain as to the best way in which to deal with the case of Aymé: his name appears on none of the blacklists of proscribed writers published by *Les Lettres Françaises* in their editions of 9 September 1944, 16 September 1944 and 21 October 1944, in spite of a vote in favour of his inclusion by the journal's director Claude Morgan.[7] This uncertainty was due in large part to the fact that Aymé's collaboration was exclusively literary, rather than ideological, and in many ways conflicted with the ideology of collaboration, and to conscious attempts to disinculpate himself whilst still writing for the collaborationist press. Thus, on the question of anti-Semitism, Marcel Aymé stood out throughout the Occupation against the prevailing right-wing ideology. As Roger Nimier comments: 'Marcel Aymé, bien qu'il soit assez bête en matière de politique, n'est past antimsémite,[8] and Georges Robert and André Lioret point to a more fundamental concern on Aymé's part with justice: 'Il prit la défense des Juifs sous l'occupation allemande à Paris, et engagea la campagne en faveur de Maurice Bardèche, condamné à un an de prison pour son livre *Nuremburg ou la terre promise*.'[9] In Aymé's story 'En Attendant', in the collection *Le Passe-Muraille*, published in 1943, a queue of Parisians waiting for their meagre ration of bread, air their grievances. In the midst of lengthy complaints about rationing, housing, fuel shortages, which provide a concise kaleidoscope of the Parisian Occupation experience, there is the single lapidiary line: 'Moi, dit un Juif, je suis Juif'.[10]

Nevertheless, if Aymé's denunciation of French anti-Semitism during the Occupation testifies to considerable political independence and courage, other declarations and procedures point to more strategic concerns. At the very end of the Occupation, in June and July 1944, *La Gerbe* published a two-part investigation on the attitudes of major personalities towards Allied bombing of French targets, 'Les Elites françaises devant le sacage de la France'. In the second of these surveys, which appeared on 13 July 1944, Marcel Aymé commented: 'Pour nous consoler, disons-nous que la de-

---

7. See Claude Morgan, *Les 'Don Quichotte' et les autres*, Paris, 1979, p. 163.
8. Roger Nimier, 'Marcel Aymé', in *Journées de lecture*, Paris, 1965, p. 41.
9. Georges Robert, André Lioret, *Marcel Aymé insolite*, Paris, 1958, p. 16.
10. Marcel Aymé, 'En attendant', in *Le Passe-muraille*, Paris, 1943.

struction de tant de quartiers pittoresques et photogéniques est en
même temps celle d'ignobles taudis où des centaines de milliers de
Français croupissaient sans air ni lumière, à l'ombre des notaires et
des probloes rogneux',[11] a reply which brought an angry and
bewildered response from *La Gerbe* itself. At the same time, Céline,
who had contributed an equally disconcerting reply to the *La Gerbe*
survey and was himself no amateur at self-defence, reacted violently
to Aymé's use of him as a character in certain of his stories in order
to disinculpate himself. In the recently-published fragment *Maudits
soupirs pour une autre fois*, Céline depicts Aymé under the name of
Marc Empième and comments:

> il m'en a foutu deux trois coups là qu'étaient vachards . . . des vapes dans
> ses contes, des soi-disant burlesqueries, des petites nouvelles mine de
> rien . . . où je me promène gentiment servi . . . "Mort aux Juifs" que je
> hurle par hasard, comme ça pour faire rire le monde . . . Pas mieux pour
> me faire assassiner . . . le monde comprend la plaisanterie . . . il est
> facétieux au possible . . . Ça m'a fait de la peine tout d'abord, et puis j'en
> ai vu tellement d'autres . . . je lui en ai voulu à Marc . . . enfin deux trois
> jours . . . le temps que j'ai dans mes rancunes . . . Seulement au moment
> n'est-ce pas, dans *Je suis partout* où il écrivait, ça faisait une coquine
> d'impression, ça m'atigeait un peu plus, lui il se dédouanait du même
> coup . . . la preuve qu'il s'en est bien tiré . . .[12]

Certainly, in Aymé's story in *Le Passe-muraille*, 'En Attendant',
Céline figures amongst the disgruntled Parisians vociferating against
the Jews, and in 'Avenue Junot', which appeared in *Je suis partout*
on 14 August 1943, Aymé uses the opportunity of an evocation of
the painter Gen-Paul's studio in Montmartre to provide a pastiche
of Céline's spoken style:

> 'Salut les hommes, vous avez vu ça, les journaux, ils nous balancent un
> drôle de bignolage, une fanfare au caillé noir qui baratine l'enfer dans les
> petites têtes de trèpe, qu'avant six mois, oui mes vaches, avant six mois,
> les tinettes à Lebrun, elles dégorgeront du sang frais et de la fricassée et
> du mutilo et vas-y Durand, mes tripes d'un côté, mes gambilles de
> l'autre, Löwenstein à Valparaiso, et marrez-vous bien, la merde qui
> monte, plus d'hommes, plus de Francecaille, un dernier glouglou, un joli
> glouglou bien merdeux, fini, plus question. En attendant, sus aux bar-
> bares, sonnez clairons, emballez mes os et plantez un saule'.

11. *La Gerbe*, 13 July 1944, p. 4
12. L.-F. Céline, *Maudits soupirs pour une autre fois*, Paris, 1985, p. 156.

Céline prit respiration.[13]

It is doubtful, however, even without this exculpatory device, whether political stances alone would have accounted for the relatively low critical standing of Aymé's work. Céline himself was rehabilitated in the 1970s, along with other collaborationist writers such as Drieu la Rochelle and even Rebatet and Brasillach. Rather, the answer lies elsewhere, in the gap between Aymé's status as a genuinely popular writer, as testified to by his success in paperback, the presence of his work in anthologies and the number of feature films based upon his fiction, and critical recognition, and this can only be explained by sociological and aesthetic factors. It is essential, for example, that Aymé's work be seen in the context of the culture of Montmartre in the inter-war years and the immediate post-war period: it was to Montmartre that Aymé, the 'peasant' novelist, immediately gravitated when he came to Paris in the 1920s and it was on the Butte de Montmartre that he lived for the rest of his life. As a Montmartrois in the inter-war years, he was a member of a well-defined if largely forgotten artistic community. The great days of the pre-war 'Bohème' had gone: the Cubist bandwagon had rolled on and it was now Montparnasse which was the capital of the avant-garde and the Left Bank in general which was the centre of intellectual life.[14] Nevertheless, there remained in the 'village' of Montmartre, which looked down upon the 'cosmopolitain' city beneath, a group of writers and artists which constituted in its way as a vibrant a community as its more publicised Left Bank equivalent. This group was made up of novelists such as Pierre Mac Orlan, Roland Dorgelès, Francis Carco, Céline and Aymé himself; painters like Pascin, Vlaminck and Gen-Paul; the actor Robert Le Vigan; and, crucially, illustrators and caricaturists, Gus Bofa, Chas-Laborde, Daragnès and the cartoonist for *Je suis partout*, Ralph Soupault. These figures, who congregated in the Restaurant Manière in the rue Caulaincourt, in the same way that the Left Bank writers met in the Flore or the Deux Magots, shared certain essential characteristics: they were all representatives of a certain Bohemianism in which the anti-bourgeois stance had turned to anti-radicalism and anti-republicanism; many were Ancien Combattants and

13. Marcel Aymé, 'Avenue Junot', *Je suis partout*, 13 August 1943, pp. 3-4. Ironically, Céline knew what he was talking about, having destroyed Gen-Paul's reputation through much the same procedures in *Bagatelles pour un massacre*.
14. See Herbert R. Lottman, *La Rive gauche*, Paris, 1981.

brought to bear a mixture of patriotism and pacifism which, again, predisposed them towards the political Right; most crucially, the influence of the humourists and caricaturists amongst them led to a development of the whimsical and fantastic which became one of the hall-marks of Montmartre writing during the inter-war years.

If Marcel Aymé's status as a Montmartre writer renders him immediately unfashionable and tends to obscure the importance of his work, these characteristics of Montmartre writing point to aesthetic elements at the heart of Aymé's fiction which act as a further barrier. His literary reputation has been dominated by his novel of 1933, *La Jument verte*, which immediately served to categorise him as a 'Rabelaisian' author, specialising in scenes of peasant ribaldry. As Roger Nimier comments: 'Marcel Aymé fut découvert par le grand public avec *La Jument verte*. On le prit pour un auteur gaulois et la confusion fut si forte qu'il s'y trompa lui-même.'[15] This marginalisation of Aymé was compounded by his use of the Jura as a privileged setting in a large body of his fiction (of which *La Vouivre* is the best example), which automatically rele-gates him to the status of regional novelist. Most important, how-ever, of all the barriers to authentic critical understanding of Aymé's fiction is that characteristic device of Montmartre culture, the blending of realism and fantasy, and this, for Nimier, is Aymé's major transgression: the critic is perfectly willing to accept the use of the fantastic in fiction which uncomplicatedly announces itself as exclusively fantastic, but 'ce qui devient insensé, c'est l'insertion du merveilleux dans la vie quotidienne'.[16] Aymé's starkly realist fiction is at the same time peopled with characters who walk through walls ('Le Passe-muraille'), produce paintings which alleviate hunger ('La Bonne peinture'), or spend half their life on the coldest and most malevolent planet in the solar system (*Uranus*), and the lesson has been imperfectly absorbed by his critics. The fact is that the proce-dure of introducing fantasy into realistic portrayal tends to occur most in Aymé's fiction when he is attempting to evoke particularly bleak and complex historical situations and is therefore a natural device in the depiction of the Occupation and the historical period surrounding it. As such, rather than constituting a gratuitous blend of two irreconcilable registers, the introduction of fantasy into realism is an important manoeuvre: at its most basic level, it pro-

15. Roger Nimier, *Journées de lecture*, pp. 56-57.
16. Ibid., p. 47.

vides indispensable camouflage for an author approaching politically dangerous subject-matter; more centrally, the clash between the fantastic and the realistic is also that between the universal and the socially-specific: it enables Aymé to adopt a vantage-point from which historical detail may be portrayed in a broader moral and metaphysical context; finally, it is arguable that this deliberate infringement of artistic laws is the only way in which the *strangeness* of the historical situation itself may be chronicled, the only way in which the unwritable may be articulated. In this context, Aymé's most faithful imitator is undoubtedly the American novelist Kurt Vonnegut who, in *Slaughterhouse 5*, can only convey the inherent otherness of the bombing of Dresden by juxtaposing realist autobiography with science fiction. Aymé's portrayal of the 'années noires', therefore, is made up both of documentary material, often of considerable value for the historian of the period, and of the more disturbing connotations of darkness itself, fantasy, dreams and nightmares.

Of all Marcel Aymé's work published during the Occupation, it was his novel *Travelingue* which was the least likely to endear him to the Comité National des Ecrivains and *Les Lettres Françaises* after the war. The novel was serialised in *Je suis partout* from 20 September 1941 to 17 January 1942, with an enthusiastic advance notice by Brasillach on 13 September 1941. When the novel appeared in volume form it also received a warm review from Gonzague Truc, writing in *La Gerbe* on 22 January 1942. Nor is it difficult to see why the work should have so appealed to the extreme French Right: on one level, at least, it reads as a straightforward satire on the Front Populaire and the Radical Republican politics of the inter-war years which produced it. Aymé charts the downfall of a powerful bourgeois dynasty at the time of the Front Populaire: the Lasquin family, owners of an ill-defined factory in the suburbs of Paris, are weakened, first by the death of the paterfamilias at the dinner party which opens the novel and subsequently by the marriage of the daughter, Micheline, to Pierre Lenoir, the son of a fellow-industrialist, whose interest is directed not to the world of commerce at all but to his one passion, athletics. The destruction of the family, however, is consummated by their meeting with the Ancelots who combine deviousness bordering on criminality, emotional weakness, snobbishness and intellectual pretension – summed up by their ecstatic belief that the most banal scene would obtain beauty in filmic terms if only translated by a tracking-shot, the 'travelingue' from which the novel takes its title. It is through the wife and daughters of Ancelot that Aymé mercilessly satirises the fashionable Parisian Left of the 1930s, with their worship of the cinema, particularly in its Soviet form, their empty intellectual jargon and their confused enthusiasm for all things proletarian, a confusion in which eroticism and pretension are equally mixed. In *Travelingue*, therefore, Marcel Aymé shows the destruction of a solid, successful and unreflective bourgeois family through its rapid infiltration by an inauthentic world of ideas and art. In this way, he produces a burlesque version of Thomas Mann's *Buddenbrooks*, in which equally a bourgeois dynasty is destroyed by art, and he looks forward to the ideas he will develop in more detail in the fictionalised essay *Le Confort intellectuel*, of 1949, where Romanticism is attacked by the protagonist, M. Lepage, for standing at the head of an entire modern tradition of misuse of language. In other words, from his vantage-point of the débâcle of 1940, Aymé is able to depict the French bourgeoisie of the inter-war years which has both given rise to the intellectual underpinning of the Front Populaire and has weakened itself to the extent that it is unable to resist it. The implication in 1941 and 1942 as the novel appeared is that this bourgeoisie, which had replaced its sense of order and rightness by confusion and pretension and self-doubt, was even less able to oppose the Germans in 1940. Indeed, the fate of Aymé's family, the Lasquins, is such that they can only be saved from the scandal which threatens to destroy them by the miraculous intervention of a fantastic deus ex machina: a barber, Félicien Moutot, who apparently wields supreme power in France, dispatching orders to all the ministries from his shop near the Gare de l'Est and holding cabinet meetings in his back room. This creation of the all-powerful barber is a typical Aymé device. Its fantastic qualities stem from the pushing to logical extremes of a familiar phenomenon, in this case, the traditional monologue of the barber to his client in which he comments upon the political situation of the day and sets it to rights. The novel itself closes with just such a monologue. What Aymé has done, however, is to translate that monologue into concrete reality: the barber Moutot is no longer a mere commentator but possesses the power behind his language. Clearly this serves, not merely a comic and fantastic, but also a bitterly satirical purpose: the barber, the representative of the common man, but also with sinister overtones of the 'homme providentiel', is the only figure who can restore order to a nation whose politics have run out of control.[17]

Yet, if Aymé's publishers and critics were correct in seeing *Travelingue* as a satirical attack upon a decadent bourgeoisie which had lost its sense of direction and a bourgeois régime which had lost its sense of control and order, they tended to play down one strain of the narrative which introduces a more anguished sense of complexity and which goes nearer to the heart of the Occupation experience. There are in the novel two former professional soldiers: Chauvieux, Lasquin's brother-in-law, who has been given a grace-and-favour appointment in the family company, and a former colleague of his, the ex-lieutenant Malinier, whose confused decline will continue throughout *Travelingue* and into *Le Chemin des écoliers* of 1946. The two comrades, who have not seen each other for many years, meet by one of the chances with which the novel is studded at a Front Populaire demonstration. Chauvieux, an ex-sergeant, has the role of 'raisonneur' in the novel: a genuine Bohemian, never happier than when living in a hotel bedroom, he is brought reluctantly into the world of the industrial bourgeoisie and retains the status of detached observer and commentator. He is also, after the death of Lasquin, the only member of the family capable of decisive action, the only member untouched by the pervasive decadence of the Ancelots. This independence and energy emerge in a key scene in the novel, in which Aymé shows himself to be nowhere near so naive in politics as Roger Nimier suggests and where he joins a major strain of French thought of the inter-war years. Describing Chauvieux coming by chance across the demonstration, Aymé writes:

Vers six heures un quart, passant place de l'Etoile, il vit une troupe de gardes mobiles, massée à l'angle des Champs-Elysées et de l'avenue de Friedland. Les trottoirs de la rue de Tilsitt étaient couverts d'uniformes sombres. Des cars, remplis de têtes casquées, stationnaient dans l'avenue de Friedland. Depuis quelque temps, des bagarres éclataient en fin d'après-midi sur les trottoirs des Champs-Elysées. Chauvieux, qui avait passé une partie de sa vie à se défendre contre les abus de la morale, méprisait d'instinct toutes les religions sociales où il ne distinguait que venin de cuistres, aigreurs de curés et larmoiements d'eunuques. Les invocations à un idéal de justice lui étaient aussi pénibles que la dignité raisonneuse du droit menacé, mais il lui semblait qu'une fois les partis

17. The shift from 'Français moyen' to leader is accompanied textually by the displacement of one consonant: 'Mouton' becomes 'Moutor'.

212

engagés dans une guerre sanglante et sans merci, chacun d'eux trouverait une excellente raison-d'être dans l'effort de la lutte. Il espérait secrètement que cette aventure serait aussi la sienne, car il ne se sentait pas à sa place aux usines Lasquin et, sans trop s'en douter, attendait du nouveau.[18]

The message is clear: 'engagement' creates its own 'raison-d'être' and its place in the political spectrum is irrelevant; action is the solution to detachment and decadence, whatever the direction it takes. Through Chauvieux, Marcel Aymé is describing that fascination with action and commitment as values in their own right which touches Malraux's fiction and allows Drieu la Rochelle to praise in the same paragraph of *Notes pour comprendre le siècle* Soviet commissars, German 'Wandervögel' and British colonialists.

For Chauvieux, this adventure, this blurring of the distinctions between Right and Left, will be a commitment which he can entirely control. His friend Malinier, like Drieu himself, is considerably less well-equipped. Whereas Chauvieux has the detachment and lucidity of the 'raisonneur', Malinier is obsessed with the decline of France and the threat posed to patriots like himself by the Front Populaire. Chauvieux himself quickly discerns personal reasons for this political obsession: Malinier has never recreated in civilian life the warmth and the purpose of his time in the army; his low-paid and insignificant post as an insurance-company clerk has echoes of the humiliations meted out to the narrator's father in Céline's *Mort à crédit*, of 1936; and, if Chauvieux is the 'raisonneur' in a latter-day Molière comedy, Malinier, as the 'obsédé', feeds his obsession with a sexual frustration and jealousy stemming from his marriage to a younger and unfaithful woman. His patriotic obsession, however, serves him ill in 1936: initially comic, it rapidly declines into something more sinister approaching madness. One day, Chauvieux finds him in his apartment, seated behind a barricaded window with a rifle, waiting for the assault of the Communists. What is disturbing about Malinier's obsession, however, is that it is not only blind, but exceedingly volatile: with a few words of argument, Chauvieux is able to persuade Malinier to abandon his overt aggression and, for the good of the patriotic cause, to infiltrate Front Populaire movements. Writing at the beginning of the Occupation, Aymé is already aware that individuals are ill-served by

18. Marcel Aymé, *Travelingue*, Paris, 1973, p. 38.

political passion, which does not enable them to see clearly through the growing obscurity and which is subject to extreme changes in direction. When he comes to depict Malinier in Occupied Paris, in *Le Chemin des écoliers*, the process begun in *Travelingue* will merely accelerate.

If *Travelingue* reads as a modern Molière comedy, with its 'précieuses ridicules', its 'raisonneur' and its 'obsédé', it has a particularly historical purpose. Aymé is looking back on a society which lost direction in the inter-war years: its language and thought were deformed, its social structures blurred, its political signposts lost. If this paved the way for France's defeat in June 1940, it also looked forward to the confusion which the French found themselves in during the Occupation itself.

For Marcel Aymé, the Occupation is above all night-time: the night-time of despair, of moral and political obscurity, but also the literal darkness of the blackout, and this aspect of the Occupation, which assumes a central function in Aymé's work, is conveyed at its most emphatic in the short story 'Traversée de Paris' in the collection *Le Vin de Paris*, of 1947. Here, Aymé describes the long journey of two black marketeers, Martin (a recurrent surname in Aymé's work) and his assistant Grandgil, through the blackout from the Boulevard de l'Hôpital in the 15e Arrondissement to the rue Caulaincourt in Montmartre with a clandestine cargo of pork. Nowhere is there to be found a better evocation of the inherently sinister quality of the black market or of the frightening nature of Paris in total darkness under the German Occupation. The sinister quality is conveyed at the very beginning of the story by a deliberate confusion between the body of the pig in the butcher's cellar and a human corpse: 'La victime, déjà dépecée, gisait dans un coin de la cave sous des torchons de grosse toile, piqués de taches brunes.'[19] The darkness is accentuated, paradoxically, by a precise emphasis on the exact topography of the itinerary from the Boulevard de l'Hôpital, across the Seine, through the Marais and the Temple, and up towards Montmartre itself. The tension is there already, in the nature of the mission itself; as Martin warns his companion: 'Entre nous, tant qu'on n'est pas arrivé chez le boucher, c'est à la mort.'[20] But the tension is immeasurably increased by the inexplicable antics of Grandgil. Hired by Martin only the same day, Grandgil proves

---

19. Marcel Aymé, 'Traversée de Paris', in *Le Vin de Paris*, Paris, 1983, p. 29.
20. Ibid., p. 72.

to be an unorthodox black marketeer: far from remaining furtive and unobtrusive, he goes out of his way to attract attention and court disaster. The mystery is finally solved, however, when, near the end of their journey, there is an air raid warning. Grandgil then reveals that he lives near by, in the rue Trudaine, and when they enter, Martin discovers that his accomplice is not the footloose petty criminal he took him for, but a Montmartre painter, Gilouin. The dénouement comes when Martin overhears the painter on the telephone: '– Louise? disait Grandgil. Bonsoir . . . Je n'étais pas là . . . une soirée de vacances. Je me suis déguisé en gangster . . . ma parole, ne ris pas, j'ai même ramené un joli butin . . . j'ai joué au méchant, à l'anarchiste, au dur intégral . . . Très amusant, je t'assure . . . Pas du tout, c'est au contraire très facile, trop facile. Ce sont les mous qui font les durs.'[21] It is the incursion of the inauthentic world of *Travelingue*, the world of snobbishness, pretension and frivolity, but directed this time, not at the dynastic bourgeoisie, but at the petty criminal. The problem for Grandgil is that the petty criminal has more solidity and more sense of order than his bourgeois counterparts. Martin is outraged, not merely because his life has been put at risk, but because his professionalism has been mocked: 'Moi, je gagne mon bifteck, j'ai du mal. Toi, tu t'es roulé dans mon travail, tu as tout fait pour me griller.'[22] He begins to slash Grandgil's paintings and when Grandgil attempts to resist, he murders him. With this act, Martin has reasserted himself and, above all, the sense of order which he represents: even when arrested shortly after, he feels a sense of serenity: 'Jamais il n'avait eu une foi aussi entière en la vertu de ses semblables.'[23] In other words, 'Traversée de Paris' constitutes an affirmation of order through work which has been so seriously undermined in *Travelingue*. That this sense of order can be affirmed only through the professional ethics of a petty criminal constitutes a further indictment of the decadence of the bourgeoisie and reinforces the picture of the inverted world of the Occupation. At the same time, Martin's insistence on the value of 'travail' as the guarantor of order contains an implicit allusion to the ideology of the Vichy régime itself and points to a conservative reading of the text in spite of its ironies.

The importance of 'Traversée de Paris' in the literature of the Occupation lies in the fact that it raises one of the most painful and

21. Ibid., p. 73.
22. Ibid., p. 75.
23. Ibid., p. 82.

ambiguous aspects of the period, the black market. It was ambiguous because, as Aymé points out in *Uranus* (1948), it continued, with the same personnel, untouched by the 'Epuration,' well into the postwar period and thus served to undermine the high moral stance of ex-Resistants and post-Liberation governments alike. As Jacques Debû-Bridel emphasised in his *Histoire du marché noir 1939–1947*, published in the early years of the Fourth Republic, 'A la Libération, le gang subsiste.'[24] Yet even during the Occupation, the black market was ambiguous, for, as 'Traversée de Paris' suggests, it constituted the concrete economic link between the literal darkness of the blackout and the moral and political obscurity in which the Parisian population, particularly, found itself.

It is inevitable that all periods of privation generate a black economy, with clandestine systems of production, distribution, labour and exchange. Socially and politically, such a system is by definition subversive, in that it both undermines the official economy and represents the anarchic assertion of the individual over the collective good. In this context, therefore, the proliferation of the black market in occupied France and especially Paris constitutes an extreme example of that breakdown of social and moral order denounced in *Travelingue*. There is no denying that the hardships suffered by the urban population were real enough. As Robert Aron records:

> Les rations alimentaires permettent à peine aux Français de subsister:
> Pain: 250 grammes par jour.
> Viande: 180 grammes par semaine.
> Matières grasses: 15 grammes par jour.
> Fromage: 40 grammes par semaine.
> Sucre: 500 grammes par mois.[25]

and: '1,700 calories correspondaient, selon les Allemands eux-mêmes à *'un régime de famine lente conduisant à la mort'*; 3.000 à 3.500 calories sont nécessaires pour un homme menant une existence sédentaire, 4.000 à 4.500 pour des travailleurs de force. Dès septembre 40, la ration quotidienne est réduite à 1.800 pour les Français adultes.'[26] At the same time, fuel rationing was equally rigorous: 'Les organismes mal nourris souffrent cruellement du

---

24. Jacques Debû-Bridel, *Histoire du marché noir 1939–1947*, Paris, 1947, Ch. VI.
25. Robert Aron, *Histoire de Vichy*, Paris, 1954, p. 192.
26. Ibid., p. 193.

froid. Dans l'hiver 1940–1941, un des plus rigoureux que la France ait connus depuis longtemps, les rations de combustible sont à peine suffisantes pour assurer par famille le chauffage intermittent et médiocre d'une pièce pendant quelques semaines: 11 degrés est considéré comme un luxe.'[27]

The initial rationing of 1940–1, however, was mild compared with that imposed after the German occupation of the Southern Zone and the capitulation of Italy in 1943. As Georges Delarue states:

Cette fois, la France était saignée à blanc. Les rations alimentaires officielles diminuaient régulièrement. Les Français n'étaient pas encore réduits à "bouffer de vieilles selles de Cosaques", mais, en 1943, la ration alimentaire correspondait à mille cinq cents calories par jour, soit mille calories de moins que le minimum vital. La ration de pain allait bientôt atteindre deux cent cinquante grammes par jour, et celle de viande quatre-vingt-dix grammes par semaine. Encore, les rations annoncées n'étaient pas toujours servies, pour les corps gras, par exemple. A Lyon, de 1939 à 1943, la mortalité des nourrissons augmenta de 50 per cent; à Paris, la mortalité par tuberculose augmenta entre 1939 et 1943, de 69 per cent chez les adultes, de 87 per cent chez les vieillards et de 104 per cent chez les adolescents, qui souffrirent le plus tragiquement des carences alimentaires prolongées . . . Les hivers 1942–1943 et 1943–1944 virent de véritables hécatombes de petits rentiers tués par la sous-alimentation. Combien de ces braves petits bourgeois, paisiblement installés dans la tranquillité de leurs petites rentes auraient imaginé qu'ils mourraient un jour de faim?[28]

In this situation, any recourse to alternative means of supply was a legitimate act of self-defence and a necessary means of survival: 'Dans les grands centres, seuls ceux qui recevaient un petit supplément expédié par des parents ou des amis vivant à la campagne, ou qui pouvaient acheter ce supplément au marché noir, arrivaient à survivre.'[29] And Robert Aron justifies a modest recourse to the black market as the only means of surviving in the face of unrealistic rationing: 'Ce rationnement, s'il n'avait été corrigé pour certains par bien des fraudes nécessaires, aurait conduit à la mort lente de la population toute entière.'[30] In other words, for the

27. Ibid.
28. Georges Delarue, *Trafics et crimes sous l'Occupation*, Paris, 1968, pp. 91–92.
29. Ibid., p. 92.
30. Aron, *Histoire de Vichy*, p. 193.

mass of the population, involvement in the black market, albeit at a modest level, appears as an indispensable alternative to slow starvation, a means of circumventing the draconian measures imposed by the occupying forces, a further example of the famous 'système D', the triumph of French ingenuity over Teutonic cruelty.

The problem in France in the period 1940–4, however, was that the black market had very specific causes and characteristics which conflict with the somewhat cosy myth. Articles 17 and 18 of the Armistice laid the ground for a total economic exploitation of France by Germany:

> Article 17. – Le gouvernement français s'engage à empêcher tout transfert de valeurs à caractère économique et des stocks, du territoire à occuper par les troupes allemandes dans les territoires non occupés ou à l'étranger. Il ne pourra être disposé de ces valeurs et stocks se trouvant en territoire occupé qu'en accord avec le gouvernement du Reich, étant entendu que le gouvernement allemand tiendra compte de ce qui est nécessaire à la vie des populations en territoire non occupé.
>
> Article 18. – Les frais d'entretien des troupes d'occupation allemandes sur le territoire français seront à la charge du gouvernement français.[31]

As Georges Delarue explains: 'L'article 17 allait permettre un contrôle rigoureux de toutes les richesses françaises; l'article 18, exploité au-delà des limites de l'imaginable, permit de lever en France un impôt quotidien démesuré qui faillit consommer notre ruine et fit la fortune de quelques-uns.'[32] This daily charge was fixed at 400 million francs per day, to which were added a whole series of supplements. The effect of this was to give the German occupation forces, and in particular certain units, sums of money so vast that they ceased to have any real economic value. The Germans used this money to buy up literally everything they could in France: what Jacques Debû-Bridel refers to as 'la pompe aspirante allemande',[33] with the dual effect of producing galloping inflation, since money was no object, and massive shortages. In other words, in the first year of the Occupation, the Germans had achieved a near-monopoly of French supplies of all ranges and had imposed their own black economy, run by all units of the occupying forces but particularly by the intelligence and secret police networks, the Abwehr

---

31. Delarue, *Trafics et crimes sous l'Occupation*, p. 20.
32. Ibid., p. 20.
33. Debû-Bridel, *Histoire du marché noir 1939–1947*, Ch. III.

and the Gestapo. Under these umbrellas, grew up official or semi-official bureaux, of which the 'Bureau Otto', linked to the Abwehr, was the most famous, which recruited French agents and specialised in an inextricable mixture of espionage and counter-espionage, expropriation and black marketeering. It was around these bureaux that grew up the 'demi-monde' of the Occupation, in which secret policemen, shady businessmen, petty criminals and prostitutes rubbed shoulders. The important point, however, is that, far from being an example of French resilience, the black market in Occupied France was German-run, with the precise aim of ruining France economically and enabling infiltration of all levels of French society by secret police and intelligence networks. To participate in the black market, therefore, as most Frenchmen were obliged to, was, inevitably, to collaborate and it is here that one of the great ambiguities of the Occupation is to be found: even the purest Resistants had recourse to the black market for their own survival and the survival of their family. Yet the modest supplements of butter, meat and eggs could eventually be traced back to the warehouses on the quai de Bercy owned by the 'Bureau Otto' or to the 'Gestapo' of the rue de Lauriston. To call attention to the black market during the Occupation, therefore, is automatically to call into question the simplified historical account of the period, not least because that black market continued to run under the Fourth Republic when literary or intellectual collaborators were being imprisoned or shot. When, in 1946, therefore, with his novel *Le Chemin des écoliers*, Marcel Aymé raised the question of the black market in occupied Paris, he was pointing very much to the Achilles' heel of the Resistance and setting a pattern which later writers, particularly those of the 'mode rétro', would follow.

Le Chemin des écoliers is Aymé's most complete picture of daily life in Paris during the Occupation; it is also, arguably, his most cynical. It depends on two central devises: the inversion of conventional values and assumptions, signified by the title itself of a novel in which the children are deeply enmeshed in the black market, and the emphasis on individual personal concerns rather than global political or historical ones. Its central characters are two middle-aged friends, Michaud and Lolivier, who run a seedy apartment-management business. This profession itself, which necessitates repeated visits by Michaud and Lolivier to numerous tenants and contractors, enables Aymé to draw a broad picture of various levels of Parisian society under the Occupation as well as providing a particular perception of the operation of the black market in the construction industry. The two friends are dominated by personal worries, though initially they differ in their responses. Lolivier has been battered into cynical pessimism by his wife, Josy, a failed pretentious actress, the successor to Madame Ancelot, in *Travelingue*, and his son, Tony, a sadist who begins by torturing his pets and finishes by commiting a particularly horrific murder: 'Il habitait une cave de la Charbonnière avec une fille et un Arabe. Il avait eu la gentillesse de me l'écrire. L'Arabe et lui, ils ont tué la fille et ils l'ont vendue par quartiers, comme viande de boucherie. C'est en essayant de vendre les morceaux qu'ils se sont fait prendre.'[34]

In this situation, Lolivier's concerns are purely personal, as he explains to Michaud:

> Si tu avais chez toi un enfer comme le mien, tu commencerais peut-être à comprendre. J'ai beau me dire que le monde est en feu, la vie, pour moi, c'est d'abord cette besace de boue et de malheur que je traine dans la nuit de mon tunnel . . . Roosevelt peut sourire au ciel de nos destinées et Hitler occuper Tombouctou, j'ai ma petite vie bien à moi et qui ne me laisse pas le temps de rêver.[35]

His colleague is apparently more complex: through Michaud, Aymé presents the portrait of a figure clinging to the last vestiges of liberalism before giving in to reality. An ex-teacher, driven into commerce by poverty, he was an enthusiastic supporter of the Front Populaire and still clings to certain progressive values. Unlike the practical, if cynical, Lolivier, he is reluctant to allow his business to have any dealings with the black market even though it is endemic to the profession. Like Lolivier, however, he too is dominated by domestic concerns – the illness and hospitalisation of his wife, Hélène, and the problems of bringing up his three children, Frédéric, Antoine and Pierrette. Where Lolivier is tormented by precise knowledge of his son's decadence, however, the liberal Michaud is shielded from the truth: he ignores the fact that Frédéric, his eldest son, a student of mathematics, is a member of the Resistance, and has only a partial perception of the corruption of his youngest son, Antoine.

If the daily operation of the partners' business necessarily brings

---

34. Marcel Aymé, *Le Chemin des écoliers*, Paris, 1977, pp. 239–40.
35. Ibid., p. 162.

them into contact with the black market, the precocious career of Antoine takes the reader into its luxurious 'demi-monde'. At the lycée, Antoine is the friend of Paul Tiercelin, whose father owns an expensive black market bar and restaurant. Here, Antoine is not merely drawn into black market operations, which bring him fabulous sums of money, but is led into an affair with Yvette, the wife of a French prisoner of war. Each night, when he should be studying, Antoine goes to Tiercelin's bar with Yvette and joins the regular clientèle of criminals, prostitutes, Gestapo agents and black marketeers. The dénouement, with Yvette leaving Antoine for a German officer and Antoine consoling himself by taking her little daughter Chou to the Cirque Médrano, appears to mark a return to Aymé's much-cherished sense of order, by which children revert to their natural childishness and escape the cruel and puzzling world of the adults. Yet there is a sting in the tail. In the last of the footnotes which accompany the narrative throughout, Aymé spies on Michaud's future:

> Michaud et Lolivier sont actuellement à la tête d'une quinzaine de millions chacun. Leurs femmes ont des diamants, des étuis à cigarettes en or, des robes de la rue de la Paix et se voient très souvent, ce qui leur arrivait jadis une fois par an. Les deux associés sont moins généreux avec leurs maîtresses. Michaud, qui s'est mis tard à la bonne chère, a vingt de tension et son foie le tourmente. Il a l'illusion d'être encore l'ami des classes laborieuses et d'aspirer à l'avènement de la justice sociale. 'Je suis un scaphandrier de la fortune, dit-il. Elle ne m'atteint pas'. Mais l'aversion qu'il a toujours eu pour le communisme ne s'inspire plus des mêmes raisons qu'autrefois. Lolivier se moque de lui: 'Il t'arrive une aventure insignifiante. Tu étais un bourgeois de gauche et tu es devenu un bourgeois de droite'.[36]

The black market has not only triumphed over Michaud, it has revealed itself as the only authentic expression of the class to which he belongs.

Through the converging fortunes of Michaud and Lolivier, Aymé provides a detailed picture of life under the Occupation, with its petty, day-to-day privation, the constant fear of arrest in the curfew, the persecution of the Jews by Germans and French alike and the all-pervasive operation of the black market. At the same time, the arbitrary fate suspended over the Parisian population and their

36. Ibid., p. 252.

occupiers is translated by the unique device of the footnotes to the novel. Often, but – significantly – not always, passing references to secondary characters, chanced upon as Michaud and Lolivier make their rounds through Paris, are followed up by footnotes which reveal their fate. Occassionally that fate is benign and their problems are resolved; more often, it is catastrophic, as in the case of a beautiful woman seen fleetingly when Michaud visits one of his apartment buildings and of whom Aymé notes:

> Un jour de décembre 1943, la belle jeune femme rencontra, dans un magasin des Champs-Elysées, un important fonctionnaire de la gestapo française, qui lui offrit de coucher avec elle. Ayant essuyé un refus, il la fit arrêter et transporter dans un local où il la viola et la dépouilla de ses bijoux. Au bout d'une quinzaine, il la repassa à ses subordonnés et, au bout d'un mois, la fit mettre à mort. Le cadavre fut jeté à la Seine après avoir été coupé en plusieurs morceaux pour la commodité du transport.[37]

As Roger Nimier notes, this is a means of introducing the fatalism of tragedy into the historical chronicle: 'On se heurte à des cadavres vivants: heureux dans le texte, ils sont torturés, pendus dans les notes.'[38] Overlaying the gloom of the historical evocation, there is an even more pessimistic metahistorical perception: Aymé's characters are subjected to a fate which they cannot possibly foresee and which is completely arbitrary.

Yet if this is true for the metahistorical situation, it equally holds good for the confusion in which the characters, and the reader, find themselves during the Occupation. The inversion of values introduced by the title continues throughout the novel: Aymé's children are not innocent, but corrupt; the Resistant Frédéric is ploddingly dull, whilst his younger brother Antoine, the black marketeer and frequenter of Germans, is attractive; the liberal morality of the pre-war bourgeoisie is worn out and it is the cynic Lolivier, and not the progressive Michaud, who is of most practical help to their Jewish client, Lina, when she begins to suffer the effects of French anti-Semitism. Indeed, the very concept of liberalism is derided as the mere attribute of one particular class: the 'bourgeois de gauche' becomes a 'bourgeois de droite'.

One of the symptoms of this confusion is that apparently disinterested acts take on a whole new political significance. This is the

37. Ibid., p. 59.
38. Roger Nimier, *Journées de lecture*, pp. 44–5.

case of M. de Monboquin, one of Michaud's tenants, who is both an ex-colonel of the French cavalry and an innocent amateur in the study of Celto-Ligurian archeology in the département of the Eure. When the colonel's wife with Michaud's help reminds him of the collaborationist implications of his publishing a book on the subject, to say nothing of attending a seminar at the German Institute, he reluctantly bows to the argument, though not without the comment: 'Mais tout ce que nous faisons: manger, dormir, circuler, ce n'est qu'autant qu'ils le veulent bien',[39] which logically extends the definition of collaboration to the very fact of existing. The last Michaud sees of him is a pathetic, half-shaved figure, who is shortly to die of a broken heart and sheer bewilderment.

Yet the colonel's confusion is nothing when compared to the disorientation of Malinier, who haunts *Le Chemin des écoliers* as he haunted *Travelingue*. He erupts into the novel, like 'une statue du Commandeur',[40] as a colleague of Yvette's prisoner-of-war husband, whose previous obsession with the fate of France in *Travelingue* has now turned, after 1940, to neurotic grief: 'La plûpart du temps, il parlait seul, avec une violence désolée, et ses yeux fiévreux, sa voix rauque faisaient penser au délire d'un moine visionnaire. Les malheurs de la France lui étaient toujours présents. Il les ressentait dans son coeur et dans sa chair, il en souffrait comme peut souffrir une mère qui surveille l'agonie de son enfant.'[41]

It so happens that in Yvette's apartment there is an old Jewish primary-school inspector, M. Coutelier, who on being insulted by Malinier as a "vieux cubiste enjuivé",[42] delivers an impressive harangue on patriotism, so impressive, in fact, that Malinier, in spite of himself, is won over. This persuasion at the hands of a 'suppôt de la judéo-maçonnerie'[43] completes the process of disorientation in Malinier's brain:

> Il commençait à entrevoir une région de l'esprit où les contraires, à l'abri des rigueurs d'une ligique implacable, se composaient intimement sans rien perdre de leurs exigences respectives. L'idée d'un tour de passe-passe ou d'une abdication déguisée ne l'effleurait pas, mais il envisageait le problème de cette fusion sous des espèces vaguement esthétiques qu'il ne

39. Marcel Aymé, *Le Chemin des écoliers*, p. 55.
40. Ibid., p. 97.
41. Ibid., pp. 97–8.
42. Ibid., p. 104.
43. Ibid., p. 105.

se sentait pas encore en état de formuler,[44]

and its natural metaphor is that of night-time: 'La nuit, comme un manteau de Noé jeté sur la défaite, le séparait des réalités humiliantes, noyait les ombres du maleur et épaissisait l'espace de telle sorte que la victoire allemande y perdait toute resonance. Il lui semblait que dans une nuit perpétuelle, la présence du vainqueur eût été tellement diminuée qu'elle aurait perdu sa signification.'[45]

This 'nuit perpétuelle' which befuddles Malinier's brain leads him to completely misinterpret the logic of the inspector's speech and the next time that they meet, Malinier is dressed in the German uniform of the LVF. Like so many others of Marcel Aymé's victims in the novel, his fate is confined to one of the footnotes:

Malinier ne devait pas mourir en Russie. Fait prisonnier par les Américains après la débâcle allemande, il fut remis aux autorités françaises. Dans l'une des prisons qu'il connut successivement, il fut maltraité. Récit d'un témoin: "Le soir, les hommes de la L.V.F., complètement nus, étaient alignés dans la cour et à moitié assomés à coups de trique. Ils passaient toute la nuit dehors dans la même tenue et leurs gardiens, presque tous des jeunes gens, venaient de temps à autre les rouer de coups. Au cours d'une même nuit, j'ai été réveillé plusieurs fois par un concert de hurlements. Le matin, avant de les faire réintégrer leurs cellules, les gardiens les obligeaient à se rouler dans des débris de verre. Je les voyais de ma fenêtre. De toutes parts, le sang ruisselait des chairs déjà tuméfiées par les coups. L'aumônier de la prison, qui était au courant de ces pratiques, feignait de les ignorer et peut-être y prenait-il plaisir. J'allai le trouver et lui reprochait sa passivité. Je le priai de faire mettre fin à ces mauvais traitements ainsi qu'à ceux, équivalents, infligés aux femmes. Il me promit que les gardiens seraient punis et les prisonniers humainement traités. Je ne sais ce qu'il en est advenu". Malinier passa en jugement au mois de décembre et fut condamné à mort. A maintes reprises, au cours de l'audience, il protesta de son patriotisme, ce qui fit d'abord sourire les jurés et finit par les agacer.[46]

In the dark night of the Occupation, with the general inversion of all values, the tragic irony of Malinier's situation is that it is his excessive patriotism which leads to his treason. The message of the novel as a whole is that relativism and opportunism are all and

44. Ibid., pp. 107–18.
45. Ibid., p. 110.
46. Ibid., p. 177.

adherence to values disastrous. Michaud and Lolivier survive and prosper by espousing the code of the black market and not by fighting against it in the name of a fictitious liberalism.

Nor does the punishment meted out to Malinier's comrades in the LVF indicate that any lessons have been learnt at the Liberation, a point which Aymé reinforces in his evocation of an imaginary community, Blémont, in the aftermath of the war, in *Uranus*, (1948), where the victors of the Liberation employ the same techniques as their persecutors during the Occupation and where the black market still operates unchecked. In an important essay, 'Le Trou de la serrure', published just after the Occupation, Aymé reflected that the traditional role of the novelist was to observe his characters as if through a keyhole: 'Le roman psychologique lui-même se contentait de décrire un mécanisme conforme aux habitudes et aux exigences de la vie en société.'[47] Yet: 'L'année dernière, le trou de la serrure a sauté et, du même coup, la porte et la muraille derrière lesquels s'abritait une vieille humanité clandestine. Le monde, étonné ou feignant de l'être, a découvert les camps d'extermination et de torture: Auschwitz, Dachau, Buchenwald et autres.'[48]

The point, however, is that these camps were staffed by ordinary Germans who 'avaient l'air de gens comme tout le monde.'[49] In other words, the phenomenon of the concentration camps lifts the lid on an unpalatable vision of ordinary humanity: 'Si on lit aujourd'hui *Cousine Bette*, en pensant au camp d'Auschwitz, on en sait évidemment un peu plus long que Balzac sur le compte de son héroïne.'[50] Hence:

> il y aurait à écrire le roman d'un brave homme gagnant soucieusement le pain de ses enfants chéris; mobilisé, les hasards d'une affectation l'amènent à tuer, à torturer et à dépenser avec allégresse une partie de ses inépuisables réserves de cruauté et de sadisme; rendu à la vie normale, il retrouve sa petite famille avec des larmes de joie et se remet courageusement au travail.[51]

The 'années noires' of the Occupation for Aymé, therefore, are not

47. Marcel Aymé, 'Le Trou de la serrure', Paris, Les Tirages à part du 'Palimugre', n. d., reprinted in Georges Robert, André Lioret, *Marcel Aymé insolite*, p. 129.
48. Ibid., p. 129.
49. Ibid.
50. Ibid., p. 131.
51. Ibid.

merely a period of confusion and obscurity, in which lucidity is difficult, if not impossible, but the revelation of a 'heart of darkness' beneath the surface of ordinary life.

In his fictional evocations of the Occupation and the period surrounding it, Marcel Aymé appears as a formidable chronicler who carefully rectifies the conventional historical myths propagated by the victors. For Aymé, the social fabric of France was falling apart even before the Occupation and the predominant philosophy of liberal humanism was already outdated and irrelevant. The reality of the Occupation experience was one of confusion, where all action and motivation was ambiguous and survival all-important. Clearly, by emphasising the pervasiveness of the black market, the primacy of individual concerns and the dubious morality of much post-Liberation activity, Aymé was making a partisan political point taken up by other authors of the Right after the war. Yet his importance goes beyond the specifically political: Aymé's world, from *Travelingue* to *Uranus* and in the post-war plays, is one in which language is debased, integrity seriously menaced, and where there is no humanism to counter the horror of it all. At this point, the satirist and historian becomes a moral visionary of a very high order.

13

SIX HEURES À PERDRE (1944): ROBERT BRASILLACH'S LAST NOVEL AND THE END OF THE OCCUPATION

Margarete Zimmermann

Six heures à perdre, Robert Brasillach's last novel, was serialised in the literary and political weekly *La Révolution Nationale*[1] from 11 March to 10 June 1944. At that point the end of the Occupation was already in sight, since the invasion of Normandy on 6 June 1944 had just marked a definitive turning-point in the war in the west. The novel is therefore a final literary portrait of occupied France, by an author who in the thirties had risen against the Republic and who after 1940 became involved in intellectual collaboration, putting the prestige of the French writer at the service of Fascism. Robert Brasillach must be considered as a key figure in French Fascism, who continues to create controversy more than forty years after his death. As early as 1945, the 'Brasillach case' was being exploited by the extreme Right in France.[2]

Born in 1909 in Perpignan, the eldest son of an army officer Arthémile Brasillach and his wife Marguerite, Robert spent part of his childhood in Morocco. After his father's death at the battle of El-Herri in 1914, the family returned to Perpignan, until his mother's remarriage, when they moved to Sens in Burgundy. In 1925, Brasillach became a pupil at the famous Lycée Louis-le-Grand in Paris and in 1928 he entered the Ecole Normale Supérieure. He owed his intellectual and political training to Charles Maurras and

---

1. See M. Bardèche's preface to the *Oeuvres Complètes*, vol. 3, Paris, 1963, pp. 341–45. All quotations are from this edition, and page references are given in brackets after quotations.

2. See G. Loiseaux, *La littérature de la défaite et de la collaboration*, Paris, 1984, p. 496.

to the intellectuals surrounding the Action Française; in 1932 he published his first novel, *Le Voleur d'Etincelles*.

During the course of the 1930s, a strong politicisation of Blasillach and of his work may be observed; as for other intellectuals of his generation, the experience of the riots of February 1934 was decisive: along with Drieu La Rochelle and Lucien Rebatet, he saw in them a 'lost opportunity' for a Fascist revolution in France and throughout his life he always commemorated 6 February.

Other important events in Brasillach's life were the Spanish Civil War and the birth of Fascist movements in Italy and Germany. In October 1937, he attended the Nuremberg 'Reichsparteitag' and published his impressions in an article entitled 'Cent Heures chez Hitler', from which he reproduced certain passages in his novel *Les Sept Couleurs* (1939), and in his book of memoirs *Notre Avant-Guerre* (1941). He was also one of a small number of French authors whose work was translated into German after 1933.[3] From 1936, he contributed to the weekly *Je suis partout* which, following the victory of the Front Populaire and under the directorship of Pierre Gaxotte, became the mouthpiece of the opponents of the Third Republic.[4]

From June 1940 until March 1941 Brasillach was a prisoner of war in Germany. After his return to France, he became chief editor of *Je suis partout*, with a daily circulation of 300,000 copies during the Occupation. His editorials were mainly devoted to anti-Semitism, accusing and denouncing his political opponents (members of the Resistance, socialists and Communists) and the propagation of French Fascism. In August 1943 he ended his association with *Je suis partout* since he no longer believed in a National Socialist victory; henceforth he would write for *La Révolution Nationale*.

Brasillach's last two novels bear the mark of the political climate of the Occupation; thus, *La Conquérante*, published in 1942, recounts in epic form the colonisation of Morocco; it is a literary monument to his mother, as well as being a hymn in praise of warlike virtues and the 'healthy' France of the provinces. *Six Heures à Perdre*, the second novel presents a political assessment of the final phase of the Occupation.

After the Liberation, Brasillach gave himself up and spent the

3. See Loiseaux, *La littérature de la défaite et de la collaboration*, pp. 48, 76.
4. See P.-M. Dioudonnat's monograph, *Je suis partout 1930–1944. Les Maurrassiens devant la tentation fasciste*, Paris, 1973, and P. Sérant, *Les Dissidents de l' 'Action Française'*, Paris, 1978.

period before his trial in prison at Fresnes. There he studied the work of the poet André-Marie Chénier, guillotined in 1794. Brasillach compared his own fate to that of Chénier and wrote his *Poèmes de Fresnes*, published posthumously and initially circulated 'under the counter'. Also dating from this period is the *Lettre à un Soldat de la Classe Soixante* (published in 1946). Brasillach was condemned to death for 'secret dealings with the enemy' and, despite the appeals of numerous French intellectuals to General de Gaulle, he was shot on 6 February 1945.

In 1948 the Association des Amis de Robert Brasillach was founded in Lausanne, followed in June 1950 by the appearance of the *Cahiers des Amis de Robert Brasillach*, the latter strongly influenced by his brother-in-law, Maurice Bardèche. These were the vehicles for an unsubtle policy of rehabilitation.[5] It is only in the last ten years, and independently of the *Cahiers des Amis de Robert Brasillach*, that a properly scientific discussion of his work has begun – an approach to the texts which tries to shake off two equally paralysing attitudes: vindication and hagiography on the one hand, with a categoric refusal to consider the term 'traitor' on the other.

As the 'last novel' of an intellectual committed to collaboration, *Six Heures à Perdre* may be compared with Drieu la Rochelle's *Chiens de Paille* and Céline's *Guignol's Band I*, although the degree of committment differed between the three authors. All three novels are literary attempts to describe the appropriate position to take when faced with a disintegrating world; three examples of 'dandiner dessus les abîmes',[6] to quote an expression by Céline.

Constant Trubert is the protagonist of *Chiens de Paille*, a 'vieil anarcho édenté'[7] and disenchanted hero who does no more than cast a detached glance at his entourage, that is, at the activities of the different political divisions in France at the end of the Occupation. Unlike the principal character of *Gilles* (1939), conceived by Drieu as a committed observer with a dream of political activism, Constant Trubert has broken off all ties with the civil war in France. Through this character, the author expresses a desire to withdraw

---

5. On this point, see my paper on research in progress: 'Littérature et fascisme: le destin posthume de Robert Brasillach' in *Romanistische Zeitschrift für Literaturgeschichte*, Heft 2/3, 1981, pp. 340–59; this publication provoked an extremely polemical 'Réponse à Margarete Zimmermann' whose author concealed his identity behind the pseudonym 'Sirius' (published in *Les Cahiers des Amis de Robert Brasillach*. no. 29, spring 1984, pp. 65–72).
6. L.-F. Céline, *Guignol's Band I*, Paris, 1944, p. 27.
7. P. Drieu la Rochelle, *Les Chiens de Paille*, Paris, 1964, p. 120.

from political events, an attitude which reflects his own behaviour at the end of the war.

It is different with Céline. At first glance, *Guignol's Band I* seems to be another work which bears witness to a deliberate retreat from a situation which had become too 'heated': the novel is set in London in 1915. But it also fits into a continuous sequence, since after the 'accursed writings' phase of anti-Semitic and anti-democratic lampoons between 1936 and 1941, Céline resumed his plans for an autobiographical novel begun with *Voyage au bout de la nuit* (1932) and *Mort à Credit* (1936). However, that is not all. In the first chapters of the novel, which describe the bombing of Paris, Céline poses as the 'chronicler' of an apocalyptic era and tries to convey these new realities in a new language, to communicate these new experiences by means of a ragged syntax and violent language. So, far from marking the end, Céline's last novel to appear during the Occupation points instead to new aesthetic directions and paves the way for the post-war Céline of the 'German trilogy' of novels: *D'Un Château l'autre* (1957), *Nord* (1960), and *Rigodon* (1969).

Six Heures à Perdre, although it borrows from the detective genre, is first and foremost a political treatise in novel form and contains a critical assessment of France in the autumn of 1943. The presentation of the fate of one individual, Marie-Ange Olivier, serves only as a pretext for the primarily political message of the novel. Brasillach revives such topical subjects as the presence of the Germans in France, the occupation of Paris, and prisoners of war, subjects which may also be found in the poetry of the Resistance where, needless to say, they receive a rather different treatment. But at the level of political concepts, *Six Heures à Perdre* expresses a change: unlike *Notre Avant-Guerre* (1941) and his novels of the thirties, the acceptance of Fascism as a political ideal is less in evidence here, and it is legitimate to see in this attitude a literary reaction to the break with *Je suis partout* in 1943.

As with Drieu's last novel, *Six Heures à Perdre* achieves nothing new in either form, language or style as a novel. This seems to highlight the connection between Drieu and Brasillach – and at the same time to distinguish them from Céline whose 'last novel' by contrast broke new ground. With *Guignol's Band I*, he 'goes beyond' the period of the lampoons; on the one hand, he puts into action the aesthetic principles already outlined in these texts, especially in *Bagatelles pour un massacre* (1937); on the other, he incorporates lampoon-type passages into his novels and stresses his role as chronicler of a crumbling world. These two characteristics pave the way for the post-war Céline.

In *Six Heures à Perdre* the author tells the story of a six hour visit to Paris by a former prisoner of war returning to a Paris that has become an alien and enigmatic place to him; so the fragments of reality which he takes in are presented as a 'un petit amas d'énigmes, pareil à un puzzle' (p. 384). Formally, the novel is quite heterogenous, since Brasillach borrows from the serialised novel, from the detective genre, from the novel of current affairs and, especially in the final chapters, from the political editorial. [8] Over the course of the novel, the different pieces of the puzzle which make up 'France in November 1943' come together to form a more coherent picture. Brasillach succeeds, thanks to the many descriptive passages, by using the device of an enquiry being led by the narrator, and flashbacks. If at several moments in the novel the author changes tone and blends political discourse, often of an extremely polemic nature, into the narrative of the novel, this shows the degree to which he confused the role of novelist and journalist.

In *Six Heures à Perdre*, for the first time Brasillach presents events from the point of view of a narrator – 'Robert B.' – who draws the reader's attention to himself as a 'spectateur impartial' (p. 539). This so-called impartiality distinguishes him from the heroes of the novels of the thirties, and it seems as if by the choice of this perspective, the author were attempting to regain a certain 'innocence'.

But let us take a closer look at the plot of the novel. The 'ghost' Robert B. uses his brief stay in Paris to begin searching for a mysterious young woman, Marie-Ange Olivier. He does so at the request of Bruno Berthier, a prisoner of war detained in Germany, who had met and fallen in love with Marie-Ange when on leave in February 1940. This female character, whom the narrator identifies as 'la figure votive de notre époque contrastée', quickly becomes the central figure of the novel, to such an extent that to solve the mystery of Marie-Ange is to understand the enigma of France in the autumn of 1943. And as the image of France emerges from a gradual piecing together of the disparate elements which the narrator records, so the fragments of information about Marie-Ange contribute bit by bit to forming a clearer picture.

Marie-Ange Olivier, whose name symbolises both her provincial background and the innocent purity which Brasillach likes to as-

8. M. Bardèche (in his preface to *Six Heures à Perdre*, p. 343) stresses the importance of G. Simenon's influence on Brasillach.

sociate with women, lives in rather shady circumstances; she maintains a relationship simultaneously with the 'young lads' of the Resistance and with her ex-husband, the Dutchman Hooten, a rather suspect character and black market dealer, who was also responsible for the death of their son Bruno. Repetition of names is a technique often found in Brasillach's novels; here Marie-Ange's lover and her son share the same name.

The last chapter of the novel, *L'Aube*, a chapter of great dramatic intensity, tells the story of a journey by lorry during which Marie-Ange kills Hooten. The novel ends with the narrator saying goodbye to Marie-Ange, who wishes now to devote the rest of her life to caring for French soldiers fighting on the side of the Germans. Robert B. leaves Paris, taking with him the indistinct impression of a rediscovered Paris, suddenly filled with the violent colours of a new age (p. 544).

The heroine of the novel, Marie-Ange, is on the one hand the incarnation of certain elements of Brasillach's personal mythology, on the other hand she carries a political message, so that it is impossible to read *Six Heures à Perdre* as merely a 'charming' and 'cavalier' literary presentation of occupied Paris, as Maurice Bardèche advised readers to do in the 1960s.[9]

Marie-Ange is the last and most complex personification of the myth of childhood which occupies a dominant position in Brasillach's imagination. This gives rise to a constant set of themes which he varies throughout all his novels, renewing and adapting them to different contexts.[10] This regressive obsession with childhood can be explained by looking at the author's life. In addition, this rejection of the aging process and of old age itself, with a corresponding cult of youth and youthful ways of life, help in some part to explain Brasillach's political orientation. One of the reasons for which he was drawn to Fascism was that he saw in it an ideology which answered the needs of a certain category of young people. Brasillach, captivated by the spectacle at the 'Reichsparteitag' in Nuremberg, looked on with fascination at the 'fine display' being performed by handsome, virile men with perfect bodies. This cult of youth goes hand in hand then with his violent rejection of the Third Republic which, in Fascist-inspired caricatures, was often portrayed

9. See his preface, p. 342: '. . . cette vue cavalière du Paris de l'occupation est charmante'.
10. See S. Kushnir, 'L'archétype de l'enfant dans l'oeuvre de Robert Brasillach' in *Revue de l'Université Laurentienne* 3, no. 2, November 1970, pp. 38–47.

as hideously ugly old woman. His Fascism therefore contains a strong aesthetic dimension, and 'image' is a key term in this context; there is, furthermore, a distinct undercurrent of homosexuality.[11]

In *Six Heures à Perdre*, the first impression of Marie-Ange is of a 'mystérieuse enfant' (p. 362). Over the course of the novel, this aura of mystery is dispelled, but at the same time Marie-Ange comes increasingly to personify a kind of ageless childhood. Marie-Ange possesses what Brasillach calls the 'don de l'éternelle enfance' (p. 422), a quality shared by all his heroes and one which serves to identify these characters. In a phrase filled with pathos, where the female character's 'réduction infantile' becomes a sign of the times, the author describes her as 'une enfant abandonnée et flottante à tous les vents de la catastrophe' (p. 476).

The characters who possess this 'gift of eternal childhood' are distinguished by their indifference to material needs, a slightly Bohemian lifestyle and by their childlike physique, all of which amounts to what might be called a completely asexual charm. Marie-Ange, who has all the qualities of this infantilism, attracts in turn other characters with the same qualities: thus Bruno Berthier, 'little' Cresnay and also the narrator, an adult searching for his Parisian youth.

At the opposite end of the scale, we find the sinister Dutchman Hooten, the relentless enemy of the world of childhood. Hooten is an old 'pervers' (p. 470), greedy for material gain; he has caused the death of his own child and, during the Occupation, that of 'little' Cresnay. These two characters, the young member of the Resistance and the dead child, are one and the same; in each case, responsibility for their deaths lies with Hooten. In this way, Marie-Ange becomes the avenger of the much-threatened world of children.[12] By this stage, it should be clear how the childhood theme is used with reference to the political conditions of the day: firstly Brasillach suggests that behind every Resistance group, there are shady characters such as Hooten;[13] then, in choosing to have the latter assassinated by Marie-Ange, the ultimate 'childlike' character, he would have us believe in the possibility of the beleaguered world being freed and 'purged' by these childlike heroes. The murder makes it

---

11. See P. de Senarclens' excellent article, 'Brasillach. Le fascisme et l'Allemagne. Essai d'interprétation', in *Les Relations Franco-Allemandes 1933–1939*, Paris, 1976, pp. 179–209.
12. See *Six Heures à Perdre*, p. 524 and p. 529.
13. See ibid., chap. 5, p. 512.

possible for Marie-Ange to return to Bruno Berthier, her lover at the beginning of the war, who just happens to have the same first name as her dead child. Berthier is presented as a Frenchman who has been moulded by reading Drieu and Montherlant,[14] as a representative of a 'wholesome' France. But the character is also 'absent' – a prisoner of war in Germany – and the murdering heroine must first of all envisage a period of purification, in the form of working as a nurse with soldiers from the Legion of French Volunteers. This 'open-ended' conclusion to the novel (as regards the future of the two lovers) seems to reveal something about Brasillach's partial disorientation in 1944. However, this in no way suggests that he had broken with Fascism, as is sufficiently clear from his *Lettre à un Soldat de la Classe Soixante*. Nevertheless, the heroes of his earlier novels, in their rejection of the 'old' Republic and their enthusiasm for 'young' forms of Fascism, had a clearer political frame of reference. The situation had become rather more complicated in 1944, with the failure of the National Revolution for which Brasillach had been the propagandist, and most of all with the defeat of Italian Fascism and the end clearly in sight for National Socialism.

By looking more closely at how France at the end of 1943 is presented certain political ideas in the novel can be clarified. How France appears to the narrator is conveyed by means of a certain number of encounters, often with women; in their context, there is a predominance of the words 'welcome' and 'to welcome' which suggest the reintegration of the 'ghost' into the national community. If account is taken of the political estrangement established by Brasillach since 1940, one can see in the accumulation of these moving scenes describing meetings with various representatives of the 'French people', an expression of his own desire for reintegration.[15]

Besides, he proceeds to interpret the situation in France in a manner as simplistic as it is biased, and it is particularly in these passages that the boundaries between Brasillach as novelist and as the violent, polemical journalist of *Je suis partout* become blurred: in hindsight, he presents the defeat of 1940 and the Vichy government as a huge benefit, whose fruits, unhappily, were not allowed to

---

14. A description of Bruno is also to be found ibid. p. 395.
15. See ibid. p. 355, the narrator Robert B.'s reference to a waiter in a café: 'Cher garçon! . . . je le regarde avec attendrissement, traînant sur ses savates, avec son tablier blanc et sale écarté sur ses jambes noires, son bec d'oiseau, son crâne chauve. C'est la France qui m'accueille, après tout . . . Mon pays est retrouvé.'

mature after the political developments of 21 June 1941, and the declaration of war by the USSR. According to Brasillach, it was Communist terror which from then on replaced the benefits of the National Revolution:

> les assassinats crapuleux déguisés en attentats politiques, les . . . enfants tués à la porte de leurs parents par les terroristes, les femmes attaquées, des hommes et des femmes sans activité publique, pourtant, assaillis et égorgés. Tout cela dans le désordre moral le plus complet. Et petit à petit le pays se vidant de toute sa substance . . ., tout le bienfait, tout le sursaut possible de 1940 à peu près radicalement annihilé. . . . (pp. 501ff.)

By presenting things in this way Brasillach keeps his distance vis-à-vis changes taking place after June 1941, and his literary double, the narrator Robert B., can even delight in his role of judging harshly the 'déchaînement de l'intérieur' (p. 499). In conceiving a character who displays behaviour typical of the intellectuals of the extreme Right or Fascists (those who 'know better'), the author attempts to rid himself of all responsibility for the condition of France in 1944.

In this context, it is hardly surprising if the presence of the Germans in Paris (also one of the major themes of Resistance poetry) is summed up by the phrase 'rien de désagréable' (p. 358). The same benevolent tolerance can be seen in the novel whenever the Germans are mentioned, as for example in a scene when the narrator meets an NCO. Both are in search of the scenes of their youth in Paris. By his 'sourire enfantin et charmant' (p. 387), the German is immediately admitted to the community of privileged beings who possess the 'don de l'éternelle enfance' and Robert B. very soon feels a 'sympathie réelle' (p. 387).

A similar tendency is shown when the narrator refers to his captivity in Germany: the 'ghost' Robert B. does not neglect to mention his sturdy appearance ('ma bonne mine le prouvait, je me portais fort bien', p. 363); his captivity is celebrated in hindsight as a community experience, even as a 'rajeunissement' (p. 394). In Robert B.'s anecdotes, the guards in these camps are people full of humour who react with a childish joy to their prisoners' attempts to escape (c.f. pp. 505ff). It is enough to mention in passing that the poems in the 'Poètes Prisonniers' collections published by Pierre Seghers in 1943 and in 1944 use a totally different language.[16]

16. See my interview with P. Seghers, 'L'action et le rêve vont ensemble, pour un

In his last novel therefore, Robert Brasillach has once again declared himself to be a 'committed' author, forever slipping between the fictional world of the novel and the political treatise with lampoonist tendencies. So *Six Heures à Perdre* should be considered as an example of a certain kind of 'trahison des clercs', the danger of which Julien Benda had already clearly announced in 1927.[17]

In his essential study of the cultural policies of the occupying Germans, Gerard Loiseaux has stressed the extent to which extra-literary factors (such as the suicide of Drieu and Brasillach's execution) favoured a 'vision légendaire de la collaboration littéraire'[18] almost as soon as the war had ended, and how much this influenced the reception given to these authors. Among intellectuals of the extreme Right, Robert Brasillach became the 'martyre du 6 février' and the figurehead of a certain vindictive right-wing faction. It is hardly surprising that such utilisation of the author for political ends has not led to a better understanding of the works.

For some years now a slight opening-up in the area of scientific work on Brasillach can be observed. There is however one very revealing factor: the abundance of biographies.[19] This biographical fervour is evidence of a certain stagnation in research; it also prevents the asking of more important, and perhaps more difficult, questions.[20]

Taking account of these factors and also of the near silence on the part of liberal literary critics, it seems equally unsurprising that the problem of Brasillach's literary ranking, of the aesthetic quality of the texts should have been avoided since 'sympathisers' as much as adversaries refuse to address the question or merely put forward answers which are too simple. Peter Tame, a British researcher totally above suspicion politically, published a monograph on Brasillach in 1986[21] in which he places the latter among the most

---

poète. Entretiens sur la poésie et la Résistance (juin 1980)', in *Lendemains* 21, February 1981, pp. 3–29; see especially p. 17.

17. See on this point M. Zimmermann, *Die Literatur des französischen Faschismus. Pierre Drieu la Rochelles politische und literarische Entwicklung 1917–1942*, Munich, 1979, pp. 114–16.

18. Loiseaux, *La littérature de la défaite*, p. 107.

19. See A. Brassie, *Robert Brasillach, ou: Encore un instant de bonheur*, Paris 1987; another biography, by P. Pélissier, is due from Denoël in 1988.

20. New avenues of research are suggested by L. Rasson in 'Désir discursif et récit de l'échec: *Le marchand d'oiseaux* de Robert Brasillach', *Romanistische Zeitschrift für Literaturgeschichte*, No. 1/2, 1985, pp. 114–61.

21. P.D. Tame, *La Mystique du fascisme dans l'oeuvre de Robert Brasillach*, Paris, 1986.

important writers of the inter-war period[22] and sets him on a pedestal (doubtful enough in any case) as the 'plus grand peintre français du fascisme comme phéomène de ce siècle'.[23] Faced with such judgements, it is necessary to introduce some further considerations to the discussion.

Any literary historian is faced with the difficult problem of choice, particularly so in twentieth-century literature, as to what he should make known and loved, what he should introduce to the literary canon of his day. The factors governing this choice, in which there is always a fair proportion of subjectivity, must be considered. For one section of the 'dark years', that which was written by collaborating writers, the question is rather pointed.[24] As regards Robert Brasillach (and the same may be said for Drieu), a certain tendency over the last few years which aims to mythologise the lives of these authors in order then to reassert the value of their work without any justification,[25] must be opposed. Neither Drieu nor Brasillach are 'great authors' of the 1930s and '40s, as some critics would have us believe: they are at most 'interesting cases' from the political and intellectual history of their time. Let us try to justify this judgement.

The formal and thematic range of Robert Brasillach's work is relatively limited; his preferred genre is the (mostly) traditional novel, despite a few timid attempts at innovation in *Les Sept Couleurs* (1939). It is indeed to be hoped that someone will undertake to study the relationships between these writers, their rejection of the avant-garde of their time, and their political positions. Brasillach's themes are no more than the variation, often poorly disguised, of certain autobiographical elements repeated endlessly within a work. For the reader, this creates the impression of a certain déjà-vu, since some motifs recur several times, and sometimes whole sentences or passages from one work are repeated in another. Moreover, Fausta Garavini has shown how closely Brasillach allies literary creation to his political beliefs.[26]

22. See ibid. p. 25: 'Son originalité réside en ce qu'il fut parmi ces écrivains les plus doués de la France de l'entre-deux guerres. . . . '
23. Ibid., p. 25.
24. See on this point S. Suleiman, 'Ideological dissent from works of fiction: Towards a rhetoric of the Roman à thèse' in *Neophilologus* 60, 1976, Cahier 2, pp. 162–177.
25. A similar position, with regard to Drieu la Rochelle, is found in C. Koch's 'Abgeschlossener Fall: Drieu la Rochelle', *Merkur* 457, No. 3, 41st year, March 1987, pp. 227–31.
26. See F. Garavini, *I sette colori del romanzo*, Rome, 1973.

This raises a further problem: as far as ideas and themes are concerned, Brasillach's work bears the mark of the times very strongly. In other words: his political ideas are present without really having undergone an aesthetic transformation, as is the case for example with Thomas Mann's *Doktor Faustus* (1947) or Marcel Aymé's *Travelingue* (1941). As a result, Brasillach's novels have aged very rapidly. But above all, faced with the historic consequences of the Fascism which the author tries to pass off as a nice, new form of 'mal du siècle', today it is impossible to accept the political ideas which underlie his work as being nothing more than a reflection of the times, or even to disregard them.

Finally, if one considers literature and art in general as the means by which we may conceive of places where the imagination reigns, create utopias and experiment with new forms of social life, then Brasillach's novels do not fulfil these conditions. They are moreover the mouthpiece of an ideology which aims precisely at destroying such possibilities. His works are extremely biased documents of their time, and their interest is limited to this historical dimension.

After the Liberation, collaborating intellectuals, whose political responsibility we are attempting to assess, were put on trial. What is often forgotten today is that these events and discussions of 1944/5 are merely, in the last analysis, a return to the 'querelle des mauvais maîtres' of the years between 1940 and 1942.[27] These were the trials which took place during the aftermath of the disaster of 1940, of writers such as Gide, Mauriac and Cocteau, accused of having 'corrupted' French youth. It is important to recall here that it was the right and, in particular, Robert Brasillach's political mentor, Henri Massis, who raised with considerable vehemence the question of the responsibility of the writer.

Robert Brasillach's death does not make him one of the 'great authors' of the first part of the century, whose work might enrich the imagination of generations to come. His last novel, *Six Heures à Perdre*, marks a highpoint in the sense that it is a final reworking of the principal themes of the earlier works, at the same time showing how the efforts of the literary imagination are stifled by too much politics. *Six Heures à Perdre* may therefore be read as evidence of a literary death – and consequently as, truly, a final novel.

---

27. See W. Babilas' excellent study 'La Querelle des mauvais maîtres' in *Romanische Forschungen*, vol. 98, No. 1/2, 1986, pp. 120–52.

14

THE VIEW OF COLLABORATION DURING THE 'APRÈS-GUERRE'

Michael Kelly

Viewed from the comfortable distance of postwar London, the French collaboration could look like a simple affair. A handful of traitors had made hay while the Nazi sun shone, only to get their comeuppance when their country was liberated by the Allies. The same story, in essence, as could be told for the rest of German-occupied Europe. Viewed from liberated Paris, the collaboration did not look so simple. Its complexities and ambiguities enabled it to support a variety of conflicting interpretations, each passionately championed by one or other of the movements which were contending for dominance in postwar France.

History always involves political judgements. Even in the late 1980s the issue of collaboration is highly political and deeply divisive. In the late 1940s it was a central question in French political life, and no account of it could avoid the political implications of the interpretation it followed. This chapter examines some of the most influential accounts of the nature of collaboration, and the positions that should be adopted towards it, in the first three years after the Liberation. It looks at the strategies adopted to narrate the events and form attitudes toward them. And it tries to show how the competing views reflect the social and political struggles of the period, in particular the significant shifts of balance which prepare the pivotal year of 1947.

What was the collaboration? It might be expected that in the postwar period there should be some debate about what collaboration consisted of, some attempt to fix the boundaries. Such issues were not entirely absent, but for the most part they were largely assumed to be a matter of common agreement. In the immediate aftermath of the Liberation, discussion was overwhelmingly focused on what should be done with collaborators, rather than what they were. Several detailed studies of the 'Epuration' now exist. The most recent is an anecdotal but balanced study by Herbert Lottman. The best-known French study is Robert Aron's *Histoire de l'épuration* in three volumes, a compilation of much anecdotal material with an ill-concealed pro-Vichy stance. Peter Novick's *The Resistance versus Vichy* is a shrewd scholarly appraisal. *La Libération de la France* contains several useful papers from a conference held in 1976.[1] The 'Epuration', ostensibly aimed at purging erstwhile collaborators, aroused high passions.

The hawks, led by the Communists, demanded the full rigours of retributive justice. In the process, they invoked the example of Robespierre, and argued the need for measures of public safety, which might be thwarted by excessive regard for the legal niceties.[2] For the most part they were driven much less by a desire for revenge than by political objectives. On the one hand was the need to restore the reputation of France in the eyes of the world. As the left-wing writer Jean-Richard Bloch put it:

> Si quelque chose a menacé la France de perdition dans le monde, ce fut l'épouvantable défection d'écrivains auxquels certaines réussites formelles avaient donné à l'étranger une maniére de gloire. Un Maurras, un Giono, un Montherlant, un Paul Morand, un Céline..., je ne puis continuer cette énumération dont la honte m'étoufferait. Ceux-là ont joué, vis-à-vis de notre pays, le rôle de ces pierres dont les auteurs d'un drame crapuleux alourdissent les poches de leur victime pour étre sûrs qu'elle ira au fond et ne remontera jamais à la surface.[3]

On the other hand, there was a determination to prevent the cadres of Vichy and the collaboration from resuming influential political positions in the post-war dispensation. After the 'rentrée' of 1947, this became a largely symbolic, rearguard battle.

The doves, led by the Catholic church and the Christian democratic MRP, invoked the values of forgiveness and reconciliation. Leading Catholic philosophers such as Gabriel Marcel argued that it was important to avoid motives of revenge, that almost anyone who

1. See Herbert Lottman, *L'Epuration*, Paris, 1986; Robert Aron, *Histoire de l'épuration*, Paris, 1967–1975; Peter Novick, *The Resistance versus Vichy*, New York, 1968; *La Libération de la France*, Paris, 1976.

2. See Roger Garaudy, 'Du procès de Louis XVI au châtiment des traîtres', *Les Cahiers du communisme*, January 1945, pp. 83–9.

3. J.-R. Bloch, 'Responsabilité du talent', *Europe*, août 1946, reprinted in Jean Albertini, *Avez-vous lu Jean-Richard Bloch?*, Paris, 1981, pp. 328–33, p. 331.

had lived through the Occupation was to some extent in complicity, and that no one was therefore in a position to cast the first stone.[4] In practice, leading Catholic resistance figures such as François Mauriac and Mgr Saliège were prominent in campaigning to attenuate the severity of the purging process. Mauriac earned from the satirical weekly *Le Canard enchaîné* the nickname 'saint François des Assises' for what became a crusade to rescue those who fell foul of the 'Epuration' process. Not all Catholics were of the same view, and Mauriac found himself several times in polemics with progressive Catholics such as Roger Secrétain, and others of the 'Esprit' group.[5]

The centre ground, including Camus, Sartre, the existentialists and the socialists, tended to favour the principles of understanding and mercy. Camus initially argued for a strict approach, despite personal reservations, declaring in *Combat*: 'Notre conviction est qu'il y a des temps où il faut savoir parler contre soi-même et renoncer du même coup à la paix du coeur.'[6] Subsequently, Camus was increasingly inclined to listen to his own qualms, and was one of the leading signatures in the unsuccessful petition to commute the death sentence passed on the prominent pro-Nazi journalist Robert Brasillach in early 1945, and in subsequent, more successful campaigns.[7] Jean Paulhan, a fellow signatory and formerly a leading figure in the intellectual resistance, undertook a highly publicised attack on the policy of the writers' association, CNE, to boycott collaborationist writers and their works, and the drawing up of 'blacklists' to this end.[8]

In the event, after the first chaotic days of Liberation, the tide ran increasingly for the doves. The best estimates suggest that perhaps 9,000 collaborators were summarily executed in the weeks of fighting, but that of 6,763 death sentences subsequently delivered

4. See Gabriel Marcel, 'Spectroscopie de la trahison', *Temps présent*, 1 September 1944, 7; R.H., 'L'heure de justice ne doit pas être l'heure de la vengeance', *Témoignage chrétien*, 9 September 1944, pp. 1–3.

5. See Roger Secrétain, 'Echec de la Résistance', *Esprit*, June 1945, pp. 1–15; Jean Lacroix, 'Les catholiques et la politique', *Esprit*, June 1945, pp. 70–78.

6. Unsigned editorial, *Combat*, 20 October 1944.

7. Brasillach was executed on 6 February 1945. The petition, organised by François Mauriac and Thierry Maulnier, attracted support from Albert Camus and Jean Paulhan in particular. A later petition on behalf of fellow journalists Lucien Rebatet and Pierre-Antoine Cousteau obtained the commuting of their death sentences.

8. See Jean Paulhan, *De la paille et du grain* Paris, 1948, and *Lettre aux Directeurs de la Résistance*, Paris, 1952.

by the courts, only 767 were actually carried out.[9]

Probably the best-known attempt to explain collaboration is an essay which Jean-Paul Sartre wrote in the summer of 1945. Entitled 'Qu'est-ce qu'un collaborateur?',[10] it contained almost no mention of anything the collaborators had done, or what it was that conferred the status of collaborator. Instead, Sartre examined in detail the social and psychological factors which had motivated them, arguing that collaboration was a normal phenomenon to be found in any collectivity, such as criminality or suicide. It was, he argued, an inherent propensity in certain individuals, lying dormant until the necessary social conditions arose for it to be manifest.

This approach enabled him to assert that, while collaborators came almost exclusively from the bourgeoisie, their decision was based on the psychology of individual deviants, rather than on a collective pursuit of class interests. He summarised the psychological components as: 'Réalisme, refus de l'universel et de la loi, anarchie et rêve d'une contrainte de fer, apologie de la violence et de la ruse, fémininité, haine de l'homme.'[11] The political consequences of his analysis boil down entirely to a plea for principled rather than pragmatic attitudes on the part of politicians. Beyond that, collaboration is seen in terms of an individual pathology explicable by existential psychoanalysis. Modern readers might be less attracted to Sartre's argument that it sprang from a feminine or (interchangeably) a homosexual desire to seduce the strong masculine invader, but the link was frequently suggested by contemporary commentators. Guéhenno, a usually perceptive commentator, observed in his diary: 'Problème sociologique: Pourquoi tant de pédérastes parmi les collaborateurs? C . . ., F . . ., D . . . (qui, à ce qu'on dit, tàte de l'un et de l'autre). Attendent-ils de l'ordre nouveau la légitimation de leurs amours?'[12] Whether or not homosexuality was more prominent in fact, it was widely perceived as a common characteristic of collaboration. So it was not exceptional that Daniel Séréno, the major homosexual character in Sartre's *Les Chemins de la liberté* novel sequence, should eventually be depicted

9. These figures are accepted by Jean-Pierre Rioux in his *La France de la Quatrième République*, vol. 1, Paris, 1980, following Novick's analysis.

10. Jean-Paul Sartre, 'Qu'est-ce qu'un collaborateur?', *La République Française* New York, August 1945, reprinted in his collection *Situations, III*, Paris, 1949, pp. 43–61.

11. Ibid., p. 60.

12. Jean Guéhenno, *Journal des années noires (1940–1944)*, Paris, 1947, p. 123. The undeveloped initials are in Guéhenno's published text.

strutting round Paris in his German uniform.[13]

There was something of a general consensus in identifying a sexual dimension to collaboration. Gabriel Marcel, an existentialist of the right-wing Catholic variety, took a similar view to Sartre. He thought there was a small minority of extreme collaborators who were guilty of a lack of judgement springing from some psychological flaw. He concluded: 'La psychologie du transfuge reste à élaborer. . . . Je soupçonne fortement que cette psychologie est à bas érotique et même masochienne.'[14] On this reading, collaborators become something akin to the mentally ill, whose plight ought to elicit pity rather than blame. An even simpler view is also implicit in the notion of a lack of judgement, that they were people who unluckily backed the wrong horse. These two views inevitably made up a large part of the arguments put forward in the public media and in the court-room, in defence or attenuation of the activities of erstwhile collaborators.

Most fictional narratives which dealt with the question of collaboration tended to use the sexual connection. Since narrative fiction is bound to present social relations as personal relations, it is not surprising that the sexual should mediate the political. But it is primarily a means of moulding attitudes rather than an attempted transcription of historical events. Undoubtedly, the postwar attitudes to collaboration were largely formed by narratives, usually informal and usually oral. Those narratives which have survived are, of course, overwhelmingly the written public narratives of prose fiction.

Fictional representations of the war formed a large, though by no means preponderant, part of France's literary output in the two or three years after liberation. Among the reasons were a flourishing demand for reprints of clandestine works which had usually been difficult to obtain; a ready supply of texts written but not published during the Occupation; and the attraction of accounts of wartime events, which provided exciting and still topical subject matter. For the first year or so the literary scene was left to writers who enjoyed Resistance credentials. Jean-Paul Sartre observed in November 1945: 'il n'est pas d'écrivains aujourd'hui en exercice qui n'aient coopéré de près ou de loin aux mouvements de la résistance; à tout le moins avait-il un cousin dans le maquis'.[15]

13. See J.-P. Sartre, *La Mort dans l'âme*, Paris, 1949.
14. Gabriel Marcel, 'Spectroscopie de la trahison', *Hebdomadaire du Temps présent*, 1 September 1944, p. 7.
15. Jean-Paul Sartre, 'La nationalisation de la littérature', *Les Temps modernes*,

Michael Kelly

Clandestine novels, though written and published during the Occupation, really came into their own after the Liberation, and exercised a powerful influence on how the collaboration was viewed. Surprisingly, they rarely depicted collaborators in much detail, and usually treated the issue of collaboration with some discretion. The best known clandestine novel, Vercors's *Le Silence de la mer*, depicts an elderly Frenchman and his niece maintaining their decision not to communicate with the German officer billeted with them, despite the human and emotional pressures to speak. The sexual dimension is suggested in the officer's discreet wooing of the girl, whom he tries to cast in the role of Beauty to his Beast. Collaboration in this context is the temptation, firmly rejected, of a human relationship with the occupant.

Claude Morgan's *La marque de l'homme*, published clandestinely under the pseudonym 'Mortagne', deals with life in a prison camp. The narrator's wife appears, through her letters, to be associating with Germans, wooed by music and culture. Ultimately she is dissuaded from collaboration by hearing volleys of shots from the firing squads in nearby Mont-Valérien prison. Her husband is also persuaded by a friend's example to take a Resistance stance. Again, collaboration takes the form of yielding to a seduction, and is finally rejected.

Louis Parrot's novel of 1943, *Paille noire des étables*, originally signed pseudonymously 'Margeride', depicts the encounter of Elie Chaméane, a Resistance worker, with Catherine, a destitute girl used by the Germans to collect intelligence on the Maquis. Under threat of starvation, torture and death she has agreed to seduce unsuspecting young Maquisards who come into town, and glean all she can about their activities. Elie's kindness impels Catherine to confess her situation to him, but before he can rescue her she flees, probably going away to drown herself. Collaboration here is the product of irresistible coercion, and uses the methods of seduction to achieve its objectives. Though the girl is objectively collaborating, her heart is not in it and she is a victim of degradation and exploitation.

Without exhausting the variety of clandestine literature, these three tales are characteristic examples of how collaboration is depicted in it. The existence of French collaborators in the form of spies, traitors and the dreaded Milice is acknowledged as part of the

November 1945, pp. 193–211, p. 206.

wartime context. But direct representation of collaboration is usually quite discreet, showing it as a the result of weakness in the face of threats or temptations. The reasons are not difficult to find. A major objective of resistance writing was to lead people away from the ever-present inducements to collaborate, especially in the early part of the Occupation when collaboration was the policy of a French leader who still enjoyed widespread popular support. A corollary of this was the need to identify the German occupying forces as the enemy, thus focusing attention on the primary aim of the Resistance as the war against the invader. Moreover, it was prudent not to paint the collaboration in too lurid colours, in case potential resisters might be dismayed or demoralised.

The effect of clandestine writing in post-Liberation France was therefore ambiguous. Whilst it served to affirm that the spirit and culture of France had never been wholly conquered, its actual message was no longer the same when the German invader had been expelled and the collaborationist government discredited and overthrown. The effect was to minimise the moral and political danger of collaboration, suggesting that understanding rather than punishment was an appropriate response.

The significant shift of meaning can be seen at work in the film version of *Le Silence de la mer* produced in 1947 by Jean-Pierre Melville. Where the novel points to real perils of war and Occupation, cunningly masked by the culture and humanity of the German officer, the film shows the same situation in reverse, with the human qualities of the officer struggling to shine through the harsh exigencies of war. With very little modification, a call to resistance is transformed into a plea for Franco-German understanding. In similar fashion, the warnings of Parrot or Morgan against collaboration as a temptation or a trap, might easily furnish excuses or alibis for those who in the event had collaborated, reluctantly or not. Whatever the arguments for renewing links with post-war Germany, the issue was not central to French political life, whereas the question of how to deal with former collaborators and the forces associated with them was very much to the fore in post-war political debate. For the most part, Resistance writers themselves were not anxious to offer succour to collaborators, and there is a painful ambiguity in the post-war impact of their wartime work.

Among the resistance sympathisers in the circles of existentialism, the fictional presentation of collaboration tended to follow the direction of Sartre's essay, attempting to analyse the problem in terms of individual pathology. Simone de Beauvoir's *Le Sang des autres* (Paris, 1945) centres on the problems of individual choice and responsibility. Collaboration is an option considered by a female protagonist, Hélène, in an attempt to assert her personal independence and dignity. Preparing to work for a German businessman in Berlin, she realises her mistake when the decisive dinner engagement appears to her most forcefully as an attempted seduction. Her reconciliation with Jean Blomart is also a commitment to the Resistance, in which cause she eventually dies.

Individual pathology is implicit in the approach of Albert Palle, whose short story 'Le Milicien' was published in two parts by Sartre's review, *Les Temps modernes*.[16] His portrayal of Miliciens hanging around in the Vercors on the fringes of combat with the Maquis emphasises physicality. Their experience is sordid and aimless, isolated from the people, punctuated by arbitrary brutality and perfunctory sex. Political and military issues are largely incidental to the experience of personal and collective disintegration. Palle's tale is reminiscent of Sartre's story *L'Enfance d'un chef* in its attempt to grasp the subjective reality of Fascism from within, and is one of the few fictional narratives to focus on characters whose collaboration was beyond doubt. Jean-Louis Bory's *Mon village à l'heure allemande* (Paris, 1945), which won the prestigious Goncourt literary prize in 1945, is another.

Bory's novel attempts to enter the experience of collaborators, as one dimension of a wider intersubjective mosaic. Events in a small village somewhere beyond Orléans in the spring of 1944 are presented from the point of view of various of its inhabitants, as well as that of German officers, local Maquisards, a narrator, the village itself personified, and even a dog. The collaborators include Denise Véchard, who cleans for the local Germans and is having a secret affair with their interpreter; Lécheur the confectioner, who gleefully provides his best fare for the occupying officers; and Auguste Boudet, the hate-filled farmer's son who joins the Milice. All the villagers have to reach some modus vivendi with the Germans. Working people, like Denise Véchard, are tempted by the prospects of gainful employment. Among the tradesmen and farmers, the temptation is strong to develop advantageous commercial relations,

---

16. Albert Palle, 'Le Milicien', *Les Temps modernes*, April 1946, pp. 1202–27; May 1946, pp. 1432–56.

even at the price of demonstrating public acceptance of the Occupation. Lécheur exemplifies this, though he also relishes the gestures of public defiance it permits. Though both Lécheur and Véchard collaborate, neither is roundly condemned. This is because they establish a kind of perverse integrity, and because both are victims who eventually die: Véchard in a fire while she is waiting for her lover, Lécheur hounded by a former employee who uses the Resistance as a cover to pay off a grudge. Auguste Boudet remains as the demon, not so much because he joins the Milice as because he uses his position to exact personal revenges on his family and friends, and to enrich himself in a black-market petrol swindle.

Sexual relations are closely linked to collaboration in Bory's novel, but it is the personal which dominates the political in the hothouse village atmosphere, to the extent that political commitments appear almost as personal gestures, and are judged largely on that basis. Hence Denise Véchard is exonerated by the genuine tenderness between her and Walter Prinz, who is last seen desperately seeking her near the fire and calling out piteously 'Tenise Féchard! . . .'[17] Conversely Auguste is condemned for his cynical sexual exploitation of the family's simple-minded servant, for maliciously destroying a treasured rose bush which his sister had inherited from her dead mother, and for finding excuses to arrest Pierre Le Meur, his sister's boyfriend.

Understandably, immediate post-war depictions in the work of former Resistance members generally showed collaboration in a most unattractive light. Perhaps the most uncompromising representation of it was in a collection of short stories by Jean Fréville, entitled *Les Collabos* (Paris, 1946). The first story, from which the collection takes its title, depicts the base opportunism of the mayor and council of a Normandy village. In reprisal for a supposed act of minor sabotage, the local German commanding officer decides to shoot either one Jew, or two Communists, or three leading citizens, including the mayor: the choice is the council's. After much squabbling, unable to find any Jews or Communists not already in German prison camps, they settle on the local blacksmith's Arab apprentice, who is duped into declaring himself as Jewish, and is duly shot. The mayor takes advantage of the episode to conclude a profitable business deal with the Germans. The story embodies the

---

17. J.L. Bory, *Mon village à l'heure allemande*, Paris, 1945, p. 267 in the 'J'ai lu' edition.

view Fréville expresses in his Preface, that: 'Leur commun dénominateur à tous fut la lâcheté, l'égoisme, l'intérêt personnel et l'intérêt de classe, la haine et la crainte du peuple, l'anti-communisme, le goût de la servitude, de la servitude qui, comme l'écrit Vauvenargues, "abaisse les hommes au point de s'en faire aimer."'[18]

The denunciatory tone of Fréville's stories expresses the mood of deep anger widely felt in resistance circles, rather than any attempt to offer objective analysis. A similar passion informs Loys Masson's *Le Requis civil* (Paris, 1945), which depicts a self-righteous bourgeois Pétainist who is brought face to face with the shame of his collaboration, particularly in the form of his own son who joins the Milice. The corruption and destructiveness of extreme pro-Nazism goes beyond anything even he can stomach, but is clearly shown to be directly in the logic of his view and commitments. Masson's unique blend of Catholicism and Communism gives the novel a ring of biblical authority and prophetic force.

As well as passion and denunciation there were, among the most committed Resistance writers, serious attempts to understand and explain the social roots of collaboration. Louis Aragon's novel, *Aurélien*, which was written during and after the final stages of the Occupation, and published in Paris in 1945, provides a detailed picture of a section of the French bourgeoisie which had fought in the First World War. Underlying their personal relationships in the interwar period is a growing appreciation of where their business interests lie. As the novel concludes in the débâcle of June 1940, they are preparing to take advantage of the commercial opportunities which the German occupation is likely to bring them. Mixing astute psychological observation with at times caustic social comment, Aragon reconstitutes the trajectory of part of the French propertied classes. Drawing, as he later revealed, on the development of the collaborationist writer Drieu la Rochelle, he leads the reader through a gradual withdrawal of the esteem for the title character as he declines from disorientation into venality.

Perhaps the best-known of the post-war novels by resistance writers is Roger Vailland's *Drôle de jeu*, which won the Interallié Literary Prize in 1945. The ambiguities of Resistance work and the strange forms of heroism it inspires are set against a background of deception and betrayal, in which sexual and political motives are intricately interwoven. The Gestapo's informant is finally identified

18. J. Fréville, *Les Collabos*, Paris, 1946, pp. 6–7.

as Mathilde, the former mistress of Marat, the central Resistance character. The destructiveness of Mathilde's sexual behaviour is not radically different from that of Marat's, however, and her treachery is established in logical rather than emotional terms. The pattern of sexual relations runs athwart the political relations and by virtue of its symbolic power, invests the activity of the Resistance workers with a disturbing ambiguity. Vailland both uses and disrupts the strong association between sexual and political virtue to produce a complex text for which he disclaimed any polemical (that is, political) value: 'Mais *Drôle de Jeu* n'est pas un roman *sur* la Résistance. Il ne peut donc fournir matière à aucune espèce de polémique, – autre que purement littéraire – et tout argument d'ordre historique ou politique qu'on y puiserait serait, par définition, sans valeur.' [19] How seriously this disclaimer may be taken is a matter of doubt. If not disingenuous, it is certainly naïve – and Vailland was capable of being both. Though it risked controversy by presenting the resisters as less than paragons, his novel dramatised the political gulf separating them from the collaborators, in contrast to the similarities at the level of personal, and in particular sexual, relations.

Standing somewhere between the existentialists and the Communists is Romain Gary's novel *L'Education européenne* (Paris, 1945) which won the Prix des Critiques of that year. Set in occupied Poland, it examines the dilemmas of Resistance and collaboration in terms which suggest a parallel with France. Interpretation of the text is complex, however, and not only because Gary himself served with the Free French army rather than in the metropolitan Resistance. The main difficulty is that the occupation of Poland, with which Gary was familiar, differs in significant respects from that of France, where relations with the Germans were much more ambiguous. Furthermore, the novel has been very substantially rewritten, so that versions currently available differ significantly in tone and import from the one published in 1945. None the less, a major theme of the novel is the often brutal sexual exploitation of women by German occupying forces and by the obsequious pro-German bourgeoisie. Driven to compliance by fear and hunger, women are degraded by men who by so doing confirm their own degradation in collaboration.

After the first two years of liberation, direct representations of the collaboration in literature became less common. Most probably

---

19. Roger Vailland, *Drôle de jeu*, Paris, 1945, p. 7 of 'Livre de Poche' edition.

the audience for writing on this sensitive subject was dwindling. Among the writers, those who felt strongly against collaboration had already said what they wanted, those who did not feel strongly were not interested, and those who might wish to defend collaboration still had a long way to go before they could do so with impunity. For the most part, these latter focused their attention on real or imagined shortcomings of the Resistance, or the claimed excesses of the 'Epuration'. However, as early as 1946, a series of works by Marcel Aymé signalled the beginning of an offensive aimed at discrediting the Resistance and, if not exonerating the collaborators, at least arguing that they were no worse than anyone else.[20]

Aymé's work marks the beginnings of the re-emergence of former collaborators into print and coincides with the first major attenuation of the 'Epuration'. The major show trials being over, court verdicts and sentences grew daily more lenient. In the summer of 1946, Communist jurors withdrew from the courts in protest. The leading Communist lawyer, Maurice Kriegel-Valrimont, explained: 'La démission des jurés communistes de la Haute Cour de Justice a troublé le cours solennel mais régulier des mises en liberté, des aquittements et des peines dérisoires dont bénéficiaient les personnages les plus marquants de la trahison.'[21] Every passing month brought a more indulgent attitude to those accused of collaboration, at least on the part of the courts and the authorities of the Fourth Republic. The cautious re-emergence of former Vichy supporters into public life no doubt played a part in accelerating the process, and in promoting the growing desire to draw a veil over the whole unfortunate episode. By the following summer, some sections of Catholic opinion were becoming alarmed at the collapse of any vestiges of justice in dealing with former collaborators. The left-wing Catholic review *Esprit* published a special issue asking 'Y a-t-il une justice en France?', and its indignation ran to a second special issue three months later.[22]

The year 1947 was a turning-point in French attitudes to collaboration, as it was in every dimension of French political and ideological activity. The onset of the Cold War brought the end of

20. An excellent account of Aymé's activity is given by Nicholas Hewitt in chapter 12 above.

21. Maurice Kriegel-Valrimont, 'Epuration et justice de classe', *Les Cahiers du communisme*, August 1946, pp. 721–32, p. 721.

22. *Esprit*, August 1947, and November 1947.

the political alliances on which the Resistance and the Liberation had been built. An important part of the realignments of that year was the return of collaborationist forces into political activity, often alongside the Gaullists who had so recently been arrayed against them. A key theme of the new dispensation was the Grandfather Rabbit view, with which this chapter began, and which Colin Nettelbeck has so shrewdly depicted,[23] according to which collaboration was limited to a small minority of clearly identifiable traitors, who were severely punished at the Liberation. As an accurate representation of historical events, it does not bear close scrutiny. But it suited the international and domestic political purposes of France's ruling groups, and the personal and collective moral purposes of the majority of French people. For those reasons it served as the guiding myth behind most literary and discursive representations of the collaboration for the next twenty years.

23. See the article by Colin Nettelbeck in this volume, pp. 252–93.

15

GETTING THE STORY RIGHT: NARRATIVES OF THE SECOND WORLD WAR IN POST-1968 FRANCE

Colin Nettelbeck

It is impossible to enumerate all the elements that go into making up the collective memory of an experience as large, varied and traumatic as the Second World War was for the French. The way in which ordinary individuals experienced it is imponderable, and there is most frequently no way of knowing what stories they told their children or their friends. Published journals are not easy to evaluate, and sometimes no easier to identify as 'fact' than a 'fiction' as self-avowed as the celebrated Calvo–Dancette *La Bête est morte*, the 1945 comic-book account of the Second World War in the animal kingdom, as told by Grandfather Rabbit.[1] There are many things that one cannot readily trace, ephemeral things such as radio broadcasts, newsreels, speeches by public figures, and so on. And these difficulties are compounded by others: even to reach a consensus about what happened and when took an extraordinarily long time – witness the fact that not until 1979 was a straightforward and accurate historical account of the 1938–44 period available to the French reader,[2] witness also that it was not until 1983 that French schoolchildren – and then only in their final year of high school – would have to learn, for examination, any comprehensive coverage of the period. The 1945 Bernard and Redon *Nouvelle Histoire de la France* for primary-school students (*cours moyen*), published by Nathan, Paris – a textbook still in use in the early 1950s – offered

---

1. The Calvo-Dancette comic 2 vols, Paris, 1945 gives a surprisingly full, albeit simplistic, version of events, not unlike the Gaullian version described below.
2. Jean-Pierre Azéma, *De Munich à la Libération*, Paris, 1979.

two brief chapters on the war, the first subtitled '1939 La deuxième guerre mondiale', and the second '1944 Libération de Paris'. After a description of the lightning defeat of the French army, the key statements of the narrative are as follows:

> Le maréchal Pétain, chef du gouvernement français, demande l'armistice. C'est, pour toute la France, une journée de deuil.
> La moitié du pays est occupée; deux millions de nos soldats sont prisonniers.
> Le gouvernement du maréchal Pétain s'installe à Vichy.
> Mais la France n'acceptait ni la défaite ni l'esclavage.
> De Londres, un ancien ministre, le général de Gaulle, lance un appel à la résistance française: "La France a perdu une bataille, elle n'a pas perdu la guerre."
> Et, en effet, la guerre allait continuer. (p. 204)

> Le gouvernement du maréchal Pétain se rapproche de l'Allemagne: c'est la politique dite "de collaboration".
> Mais les Français, eux, se refusent à collaborer avec "l'occupant", qui les traite en esclaves.
> Les Allemands ... veulent forcer les ouvriers français à partir en Allemagne, afin d'y travailler dans les usines de guerre.
> Des milliers de patriotes sont arrêtés, torturés, déportés en Allemagne, où ils meurent de misère et de faim dans les camps de concentration.
> En France, les résistants organisent une lutte incessante de guérillas: ils se réfugient dans le maquis, c'est-à-dire dans les bois et les montagnes.
> Les Allemands ripostent en fusillant des otages innocents.
> Le 6 juin 1944, une grande armée, comprenant des troupes américaines, anglaises et françaises, réussit, malgré la défense allemande, à débarquer en Normandie. (pp. 205–6)

The Germans are beaten, Paris is liberated, and France, although faced with a huge reconstruction effort, goes on. Even Calvo's story was not quite as far-fetched.

If it can now be said, with some confidence at least, that there are narratives in the France of today that have at last got the story of 1938–44 right, it will be some time yet before that story is widely accepted as truth, and furthermore, the 'truth' will have emerged only after a long and painful struggle. Part of the struggle has to do with the French gradually learning to face and cope with the more traumatic aspects of the experience; and part of it results from a political conflict about who was going to have the right to tell the story: the role of Grandfather Rabbit was not as uncontested as

Calvo thought. The deeper one delves into the period, the more obvious it becomes that what was at stake was a question not so much of ideology, but of the very identity of France. It is not an idle symbol that 1983 should mark not only the official entry of the wider French experience of the war in school textbooks, but the time when the nation was able (albeit in a cautious manner, as if somehow still convalescent) to open one of the most entangled cases in its judicial history – the trial of Klaus Barbie, the so-called 'butcher of Lyon'. Despite many hesitations, and many unseemly legal manoeuvres, the extensive media coverage of the trial in 1987 showed that France, collectively, is prepared now to remember what for a long time it went to great lengths to block out.

If 1968 has been chosen as the watershed, it is not because of the mini-revolutions of that year, but rather because it is a significant turning in history – a turning of which the student and worker agitation is only one expression. It is the end of the decade of Charles de Gaulle's rule, but more importantly, it is the end of what can be called the 'Gaullian' myth of history – not because he was the only one to espouse it, but because he was its most eloquent, persistent, and politically powerful exponent. It was a version of history that had the story very wrong, and de Gaulle's departure marked the beginning of a veritable flood of war-narratives of all sorts: memoirs, historical studies, documentary and fictional films, novels.[3]

The diversity of this corpus is immense, and the daunting methodological problems can be measured by two works that have limited themselves to studying the fiction. The American critic, Frederick J. Harris,[4] has chosen to group his material by topics, following the chronology of the events and using the literature essentially as an illustration of the history. He admits as one of the disadvantages of this approach the dividing up of literary works – we get Sartre on the defeat, for example, and then Sartre on the camps a few chapters later – but there is a more serious problem of

---

3. A comprehensive bibliography would occupy many pages. There is a useful one in Pascal Ory's article 'Comme de l'An quarante. Dix années de 'retro satanas', in *Le Débat*, no. 16 (Nov. 1981), pp. 109–17. It can be supplemented, for films, by Stéphane Lévy-Klein's article in *Positif*, no. 170 (June 1975), pp. 36–59: 'Sur le cinéma français des années 1940–44: II – les réalisations.' And there is a useful checklist of novels in the thesis of Daniel Brandi, *La Guerre de 1939–45 dans les romans de Camus, Céline, Gracq, Simon, Tournier: la guerre transposée*, Doctorat de troisième cycle, Université de Paris IV, 1980.

4. Frederick J. Harris, *Encounters with Darkness*, Oxford, 1983.

which he seems unaware: namely his failure to take any account of when the various fictional accounts were written. Thus, in his chapter on the lack of enthusiasm in the French Army, he quotes first from Tournier's *Le Roi des Aulnes* (1970), then from Dutourd's *Taxis de la Marne* (1956), P.-H. Simon's *Portrait d'un officier* (1958), Jacques Perret's *Caporal épinglé* (1947), and Sartre's *La Mort dans l'âme* (1949) – in that order. Still, despite its flaws, this book does give a good idea of the range of human experience involved. A different, and rather more fruitful approach is taken by Daniel Brandi,[5] who delineates two periods (before and after 1950) as part of a general evolution towards a greater literary perspective on the war. He is less interested in the war itself than in the way in which a chosen group of authors transpose the experience into a literary version.

Beginning with Camus's allegorical fable, *La Peste* (1947), he works forward to Tournier's *Le Roi des Aulnes*, via Céline, Gracq and Claude Simon. This is certainly a more convincing way of dealing with literature, and although it does not say so in as many words, its structure implies that Brandi has understood that any account of this literature of history must be set in the context of the history of literature.

Rather than Brandi's date of 1950, however, it is preferable to see the first period as extending to 1958, since it is de Gaulle's return that marks a change in attitude to history. It is impossible to assess in any scientific manner to what extent this early corpus of novels, along with a long list of narrative films, constitute a real contribution to the collective memory, but they do offer considerable understanding. At the same time as the political, legal, and educational structures of society were trying to simplify the situation by pushing unpleasant truths into oblivion, novelists and film-makers were telling an enormous range of stories, which remain as a significant expression of what has collectively been remembered. And although, taken separately, they may be no more than the account of a subjective experience – this man caught as a prisoner-of-war, this one carting a butchered pig across Paris in a suitcase, this little girl losing her parents in a stukka attack on a civilian refugee column, this young woman falling in love with a German soldier[6] – together they add up, not just to the chronicle of events

5. Brandi, *La Guerre de 1939–45*
6. As in Sartre's *La Mort dans l'âme* (or Perret's *Le Caporal épinglé*), Aymé's *La Traversée de Paris*, *Les Jeux interdits* and *Hiroshima mon amour* respectively.

that Frederick Harris outlines, but to a tragic and enormous sense of loss. While some aspects of Fourth Republic policy seem to have aimed at getting life back to 'normal' after the eruptions of the war,[7] what is commonly expressed in the narratives of this time, beyond all the diversity, is that the changes wrought by this war were definitive, and that France would never be the same again.

There can be little doubt that de Gaulle's total occupation of the political and historical stage effectively prevented the telling of other versions of the story: for ten years, he monopolised the role of Grandfather Rabbit. Briefly, the Gaullian myth of history can be expressed as follows. France, after being badly demoralised in the 1930s by incompetent leadership and the divisive struggles of party politics, was crushed in 1940 by superior weaponry, and rather let down by its British allies. Even while she was being bled dry by the brutally repressive army that occupied her for four years, she resisted bravely: from the outside, with de Gaulle's Free French, and from within, through various clandestine movements. This France regained her freedom and honour by driving the Germans out – with a little help, of course, from the Allies. The few villains who had helped the Germans were purged: the collaborationist Vichy government in the first place, with the ignoble old Marshal Pétain being sent off into exile, and the even more ignoble Laval being shot; scurrilous intellectuals, too, like the novelist-journalist Brasillach, were sent before the firing squad or to jail. France could once again stand proudly as a united people, joined by their historic participation in the unrelenting struggle against the Hitlerian occupant. This is the France of Destiny, the Eternal France that saw its role as the leader of a new European community that would be strong enough to resist the threat from the East as well as American and British hegemony.

In retrospect, the rhetoric sounds hollow, and even a little ridiculous. De Gaulle's electoral successes, moreover, may well have depended less on his selective version of history than on what this latter shared with a more general shying away from the traumatising experiences of the war itself. It can surely be no accident that the de

7. This is particularly evident in the generous amnesty policies, which saw the number of collaborationist prisoners reduced from 43,000 to 13,000 by December 1948, 8,000 a year later, 4,000 at the beginning of 1951, 1,500 in October 1952, 61 in 1956 and 19 in 1958. See Marcel Baudot, 'La Répression de la Collaboration et l'Epuration politique et économique', in *La Libération de la France*, Actes du Colloque international tenu à Paris du 28 au 31 octobre 1974, Paris, 1976, p. 781.

Gaulle decade coincides with the boom of the anti-narrative constructions of the 'Nouveau Roman' and the 'Nouvelle Vague' in cinema, as well as with the anti-historical developments of the structuralist movements. Nevertheless, for ten years, a majority of the French (although the majority dwindled with time) seemed to find in the image of France projected by de Gaulle a compensation for the objective shrinkage of France's power in the world, and a stabilising influence that permitted a degree of psychological healing, and considerable economic recovery. There had been little such stability, healing, or recovery in the years preceding de Gaulle's taking of power, and the France of the Fourth Republic years was neither as proud nor as united as the later Gaullist myth would portray it. The war itself, far from reducing the ideological cleavages that are so deeply scored into French history, actually brought them to a head, and post-war France very much still fragmented by its experience of the defeat and the Occupation, unable to agree on what the experience had been, let alone what it had meant, was caught up in the throes of perhaps the greatest identity crisis in its history. There were also external problems, like the Cold War, or the difficulties of colonial withdrawal, and such factors served to exacerbate inner conflicts by sharpening political factionism. This flourished under the Fourth Republic constitution, which, like the Third Republic before it, encouraged a multiplicity of political parties, and made coalition governments of some kind almost inevitable.

In order to grasp why it has been difficult to 'get the story right', it is worth recalling just what a complicated and entangled story it was. The dark heart of the War for France is in the years 1943–4, when the major struggle was within. Although its limited scope prevents it from being considered a real civil war[8] (the majority of the population was largely passive), there was certainly a significant Franco-French conflict. Its most obvious manifestation, though not its only one, was the battle to the death between French Resistance fighters (widely thought of as terrorists by the population at large) and the French Milice, the paramilitary police force formed by Joseph Darnand with the blessing of both Vichy and the Germans. It is easy enough, especially in retrospect, to understand that the

---

8. The British journalist and France-watcher, Alexander Werth, had felt the seeds of civil war to be present in France as early as 1934. See *France in Ferment*, London, 1934, p. 283.

German Occupation was not likely to bring out the best in the occupied people, and it was of course an active part of Hitler's policy of permanently humiliating France, to provoke as much divisiveness as possible. Not counting the areas occupied by Italy, France, from the beginning, was divided into four zones that had little communication between them. Alsace-Lorraine was simply annexed, and its young men forced into the armies of the Reich; the north was placed under the German military command in Belgium; half of the rest was occupied, at French expense, by a very large German army; and even the so-called 'free' zone in the south, governed from Vichy, was the victim of such draconian economic demands from the Germans that the freedom was more illusory than real. At that stage, France's colonial empire was largely intact, but reduced, by the terms of the armistice, to the role of impotent spectator. This was underlined, in July 1940, by the British operation that sank the French fleet at Mers-el-Kébir, and killed 1,300 powerless French sailors. This same event served to play on endemic French anglophobia, as did the later British invasion of Syria, with the result that public opinion about who was the enemy in the war, and who were the allies, was also deeply divided. For many, de Gaulle was far from a hero: he was something of a traitor who had not only abandoned his command in France, but compounded his crime by throwing his lot in with the treacherous British.

All this notwithstanding, neither the divisions imposed by the Germans, with their concomitant difficulties of communication, nor the economic problems, prevented France from being a reasonably united nation during the first two years of the Occupation – up to November 1942, when the Germans, in response to the Allied invasion of North Africa, took over the whole of mainland France. Unified in its relief to be out of the war, and in its belief, as Paxton and others have amply shown[9], that Pétain and the Vichy government were the best means of assuring a decent and honourable return to normalcy, as well as the most likely way of securing the return of the millions of prisoners of war. To understand the completeness of this illusion, account must be taken of the religious veneration that surrounded the octogenarian Pétain, the hero of Verdun who had

9. Robert O. Paxton, *Vichy France*, New York, 1972. (Translated as *La France de Vichy*, Paris, 1973; new edn, coll. 'Points-Histoire', 1977.) See also Henri Amouroux, *La grande histoire des Français sous l'occupation, ii: Quarante millions de petainistes*, Paris, 1977, *passim*. Roderick Kedward's *Resistance in Vichy France: A Study of Ideas & Motivation in the Southern Zone 1940–42*, Oxford, 1978.

returned to save France from its shame, and to restore the great values of family, work, and patriotism. It would take time before the majority of French people would realise that their messiah was a dithering, pious, and incompetent geriatric, and that his government was not merely a puppet of German policy, but actively committed to an ideology of collaboration. To use the word 'realise', moreover, is only possible with hindsight: most people had very little idea of what was going on. From where would they have taken their information? Newspapers were full of propaganda, and they knew it, and the same was true for the radio, whether from Vichy, Paris, or London. What they knew was their clocks had been adjusted to Berlin time, that their prisoners didn't come home, that it got harder and harder to feed and clothe oneself unless one could take advantage of the black market.

During these first two years, resistance against the Germans was sporadic and largely disorganised. We must remember that the Communists, glued as closely as ever to the pro-Moscow line, were in the embarrassing situation of being tied by the German-Russian pact until the German invasion of Russia in mid-1941 – and the Communists although clandestine, were the best-organised of political groupings within France. Whatever measure one takes, it is impossible to avoid the image of disintegration. This France, which had thought of itself as a great power in every sense of the word, and which was moreover thought to be so by its friends and enemies alike, was, largely without realising it, falling into bits.

The geographical divisions were compounded by social, political, and racial ones. If one were rich enough, one could eat and wear what one wanted, and even drive a car; if one were well enough connected, survival, and even relative comfort, were assured.[10] Sartre, Simone de Beauvoir and Camus, in Paris, were never at serious risk, which is not to say that life was easy,[11] and nor was Jacques Lacan, when he demanded back from the Gestapo the dossier of his wife Sylvie, who had been unwise enough to declare herself Jewish.[12] Gide, in the south, was safe and comfortable, and so was Malraux, until he launched into active resistance very late in

10. The memoirs of Maurice Sachs are illuminating in this regard, and particularly *La Chasse à courre*, Paris, 1949. See also Jacques Delarue, *Trafics et crimes sous l'Occupation*, Paris, 1968, especially Part I: 'Les dessous du marché noir'.
11. See Simone de Beauvoir, *La Force de l'Age*, Paris, 1960, chs 7 and 8.
12. See Catherine Clément, *Vies et légendes de Jacques Lacan*, Paris, 1981, pp. 30–31.

the war.[13] If one was identified as a refugee or a Communist, one could be jailed, or put into a concentration camp, or onto a list of hostages,[14] if one was a Jew, one's identity papers said so, and so did the yellow star one was obliged to wear prominently displayed on one's chest – and one was likely to be picked up at any time, and taken away. And it must be remembered that Vichy's anti-Semitic laws were formulated in advance of German demands, and that the first big raid in Paris, in July 1942, in which more than 20,000 Jews were rounded up into the Vélodrome d'hiver, was carried out by French police, 9,000 strong.[15]

It was a time of pain and paradox. Again, it is only in retrospect that the terms of the dilemma can be clearly formulated. For the French of the time – except perhaps for the few tens of thousands by choice or chance in exile – nothing was clear. There was unavoidable ambiguity for instance, for singers like Edith Piaf or Charles Trenet, knowing that part of their audience was made up of German military personnel, but aware of a duty to give heart to their compatriots. The French film industry continued to produce large numbers of films, even though it had to submit to German censorship, and often enough to the pressures of varying degrees of German ownership,[16] believing that French actors should have work, and that French audiences should be able to see their own films in their own language, rather than subtitled German ones.

On another level, during the bleakest period of the Occupation, in 1943–4, when there were 2,200 German gestapists in France, there were 30,000 French agents working for the Germans.[17] It is obvious, with hindsight, that that was wrong, but one has only to read accounts of the trials of Pierre Laval or of Robert Brasillach,[18] the pragmatic politician and the committed ideologue, to realise that at the time, even the most grotesque and heinous behaviour was no longer shocking, so blurred had the contours of moral identity

13. See Jean Lacouture, *André Malraux*, Paris, 1973, pp. 273–82.
14. There is a moving account of some aspects of these fundamental insecurities by Hélène Elek, mother of Thomas Elek, one of the Manouchian group:*La Mémoire d'Hélène*, Paris, 1977.
15. See, for the story of the politics of Jewish repression in France, M. Marrus and R. Paxton, *Vichy France and the Jews*, New York, 1981.
16. Over two hundred films were made in France during the Occupation. See J. Siclier *La France de Pétain et son cinéma*, Paris, 1981. See also Chapter 8 above.
17. See *Le Monde*, 18 May 1978: Claude Sarraute's report on a 'Dossiers de l'écran' programme on the Occupation.
18. Robert Aron, *Histoire de l'Epuration*, vol. 2, pp. 322–54 (Brasillach) and pp. 534–68 (Laval).

become. For the occupied French, actions and attitudes were dictated less by principle than by circumstances. It is widely accepted, for example, that one of the important reasons – and perhaps the most important reason – why the Resistance ranks began to swell so dramatically from 1943 on, was that the underground was the only alternative for young men who would otherwise have been shipped off to work in Germany through the obligatory labour programme (Service de Travail Obligatoire). To present such men as patriotic heroes is to twist words, and history.

The more deeply one goes into the period, the more difficult it is to describe any behaviour or destiny as typical or exemplary. There are no easily definable paradigms, and if one were to seek a term to define the experience of the collectivity, it would have to be a term like 'dissociation'. How deeply the conflict penetrated into the fabric of French society is shown in the post-Liberation purge, which the Resistance forces, Communists and Gaullists alike (if not together), organised as a kind of national catharsis, but which in retrospect appears as a clumsy and grotesque attempt to hide as many skeletons as possible in the national closet. Aron's now-classic history of the 'Epuration' abounds in stories of atrocities committed in the name of justice, and of blatant injustices committed for reasons of political expediency. Aron exaggerates the number of people affected. He suggests almost 100,000, enough victims, he opines, to create a psychosis that will continue to weigh in the memory of the survivors.[19] The real figure was probably more like a half of that,[20] but Aron is right about the psychosis. In retrospect, it is hard to find justification for shaving women bald and parading them naked just because they happened to fall in love with a German soldier; and even if one is understanding about such manifestations of popular vengeance-lust, it is not easy to accept that the authorities of justice found it necessary to pump Pierre Laval's stomach after he had taken cyanide, so that he could be stood up in front of a firing-squad. Any overall assessment of the 'Epuration' would have to conclude that it did more harm than good, and while it did provide one of the bases of the Gaullian version of history, with its simplified image of a

19. Ibid., iii/2, 371.
20. According to Baudot, 'La Répression de la Collaboration et l'Epuration politique et économique' (ref. 7) p. 783, about 10,000 were executed and there were 43,000 prison sentences. Baudot's research was sparked by the American Peter Novick (*The Resistance versus Vichy*, pp. 207–8), one of the 'liberators' of French history of this period. See *infra*.

prompt and just punishment being meted out to those who had betrayed their country, its attempt to play a role as a unifying force was counterproductive.

Contemporary commentaries critical of the 'Epuration' are rare, understandably so, since anyone criticising the process openly could easily appear suspect. One such critic, however, was Roger Grenier, who wrote for Camus's *Combat*, and who during the purge was working as a court reporter. As well as pointing out that most of the magistrates judging the people accused of collaboration had also worked as judges under Vichy, Grenier is already aware of an emerging historical myth: he writes that since the Liberation, the fiction has been established of a people struggling without respite for four years. In fact, he claims, the Resistance was a preoccupation that entered into the collective consciousness of the country after the Liberation. During the Occupation, it was of concern only to a few particular consciences. The collective conscience was dulled by an inertia that made it lean somewhat towards hostility against the occupying forces that hampered it, but that could hardly be called Resistance.[21]

Such honesty was not in tune with the spirit of the times. The general mood seems to have been formed from a desire to forget the war as soon as possible, to erase the differences, and heal the wounds. Sartre's immediate postwar essays are conciliatory in the extreme:[22] certainly there were problems under the Occupation, but they weren't that bad; probably no more people had been involved in active collaboration than in active resistance – say about 2 per cent on each side; now that the Germans had been booted out, it was time to settle down and rebuild. Sartre seems to assume that with the ejection of the external enemy (the Germàns), French unity would automatically occur. He would soon discover that the story was not as straightforward: indeed, his own inability to tell the story comprehensively was to be ironically and dramatically illustrated in his abandoning of *Les Chemins de la liberté*, which begins boldly enough, but bogs down in the beginning of its fourth volume in a prisoner-of-war camp, leaving the major questions of France's comportment after 1940 begging. Sartre is a pertinent case because he was to become the master-thinker of the post-war generation, and his views and reactions can be considered symptomatic.

21. Roger Grenier, *Le Rôle d'accusé*, Paris, 1948, pp. 106–7.
22. J.-P. Sartre, 'Paris sous l'Occupation' and 'Qu'est-ce qu'un collaborateur', in *Situations III*, Paris, 1949.

An equally interesting illustration of the belief that once the Germans were gone all would be well is evident in the way in which the internal resistance fighters were welcomed into the Liberation armies of Leclerc and Delattre. Known as the 'Amalgame', it involved the receiving into the regular armies of tens of thousands of volunteers from all areas of the Resistance. This took place in an atmosphere of considerable confusion and pragmatism,[23] but of great enthusiasm, the assumption being that all these French people were basically on the same side. By December 1944 there were more than 100,000 such volunteers integrated into the armies that were driving the Germans back, and the image of unity is very strong indeed. This did not outlast, however, the period of combat, and as early as 1946, discriminatory measures began to surface, aimed at keeping in subaltern positions those officers who had come from the internal resistance movements.[24]

This conflict between those who had resisted from within and those who had resisted from without was probably mirrored in all aspects of French life, and one of the most significant aspects of the struggle for power in post-war France, going beyond the traditional 'Communist' – 'Gaullist' opposition. In any case, it is clear that, even if getting rid of the Germans was a necessary condition for France to regain it own unity and identity, it was certainly not a sufficient one. France had gone into the war as a badly divided nation, and its experience of the Occupation had fragmented it further. It is not surprising that once the enthusiasms of the Liberation had died away, the divisions should reappear. As far as the 'Epuration' is concerned, one can understand it, now, as part of the collectivity's attempt to cope – a naïve and inappropriate way of trying to rid itself of a shame and a guilt whose depth and spread it underestimated.

The difficulty that postwar French society had in dealing with its experience of fragmentation could be demonstrated in many ways, but none more telling than the story of Joseph Joanovici, the major scandal-figure of the Fourth Republic.

It is a story of hedged bets, of multiple betrayals, of self-interest, compromise, and corruption in high places extending from before the war to the time of Joanovici's final disgrace in 1958 – a nice, if coincidental symbol of the end of the Fourth Republic. It would be

23. Lt-Col. Roger Michalon, 'L'Amalgame FFI-1ère Armée et 2è D.B.', in *La Libération de la France*, pp. 593–667.

24. Col. E.R. Rol. Tanguy, ibid., pp. 684–5.

some time before a synthesis of this story could be told,[25] for reasons candidly summarised by one of the public prosecutors: 'Dans cette affaire, la justice n'est pas à trouver la vérité, mais à assurer la tranquillité des Français. Et cette affaire-là est de nature à troubler le pays.'[26] No one would doubt that this régime produced some fine things and benefited from the work of some scrupulously honest politicians: the Auriols, or the Mendès-Frances, for example. None the less, as an expression of the society of the time, it reflects the uncertainties and conflicts, and above all, the inability of the French collectivity to manage its traumatic experiences with any kind of coherence. As a régime, the Fourth Republic would appear to have encouraged polarisation and fragmentation, rather than any new unity of the French identity.

Artistic intuitions of the direction French history was taking achieved only rarely a synthesised expression in any given work, and two such works will be considered shortly. The major characteristic of the narratives of this period is their variety, both in form and content. As an example, let us examine, briefly, three novels that appeared immediately after the Liberation: Jean-Louis Bory's *Mon Village à l'heure allemande*, Romain Gary's *L'Education européenne*, and Roger Vailland's *Drôle de jeu*.[27] Each of these works reflects, naturally enough, its author's war experience and point of view, and each was a considerable popular and critical success. At first sight, however, they are so different in every way that they do not even appear to be talking about the same war.

Jean-Louis Bory spent the war in France, mostly in his village near Orléans. He was not actively involved in the Resistance. He wrote his novel, which won the Goncourt Prize in 1945, during the crucial months of May, June and July 1944: that is, in the period covering the expectation of the Allied landing in France and the landing itself, but stopping short of the Liberation. It ends ambiguously, uneasily balanced between hope and fear, and it is significant that Bory did not think fit to add to it once the Liberation had

25. See Philippe Bernet, 'Le mystère de Monsieur Joseph', in G. Guilleminault (ed.), *La France de Vincent Auriol*, Paris, 1970, pp. 177–257. The degree to which the Fourth Republic was troubled by the Joanovici affair can also be gauged from the frequent allusions to it in Auriol's own memoirs: *Le Journal du Septennat: 1947–1954*, Paris, 1970–79, *passim*.

26. Bernet, 'Le mystère de Monsieur Joseph'.

27. Jean-Louis Bory, *Mon Village à l'heure allemande* Paris, 1945. Romain Gary, *L'Education européenne*, Paris, 1945; new edn, 1956. Roger Vailland, *Drôle de jeu*, Paris, 1945.

actually taken place. The kaleidoscopic construction of the novel reflects the vision of a world that has been fragmented by the war, and that can only be reconstituted by active participation. 'Liberation' is not to be achieved by the mere fact of the Allied invasion.

In the light of the cumulative knowledge available from more recent sources, the book seems to have considerable documentary value as a fair, balanced and accurate account of what life was like in a war-time French village. Beyond the daily problems and the conflicting attitudes of the villagers, the novel shows the whole village as being corrupted by fear. The German presence distorts personalities and relationships, and magnifies petty jealousies and irritations into monstrous hatreds: the Germans, as well as using the village, are used by the villagers as a weapon against one another. Bory clearly approves of the Resistance, but there is little optimism for the future, because the religious and moral traditions and values that made the village a human community have been destroyed. The village does not have to endure great suffering, but this only underscores the pessimistic view that even in this relatively unscathed village, things will never be the same again. Occupied by the Germans, bombed by the Allies, the villagers are so powerless in respect to their own destiny, so little 'at home', that they appear almost superfluous. Perhaps the novel's popular success resulted from the fact that its way of telling history was, to a significant degree, representative, although, at the time, it had not yet been shown, by historians, to have been so.

Romain Gary's novel, *L'Education européenne*, was also written during the war, and not after it, in the autumn of 1943 while Gary was operating with the Free French group 'Lorraine' in England. His viewpoint on France is doubly that of an outsider, since he was of Russian birth, and involved in the resistance from England. His novel won the Prix des Critiques in 1945. Ostensibly, it is about the Polish resistance, and the story is set in Poland, with the Russians as the 'liberators'. None the less, the comparison with the French situation is made explicit: indeed, the Polish partisans, in their struggle against the German Occupation, are shown to be part of the same struggle as the French – the struggle for freedom. On one level, the novel is very idealistic: it seeks to play down class and religious differences and national conflicts – one of its interesting techniques is to use various languages in the text (Hebrew, Polish, Russian, German and English, as well as French). On another level, it recognises the futility of such idealism in the light of what has happened. The young hero Janek survives, and the epilogue shows him as an officer in the reconstructed Polish army, but the final images of the novel are a return to the death of the poet Dobranski who was hoping to transform the war experience into some kind of European education, and whose life has been obliterated by the blind forces of a history symbolised by an army of ants crawling over his unfinished book. It is the tireless and tragic stupidity of mankind that wins out in an expression of universal pessimism:

> A quoi sert-il de lutter et de prier, d'espérer et de croire? Le monde où souffrent et meurent les hommes est le même que celui où souffrent et meurent les fourmis: un monde cruel et incompréhensible, où, la seule chose qui compte est de porter toujours plus loin une brindille absurde, un fétu de paille, toujours plus loin, à la sueur de son front et au prix de ses larmes de sang, toujours plus loin! sans jamais s'arrêter pour souffler ou pour demander pourquoi . . . "Les hommes et les papillons . . ."[28]

Between Bory's French village and Gary's Europe, Roger Vailland occupies an intermediate zone. Once again following the author's own experience, the novel is largely set in occupied Paris, and the protagonist, 'Marat', is a resistance fighter with Communist sympathies,[29] although he is working in a Gaullist network. From a technical point of view, the novel is interesting in its attempt to render the hero both from within and from the outside, with an alternation of interior monologue and objective third-person narrative. It is a technique which indicates a tension both within the hero, and between the hero and the world in which he moves. What emerges is that it is not a natural or automatic thing to be a resistance-fighter, but a matter of choice, and of choosing against what Vailland calls the 'inert mass' of the French, who have resigned themselves to their conquered status. The novel ends on a less pessimistic note than the other two, but the relative optimism is based on a faith in the solidarity of the Resistance, and not on any objective assessment of the whole situation: at the end of the novel, Marat's comrade is in the hands of the Gestapo, and Marat is drugging himself to sleep. In these circumstances, his declaration of faith is, at the very least, ambiguous. As in the other two novels, this

---

28. Gary, *L'Education européenne*, p. 245.
29. For a detailed analysis of Vailland's own evolving relationship with the Resistance and Communism at this time, see J.E. Flower, *Roger Vailland: The Man and His Masks*, London, 1975, pp. 36–43.

work contains no account of the Liberation, and, as in Bory, the obvious and visible enemies, the Germans, are shown to be less to be feared than the enemy within. There is no doubt symbolic significance in the fact that it is the hero's former lover Mathilde who emerges as the book's chief villain: she appears as a France that has betrayed, and that must be rejected. Vailland's belief in the Resistance seems to be predicated not on any commitment to the eternal glories of France but, on the contrary, on the conviction that France, as an identifiable entity, has in fact collapsed. Resistance is less against the Germans than against total despair. Vailland's novel won the Interallié Prize in 1945.

Although the success of these novels is an indication, not a proof, that their concerns were shared by significant numbers of post-war French readers, it is not unreasonable to suppose that the very lively market for war-experience stories of all kinds at this time corresponded to a need to find out what had happened. It is also more than plausible that the sense of loss, of a break in history, that underlies so many accounts of the events, corresponded to a widely-experienced reality. It would be an unverifiable conjecture to suppose that a collectivity might, in the face of a great trauma, resort to the same mechanisms of repression as an individual, and later manifest the same kinds of needs of remembrance. That is, none the less, what appears to be happening in France in the years between the end of the war and the present. As far as the first period is concerned (1944–58), there are two works of synthesis that should be mentioned, both because of their inherent importance, and because of their paradigmatic value.

The first is the war tetralogy of Céline. Céline is a story in himself, which is treated separately elsewhere in this volume. [30] The second is Alain Resnais's film *Hiroshima mon amour* (1959), the making of which coincides with both the end of the Fourth Republic and the beginning of the New Wave (Nouvelle Vague) in cinema. It is unusual for a New Wave film in that it is historically oriented, but that is not surprising, given that Resnais's first film, *Nuit et brouillard* (1955), was a documentary reconstruction of the world of the concentration camps, and part of the collective memory process. In *Hiroshima*, scripted by Marguerite Duras,[31] we watch the story of a French actress who is in Japan in the late 1950s

30. See Colin Nettelbeck, 'Céline', pp. 190–202.
31. The script is published as: M. Duras, *Hiroshima mon amour*, Paris, 1960.

to make a film about peace and who falls in love with a Japanese businessman. This affair triggers off a set of memories of another love affair, which took place fourteen years earlier, in Nevers, in central France, during the German Occupation. Painful memories, for the lover was German, and he was shot, and because the girl had her head cropped and was paraded naked. Then, since her parents felt shamed by her actions and wished to restore their respectability, they banished her for months to the cellar, before sending her away. For Duras and Resnais, this heroine incarnates the repressed memory of France, and what they have sought to do is to find a context large enough for it to be possible for the repressed material to be brought out. Using Hiroshima as an example of a shameful story that can be told, and thus transcended, they are suggesting that the story of France, like that of the woman, can also be told and transcended. A head shaven for collaboration is not as bad as one whose hair has fallen out as a result of the nuclear bomb: cropped hair grows back, and the implied message of the film is that if Hiroshima has been able to rise up again out of its ashes, then France should be able to do the same. It should be noted that the film is profoundly anti-nationalistic. Within her French setting, the woman's security and respectability – her profession and her family – depend on her forgetting. The ability to remember, which is her real 'liberation', is only accessible when she steps outside of the French context into the wider space/time of Hiroshima. Of course, repression is not authentic forgetting, and this is perhaps the film's most important historical insight: the shame can only really be forgotten if it is first remembered.

This was not the point of view of Charles de Gaulle, and it should by now be clear that his vision of history, however coherent, and however much it served the needs of France's revival, could not produce a true story of what had happened. The skeletons were bound, in time, to come out of the closet, the more so in that many of them weren't skeletons at all, but real people, like the many thousands of amnestied collaborators, or more importantly, the millions who, even as they gave themselves over to the Resistance's view of history that de Gaulle claimed as his own, knew that they had done nothing, or worse. This is a whole generation of people all too willing, in the face of the disintegration of their identity, to respond to a positive image of themselves.

The degree to which this generation was not able, or willing, to cope with remembering the more unpleasant aspects of the war experience is evident in the treatment meted out to the work that marks a major turning-point in the collectivity's attitude: *Le Chagrin et la pitié* (1971). This four-hour documentary was made by young film-makers,[32] and was a deliberate and overt challenge to the monolithic view of history that had dominated the previous decade. No reasonable viewing of the film could reach the conclusion that its authors have any pro-collaborationist sentiments. On the contrary, there is no doubt that their sympathies lie with people like the Grave brothers – committed resistance fighters – and Pierre Mendès-France or Anthony Eden. None the less – and this is what makes the crucial difference between the film and any preceding account – they also make sure that other viewpoints are expressed in as balanced a way as possible.[33] Thus we see a pharmacist (Marcel Verdier) and a schoolteacher (M. Danton), who did nothing, avoiding taking any position that might cause them risk; we see a German officer (Col. Tausend) tranquilly defending the Wehrmacht's policies and actions; we see Laval's son-in-law (Comte René de Chambrun) trying to rehabilitate the ex-Prime Minister; and, perhaps most strikingly, we see Christian de la Mazière, filmed in the castle of Sigmaringen, explaining, with urbane self-understanding rather than with regret, how he came to join the Waffen-SS.

The documentary was made for television by television specialists, but it was banned from French TV, and was to remain so for ten years, under the governments of both Pompidou and Giscard, as being dangerous to the common good. Ophuls describes how the head of the ORTF at the time, Jean-Jacques de Bresson, not only considered that 'Certains mythes sont nécessaires au bonheur et à la tranquillité d'un peuple', but refused to accept dinner invitations unless it was guaranteed that *Le Chagrin et la pitié* would not be discussed![34] By subterfuge and persistence, the film was granted its visa for screening in cinemas, so that it was, over a period of time, seen by a large number of people.[35] When it was finally released on

32. Marcel Ophuls, André Harris and Alain de Sédouy. The text of the film was first published by the *Avant-scène du cinéma* (nos. 127–8 (1972)), but a more recent version, Paris, 1980, has a very useful introduction and appendices. This is the reference in the following notes.

33. Marcel Ophuls, *Le Chagrin et la Pitié*. The first appendix (pp. 201–66), *Réponses aux questions posées par une classe du lycée Condorcet, à Paris, le 8 juin, 1979*, is a rich and enlightening analysis of the film's genesis and intentions.

34. Ibid., pp. 20–1.

35. Ibid., pp. 11–14, and p. 202.

French TV, with a considerable show of self-congratulatory liberalism from the newly elected socialist government in 1981, it no
longer had the power to shock. The 'liberation' was more symbolic
than real, for the real change had already taken place. This is not to
criticise the release of the film to television: on the contrary, the
1981 audience could see it in the spirit in which it had been made, as
a first-rate documentary, and no longer as a threat or as a subject for
acrimonious debate.

What had happened? Firstly, the audience of 1981 now included a
generation younger, and hence more distant from the events, even
than those who had made the film. This phenomenon had already
been pointed out at the time of the re-release of the film to cinemas
in 1979.[36] For the young members of the audience, the film itself
had become 'historical'. More importantly, during the period of the
banning of the film from TV, the public arena had been flooded with
stories and histories covering every aspect of the 1940–4 period. The
forbidden fruit of 1970 had, by 1981, become promiscuous fashion.

The young French historian Pascal Ory[37] has pointed out the
dangers of the resurgence, after 1968, of some of the less salubrious
aspects of the French behaviour under the Occupation: the re-
appearance of arch-collaborationists such as Darquier de Pellepoix,
for example, or the scurrilous racism of a Robert Faurisson, or the
bombing of the Jewish synagogue in the rue Copernic in 1980. It is
not certain that all these events are related, however, and it is clear
that for Ory, and others like him, such dangers are unavoidable
side-effects of what is essentially a liberation process. During the
Gaullist period, apart from the work of Robert Aron, already
mentioned, there had been, in France, very few efforts by historians
to bring into focus the more blurred experiences of the Occupation,
and they remained tentative and incomplete – preliminary fact-
gathering works rather than comprehensive histories. Thus while
pioneering books as Gérard Walter's *La vie à Paris sous l'occupation*, Henri Amouroux's *La vie des Français sous l'occupation*, or
Michèle Cotta's *La Collaboration*[38] all contain much useful information, they remain impressionistic, and not least because their

36. By a sagacious Truffaut to Ophuls, dismayed by the apparent drop in attendance: ibid., pp. 203–4.

37. Ory is the author of *Les Collaborateurs*, Paris, 1976, *La France allemande*,
Paris, 1977, and *Le Petit Nazi Illustré: 'Le Téméraire' (1943–1944)*, Paris, 1973,
L'Entre-deux-mai, Paris, 1983.

38. Respectively: Paris, 1960; Paris, 1961; Paris, 1964.

source-material was more limited than was necessary.[39] Paxton has taxed the French government for its failure to release various documents, but stressed the availability of German and Italian documents which French historians, with the exception of Henri Michel, seems to have ignored. It took the dispassionate and exceedingly thorough work of the outsider Paxton to create the major historiographical breakthrough,[40] in terms of both content and methodology: his books make abundantly clear that collaborationism, on the part of a Vichy government that was for at least two years almost universally accepted by the French people, was a deliberate, broad-based and vigorously-pursued policy; and just as importantly, it abstracts the period from the tendencious and polemical aura which surrounded it, and sets the criteria for studying it firmly in the realm of the scholarly and the scientific.

With Michael Marrus, Paxton was to make another important contribution in 1981, in *Vichy France and the Jews*,[41] where it is demonstrated that French anti-Semitic policies and legislation were independent of Nazi ones, and that repression of the Jews in France was often in advance of the occupants' demands. This book is as significant a lesson in methodology as the earlier one, but in terms of its content, it rather sums up and confirms, with scientific precision, material which had been appearing quite regularly in France over the previous decade: studies and memoirs, or films like Malle's *Lacombe Lucien* or Drach's *Les Violons de bal* – both were first released in 1974. Paxton's two books are less a historiographical frame delineating the mass of material that has appeared since 1968, than markers that indicate the high ground of collective awareness of the realities of the Occupation period – the limits, as it were, beyond which obfuscation was no longer acceptable and ignorance no longer possible, at least for historians. The extent to which the collectivity had been guilty of collaborationism and genocidal racism had been established for once and for all, and the stereotypes of the Gaullian vision of history could no longer be relevant.

As was suggested earlier, the range of histories dealing principally

39. Paxton, *Vichy France: Old Guard and New Order 1940–44*. Henri Michel, *Vichy: année 40*, Paris, 1966.
40. Paxton (*Vichy France*) recognises his own debt to other American and British historians, and particularly to Stanley Hoffmann whose seminal role in the diffusion of information in France was crucial. (*A la recherche de la France*, Paris, 1963).
41. See Marrus and Paxton. *Vichy France and the Jews* and Serge Klarsfeld's *Vichy-Auschwitz*, Paris, 1983.

with aspects of collaborationism that appear in the post-1968 period is enormous, both in subject-matter and in quality. Some, like Jacques Delperrie de Bayac's *Histoire de la Milice* (Paris, 1969) or P.-M. Dioudonnat's *Je suis partout: 1930–1944* (Paris, 1973), offer a solidly documented synthesis. Others, like Halimi's *Chantons sous l'occupation* (Paris, 1976), or Le Boterf's *La vie parisienne sous l'occupation* (2 vols, Paris, 1974) are tantalisingly anecdotal, and smack of insufficiently-directed reading of old newspapers and magazines. It is obvious, however, that there was a lively and ongoing market for this material at all levels, and the public demand can be measured by the uninterrupted flow of new titles.[42] Popularising of the historical material, through works like Amouroux's *La grande histoire des Français sous l'occupation*,[43] suggests the existence of a keen mass audience, the more so in that Amouroux has supplemented his written-word diffusion through a long-standing series of radio and television programmes. There can be no doubt that a massive transformation of the collectivity's historical vision was taking place.[44]

Of course – and the point needs to be stressed – the nature of the collectivity itself had changed, with the emergence of a new generation, and one of the major aspects of the famous generation gap of the late 1960s is precisely the historical one: the blurred identity of the generation who had lived through, as adults, the Occupation period was bound, if only by default, to thwart the identity-quest of their children. Beyond the sociological, ideological and psycho-analytical terminology that abounds at that time, beyond all the conceptual abstractions, there remain problems that are neither conceptual nor abstract, problems the more difficult to confront because they concern concrete relationships between parents and their children. Or the absence of such relationships – for we shall see that one of the recurring themes of post-1968 accounts of the war is precisely such an absence. For this new generation, the quest to define identity leads – because of the uncertainties surrounding their origins – inexorably to a turning-back, to a new examination of the people and circumstances whose children they are.

42. The most reliable overall bibliographical source is the *Revue d'histoire de la deuxième guerre mondiale* (Paris, quarterly from 1950).
43. Paris, 7 vols so far, beginning in 1976.
44. Another significative event that shows the scope of the problem of telling history was *Vichy-Fiction*, a theatrical conception (performed by Bernard Chartreux and Michel Deutsch) in October 1980 by the Théâtre national de Strasbourg. It received very extensive media coverage.

The idea of a single new generation is, of course, an oversimplification, and a more accurate description of the situation must take account of the simultaneous co-existence of several different age-groups in the emergence of the new narrations of history. Together, these form a spectrum of perspectives on the war period just as complex as the one we saw for the immediate post-war. At one extreme, there is a figure like Jacques Laurent, born in 1919, and old enough to have experienced the war as a young adult. At the other, there is a Patrick Modiano, born after the war, but also, in significant ways, born of it. And in between, a whole range of people who were children or adolescents – Bernard Clavel, Christine de Rivoyre, Michel Tournier, Evelyne Le Garrec, Louis Malle, Pascal Jardin, Claudine Vegh, etc. These, and the many dozens of kindred accounts, are not equally profound or convincing (either as individual works or as representations of the general experience), but they form a corpus whose concerns recognisably reflect those of the new 'historians' of the period – the Orys, Riouxs and Azémas: the need to take stock, the awareness of the extent of collective guilt, the sense of the failure of the accepted authority figure, the specific problem of the Jews.

But it has to be remembered, too, that from the point of view of the actual narration process, we are dealing with a phenomenon that is post-'Nouveau Roman' and post-'Nouvelle Vague': that is to say, a situation in which self-consciousness and self-questioning of literary or cinematographic expression are almost unavoidable. We have, in short, the paradoxical coincidence of, on the one hand, the need to experiment with original forms and techniques, and on the other hand, the need to return to thematic material that belonged to an earlier 'age'.

Jacques Laurent's *Les Bêtises* (Paris, 1971), winner of the Goncourt Prize, is a good example of an attempt to draw these multiple concerns into a single narrative. In respect to the war period, Laurent really belongs to the generation of Nimier, Déon and Blondin – the so-called 'hussards' with whom he is usually classified – and indeed he did publish a short 'naïve' war-novel in the pre-Gaullian period: *Le Petit Canard* (1954). Ideologically, he comes from the anarchist-bourgeois tradition, 'marginalised' in the post-war years as much by Sartrian literary ideas as by de Gaulle's haughty paternalism. Furthermore, the voluminous populist opus written under the pseudonym of Cécil Saint-Laurent has not helped his reputation. Until 1968, only his polemical writings[45], which often have an awesome sting, were taken seriously, although he does have wide-ranging historical competency. *Les Bêtises*, however, brings Laurent into the mainstream, and reveals him as a novelist of substance. His opus was consecrated by his admission to the Académie Française in 1987.

Les Bêtises is a complex work that plays with multiple levels and convolutions of meaning and structure. It is presented by an 'editor' as being a succession of four different texts written by a recently-dead friend: a short unfinished novel written between 1940 and 1946; a long 'examination' of the novel, written in 1947; a private journal of the 1952–64 period; and finally, a short philosophical treatise completed just before the narrator's accidental death in 1966. The unifying principle of the novel is a resolutely individual-istic and stoic attitude governing the vision of both life and art. The experiences of the Second World War (from the viewpoint of a member of the Armistice army) or of the war in Indochina are recounted and discussed in the same individualistic mode as the narrator's numerous amorous exploits or other encounters with people or places, or indeed his literary readings. Nevertheless, his story, for all its claim to being the truest and most profound account of his self, does have a clear social and historical dimension. The Second World War is shown as being at the origin of a radical transformation that alienates the narrator from his roots and his sense of order, and casts him into the 'in-between' role that will emerge as the symbol of his destiny. As a guard of the Demarcation Line, he is neither 'occupied' nor 'free'; as a corporal, he is neither leader nor follower. He is, in fact, a keenly intelligent observer, if not always a dispassionate one, and his story evokes the seamier political manoeuverings between Vichy and the Gaullist Resistance fighters, as well as the failure of authority figures of the previous generation (particularly the narrator's father), and the persecution of the Jews. As a writer, he is also aware of literary history: the structure of the four sections is a persuasive metaphorical portrayal of the increasing interiorisation and self-questioning of modern fiction, and in addition, significant sections of the novel are devoted to analysis of a whole range of authors, from Proust, Morand and Céline to the 'Nouveau Roman' and 'Nouvelle Critique'.

---

45. For example, Jacques Laurent, *Paul et Jean-Paul*, Paris, 1951; or idem, *Mauriac sous De Gaulle*, Paris, 1964. Laurent's autobiography, *Histoire égoïste*, Paris, 1976, offers precious insights into the whole period. His *Année 40* (Paris, 1965, with G. Jeantet), is a provocative anti-de Gaulle history.

Laurent's strengths are his intensely sensual appreciation of life and his savage polemical wit, and he has used these to place the war-experience account in a wide enough context to defuse its effects. Despite opinions that are sometimes suspect – in particular his distant, rather mocking treatment of the race question – the novel does show that for those of Laurent's generation, the war period was still, after 1968, unfinished business, and it succeeds in un-telling the grosser myths of the Gaullist era. Laurent's contribution to a general awareness of the scope of the problem and of the change in society is very considerable.

⌐ The attempt to define a context broad enough for the war experience to be transcended finds expression in most of the works of the post–1968 period. Bernard Clavel (born 1923), in his tetralogy *La grande Patience*,[46] begins with the pre-war situation of daily life in a small town in the east of France. Political events and social conflicts are distorted by the fact that the narrative view is both provincial and adolescent, and this distortion is continued throughout the work, whether the viewpoint is that of the rather fatuous young hero, Julien Dubois (vols i and iii), or that of his mother (vol. ii) or father (vol. iv). Clavel's point here is perhaps trite – that the people who lived through these events did not really know what was happening to them. It is convincingly made, however, and in fact it becomes quite telling, when the last volume reveals how devastating and definitive are the effects of the war on a whole way of life. With the death of the parents in 1945, Clavel underlines the emergence of an orphaned generation. The break is the more poignant because of the detailed documentary descriptions of what has been lost: Julien's apprenticeship before the war as a bread-maker, and the father's own work on the land. What has been broken is a tradition of stubborn faithfulness and attachment to work, family, and place (a tradition which the Vichy motto – 'Travail, famille, patrie' – made a futile attempt to preserve), values which were their own justification, but which the war has swept aside. Not only have the two sons – Julien is an artist, his brother Paul a ruthless businessman – been alienated forever from such simplicity and innocence, but they are both utterly mediocre people. Clavel does not blame individuals or institutions, but rather conveys the sense of an inevitable fate. The Occupation appears as a

46. *La Maison ι.*   ΄ι *mer*, 1963, *Le Cœur des vivants*, 1964, ʟ

manifestation of entropic forces that destroy the father's world not because it was in any way bad, but simply because its time had come. And as the title of the last volume suggests, the two sons, 'winter's fruits', do not offer much promise for the future.

A similar pessimism pervades Christine de Rivoyre's *Le Petit Matin*,[47] which also adopts an adolescent and provincial narrative viewpoint. Presented as the diary of a seventeen-year-old girl, the novel is in fact a carefully constructed metaphorical account of the collapse of a world. As with Laurent and Clavel, the elements of 'raw' experience are there – the restrictions imposed by the war, the camps, the prisoners, and even details about how to make ersatz coffee and sugar. Such details are clichés, but Rivoyre, like Clavel and Laurent, feels the need to take them up again as part of her own authentic and specific experience. But, once again, the lived experience is only one aspect of the whole subject-matter of the novel, the core of confusion and guilt that has to be transposed into a wider symbolic context.

Rivoyre's symbols are largely sexual. Her heroine, Nina, comes from a family of gentry in the Landes, a conservative, in-turned, anti-Semitic world reminiscent of Mauriac. (If one reads *Le Petit Matin* alongside *Thérèse Desqueyroux* or *Le Nœud de vipères*, the war appears less as a cause than as a catalyst that precipitates a process of fragmentation that was already at work fifteen years earlier.) Nina is full of sensuous rebellion, in love with her horses and her first cousin Jean, who has joined the Resistance. The intrusion of the Germans into this world reveals its brittleness and fragility. Jean, whose lack of sensual energy is symbolised in his hatred of horses, is displaced in Nina's heart by a German cavalry officer, who saves the life of her favourite horse, and whose charm and strength – despite her patriotic loathing of him – she does not resist. Against this background, her father, who evolves from a state of passive humiliation to active resistance, is quite irrelevant. At the end of the novel (set on the eve of the Liberation), threatened with having her head cropped, she is in a state of hallucination, not knowing whether Jean is alive or dead, tormented by thoughts of his homosexuality and by fantasies of herself murdering her departed German lover. It is through this chaos that Rivoyre reveals her vision of her generation as one which, while being spared the

47. Christine de Rivoyre, *Le Petit Matin*, Paris, 1968. This novel won that year's 'Prix interallié'.

direct brutality and horror of the war, none the less lost through it all sense of identity and purpose.

There is one element of reconciliation, in that Nina's 'fault', which from a Resistance-based historical viewpoint would have to be considered as treasonable, appears here as the result of forces whose scope is well beyond the control of individuals, or of family or national values. This portrayal of it serves to expunge the guilt: if there is no other positive result, at least the experience – a female one recounted from a female viewpoint – no longer has to be repressed, but can take its place without excessive shame among the other experiences of the collectivity.

The fragmented diary form that Rivoyre uses to transmit her heroine's experience both mirrors the fragmenting nature of the experience itself, and reveals the author's awareness that traditional narrative is not appropriate for capturing the fundamental uncertainties that underlie her vision. At the same time, the quest for new form does not lead her to abstraction: the recounting of the facts and events is part of a historical realism necessary to exorcising the demons of the past. Rivoyre's approach to this kind of material is typical of many others of this era, in that while telling what happened may not be an adequate response to the repressed trauma, it is a sine qua non.

Laurent, Clavel and Rivoyre all evoke the Occupation as a time of adventure and irresponsibility, invoking the youth of their protagonists as an absolute excuse for any mistakes they might have made. They make it abundantly clear that the rights and wrongs that emerged a posteriori were not perceivable values to their rebellious adolescents. The Parisian bourgeoisie (Laurent), the provincial petty bourgeoisie (Clavel), and the landed gentry (Rivoyre) are portrayed as having in common attitudes that were lax, though not in any way pro-German; the protagonists are all children of a humiliated country and of parents who have failed to equip them to cope with life. If Laurent's narrator comes close at times to those in power, neither he nor either of the others actually wields it. All appear as victims of circumstances beyond their control and understanding. To this extent, the three characters can be said to represent the ordinary French public, the mass of uncommitted people who stumbled through the war years as best they could, and who might have been able to say so earlier, had Gaullian ideology not driven them into an ashamed silence. Although these novels do not portray an image that the French collectivity might be proud of, it is one with which many people could identify without any particular cause for guilt. And that, in terms of collective attitudes, represents a significant change.

An even more significant, and more difficult, part of the story emerges with the children of those who were either involved with governmental power or committed to the collaborationist ideologies – those whose responsibility could not be swept aside or covered up. Such accounts are understandably rare. Pascal Jardin's *La Guerre à neuf ans*, and to a lesser extent his *Guerre après guerre*[48] illustrate some of the problems of dealing with this material. Jardin relies on his extensive experience as a filmscript writer to create a 'montage' of scenes (built around famous personages), splicing a number of episodes from the present into a largely chronological arrangement of events from the 1939–44 years. The aim is no doubt to create perspective and distance. However, from the point of view of content, Jardin has to contend with presenting his father (who is the centrepiece of the account) simultaneously as a man he loved and admired, and as the high-level civil servant who was head of Laval's department in 1942–3 and then an envoy of Vichy to Switzerland. Unfortunately, the love and admiration are so strong that they serve as a justification not only of the father's confident, boisterous, and sometimes engaging personality, but also of his misogyny and egoism and, by implication, of his whole life. The realities of his political activities are passed over. At a time when authority-figures, and fathers in particular, are widely decried, Jardin is an exception, in that he puts his own father forward as a successful man and a worthy model. There are many interesting observations on life in Vichy, less 'remembered', no doubt, than reconstructed, but none the less useful reminders of the grey complexities of a period that Gaullian mythology reduced to a uniform black. Thus, for example, Jean Jardin could have in his home (in November 1942) the German diplomat Krug von Nidda, and the Jewish intellectual, Robert Aron, who was hiding from the Gestapo.[49] And he could be equally friendly with Emmanuel Berl and his Jewish wife Mireille or the earnest collaborationist Bertrand de Jouvenel.

The younger Jardin's apologia tends to amalgamate his father with Vichy and vice-versa, bringing even Laval into an aura of basic

---

48. Pascal Jardin, *La Guerre à neuf ans*, Paris, 1971; idem, *Guerre après guerre*, Paris, 1973.

49. Jardin, *La Guerre à neuf ans*, pp. 137–9.

goodness. But the shallowness of his stance is dramatically revealed in a passage where he recounts how after the war, he was persecuted by his schoolmates for being the son of a collaborator: 'Il ne m'était pas plus aisé d'ignorer mon enfance qu'il n'était facile à un Juif d'oublier pendant la guerre qu'il était un Juif.'[50] This degree of blinkered egoism verges on the pathological and obscene, and paradoxically, the effect of Jardin's books is less to rehabilitate the character or values of Jean Jardin than to lay bare – unwittingly – the strange power continuities that permitted Jardin senior to keep his career and personality intact through all his own compromises and the vicissitudes of history. Despite himself, Pascal Jardin appears as the emotionally crippled victim of the overweening paternalism that Jean Jardin shared with the Vichy régime. Although this story is atypical in its intentions, then, it stands out in the mosaic of war accounts as an indictment of the Vichy generation, albeit an unconscious one.

There is nothing unconscious about Evelyne Le Garrec's *La Rive allemande de ma mémoire*, which uses Freudian and feminist models to work through a complicated family history (which includes some German ancestry), in an attempt to exorcise the shame and memory of a collaborationist father gunned down by the Resistance in 1943. Her investigation was sparked by a quest for roots. She had read numerous works on collaborationism: 'J'y ai appris beaucoup sur la collaboration en général, mais rien sur mon père, tant il m'était difficile d'établir un rapport entre lui, obscur militant provincial qui n'a laissé derrière lui aucune trace, et les chefs politiques, écrivains, éditorialistes . . . à Vichy ou à Paris.'[51] When her quest reveals that her father was more active than she had believed (he was a PPF official and wrote for *L'Emancipation nationale*), and hence closer than she had thought to 'collaboration in general', her reaction is to reduce her trauma to the domain of individual psychology. The historical coincidence that has thrown together her father's natural character and the ideology of Nazi Germany provides, she believes, a convenient way out of her dilemma. Assimilating paternity, paternalism, patrimony, patronym and 'patrie' into the same authoritarian image, and equating that image with her father, she implodes the historical dimension of her story, and concludes that she would have rejected her father even if he had fought for the

50. Ibid., p. 166.
51. Evelyne Le Garrec, *La Rive allemande de ma mémoire*, Paris, 1980, p. 119.

Resistance.[52]

The direction in which she seeks reconciliation (within herself, and between herself and the social world) is that of a father-less country-less vision of the world – a world like that of her mother, whose own German father had abandoned her in childhood, or like that of the Jewish victims evoked in the anti-Semitic texts she quotes to punctuate her own. There is something despairing and sterile about the willed rootlessness that is the book's final position, but less despairing and sterile than the author's point of departure. In any case, at least as telling as the conclusions is the process of investigation, which reveals the immense difficulties that the collectivity put in her way – from the laws preventing access to police records, to the hotel proprietress who refuses point-black to admit of any knowledge of what she had witnessed in 1943. The reconstruction of events and circumstances can be achieved only through stubborn and patient effort, and the impression created as Le Garrec excavates into the memory of her childhood village is that the issues which had led to her father's assassination, far from being dead and buried, had in fact been buried alive.

It was, in part, this problem that led Louis Malle (born 1932) to make *Lacombe Lucien*. In a commentary on the genesis of the film,[53] Malle tells how as a young man, after an expedition with oceanographer Jacques Cousteau, he chanced to meet Cousteau's brother Pierre and Lucien Rebatet. Cousteau was editor-in-chief of *Paris-Soir*, then of *Je suis partout*. Rebatet, ex-Action Francaise, ex-Radio Vichy, was one of the most violent polemicists of the Paris collaborationists. Both had recently been released from jail, where they had been serving sentences for collaboration, and both still passionately convinced of the rightness of their views. Malle was reminded of the dislocation of his own family during the Occupation – his parents were supporters of Pétain, while his cousins had joined de Gaulle in London, and an uncle had been deported to a concentration camp. If the seeds of his film were planted at that time, however, they grew only slowly. Other experiences enriched the original material: the upheavals of the Algerian War, when he observed the discrepancies between the rhetoric of civilisation and the brutal savagery of French soldiers; the activities of the American marines in Vietnam; the repression by vigilantes of

52. Le Garrec, *La Rive allemande*, pp. 212–13.
53. Jacques Mallecot, *Louis Malle par Louis Malle*, Paris, 1978, pp. 8–54.

student and worker movements in Mexico. In short, before becoming reconcentrated in the period of the Occupation, his creative process had passed through a more universal experience and a wider historical context.

Just how raw the collective sensibility still was in 1974 can be judged from the critical reception of the film. While over a quarter of a million people had been to see it within three weeks of its release in Paris,[54] many major critiques were severely negative on both left and right. It was accused of being historically inaccurate and ideologically suspect.[55] It provoked – along with Cavani's *Night Porter*, which appeared at the same time – a violent debate on the nature and causes of the movement that had already been nicknamed 'rétro' – the wide-spread 'looking back', which revived earlier music and clothing fashions, and which had a special focus on the Second World War.[56] The debate engaged such personalities as Michel Foucault and Jean Baudrillard.[57] Foucault saw the film as symptomatic of a 'battle for History', and blamed the existence of the battle on the French Left's lack of historical perspective. For Baudrillard, on the contrary, any preoccupation with History was 'rétro'. It was clear that this film as much as *Le Chagrin et la Pitié*, touched raw nerves. It also marks, historically, the time when the 'battle for History' enters the realm of public discussion.

The negative responses to the film are not surprising: superficially, it could be offensive to almost everybody. The lusty peasant lad, whose father is a prisoner of war, whose mother has become a neighbour's mistress, and whose request to join the underground is turned down by an overdemanding school-teacher, is easy prey for the group of French Gestapists in the nearby town. From being a nobody, he becomes a figure of power, able to bully his way into the home, if not into the heart, of the Jewish refugee family, ravishing the daughter, and reducing the father to a state of suicidal despair. But the daughter is not unambiguously a victim: she is attracted to Lucien, and sick of being Jewish,[58] and even the father tries to use Lucien's services to secure passage to Spain. The group

54. *France-Soir*, 22 Feb. 1974.
55. See, for example, *Libération* 28 Feb. 1974, p. 10; *France nouvelle*, 26 March 1974, pp. 14–15; *L'Arche*, no. 206, April-May 1974, pp. 57–61; *Etudes*, April 1974, pp. 587–90; *Cahiers du cinéma*, no. 250 May 1974, pp. 42–9.
56. See Pascal Ory, 'Comme de l'an Quarante'.
57. Michel Foucault, *Cahiers du cinéma*, nos. 251–2 July 1974, pp. 42–47; Jean Baudrillard, *Ca: cinéma et histoire*, vol 2, 1976, pp. 16–19.
58. 'J'en ai marre d'être juive!'. Louis Malle, *Lacombe Lucien*, Paris, 1974, p. 101.

of collaborators in the Hôtel des Grottes live in an atmosphere of demonic futility, where torture, black-marketeering and denunciation merge into scenes of dancing or alcoholic boredom. The Resistance sympathisers one sees – the maid Marie, or the doctor – are not particularly sympathetic.

Even on this level, however, it is obvious that Malle is not attacking the Resistance or defending Nazism or collaboration. If the film is certainly provocative, it also fulfils Malle's explicit aim of shaking people out of their complacency and of forcing his spectators 'à reconsidérer des idées reçues, par exemple qu'un collaborateur soit nécessairement un monstre coupé du corps social'.[59]

This desire to change people's ways of looking at the problems of the Occupation is built into a less-obvious dimension of the film, one that is revealed through the character of the Jewish girl, France. Her name is patently symbolic, first of her father's wish for her to be a 'true' Frenchwoman, but more subtly, of an attempt by the film-maker to create a paradigm of a 'Jewish' France whose attitude towards the dark years of the Occupation would be the same as that of the young heroine towards Lucien: not innocent, but life-affirming, and motivated by a strong survival instinct. On this level, the film looks beyond the notions of guilt and blame, and points to a more measured view of history, one that had been expressed (but not widely heard) a decade earlier by the historians Plumyène and Lasierra, who suggested that the behaviour of the French during the war – their military collapse, their general torpor and passivity during the Occupation – resulted from an instinctive movement away from the 'chemin de la destruction'.[60] Although such a theory is unverifiable, it has the advantage of being less divisive than others, and of taking into account a broad spectrum of historical facts. It also indicates the emergence of a less vindictive and less abrasive element in the collective attitude. Not that there is any evidence of the older generation changing its views. The re-release of *Lacombe Lucien* on television (May 1978 and again in May 1982) resulted in protracted media debate, some of it quite as acrimonious as at the time of the original screening.[61]

If change was occurring, then, it was partly because, with the breakdown of the Resistance monopoly of history, other voices and

---

59. Mallecot, *Louis Malle par Louis Malle*, p. 49.
60. J. Plumyène and R. Lasierra, *Les Fascismes français: 1923–1963*, Paris, 1963, p. 174.
61. Based on consultation of the *dossiers de presse* held at Gallimard.

experiences were making themselves heard, and partly because of the younger generation articulating its own reactions. Malle, already, had lived through the war as a pre-adolescent, and was bound to have a more 'innocent' experience of it than even Laurent, Clavel or Rivoyre. The distance he achieves in the film is not all of his own making, however, and he has readily admitted that the success of the work depended heavily on the script-writer, Patrick Modiano,[62] who was born in July 1945, and so had no direct experience of the Occupation at all – not even pre-natal! – with the result that the war period belonged, already, for him, to the domain of symbol and myth. The metaphorical dimension sought by the narratives of the earlier generations was Modiano's by birthright.

Modiano is in fact paradigmatic of the whole post-1968 war narrative phenomenon – which goes from the anguished resurgence of traumatic material to the gradual transcendence of these memories a decade or so later – except that he does it in a much shorter period of time. From the start, too, he was not concerned with presenting the Occupation in a realist mode – he describes it as a 'paysage' and a 'tremplin', an atmospheric device through which he hoped to evoke the uncertainties of his own age-group. And yet, paradoxically, his contribution as a historian is very real indeed. All of his first three novels – *La Place de l'Etoile* (1968), *La Ronde de nuit* (1969), *Les Boulevards de ceinture* (1972)[63] – astounded commentators by their detailed, if highly allusive, evocation of the people, places and activities of the Occupation; Modiano's knowledge of the period is prodigious. It began as an identity quest, a personal obsession growing out of a series of family traumas – a Jewish father whose wartime survival depended on secrecy and compromise, a Flemish-speaking Belgian actress mother who spent the war in Paris working for a German film company, a much-admired brother who died in late childhood, frequent absences of both parents, and then their divorce. Frustrated by the lack of direct information about his origins, he researched the period preceding his birth with single-minded zeal, years before the publication of the books that allow the curious contemporary reader to verify the accuracy of his material. His sources are the documents of the period, and its people, and he brings them to life in the same way that the narrator of *Les Boulevards de ceinture* brings to life the figures in a yellowing photograph.

62. Mallecot, *Louis Malle par Louis Malle*, p. 47.
63. All published in Paris.

As a historian, Modiano is iconoclastic and impressionistic, but his fascination with the black market-collaboration-Gestapo nexus, and with the problems of French identity and Jewish survival corresponds precisely to the areas of the Occupation that had been glossed over by official history. One might argue that his history is hardly that of the Occupation at all, since he deals neither with politics nor major events, and leaves the Germans out almost altogether, drawing his inspiration from the marginal figures that gravitated around the Bonny-Laffont gang in the rue Lauriston, or from the clique of journalists that Jean Luchaire or Robert Brasillach gathered about them. Yet Modiano captures very well not only the feeling of the period – and here his use of names of people, theatres, popular bars, drinks, etc., serves to conjure up a whole forgotten world – but also its essential spirit. In *La Place de l'Etoile*, he sketches symbolically – in stark caricature – the deep confusions in French society that the Occupation so exacerbated: on the one hand, the ossified nationalism of Vichy, and on the other, what he sees as the empty abstractions of internationalism. The only unity in the French identity is its anti-Semitism.[64] In *La Ronde de nuit*, the narrator embodies the lethargic oscillation of the collectivity between boy-scoutish resistance and the most sordid exploitation: as he drifts from one group to the other, he appears less as a double-agent than as the victim of a double passivity, caught in a web of fear and betrayal. In *Les Boulevards de ceinture*, which is set in July 1944, the whorehouse atmosphere is similar to the one that Modiano would create for Malle in *Lacombe Lucien*. It is a completely decadent world, shoddy, sinister, and cynical, a world beyond pleasure or pain, or belief in anything other than its own imminent and inevitable destruction. The narrator's successful quest to join forces with his father leads to their both being condemned, which is Modiano's wryly ironic way of putting the Occupation behind him.

Modiano's concentration on the aspects of the Occupation that had not been successfully absorbed into the collective memory is, from a subjective viewpoint, coincidental, in that the novelist was not motivated by the collectivity's preoccupation with those dark years, but rather by a desire, as we have seen, to find an appropriate set of images to render the spirit of his own time. This does not prevent him, objectively, from expressing the collectivity's unre-

---

64. This provocative notion of the youthful Modiano was taken up again by the philosopher Bernard-Henry Lévy, in *L'Idéologie française*, Paris, 1981.

solved conflicts about the war, and indeed results in his portrayal of the war being both a metaphor and an aetiology. On this level he appears as a kind of historical visionary, having instinctively understood, in the same way as the Resnais of *Hiroshima*, and well before most of the French historians, that the bad memories had to be recalled before they could be forgotten.

The relationship between the historical dimension and the literary one is very complex in Modiano's work. *La Place de l'Etoile* is an explosive, kaleidoscopic novel that mirrors the fractured vision of history that it conveys. It is full of pastiche and parody, and in a more visceral and violently humorous way than in Laurent's *Les Bêtises*, it sets about mulching the whole literary tradition from Robert de Clary to the 'Nouveau Roman', passing via Voltaire, Rousseau, Chateaubriand, Proust, Larbaud, Céline and the more minor anti-Semites, and the between-the-wars regionalist novelists. Once again, the young Modiano's inspiration is intensely personal – he is working through literary aversions and attractions in an attempt to define his own identity as a writer. But here, too, his own literary apprenticeship is revelatory of the collective quest to find a narrative form that might take the traumatic historical material into account, a story that might carry the history. In *La Ronde de nuit*, he goes one step further, inverting the logic of his original equation (fragmented history = fragmented story) to create a parallelism between the continuities of the history (the ways it reaches into the present), and a narrative that progressively becomes more linear. This principle of linearity, which will be an essential aspect of Modiano's later work, is dependent on the unblocking of specific historical material, and prefigures, yet again, the collective release and synthesising, by historians, of the same material over the next decade. In *Les Boulevards de ceinture*, finally, Modiano returns to parody, this time to self-parody, as a way of effacing the obsessional thematic material – the Occupation, the Father, the Jewish problem. In this respect, even the 'Nouveau Roman' device of using an old photograph as a pretext for the narrative is in a way self-erasing. With this work, Modiano was able to turn his back on the historical and literary past simultaneously.

In using history as a way of transcending it, by working through the specific time/place not only to exorcise it, but to turn it into synapse and myth, Modiano is in advance of the collective process, but none the less part of it. So, too, is Michel Tournier (born 1924), who in *Le Roi des Aulnes*[65] uses myth to create a historical allegory, or rather, an allegory of history. The novel is an intricate construction of symbolic devices, and Tournier uses his central figure, Abel Tiffauges, to explore a whole array of philosophical, sexual, and quasi-mystical themes. In this inverted hagiography of the becoming-of-an-ogre, history is thus only one dimension, but it is a significant one, and in itself polyvalent.

Most obviously, the history is that of Nazi Germany, its awesome power and ultimate defeat being evoked not through descriptions of military battles or political manoeuverings, but in terms of the immense primaeval energies, grotesque and bestial, of an ogre tradition that raises children to sacrifice, and equates love and beauty with death. Tournier's open and deep admiration for Germany – which he salutes in Nerval's words of 'notre mère à tous' – has its origins in his family's long-established germanophilia, and is treated at length in his later autobiographical essay, *Le Vent paraclet*.[66] There is personal bitterness in his castigation of Hitler and of the murderous anti-Semitism which brought catastrophe on the Germany of great dreams and geniuses. The Führer is the Major-Ogre, the ultimate perversion of authority, the 'father'-cannon whose 'children' become his own fodder. The Jewish-child, Ephraïm, survivor of the death camps, who rides the ogre Tiffauges down into the East Prussian marshes, is a kind of archangel of vengeance whose light shines out over a destroyed world.

On a level wider than the Nazi collapse, Tournier's symbols point to a more universal history – that of the entropic decline of the Judeo-Christian belief-system into the death-oriented ethos of contemporary Europe. From this angle, *Le Roi des Aulnes* is the story of how Abel (the Biblical 'good son'), after his destiny seems to direct him towards Saint Christopher (the Christ-bearer), becomes Tiffauges (the 'deep-eyed' ogre whose name is taken from the domain of the notorious Gilles de Rais), a figure who evolves more and more in the direction of the demonic. In *Le Vent paraclet*, Tournier claims that the 'real subject' of his novel is 'la phorie' ('bearing'),[67] but in fact, it is the progressive failure of bearing, the failure of the transmission of the belief-system, the faith without which dispersion becomes inevitable. The novel does not explain the failure, except in terms of another symbol, represented by the

---

65. Michel Tournier, *Le Roi des Aulnes*, Paris, 1970. This novel won the Prix Goncourt.

66. Ibid., ch. 2, pp. 65–144.

67. Ibid., p. 120.

character of Nestor, the evil principle of the division between the divine and human nature.[68] This is Tournier at his most mystical, less spiritual perhaps than darkly witty, the Tournier who in all his novels deconstructs, with black vision and white humour,[69] the great myths of Western civilisation.[70]

The broad symbolic dimensions of history provide a context for the more French-specific historical allegory that *Le Roi des Aulnes* contains. In *Le Vent paraclet*, once again, Tournier shows himself a harsh judge of his country's behaviour in the 1939-45 period, decrying the post-war Resistance mythology as a 'bel exemple d'autointoxication de tout un pays concernant une période peù glorieuse de son histoire',[71] and dismissing the Epuration as nothing more than despicable hypocrisy. These attitudes are now familiar to us as common elements of most post-1968 treatments of the war, and they are quite clearly built into *Le Roi des Aulnes*. With his distant German origins, Abel Tiffauges incarnates a France that follows the traditional linear history through a period of christian-isation (the collège Saint-Christophe episode), enlightenment (the Nestor episode), and industrialisation (Tiffauges as a Neuilly mechanic). The image of Tiffauges being compared with the mur-derer Weidmann and 'saved' from prosecution by the outbreak of war patently alludes to a vision of a corrupt and divided pre-war France, which is continued into the portrayal of an ethos of self-de-structiveness and incompetence in the 'phony war' episode, where Tiffauges eats his own beloved pigeons. All this disorder prepares and explains the wholehearted embracing of the German order by a Tiffauges-France whose collaborationism is not imposed but chosen.

Tournier's assessment of France's behaviour is caricatural, and too partial to be taken at face value. When he claims that there was no doubt that for 'le Français moyen des années noires (. . .) l'avenir appartenait et pour longtemps à l'Allemagne victorieuse',[72] he is being swayed by his pro-German feelings, and perhaps by disappointment at the apparently failed destiny of France. In this allegorical reading, the final image is deeply pessimistic, with

68. This figure is drawn on Nestorius, the heretical fifth-century Patriarch of Constantinople who taught the doctrine of a divided (flesh/spirit) Christ.
69. Michel Tournier's own term. On 'l'humour blanc', see *Le Vent paraclet*, pp. 192–8.
70. See Colin Nettelbeck, 'The Return of the Ogre: Michel Tournier's *Gilles et Jeanne*', in *Scripsi*, vol 2 no. 4, June 1984, pp. 43–50.
71. Tournier, *Le Vent paraclet*, p. 77.
72. Ibid., p. 78.

Tiffauges-France being driven back into the earth under the weight of a guilt that takes the form of an avenging angel of the deported Jews. Unlike the other writers we have seen, Tournier does not seem to seek reconciliation, but his vision of the French history of the war emphasises the same residual guilts – of collaboration, of betrayed authority, of anti-Semitism.

One might speculate that the chilling despair underlying Tournier's sense of history generates the baroque and grotesque imagery that permeates so much of his work. It is also possible that his pessimism is exaggerated by blind spots about the actual history: certainly it can be argued that in his evocation of the specific period of the Occupation, he overplays the pro-German thrust, by making it appear more central than it was in fact. None the less, his success, both critical and popular, indicates that his overall vision must be taken into account in an assessment of the collective view.

It would be rash to suggest that any single narrative of the French experience of the Second World War is successful to the point of making it seem unnecessary to say anything further, and yet François Truffaut's *Le Dernier Métro* (1981) has a plausible claim to doing just that. The mature Truffaut (born 1932) manages, in this film, a synthesis of descriptive history and symbolic meaning that is found nowhere else, except in the youthful Modiano. The film-maker himself believes that the originality of *Le Dernier Métro* comes from his own experience as a child.[73] He was eight years old when the Occupation began, and twelve when it ended. There may be truth in this, but Louis Malle was the same age, and *Lacombe Lucien* reveals a much rawer attitude and is a much more provocative film. Part of *Le Dernier Métro*'s strength is, rather, in the perspective it achieves by being later, rather than earlier 'rétro'. The personal reasons that Truffaut gives for coming late to this film – or more generally to a film about the Occupation – are so remarkably symbolic of the collectivity's attitudes to the period that they deserve to be quoted at length:

En 1958, écrivant avec Marcel Moussy *Les Quatre cents coups*, j'avais regretté de ne pouvoir évoquer mille détails de mon adolescence liée à cette période de l'Occupation mais le budget et l'esprit 'nouvelle vague' étaient peu compatibles avec la notion de 'film d'époque'. De ce point de vue, *Jules et Jim*, en 1961, a constitué une exception.

C'est en 1968, après avoir tourné *Baisers volés*, que l'envie m'est

73. In *Avant-Scène du cinéma*, nos. 303–4 1–15 March 1983, p. 9.

revenue de reconstituer cette époque mais, à ce moment, j'ai été stoppé net dans mon élan par un film remarquable: *Le Chagrin et la Pitié* de Marcel Ophüls.[74]

It would take more than another ten years, and the experience of many other war narratives, before Truffaut and his co-scenarist Suzanne Schiffman settled on their version of the story. By that time, Truffaut had also evolved the specifically theatrical dimension of his project, so that his film about the Occupation would also be a film about the theatre, in the same way that *La nuit américaine* (1973) had been a film about cinema. In other words, after the 1958-68 hiatus (incidentally the de Gaulle years), by the time the film comes to be made, its historical subject matter has already been distilled into an artistic context. The story of a theatre during the Occupation will be transformed into the Drama of the Occupation, a ritual re-enactment of a history already perceived (as in Modiano) as myth.

Truffaut's association of *Le Dernier Métro* with his own childhood is translated in the film's exuberance, but in terms of the detailed evocation of the Occupation, youthful memories are less important than the conscientious homework to which he confesses in his preparation of the scenario.[75] Throughout the film, there is an impressive litany of authentic details. From the opening general scene-setting images of Nazi banners hanging over the rue de Rivoli arcades (that is, registering the fact of the German presence), there is a consistent focus on the range of everyday French reactions to the imposed constraints – bicycle-taxis, black marketeering, letters of denunciation, food queues, black-outs, trips to the bomb-shelters, women painting seamed stockings on their legs, parcels for the POWs, 'coffins' sent out to collaborators, etc. The concern with realism suggests that Truffaut was aware that, for the facts to be transcended, they first had to be recognised as facts.

At the same time, there is no doubt that he considers the collective French reaction to have been sound. Both his major characters, Bernard and Marion, are positive figures. Bernard's integrity – his simple, good, unquestioned values – is there from the beginning of the film. Although he is lightly mocked as an unsuccessful 'macho',

74. Ibid., p. 4. My translation.
75. Ibid., p. 5. He mentions the memoirs of Ginette Leclerc, Jean Marais, Alice Cocéa and Corinne Luchaire, as well as Le Boterf's *La Vie parisienne sous l'occupation*.

he at no time accepts the German presence, refusing even to stay in a night-club with his friends when he observes Germans there.[76] (This point has moreover already been prepared by the scene in which the stage-manager Raymond teaches the concierge's son the list of deprecatory names for the Germans: 'boches', 'frisés', 'fridolins', 'vert-de-gris', 'doryphores'.[77] He is also instinctively and fearlessly anti-collaborationist, as is shown by his physical attack on the dangerous and powerful Daxiat;[78] and he helps the Resistance for some time before finally joining it.

While Bernard is a metaphor of a France which had its heart in the right place, Marion symbolises a more complex and calculating spirit, that has worked through the practical details of what has to be done for her husband, her actors, and her theatre to survive. There is no simplicity in Marion, and if her name is in any way meant to suggest a 'Marianne', then Truffaut, as a balance to his slightly sentimental characterisation of Bernard, is surely very close to the 'survivalist' explanation of the Occupation that emerged via the Jewish heroine in *Lacombe Lucien*.

The uneasy, but none the less strong, working relationship between Bernard and Marion is reflected in the relationship of the film's major themes. The German presence is presented as a combination of polite behaviour, political control, and police (Gestapo) repression, moving more in the last direction as the war drags on. The Resistance appears in a positive light, but as a marginal activity, sustained by the support of the 'good-hearted', but officially considered as 'terrorism' – though the widening of Resistance attitudes with the passage of time is clearly brought out. But while Truffaut seems to have no doubt that France, at least eventually, did resist, he is not sympathetic to the post-Liberation organisation of the Resistance into a political force – as is shown in the arrest, release, and re-arrest, for completely misguided reasons, of the director Jean-Loup by the FFI. On the other hand, the Collaboration, represented by the journalist Daxiat, gets very short shrift indeed. Although this character is fleshed out sufficiently to be a realistic and believable symbol of one aspect of French behaviour, he is in no

76. Ibid., p. 53.
77. Ibid., p. 44.
78. 'Daxiat' was the pseudonym used by the *Je suis partout* drama critic, Alain Laubreaux, in writing his play about Stavisky (*Les Pirates de Paris*). Truffaut is frank about this source, but does not mention that the fight between Bernard and Daxiat is based on one between Laubreaux and Marais. See Patrick Marsh, *Le théâtre à Paris sous l'occupation allemande*, (ref. 18), p. 231.

way seen as central. Rather, his sinister power is perceived as anomalous: he is a 'living paradox'.[79]

The strongest theme in the film is the Jewish question. Anti-Semitism appears as a wide-spread and insidious force: allusions to the banning of Jews from public office are reinforced by the mention of the twenty-five Jews bizarrely allowed to remain in the Paris fire-brigade because of their social usefulness; newspaper and radio propaganda feeds raids and concentration camps. The plight of the Jews in France is stressed throughout: there is the actor, Rosen, who cannot get a job, even with Marion; there is the girl Rosette, fourteen years old, who hides her yellow star under her scarf in order to care for her parents who can no longer go out at all; and above all, there is Lucas Steiner, the director-in-hiding, who when frustrated in his plans to escape by the spread of the Occupation in November 1942, becomes as suicidal as Monsieur Horn in *Lacombe Lucien*, and is only saved by the cold lucidity of his wife.

All of these factors add up to a situation of uncomfortable compromise. Survival – in this instance the survival of Steiner and his theatre – depends on playing the game according to the imposed rules – crawling to Daxiat to get the performance visa from the German censors, signing a specifically anti-Semitic contract in order to get an acting job, soliciting the German authorities to avoid a shut-down. There are no clean hands.

By setting his film at a pivotal time of the Occupation, that is, from the end of 1942 when the German invasion of the south abolished the distinction between 'occupied' and 'free' zones, Truffaut provides a somewhat paradoxical thrust towards collective unity, by emphasising the Germans as the common enemy. He avoids the dimension of the Pétain-de Gaulle conflict (which is not mentioned). Although this obviously omits what was a significant issue of the time, he seems to be suggesting that neither France's Petainism during the first two years of the Occupation, nor the subsequent Gaullian Resistance-centred view of history, are relevant to the perspective of the 1980s. The live issues are collaborationism and anti-Semitism. With the former, Truffaut's stance is reassuring, for although Daxiat survives the war and the 'Epuration', he is symbolically killed off in the 1960s by a throat cancer (punished, as it were, in the word-organ through which he has most sinned). In respect to anti-Semitism, the attention that the

79. *Avant-scène*, 45.

film pays to this theme is a warning and an acknowledgement by the film-maker of an endemic French problem, and it is especially interesting in the context of the authority theme.

The failure of authority that obsessionally preoccupies the post-1968 period is a question of which Truffaut seems superbly ignorant. There are no flawed fathers or political leaders in *Le Dernier Métro*, none of the figures that one finds in Laurent or Le Garrec or Modiano as the indicators of the disintegration of national consciousness and identity. The title of the play being performed within the film is, ironically, *La Disparue*, for the real missing figure is, of course, Lucas Steiner himself, the director of the theatre – and even he is not really missing, but hidden in the cellar. If Truffaut pays no attention at all to the socio-political aspects of authority in respect to the French identity, he is obviously concerned about it on an artistic level. Indeed, his portrayal of Steiner as director is a strong image of his continued belief in the necessity of authority in art – a belief which was one of the seminal forces of the 'New Wave'. It is important to stress, however, that it is only in the artistic context that the concept is shown to be useful. Furthermore, if the theatre, in *Le Dernier Métro*, is used as a metaphor of the way in which art can transcend history, it is a specifically non-nationalist art (a Norwegian play directed by a German Jew), and the authority of the director depends on his being accepted by a community working together in the same direction – a direction of self-transcendence represented by the play itself.

Truffaut's general view, in short, is oriented towards reconciliation, and is based on a confidence that art is a means of surviving and overcoming the historical trauma. His film will remain a landmark: the narrative point beyond which the collecting of experience into a paradigm ceases to be a vital matter for the collectivity and becomes once again a set of individual accounts, scattering gradually, one supposes, and emphasising forgetting, rather than remembering.

Individual needs will remain, and indeed, have remained. In his postface of Claudine Vegh's *Je ne lui ai pas dit au revoir* (Paris, 1979), Bruno Bettelheim points out that the consequences of the Holocaust have been felt not only in the following generation, but in the one after that. He suggests the mechanisms that make this so:

> Pourquoi les jeunes victimes étaient-elles incapables de parler de ce qui leur était arrivé? Pourquoi leur est-il encore si difficile, vingt ans, trente

ans après, de s'exprimer sur ce qui leur est arrivé quand elles étaient enfants? Et pourquoi est-il si important de parler de ces choses-là? Je crois que ces deux questions sont étroitement liées: ce dont on ne peut parler, c'est aussi ce qu'on ne peut apaiser; et si on ne l'apaise pas, les blessures continuent à s'ulcérer de génération en génération. (p. 179)

Although Bettelheim is addressing himself to the situation of the children and grandchildren of Jews who died in the camps – a horror that makes most other historical traumas seem insignificant, the model of analysis is helpful as a guide to understanding the French situation, and particularly the way in which the unresolved nature of the response among the traumatised children has kept the psycho-historical abscess active.

Resolution implies a satisfying account of events and behaviour – a synthesis, in short, that would include both a description of what took place, and a collectively believable explanation of why. I have argued that such a synthesis was not available to the 1968 nexus of generations, partly because the pre-Gaullian period did not have time to work its complex experiences into an overview, and partly because de Gaulle's Resistance-focused vision of history deflected, for a whole decade, most attempts at penetrating insight. If de Gaulle's vision was a distortion, however, it was also an order and an orthodoxy, and its displacement could only lead to a period of confusion. It is however from such confusion, perhaps, that all great myths are born. This essay has attempted to describe the birth of such a myth. It is itself a story, whose minor and major characters are authors, whose major metaphors are their works, whose thematic background is the slippery time-space continuum of the last half-century, and whose plot structure is the conflict between a host of individual memories and the slower evolution of collective attitudes.

NOTES ON CONTRIBUTORS

Roy Armes is Reader in Film and Television Studies at Middlesex Polytechnic in London. His numerous publications on film include monographs on Alain Resnais and Alain Robbe-Grillet and a recent study on the history of French cinema.

W.D. Halls has taught at Oxford, and was a senior member, and onetime supernumerary fellow, of St Antony's College. He is the author of works on French literature, history, culture and education, as well as a translator of French sociological and anthropological books. His study on *The Youth of Vichy France* (1981) was published in French translation in 1988. He is presently working on a history of French Christians during the Second World War.

Nicholas Hewitt is French Professor at the University of Nottingham. He has written extensively on the literary and intellectual history of the inter-war years and the Fourth Republic. His most recent book *The Golden Age of Louis-Ferdinand Céline* was published in 1987 by Berg Publishers.

Gerhard Hirschfeld was until recently a Fellow of the German Historical Institute in London and is now Director of the Bibliothek für Zeitgeschichte in Stuttgart. He has published widely on the history of Nazism, the Second World War and on the German emigration to Great Britain after 1933. His study on the Netherlands under German Occupation *Nazi Rule and Dutch Collaboration* appeared in an English translation in 1988 (Berg Publishers).

H.R. Kedward is Reader in History at the University of Sussex. He has published several books and numerous articles on the German Occupation of France, among them *Resistance in Vichy France* (1978) and *Occupied France* (1985). He is currently completing a major study on the French Maquis.

Michael Kelly has taught for many years at University College, Dublin, and is now Professor of French at the University of Southampton. He has written extensively on the history of ideas in France and the relationship between literature, arts and politics in the 1930s and 1940s. He is the author of books on Emmanuel Mounier and modern French Marxism.

Paul Kingston is Senior Lecturer in French and currently head of the department of Language Studies at Coventry Polytechnic. He has published books and articles on anti-Semitism in France 1930–44 and on propaganda in radio broadcasts in French during the Second World War. He is currently working on a critical edition of *Au Bon Beurre* by Jean Dutourd to be published in 1989.

Gerd Krumeich is Professor of Modern History at the University of Düsseldorf. For three years he was a Fellow of the German Historical Institute in Paris. He has written extensively on French military and political history, including a major study on *Armaments and Politics in France on the Eve of the First World War* (Berg, 1984). He has just finished a book on the cult of Joan of Arc in French nationalism during the nineteenth and twentieth centuries (*Jeanne d'Arc in der Geschichte*, 1989).

Patrick Marsh is College Lecturer in French at University College, Dublin. He has published widely on the theatre and particularly on the theatre in France during the Second World War, notably 'Le théâtre à Paris sous l'occupation allemande' in a special number of *La Revue d'histoire du Théâtre*.

Colin Nettelbeck is Associate Professor of French at Monash University, Melbourne. He has written books on Bernanos, Céline, Modiano and on the French experience of the Second World War. He has also written extensively on twentieth century French literature, film and social history.

Robert Pickering is Professor of French at University College, Cork. He has published widely in the field of French writing during the Second World War, with a particular interest in the work of Valéry. He is currently working in the area of authorised literature in France, 1940–4, and its relation to censorship and propaganda.

David Pryce-Jones is a full-time writer living in London. He is the author of *Paris in the Third Reich* (1982). He has also written books, among others, on the Middle East, on the Hungarian Revolution, a biography of Unity Mitford and a book on the Arabs, which includes a chapter on the influence of Nazism (*The Closed Circle*, 1989).

Sarah Wilson is Lecturer in the history of art at the Courtauld Institute, University of London, specialising in post-war France. She has contributed catalogue essays to recent exhibitions on Raoul Dufy, Ferdinand Legér, late Surrealism and is presently preparing a major study on art and politics in France between 1935 and 1953.

Margarete Zimmermann is Professor of Romance literature and language at the Freie Universität, Berlin. She has published both on writers sympathetic to the idea of collaboration (Céline, Brasillach, Rebatet) and on Resistance writers (Vercours, Cassou, Seghers). She has made a particular study of Drieu la Rochelle in her book *Die Literatur des französischen Faschismus* (1979).

SUGGESTIONS FOR FURTHER READING

1. Politics

Amouroux, Henri, *La grande histoire des Français sous l'occupation*, Vols. I–VII, Paris, 1976–85

Aron, Robert, *Histoire de Vichy*, Paris, 1954

Azéma, Jean-Pierre, *La Collaboration (1940–1944)*, Paris, 1975

Billig, Joseph, *La solution finale de la question juive*, Paris, 1977

Bourderon, R., and Yvan Avakoumovitch, *Détruire le PCF*, Paris, 1988

Chambrun, René de, *France during the German Occupation 1940–1944: Summaries and Important Selections from Statements on the Government of Maréchal Pétain and Pierre Laval. A Bibliographical Supplement*, Stanford (Calif.), 1986

Cobb, Richard, *French and Germans, Germans and French. A Personal Interpretation of France under Two Occupations, 1914–1918/1940–1944*, Hanover/London, 1983

Dank, Milton, *The French against the French: Collaboration and Resistance*, London, 1978

Defrasne, Jean, *Histoire de la collaboration*, Paris, 1982

Delarue, Jacques, *Histoire de la Gestapo*, Paris, 1962

——, *Trafics et crimes sous l'Occupation*, Paris, 1968

Delperrie de Bayac, J., *Histoire de la Milice*, Paris, 1969

Dioudonnat, P.M., *L'argent nazi à la conquête de la presse française*, Paris, 1981

Foreign Office, *The Review of the Foreign Press 1939–45*, Series D. and F. (France) London, 1980

Girardet, R., 'Pour une introduction à l'histoire du nationalisme français', *Revue française de science politique*, 8, No. 3, pp. 502–38

Gordon, Bertram M., *Collaborationism in France during the Second World War*, Ithaca (NY), 1980

Halls, W.D., *The Youth of Vichy France*, Oxford, 1981

Hoffmann, S., 'Collaborationism in France during World War II', *Journal of Modern History*, No. 4, September 1968, pp. 375–95

Huddleston, Sisley, *Pétain: Patriot or Traitor?*, London, 1951

Kedward, Roderick, *Resistance in Vichy France: Ideas & Motivation in the*

Southern Zone, Oxford, 1978

——, *Occupied France: Collaboration and Resistance 1940–1944*, Oxford, 1985

—— and Roger Austin (eds.), *Vichy France and the Resistance: Culture and Ideology*, London and Sydney, 1985

Klarsfeld, Serge, *Vichy – Auschwitz*, 2 vols., Paris, 1983/85

Knisel, Richard, *Capitalism and the State in Modern France: Renovation and Economic Management in the Twentieth Century*, New York, 1981

Laborie, Pierre, *Résistants, Vichyssois et autres*, Paris, 1980

Le Boterf, Hervé, *La vie parisienne sous l'occupation*, Paris, 1977

Lévy, Claude, *'Les Nouveau Temps' et l'idéologie de la collaboration*, Paris, 1974

Limagne, P., *Ephémérides de quatre années tragiques, 1940–1944*, 3 vols., Paris, 1945–6

Marrus, Michael R., and Robert O. Paxton, *Vichy France and the Jews*, New York, 1981

Mayer, A.J., *Dynamics of Counterrevolution in Europe 1870–1956: An Analytic Framework*, New York, 1971

Micaud, C., *The French Right and Nazi Germany, 1933–1939*, Durham (N.C.), 1943

Michel, Henri, *Pétain et le Régime de Vichy*, Paris, 1978

Novick, Peter, *L'épuration française 1944–1949*, Paris, 1985

Ory, Pascal, *Les Collaborateurs, 1940–1945*, Paris, 1977

Paxton, Robert, *Vichy France: Old Guard and New Order 1940–44*, London, 1972

Pryce-Jones, David, *Paris in the Third Reich: A History of the German Occupation, 1940–1944*, London, 1981

Raijsfus, Maurice, *Des Juifs dans la Collaboration, L'UGIF, 1941–1944*, Paris, 1980

Rebatet, L., *Les mémoires d'un fasciste*, Paris, 1976

Siegfried, A., 'Le Vichy de Pétain, le Vichy de Laval', *Revue française de science politique*, 6, No. 4, 1956, pp. 737–49

Sternhell, Zeev, *Ni droite ni gauche. L'idéologie fasciste en France*, Paris, 1983

Sweets, John F., *Choices in Vichy France: The French under Nazi Occupation*, New York and Oxford, 1986

Tournoux, Raymond, *Pétain et la France, La Seconde Guerre Mondiale*, Paris, 1980

——, *Le Royaume d'Otto*, Paris, 1982

Veillon, Dominique (ed.), *La Collaboration. Textes et débats*, Paris, 1984

Weber, Eugen, 'Nationalism, Socialism and National-Socialism in France', *French Historical Studies*, vol. 2, No. 3, 1962, pp. 273–307

2. The Church

Bédarida, R., *Les Armes de l'Esprit: Témoignage Chrétien (1941–1944)*, Paris, 1977

Bolle, P., and J. Godel (eds), *Spiritualité, théologie et résistance*, Grenoble, 1987

Cahiers du Témoignage Chrétien, 1941–1944, 2 vols., Paris, 1980

Dansette, A., *Destin du catholicisme français, 1926–1956*, Paris, 1957

Duquesne, J., *Les Catholiques français sous l'occupation*, Paris, 1966 (2nd rev. edn, 1987)

Eglises et Chrétiens dans la deuxième guerre mondiale: La région Rhône-Alpes, Lyon, 1978

Eglises et Chrétiens dans la deuxième guerre mondiale dans le Nord/Pas de Calais, Colloque de Lille, *Revue du Nord*, Nos. 237 (April–June 1978) and 238 (July–Sept. 1978)

Eglises et Chrétiens dans la deuxième guerre mondiale: la France, Lyon, 1982

Halls, W.D., 'Catholicism under Vichy: A Study in Diversity and Ambiguity', in Kedward and Austin (eds.), *Vichy France and the Resistance* (see Politics section)

Latreille, A., *De Gaulle, la Libération et l'Eglise catholique*, Paris, 1978

Riquet, M., *Chrétiens de France dans l'Europe enchaînée*, Paris, 1972

3. Joan of Arc

Atkin, Nick, 'The Cult of Joan of Arc in French Schools, 1940–44', in Kedward and Austin (eds), *Vichy France and the Resistance*, pp. 265–8 (see Politics section)

Jacobs, Gabriel, 'The Role of Joan of Arc on the Stage of Occupied Paris', in Kedward and Austin (eds.), *Vichy France and the Resistance*, pp. 106–22 (see Politics section)

Krumeich, Gerd, *Jeanne d'Arc in der Geschichte: Historiographie – Kultur – Politik*, Stuttgart, 1989

Marsh, Patrick, 'Jeanne d'Arc during the German Occupation', *Theatre Research International 2* (1976–7), pp. 139–46

Warner, Marina, *Joan of Arc: The Image of Female Heroism*, New York, 1982

4. The Fine Arts

Arno Breker, 60 ans de sculpture, Paris, 1981

Bertrand-Dorléac, Laurence, *Histoire de l'Art, Paris, 1940–1944*, Paris,

1986 (with a comprehensive bibliography)

Breker, Arno, *Paris, Hitler et moi*, Paris, 1970

Cone, Michèle, *Art and Politics in France during the German Occupation*, Ann Arbor (Mich.), 1988

Exposition Résistance-Deportation, Paris, 1980

Fauré, Michel, *Histoire du surréalisme sous l'Occupation*, Paris, 1982

Hinz, Berthold, *Art in the Third Reich*, London, 1979

Valland, Rose, *Le Front de l'Art: Défense des Collections françaises, 1939–1945*, Paris, 1961

Wilson, Sarah, 'La vie â Paris pendant l'Occupation' and 'Les jeunes peintres de tradition française', plus selected documents in *Paris-Paris, Créations en France, 1937–1957*, Centre Georges Pompidou, Paris, 1981

5. The Cinema

Bertin-Maghit, Jean-Pierre, *Le Cinéma français sous Vichy*, Paris, 1980

Chirat, Raymond, *Le Cinéma français des années de guerre*, Paris, 1983

Courtade, Francis, *Les Malédictions du cinéma français*, Paris, 1978

Ehrlich, Evelyn, *Cinema of Paradox*, New York, 1985

Garçon, François, *De Blum à Pétain*, Paris, 1984

Jeancolas, Jean-Pierre, *15 ans d'années trente*, Paris, 1983

Léglise, Paul, *Histoire de la politique du cinéma français*, volume two: *Entre deux républiques, 1940–1946*, Paris, 1977

Régent, Roger, *Cinéma de France*, Paris, 1948

Siclier, Jacques, *La France de Pétain et son cinéma*, Paris, 1978

6. The Theatre

Anouilh, Jean, *Nouvelles Pièces Noires*, Paris, 1958

Beauvoir, Simone de, *Les Bouches Inutiles*, Paris, 1945

——, *La Force de l'Age*, Paris, 1960

Claudel, Paul, *Théâtre I*, Paris, 1967

——, *Théâtre II*, Paris, 1965

Cocteau, Jean, *La Machine Infernale*, London, 1957

Galster, I., *Le Théâtre de Jean-Paul Sartre devant ses premiers critiques*, Tübingen, Paris, 1986

Gide, André, *Journal 1939–49*, Paris, 1954

Giraudoux, Jean, *Littérature*, Paris, 1941

——, *Pleins Pouvoirs*, Paris, 1939

Guitry, Sacha, *Quatre ans d'occupations*, Paris, 1952

——, *Soixante jours de prison*, Paris, 1949

Montherlant, Henry de, *Le Solstice de Juin*, Paris, 1941

——, *L'Equinoxe de Septembre*, Paris, 1947
——, *Textes sous une occupation (1940–44)* Paris, 1953
——, *Carnets: années 1930 à 1944*, Paris, 1957
Rougemont, Denis de, *Journal d'une Epoque, 1926–46*, Paris, 1968
Sartre, Jean-Paul, *Situations I*, Paris, 1947
——, *Bariona*, Paris, 1967
Vermorel, Claude, *Jeanne avec nous*, Paris, 1942

7. Literature

Atack, Margaret, *Literature and the French Resistance – Cultural Politics and Narrative Forms, 1940–1950*, Manchester, 1989
Babilas, W., 'La Querelle des mauvais maîtres', *Romanische Forschungen*, vol. 98, No. 1/2, 1986, pp. 120–52
Bremer, Th. (Ed.), *Europäische Literatur gegen den Faschismus. 1922–1945*, Munich, 1986
Buckley, William (ed.), *Critical Essays on Louis-Ferdinand Céline*, Boston, 1988
Dunne, Tom (ed.), *The Writer as Witness*, Cork, 1987
Faure, Christian, *Littérature et société – la mystique vichyssoise 'du retour à la terre' selon l'oeuvre d'Henri Pourrat*, Ambert, 1988 Régionale du Livradois-Forez, Revue Archéologique Sites, 1988
Flügge, M., *Verweigerung oder Neue Ordnung. Politik, Ideologie und Literatur im Frankreich der Besatzungszeit 1940–1944 am Beispiel der 'Antigone' von Jean Anouilh*, 2 vols., Rheinfelden, 1982
Gibault, François, *Céline*, 3 vols., Paris, 1977–85
Godard, Henri, *Poétique de Céline*, Paris, 1985
Guéhenno, Jean, *Journal des années noires*, Paris, 1947
Hamon, Philippe, *Texte et idéologie*, Paris, 1984
Hewitt, Nicholas, *The Golden Age of Louis-Ferdinand Céline*, Oxford, 1988
Higgins, Ian (ed.), *Anthology of Second World War French Poetry*, London, 1982
——, *The Second World War in Literature*, Edinburgh, 1986
Kohut, K. (ed.), *Literatur der Résistance und der Kollaboration in Frankreich*, 3 vols., Wiesbaden and Tübingen, 1982–4
Loiseaux, Gérard, *La Littérature de la défaite et de la collaboration*, Paris, 1984
Lottman, Herbert R., *La Rive gauche*, Paris, 1981
McCarthy, Patrick, *Céline: A Critical Biography*, London, 1975
Morgan, Claude, *Les 'Don Quichotte' et les autres*, Paris, 1979
Nimier, Roger, *Journées de lecture*, Paris, 1965
Rieuneau, Maurice, *Guerre et révolution dans le roman français 1919–1939*,

Paris, 1974

Robert, Georges, and André Lioret, *Marcel Aymé insolite*, Paris 1958

Seghers, P., *La Résistance et ses poétes. France 1940–1945*, Paris, 1974

Thiher, Allen, *Céline: The Novel as Delirium*, New Brunswick (NJ), 1972

Tucker, W.R., *The Fascist Ego: a Political Biography of Robert Brasillach*, 1975

Vandromme, Pol, *Aymé*, Paris, 1960

——, *La Droite buissonnière*, Paris, 1960

Zimmermann, M., *Die Literatur des französischen Faschismus. Untersuchungen zum Werk Pierre Drieu La Rochelles 1917–1942*, Munich, 1979

——, 'Littérature et fascisme. Le destin posthume de Robert Brasillach', *Romanistische Zeitschrift für Literaturgeschichte* 2/3, 1981, pp. 340–59

——, 'Pierre Seghers: "L'action et le rêve vont ensemble, pour un poète". Entretiens sur la poésie et la résistance (juin 1980)', *lendemains* 21, February 1981, pp. 3–29

——, 'Céline et les céliniens: un bilan', *Romanistische Zeitschrift für Literaturgeschichte* 3/4, 1982, pp. 459–89

8. Post-War Perspectives

Aron, Robert, with Yvette Garnier-Rizet, *Histoire de l'Epuration*, 3 vols., Paris, 1967–75

Azéma, Jean-Pierre, *De Munich à la Libération*, Paris, 1979

Baudot, Marcel, 'La Répression de la Collaboration et L'Epuration politique et économique', in *La Libération de la France*, Paris, 1976

D'Astier, Emmanuel, *De la chute à la Libération de Paris*, Paris, 1965

Lottmann, Herbert R., *L'Epuration*, Paris, 1986

Novick, Peter, *The Resistance versus Vichy: The Purge of Collaborators in Liberated France*, New York, 1968

Ophuls, Marcel, *Le Chagrin et la Pitié*, Paris, 1980

Rioux, Jean-Pierre, *La France de la Quatrième Republique*, vol. 1, Paris, 1980

Rousso, Henry, *Le syndrome de Vichy. 1944–198 . .*, Paris, 1987

INDEX

303

Index

306

Index

Index